Themis Bar Review
Illinois Volume One

Administrative Law
Agency
Civil Practice and Procedure
Commercial Paper
Conflict of Laws
Corporations
Equity
Family Law

ISBN 978-1-935445-97-5
1-935445-97-9

Administrative Law

ADMINISTRATIVE LAW

Table of Contents

BAR REVIEW

ADMINISTRATIVE LAW

This outline discusses the laws governing federal agencies and their actions, and covers the basic principles involved with administrative agencies, including: agency creation, authority, rulemaking, investigations, adjudication, judicial review, and agency accountability. The Administrative Procedure Act ("APA"), 5 U.S.C. § 551, *et. seq.* (*cited herein as* "APA § xxx"), provides the uniform general framework for federal agency rulemaking and enforcement proceedings, as well as guidance to most states.

I. INTRODUCTION

Administrative agencies exist at all levels of government and carry out many of a government's complex day-to-day functions and tasks. They are given authority through legislation, called an **"enabling act,"** and are charged with overseeing and administering government functions within a particular area of substantive law (e.g., environmental regulation, telecommunications, etc.). While the areas of expertise and authority vary greatly from agency to agency, the procedural requirements and constitutional limitations on agency action often apply uniformly.

Agency powers delegated through enabling legislation may include **quasi-legislative** (rulemaking) and **quasi-judicial** (adjudicative) powers.

A. AGENCY TYPES

While agency control is not entirely confined to any one branch of government, agencies can usually be categorized as either **executive agencies** or **independent agencies**.

1. Executive Agencies

In the federal government, most agencies operate under the general control of the President or are within another executive branch agency (e.g., the U.S. Fish & Wildlife Service is within the Department of the Interior and under the authority of the Secretary of the Interior). Heads of executive agencies are appointed by the President and generally may be removed at the President's discretion (i.e., with or without cause).

2. Independent Agencies

Congress has decided that certain regulatory agencies, because of the subject matter within their jurisdiction, require more separation from the political process than most agencies. These agencies operate relatively independently of the President and are described as **independent agencies**. Rather than having one director, an independent agency is headed by a group of "members" or "commissioners." Independent agency members are appointed by the President and must be confirmed by the Senate. Often, the terms of board members are staggered to ease the effects of member turnover.

Members of independent agencies are typically insulated from direct presidential supervision. To remove the head of an independent agency, the President must meet whatever special requirements are listed in the agency's enabling act (typically good cause, neglect of duty, or malfeasance). Sometimes, courts will impose such restrictions on removal even when the enabling act is silent. This check on presidential control allows independent agencies to engage in their regulatory duties without undue political pressure from the executive branch.

B. THE ADMINISTRATIVE PROCEDURE ACT (APA)

In addition to its enabling legislation, every federal administrative agency must follow the procedural requirements of the Administrative Procedure Act ("APA"). Enacted in 1946, the APA establishes uniform rulemaking, investigatory, and adjudicative procedures that pertain to all federal agencies. The APA also expressly authorizes persons to challenge final agency actions in federal court once they have exhausted all remedies available within the agency itself.

The APA directs an agency as to procedures that must be followed in all agency actions when the agency's enabling act is silent.

C. GENERAL CONSTITUTIONAL CONCERNS – DUE PROCESS

The United States Constitution guarantees that the government may not deprive any person of "life, liberty, or property, without due process of law." U.S. Const. amend. XIV. The fundamental requirements of procedural due process in an administrative law context are (i) **notice** and (ii) **the opportunity to be heard** at a meaningful time and in a meaningful manner (i.e., a proper hearing).

1. Liberty

Besides basic physical freedom, "liberty" includes aspects of life that are considered to be fundamental to the pursuit of happiness (e.g., the right to travel, work, procreate, or marry). Courts have expanded the concept of liberty and have required a proper agency hearing for the following:

i)   Suspension or expulsion from school;

ii) Deportation of illegal immigrants; and

iii) The creation of a stigma affecting a person's ability to obtain employment.

2. Property

"Property" includes tangible items, such as real estate, consumer goods, and money. The concept of property also extends to certain intangible items, such as entitlements to government benefits.

Professional licenses are deemed to be "property" for due process purposes. Agency actions that threaten the deprivation of such licenses require, at minimum, notice to all affected parties and the opportunity to be heard.

3. Exception – Emergency Circumstances

If an emergency actually exists, an agency may deprive a person of liberty or property before giving notice and conducting a hearing. After the emergency situation has been resolved, the agency must conduct a hearing as soon as possible. The emergency must be real (i.e., provable by facts) and not merely the result of rumors.

4. Required Procedures

Courts consider three factors in determining the amount of process that is due:

i)   The private interest affected by the governmental action;

ii) The risk of erroneous deprivation of that interest using current procedures and the probable value of additional or substitute safeguards;

iii) The burden (fiscal and administrative cost) involved in providing the additional process.

The greater the importance of the threatened interest, the greater the likelihood that courts will require extensive procedural safeguards prior to the termination of the interest. Generally, the person whose interest is being deprived is entitled to notice of the government's action by an unbiased decision maker and an opportunity to be heard, although the hearing need not necessarily occur before the termination of the interest.

II. AGENCY CREATION

A. ENABLING OR ORGANIC LEGISLATION

Agencies are legislatively created entities. Authority is delegated to an agency by Congress through the agency's "**enabling act**" or "**organic act**," along with any subsequent legislative enactments that may broaden or limit the agency's jurisdiction, policies, or procedures. An enabling act brings an agency into existence, giving it the authority to create rules, investigate offenses, and adjudicate matters. The enabling act may give express directions regarding procedure that an agency must follow before finalizing an action. Judicial review of final agency actions is often authorized within the language of an agency's enabling act.

1. Congressional Delegation of Authority

Congress's authority to delegate its power to other governmental agencies comes from Article I, Section 8 of the Constitution, the Necessary and Proper Clause, which gives Congress the power "to make all Laws which shall be necessary and proper for carrying into Execution the foregoing Powers, and all other Powers vested by [the] Constitution in the Government of the United States, or in any Department or Officer thereof." U.S. Const. art. I, § 8.

2. The Non-Delegation Doctrine

Congress's power to delegate its authority to administrative agencies is not without limits. The "non-delegation doctrine" requires that Congress include an **intelligible principle** within enabling legislation to guide the agency in its functions. Without such guidance, an enabling act and its Congressional delegation of authority are unconstitutional and may be challenged.

B. CONTROL OVER AGENCIES

Federal agencies are part of the executive branch. Independent agencies operate with greater independence from the President than do executive agencies. All agencies, whether executive or independent, are subject to various forms of control exercised by the executive, legislative, and judicial branches.

1. Executive Control

a. Appointment

Principal officers (e.g., cabinet secretaries and commissioners of independent agencies) are appointed by the President, subject to Senate approval. **Inferior**

officers (i.e., those who exercise significant authority but whose jurisdiction is narrowly limited by statute, or whose work is directed and supervised by another) are appointed by either the President, the heads of departments, or the courts, as decided by Congress. Mere **employees** are not required to be appointed by any particular methods; they are simply hired by their immediate supervisors.

b. Removal

Congress may place limits on the President's ability to remove federal officers. For example, members of independent agencies may usually only be removed for good cause.

Statutory limits on the President's power to remove federal officers are unconstitutional if they impede the President's ability to carry out his constitutional duties. Accordingly, core executive officers, such as cabinet secretaries, may be removed by the President at will.

c. Executive orders

Presidents may also exercise control over agencies by issuing executive orders.

2. Legislative Control

Through the enactment of legislation, Congress has the power to (i) create or dissolve administrative agencies, (ii) implement procedures and directives for their actions, and (iii) set standards of judicial review. Additionally, the Senate votes to confirm principal agency officers.

Congress may not participate in the process of appointment of federal officials (except for the Senate's role in confirming principal officers) nor in the process of removal (except by impeachment). Congress may, however, appoint and remove officials (such as the Librarian of Congress) who serve merely as fact-finders in aid of Congress's performance of its duties.

Members of Congress cannot serve as officers or judges of the United States while they keep their seats in Congress. U.S. Const., art. I, § 6.

Congress also has other control mechanisms at its disposal, such as the ability to limit or cut funding to an administrative agency and subpoenaing agency officers to appear at oversight hearings.

3. Judicial Review

Persons aggrieved by an agency action may seek relief from the judiciary. APA § 702. Unless there are further directives contained in the language of an agency's enabling act, the APA directs courts to set aside agency actions that are:

(i) Arbitrary, capricious, an abuse of discretion, or otherwise not in accordance with law;

(ii) Contrary to constitutional right, power, privilege, or immunity;

(iii) In excess of statutory jurisdiction, authority, or limitations, or short of statutory right;

(iv) Without observance of procedure required by law; or

(v) Unsupported by substantial evidence in a case involving formal adjudication or rulemaking.

APA § 706.

4. Separation of Powers

The doctrine of separation of powers requires that each of the three branches of government serve a designated role. A branch may not interfere with the functions of the other branches, unless authorized by the Constitution's system of checks and balances (e.g., impeachment, judicial review, veto power, etc.).

In delegating its authority to administrative agencies, Congress is limited to a strictly legislative role and may not retain direct power over an agency's decisions, policies, or actions. For example:

i) Congress cannot delegate authority to an administrative official who is answerable only to Congress;

ii) Congress cannot appoint administrative officials to agency positions;

iii) Members of Congress may not serve as officers of an administrative agency;

iv) Congress must go through proper impeachment proceedings to remove agency directors and officials; and

v) Congress may not reserve the power of the legislative veto over agency actions.

5. Federal Preemption

Many substantive areas of law are administered on a federal and state level simultaneously (e.g., environmental regulation). If conflicts exist between agency rules and state law, **preemption** dictates that the federal policies will control, unless Congress or the federal agency consents to the authority of state law.

III. THE ADMINISTRATIVE PROCESS – AGENCY ACTIONS

A. IN GENERAL

The day-to-day operation of any agency involves a variety of functions necessary to carry out the legislative directives to which it is assigned. The three most prevalent agency actions are: rulemaking, investigation, and adjudication. Many agencies are authorized to conduct actions in all three categories.

When Congress authorizes an agency to use either rulemaking or adjudication, the choice between these two actions in any given instance lies within the agency's discretion. An agency may choose to use rulemaking, for example, to resolve a general issue that it would otherwise be required to revisit again and again in adjudication.

Agency action requires certain procedural safeguards to ensure that due process and agency efficiency are preserved. Agencies must conduct their actions according to procedural requirements contained in their enabling act, self-adopted rules, the APA, and the Constitution. The APA will control federal agency actions when the other authorities are silent.

B. RULEMAKING

Agencies promulgate a massive number of rules relating to various aspects of their statutory mandates. Rules promote efficiency, give the public general notice of an agency's procedures and positions, and are necessary for agency uniformity in policy, procedural matters, and legislative interpretations.

The adoption of non-substantive rules do not require an agency to follow any formal procedure. However, when a rule is substantive, the APA and due process require agencies to follow specific procedures under formal rulemaking or informal rulemaking.

Courts may invalidate agency rules when (i) the agency fails to follow proper procedure when promulgating the rule, or (ii) the rule's substantive provisions are unlawful.

1. Administrative Rules in General

The APA defines a "rule" as an agency statement "of general or particular applicability and future effect…." APA § 551(4). Agency rules, unlike adjudications, (i) **apply generally** to all persons, and (ii) affect **future conduct**, rather than past actions. All federal rules must be published in the *Federal Register*. APA § 552(a)(1).

Rulemaking may require certain procedures to be followed, depending on whether the rule is **substantive** or **non-substantive**.

a. Non-substantive rules

Non-substantive rules include (i) rules regarding intra-agency procedure and personnel matters; (ii) interpretive rules (i.e., those that merely clarify existing rules or statutes, without creating new legal rights or obligations); and (iii) policy statements (i.e., predictions about how an agency intends to enforce its statutory mandate and are not binding on the agency or the public). Agencies may generally issue non-substantive rules without following the APA's rulemaking procedures. APA § 553(b)(3).

Non-substantive rules generally do not affect the rights or require anything of persons outside of the agency itself.

b. Substantive rules

Substantive or "legislative" rules have the force of law and affect the rights and duties of those outside the agency. When issuing a substantive rule, an agency must generally conduct either **formal rulemaking** or **informal rulemaking**.

Substantive rules affect the rights of persons or impose requirements for them to follow. Unless an exception applies, an agency must follow proper rulemaking procedure (formal or informal, depending on its legislative mandate) when adopting a substantive rule.

2. Formal Rulemaking

In rare instances, a statute will provide that an agency may issue rules "**on the record after opportunity for an agency hearing**." This triggers the requirement for formal rulemaking, in which interested parties are to be heard before an administrative law judge. The process of formal rulemaking is the same as that of formal adjudication, except that in formal rulemaking, the agency may dispense with face-to-face hearings if no party would be prejudiced thereby. See APA § 556(d). Very few agencies are required by Congress to promulgate rules through formal rulemaking. (*See* § III.D.4. Formal Adjudication, *infra* for the procedural requirements of formal rulemaking).

> Courts have determined that a statutory requirement for the issuance of a rule after a "hearing" does not invoke the formal rulemaking requirement.

3. **Informal Rulemaking**

If a statute does not require a "hearing on the record," an agency must follow the procedural requirements of informal rulemaking in order to issue a substantive rule, unless an exception applies. When promulgating a substantive rule through informal rulemaking, an agency must:

   i)   Issue notice of the proposed rulemaking;

   ii) Receive and consider comments from interested members of the public;

   iii) Issue and publish a final rule; and

   iv) Give any interested person the right to petition for the issuance, amendment, or repeal of a rule.

APA § 553.

> The APA's procedure lays out the minimum steps that an agency must follow when issuing substantive rules. An agency may face additional rulemaking requirements, imposed either by legislation or its own rules and regulations.

A court cannot require an agency to follow rulemaking procedures beyond those expressed in the APA, enabling legislation, or its own previously-adopted rules.

a. **Notice**

An agency must publish notice of proposed rulemaking in the federal register, unless all relevant parties already have actual notice. Notice must include:

   i)   A statement of the **time, place, and nature** of public rule making proceedings;

   ii) Reference to the **legal authority** under which the rule is proposed; and

   iii) Either the terms or substance of the proposed rule or a description of the subjects and issues involved.

APA § 553(b).

b. **Public comment**

The agency must give interested persons the opportunity to submit **written comments** (e.g., arguments, data, and viewpoints). The agency *is not* required to allow parties to present oral comments.

The APA requires the agency to "consider" the comments submitted, but an agency is not expressly required to incorporate information gathered by public comment in its final rule. APA § 553(c).

c. Final rule

After the agency considers all relevant information presented, it issues a final rule, which must include a "concise general statement of [its] basis and purpose." APA § 553(c).

d. Publication

To become effective, agency rules must be published in the Federal Register for at least 30 days. Exceptions to this requirement exist for (i) rules that grant exemptions or relieve restrictions, (ii) non-substantive rules, and (iii) instances for which the agency finds good cause for immediate enactment and publishes the cause with the final rule. APA § 553(d).

Publication serves as **constructive notice** to the public of a rule's existence. All persons are bound by a rule's provisions, regardless of whether they have actual notice of a rule's existence.

e. Deviation from proposed rule

The final rule adopted by an agency often differs from the initial rule the agency proposed to the public through notice. This occurs as a result of public comment and agency decision-making.

If the final rule is a **logical outgrowth** of the initially proposed rule, the agency is not required to begin the informal rulemaking process again (i.e., giving notice of the rule and the opportunity for public comment). *American Medical Assoc. v. United States*, 887 F.2d 760, 767 (7th Cir. 1989).

f. Right to petition

The APA requires that, as a part of informal rulemaking, each agency must "give an interested person the right to petition for the issuance, amendment, or repeal of a rule." APA § 553(e). The agency has ultimate discretion to grant or refuse the petition.

4. Situations Exempt from Rulemaking Requirements

Agencies may promulgate substantive rules without notice and public participation if rules involve:

i)   Military or foreign affairs;

ii) Agency and personnel management;

iii) Management of public property; or

iv) Matters relating to loans, grants, benefits, or contracts.

Notice and public comment are also not required if the agency for good cause finds that the procedure would be "impracticable, unnecessary, or contrary to the public interest." APA § 553(b)(3)(B).

C. ADMINISTRATIVE INVESTIGATIONS

Agencies require adequate information upon which to base conclusions that best serve the public interest. Their duties often involve the investigation of individuals and organizations that are suspected of violating the law.

While parties often turn information over to an agency voluntarily, agencies may need to utilize other methods to compel information, including **subpoenas, physical searches and inspections**, mandatory **reports**, and **hearings**.

Any evidence gathered through an agency investigation is subject to the adjudication process.

An agency is not limited by the requirement of a "case or controversy" to initiate an investigation. Investigations are valid upon a *mere suspicion* that a party is in violation of the agency's statute or its regulations.

1. Constitutional Concern: Self-Incrimination

Persons and entities *may not,* under the Fifth Amendment's protection from self-incrimination, refuse to disclose agency requests for records kept in the ordinary course of business. The Supreme Court has held that such records are not protected when required to be kept by agency rule, if they are the appropriate subject of governmental regulation. *Shapiro v. United States*, 335 U.S. 1 (1948).

2. Subpoenas

A subpoena is a court order requiring the production of information through documents, testimony, or both. The subpoena has become a primary tool for agencies to compel the disclosure of information from private persons and entities.

a. Authority

Authority to issue subpoenas must be expressly delegated to an agency through legislation. The APA itself does not vest authority in an agency to issue subpoenas as part of its investigations. Rather, it states that "the court shall sustain the subpoena or similar process or demand to the extent that it is found to be in accordance with law." APA § 555(d).

Nearly all agencies have been given the power to issue subpoenas through their enabling statutes.

b. Scope

The information an agency seeks through a subpoena must be within the scope of a proper investigation. Courts will only grant a subpoena to an agency "if the inquiry is within the authority of the agency, the demand is not too indefinite, and the information sought is reasonably relevant." *United States v. Morton Salt Co.*, 338 U.S. 632, 652 (1950).

An agency may compel, through subpoena, information from **any person** who may possess it, not just from persons who are the subject of an investigation.

3. Searches and Physical Inspections

Physical searches and inspections of private property often occur during agency investigations, particularly those conducted to protect public health or safety. In general, an agency is required to obtain a **warrant** before entering private property for investigative purposes. This requirement, rooted in the Fourth Amendment's protection from unreasonable searches and seizures, has several exceptions listed below.

An agency's enabling statute generally gives it the authority to search and inspect private property. This authority may extend to the entire premises or operation, or may limit the agency's search to electronic and paper records.

Agencies *are not* required to give advance notice of an inspection (unless the enabling statute dictates otherwise). Many agencies, however, do give notice of their inspections as a courtesy.

a. Constitutional concerns—unreasonable searches and seizures

The Fourth Amendment guarantees: "The right of the people to be secure in their persons, houses, papers, and effects, against unreasonable searches and seizures, shall not be violated and no Warrants shall issue, but upon probable cause, supported by Oath or affirmation and particularly describing the place to be searched and the persons or things to be seized." U.S. Const. amend. IV.

Under these protections, a person who is the subject of a physical search or inspection has the right to refuse. If the person refuses:

i) The agency must obtain a **warrant** from a proper judge or magistrate;

ii) The warrant must be supported by a **sworn affidavit** from an official with the agency; and

iii) The affidavit must describe the **general purpose and scope** of the search.

b. Burden of proof

Due process requires the government to show **probable cause** before a search warrant will be issued. In an administrative law context, probable cause exists if an agency can demonstrate to the issuing court that (i) it has a **reasonable basis to believe a violation exists**, or (ii) that the search is part of a **systematic inspection plan** being carried out by the agency.

c. Exceptions – warrant not required

An agency does not need to obtain a warrant to physically search or inspect private property if there is:

1) Consent

In a majority of circumstances, the person whose property is to be inspected will consent to the investigation and disclose the information sought by the agency. Consent from an owner or manager nullifies an agency's requirement to obtain a warrant.

2) Emergency

Emergency circumstances may compel an agency to enter private land before obtaining a search warrant. Investigations and the seizure of evidence are proper if they are a product of the agency's effort to stop or mitigate the emergency situation.

3) Violations in plain-view

Agency officials may enter areas that are open to the public without a warrant and pursue violations of law that occur in plain-view. A person's expectation of privacy is greatly diminished in these circumstances, and a warrant is not required for an agency to take proper action.

> **Example:** An agency charged with regulating air quality may enter private property without a warrant in order to inspect a smokestack, from which emissions are visible for miles. *Air Pollution Variance Bd. v. Western Alfalfa Corp.*, 416 U.S. 861 (1974).

4) Searches authorized by statute (heavily regulated industries)

Certain industries are so heavily regulated that they may reasonably expect periodic agency inspection on their premises. If authorized by statute, agencies may search and inspect the commercial properties and facilities of heavily regulated industries without obtaining a warrant if:

  i) The regulatory scheme involves a **substantial government interest**;

  ii) The inspection is necessary to further the regulatory scheme;

  iii) The statute gives the owner proper **notice** that periodic searches may be made;

  iv) The inspection has a properly defined **scope**; and

  v) The scheme **limits discretion** of inspecting officers.

New York v. Burger, 482 U.S. 691, 702-703 (1987).

> **Examples** of heavily regulated industries include automobile junkyards, banks, mines, and power plants.

D.   ADJUDICATION

1.   In General

Adjudication is an agency hearing that involves an individual or specific group and focuses on addressing conduct that occurred in the past. Typically, the agency, through an investigation, has determined that a person is in violation of the law that the agency is charged to uphold. Adjudicative hearings allow the agency to decide the rights and liabilities of parties based on past or present facts.

Agency adjudication, by its definition, affects the rights of individuals. When adjudication is utilized, agency procedure must follow guidance from its enabling act, its self-adopted rules, the APA, and the Constitution. The Constitution guarantees that an agency cannot, through adjudication, deprive individuals of life, liberty, or property without due process. In addition, statutes and agency rules often contain language that triggers particular procedures.

At the conclusion of an adjudication, the agency will issue an **order**, declaring its final decision on the matters at issue.

2. Adjudicative Decision Makers (Administrative Law Judges)

Most agency hearings are conducted by **administrative law judges (ALJs)**. ALJs are typically employed by the agency for which they hear cases and may be removed only for good cause.

In agency adjudication, an ALJ will hear parties' cases and render an **initial decision**. The agency head (e.g., the Secretary of a cabinet department, or the commissioners of an independent agency) will then review the ALJ's findings and initial decision and render a **final agency decision**. The agency head has broad discretion in reversing an ALJ's findings and generally reserves the right to make the agency's ultimate conclusion on the matter.

During the adjudication, the ALJ (or person deciding the case) must actually consider the relevant evidence presented before rendering an opinion. He may employ others to help in the hearing and analyze the evidence, but he may only make his initial decision after reviewing the evidence himself.

3. Unbiased Decision Maker

Due process requires that an unbiased decision maker preside over all agency adjudications, both formal and informal. Adjudicative bias may come in the form of (i) an **economic stake** in the outcome of a case, (ii) **preconceived judgments** about the facts of a case, or (iii) a **close relationship** with an interested party.

Upon determining that a decision maker is biased in some way, a party may file an affidavit with the agency. In the event the presiding decision maker is excused for bias, the agency shall issue its own decision in the case. APA § 556(b).

a. Separation of functions

An agency employee who has served as an investigator, prosecutor, or advocate involved with the adjudication cannot participate or advise in the agency's decision in any factually related case, except as a witness or counsel in public proceedings. APA § 554(d).

b. Ex parte communications

During the course of agency adjudication, the decision maker may not:

i) Consult a person or party on a fact in issue, unless on notice and opportunity for all parties to participate; or

ii) Be responsible to or subject to the supervision or direction of an employee or agent engaged in the performance of investigative or prosecuting functions for an agency.

APA § 554(d). An agency employee who has not served as an investigator or advocate in the hearing may, however, communicate with an adjudicative decision maker.

4. Formal Adjudication

Many agency enabling statutes require that adjudication occur "on the record after opportunity for an agency hearing." When this language is included in the statute, an agency must conduct a **formal adjudication**. The APA sets out specific requirements for all formal adjudications, including proper notice and requirements for a proper adjudicative hearing.

a. Notice

Parties subject to an agency hearing must be given timely and adequate notice, including the:

i) **Time, place, and nature** of the hearing;

ii) **Legal authority and jurisdiction** under which the hearing will be held; and

iii) **Matters of fact and law** asserted.

An agency may overcome improper notice if it can show that the proper parties *actually knew* of the adjudication and the substance of the matters involved.

An agency may not change the theory of its case during adjudication without notice to all affected parties.

When adjudication involves multiple private parties, each party must give all other parties to the proceeding prompt notice of issues controverted in fact or law. APA § 554(b).

b. Right to a hearing

Formal adjudication requires the agency to give all interested parties the opportunity for:

i) The submission and consideration of facts, arguments, offers of settlement, or proposals of adjustment when time, the nature of the proceeding, and the public interest permit; and

ii) An oral hearing before an unbiased decision maker when the parties cannot resolve an issue on their own.

Before an initial decision may be rendered, all affected parties are entitled to submit, for the consideration of the decision maker and agency:

i) Proposed findings and conclusions; or

ii) Exceptions to the decisions or recommended decisions of subordinate employees or to tentative agency decisions; and

iii) Supporting reasons for the exceptions or proposed findings or conclusions.

APA § 557(c).

c. The right to counsel

Parties to an administrative hearing generally are permitted to be accompanied, represented, and advised by counsel. There is, however, no constitutional guarantee of representation; an agency is not required to provide a party with counsel. APA § 555(b).

d. Discovery

In federal agency adjudication, there is no general discovery requirement outside of an agency's enabling legislation. Many statutes do, however, authorize affected parties to compel relevant information through the issuance of subpoenas. Parties may also utilize the Freedom of Information Act to gather information that is relevant to an adjudicative hearing.

e. Burden of proof

Unless specified otherwise by statute, the **proponent** of a rule or order has the burden of proof during formal adjudication.

f. Consideration of the record as a whole

An agency cannot impose a sanction or issue a rule or order unless it first considers the **record as a whole** and its final decision is "supported by and in accordance with the reliable, probative, and substantial evidence." APA § 556(d).

g. Standard of proof

In general, the burdened party must prove its case by a **preponderance of the evidence**. In some cases, the standard may be higher (e.g., clear and convincing evidence) if greater rights are at issue (e.g., deportation, revocation of a professional license).

h. Evidence

The admission of evidence in an administrative adjudicative hearing is much less exclusive than the Federal Rules of Evidence. As a general rule, an agency may admit *any evidence* that is **relevant** to the proceeding.

1) Hearsay evidence

Hearsay evidence is admissible in agency hearings. However, an agency's decision may not be based entirely on hearsay evidence.

If a party relies on hearsay evidence, many courts require **residuum** (non-hearsay) evidence to support hearsay evidence that is presented. While there is no strict residuum rule in federal court when hearsay evidence is presented, decisions based on hearsay evidence may lack proper "substantial evidence" for support when scrutinized under judicial review.

Constitutional Concern – Confronting Adverse Witnesses: Although hearsay evidence may be liberally introduced into an administrative proceeding as relevant, due process ensures persons the right to confront adverse witnesses. When an out-of-court statement by a non-testifying declarant is used to prove the truth of the matter asserted, there may be a violation of this fundamental right.

2) Official notice

The decision maker in an administrative hearing may take official notice of facts that are commonly known or that can be learned through common reference sources, as well as technical matters that are within the agency's area of expertise. Material that is officially noticed becomes evidence under which an agency may issue its final decision.

Upon timely request, opponent parties must be given an opportunity to rebut evidence that has been admitted through official notice. APA § 556(e).

i. The record

All evidence presented in each formal adjudicative hearing must be compiled into an official agency record. In reaching its final decision, an agency decision maker must rely solely on the record that contains all of the testimony and exhibits presented during the hearing process. Evidence not included within the record may not be considered by a decision maker, unless it is properly admitted through official notice. APA § 556(e).

For each decision, the record must include:

i) **Findings and conclusions** on all material issues of fact, law, or discretion that are presented on the record; and

ii) The **appropriate rule, order, sanction, relief**, or denial thereof.

APA § 557(c).

> The record will become the sole context by which a court may review an agency's adjudicative decision making. Courts will not infer findings that are not included in the record, nor will they accept "post hoc" rationalizations for agency decisions.

j. Binding effect of agency decisions

When parties have had the opportunity to present evidence and be heard in front of an impartial agency decision maker and the agency has issued a final decision on the matter, *res judicata* precludes the same (or substantially related) claim from being formally tried in the future.

When an agency receives an unfavorable decision through adjudication, it is precluded from re-litigating the same claim against the same party. An agency cannot retry a case that it has lost in another circuit in an attempt to receive a more favorable decision.

k. Reconsideration of agency decisions

Under the APA, a losing party in an agency adjudication may petition the agency to reconsider its decision or to reopen the proceeding. The determination of whether to grant the petition is at the agency's discretion.

5. Informal Adjudication

In many instances, an agency's enabling statute does not require formal adjudication. In such instances, the agency may conduct an informal adjudication to resolve disputes.

In cases of informal adjudication, an agency is not required to follow the APA's strict procedural steps of formal adjudication, but must at least provide all interested parties with:

i) The right to appear before an **impartial decision maker** of the agency;

ii) The right to be represented by **counsel** at the hearing;

iii) The right to issue **subpoenas** to a party upon a "statement or showing of general relevance and reasonable scope of the evidence sought";

iv) The **opportunity to confront adverse witnesses**, although cross examination may be limited; and

v) **Prompt notice** of a denial (in whole or part) of a written application, petition, or other request made in connection with an agency proceeding; notice must be accompanied by a brief statement of the grounds for denial.

APA § 555.

6. Adjudicative Fees and Expenses

Unless the decision maker finds that the position of the agency was substantially justified or that special circumstances make an award unjust, the agency conducting the adjudication must award fees and other expenses incurred to the prevailing party. The adjudicative officer may reduce the amount of fees or expenses awarded if the party, during the course of the proceedings, engaged in conduct that unreasonably delayed the final resolution. APA § 504(a).

IV. JUDICIAL REVIEW

A. IN GENERAL

The Administrative Procedure Act sets forth a strong **presumption** that final agency action is subject to judicial review. This presumption can only be overcome by clear and convincing evidence from Congress to the contrary. There is a virtually irrebuttable presumption in favor of judicial review of constitutional claims. There is no presumption in favor of pre-enforcement judicial review.

Through judicial review, courts may overturn, enjoin, or compel agency actions. A reviewing court decides all relevant questions of law, interprets constitutional and statutory provisions, and determines the meaning or applicability of the terms of an agency action.

Authorization for judicial review of agency action is usually expressly contained (or precluded) within the agency's enabling act.

Even when authorized by statute, not all agency actions may be challenged in court. The party seeking to challenge agency action in court must first show:

i) Legislative authorization for judicial review;

ii) Standing;

iii) A final agency action;

iv) Ripeness of the issues presented; and

v) Exhaustion of all available administrative remedies.

Upon review, a court may compel agency action unlawfully withheld or unreasonably delayed. The court may also *set aside agency actions* that it determines are:

i) Arbitrary, capricious, an abuse of discretion, or otherwise not in accordance with the law;

ii) Contrary to constitutional rights, powers, privileges, or immunities;

iii) In excess of statutory authority;

iv) Without observance of procedure required by law;

v) Unsupported by substantial evidence on the record, in cases involving formal adjudication or formal rulemaking; or

vi) Unsupported by the facts.

APA § 706.

B. JUSTICIABILITY

1. Statutory Authorization and Preclusion

Federal courts are courts of limited jurisdiction and may only hear **cases and controversies** arising under the laws, treaties, or the Constitution of the United States. In order for a court to review agency actions, judicial review must be authorized by statute; such authorization typically exists within an agency's enabling statute.

> Every case filed in a federal court requires a jurisdictional statute. This authority usually exists in an agency's enabling statute.

Congress may, however, be silent in its legislation as to whether it intends an agency's actions to be subject to judicial review. The Supreme Court has held that, under the APA, federal agency actions are presumed to be reviewable unless there is clear and convincing evidence that Congress intended otherwise. *Califano v. Sanders*, 430 U.S. 99, 109 (1977).

Courts may also be expressly precluded from reviewing an agency's final actions or decisions. The APA distinguishes between two types of preclusions to review: (i) matters that are expressly **precluded by statute**; and (ii) matters that have been **committed to agency discretion by law**. APA § 701(a). Agency action is committed to agency discretion by law when the agency's enabling statute is written so broadly that a court would have no meaningful standard against which to judge the agency's exercise of discretion (i.e., there is "no law to apply").

a. Agency inaction: enforcement

Challenges to an agency's failure or refusal to take action are generally not reviewable by courts. The presumption may be overcome if a statute **commands an agency to act** on a certain matter, and the agency has failed to do so, or if the agency's systematic course of inaction amounts to an abdication of its statutory mandate.

b. Agency inaction: rulemaking

Challenges to an agency's refusal to engage in rulemaking in response to a petition for rulemaking may be reviewable by courts.

2. Standing

The doctrine of standing requires that plaintiffs bringing a claim have "a personal stake in the outcome." *Baker v. Carr*, 369 U.S. 186, 204 (1962). To have proper constitutional standing, a plaintiff must have (i) suffered an actual or imminent **injury**, (ii) that was **directly linked** to the actions of the defendants, and (iii) that may be **redressed** by the court granting the relief requested. *Lujan v. National Wildlife Federation*, 504 U.S. 555, 560 (1992).

In challenging the actions of an administrative agency, a plaintiff must also demonstrate that she is within the **zone of interests** that the statute seeks to protect. *Air Courier Conference v. Postal Workers Union*, 498 U.S. 517, 519 (1991).

> The threshold requirements for a plaintiff's standing to get into federal court (injury, within the zone of interests) are stricter than for those participating in an agency adjudication or rulemaking.

a. Injury in fact

A plaintiff's injuries must be actual (not abstract) and personal (more particularized than that suffered generally by all citizens). *Valley Forge Christian College v. Americans United for Separation of Church and State, Inc.,* 454 U.S. 464, 471 (1982).

> Courts have expanded the concept of injury caused by agency action to include economic injuries, competitive injuries, environmental and recreational injuries, aesthetic injuries, and injuries stemming from the deprivation of information.

b. Zone of interest of legislation

To properly challenge a final agency action through judicial review, a party must arguably fall "within the zone of interests protected or regulated by the statute or constitutional guarantee in question." *Assoc. of Data Processing Service Organizations v. Camp*, 397 U.S. 150, 153 (1970). This means that, while a statute need not expressly state that the plaintiff in question falls under its protections, a court must determine that the plaintiff's interests and rights are among those intended to be protected through the enactment of legislation.

c. Special instances of standing

Courts have established certain instances when, although a plaintiff would normally not have standing to challenge an agency action, circumstances permit the case to go forward.

1) Taxpayer standing

Generally, citizens may not challenge actions of the federal government in federal court if their standing is based solely on their status as a taxpayer. However, a narrow exception applies if a plaintiff can demonstrate:

i) The challenged action is based on the federal government's taxing and spending power; and

ii) The action violates a constitutional prohibition on the use of that power, such as the Establishment Clause.

Flast v. Cohen, 392 U.S. 83, 102-103 (1968).

2) Third-party standing

To have standing, a plaintiff's injuries must generally be personal. Courts have allowed plaintiffs to bring third-party claims in rare instances if:

i) The injured party would have difficulty asserting his own rights;

ii) A close relationship exists between the named plaintiff and the injured party (e.g., a doctor-patient relationship); and

iii) The injured party does not have adequate resources to assert the claim himself.

3) Organizational standing

Organizations and associations will often challenge agency actions if the cost of litigation would preclude an individual from bringing her own claim. Organizations have proper standing to challenge agency actions in federal court if:

i) Their members would have standing to bring suit in their own right;

ii) The subject matter of the challenged action is related to the organization's overall purpose; and

iii) Neither the claim nor the requested relief requires the participation of individual members of the organization.

3. Exhaustion of Administrative Remedies

Generally, a plaintiff may not seek judicial review of agency action until after she has exhausted all remedies that are available within the agency itself (e.g., hearing, appeal, etc.). Courts adhere to the doctrine of exhaustion in order to promote judicial efficiency and utilize expertise within agencies, and will dismiss claims when a plaintiff has failed to first attempt all avenues of relief within the agency.

An aggrieved party must pursue all remedies available within the agency, as far as the agency will permit, before challenging the agency action in court.

Exceptions to the requirement of exhaustion exist. A plaintiff may bring a claim without first exhausting all administrative remedies if:

i) The action is brought under the APA (unless a statute or regulation explicitly requires exhaustion);

ii) Requiring exhaustion would undermine the effectiveness of eventual judicial review (e.g., it would cause irreparable harm to the plaintiff);

iii) The agency is unable to provide effective relief (e.g., the injured party requests money damages or a finding of unconstitutionality); or

iv) The challenger can show that exhaustion of administrative remedies would be futile (e.g., the agency is biased).

4. Ripeness

Courts will only hear challenges to agency actions that are ripe for review. An agency policy must first be applied before it can be challenged; this allows a reviewing court to determine how the policy is applied in practice.

In determining whether an issue is ripe for review, a court will consider the:

i) "**Fitness of the issues**" for immediate review; and

ii) "**Hardship to the parties**" that would result should the court deny review.

Texas v. United States, 523 U.S. 296, 301 (1998).

The first requirement, fitness of the issues, has two subparts: (i) the claims must be purely legal, and (ii) there must be final agency action. The second requirement, hardship to the parties, will be met if a party is forced to comply with expensive or burdensome regulation while waiting for judicial review.

5. Finality

Generally, courts will not grant judicial review of an agency action if the agency has not fully resolved the matter first; the action must be final. Agency action is final if the action marks the consummation of the agency's decision-making process and some legal consequence flows from the agency's action.

Courts may, however, permit judicial review in instances when:

i) A challenged action will threaten public health or safety;

ii) Delaying judicial review would impose a severe economic hardship on the party affected by the action; or

iii) The agency has unreasonably delayed taking action in the matter.

C. STANDARD OF REVIEW

When reviewing challenges to agency actions, courts are limited in their ability to substitute their own judgment and discretion for that of the agency administering its statutory duties. The scope of review will vary, depending on the type of agency action that is being challenged – **discretionary acts**, **findings of fact**, or **interpretations of law**.

1. Exercises of Agency Discretion – "Arbitrary and Capricious" Review

Agency actions often involve exercises in agency discretion, such as an agency's decision to adopt a new rule or regulation or a decision regarding what resources to commit to a particular issue.

When a decision is to be "committed to agency discretion by law," a court is precluded from reviewing the agency action. APA § 701(a)(2).

When agency action is not expressly committed to agency discretion by law, a reviewing court will only overturn an act if the agency decision was **arbitrary and capricious**. APA § 706(2)(A). Under this standard, courts will only overturn discretionary agency action when it determines that:

i) The agency failed to **consider all relevant factors** (including objections and alternatives) in making its decision; or

ii) The agency failed to **engage in reasoned decision-making** in exercising its discretion.

2. Findings of Fact

Through investigations and subsequent adjudicative hearings, agencies often make independent findings of fact on which they rely to draw conclusions. Courts are very deferential to an agency's fact-finding. On the federal level, unless directed otherwise by statute, a reviewing court may only overturn an agency's formal findings of fact if they are **unsupported by "substantial evidence" on the "whole record."** APA § 706.

a. "Substantial evidence"

Courts have interpreted this standard to include any amount of relevant evidence that "a reasonable mind might accept as adequate to support a conclusion." *Consolidated Edison Co. v. NRLB*, 305 U.S. 197, 229 (1938). An agency's factual conclusions must be **reasonable** in light of the evidence included in the record.

b. "Whole record"

A reviewing court must examine the whole record, including dissenting comments and contradictory data, in determining whether an agency's factual conclusions are reasonable.

c. Findings of the ALJ

When the findings of the ALJ and agency contradict one another, the "substantiality" of the evidence supporting the final decision may be lessened.

3. Agency Interpretations of Law – *Chevron* Deference

Often, Congress does not give express directions as to how an agency is to carry out its many functions in enforcing the law. Courts give agencies great deference when interpreting ambiguous statutory language intended to guide their actions.

a. Analysis

When analyzing agency interpretations of statutory language, courts will employ a two-part test, referred to as *Chevron* deference:

i) First, has Congress spoken clearly as to the precise question at issue? If the language is clear and unambiguous, the agency and court must give effect to Congress's clear intent.

ii) If the statute is silent or ambiguous with respect to the agency's interpretation, courts will only reject agency interpretations that are unreasonable. Courts will defer to **any reasonable agency interpretation** of ambiguous statutory language.

Chevron USA Inc. v. Natural Resources Defense Council, 467 U.S. 837, 842-43 (1984).

b. Exceptions to the *Chevron* defense

There are three circumstances in which *Chevron* deference generally does not apply:

i) When an agency has interpreted a statute that it does not administer; *see Gonzales v. Oregon*, 546 U.S. 243 (2006);

ii) When the agency's interpretation did not arise out of a relatively formal agency action such as notice and comment rulemaking or formal adjudication; *see U.S. v. Mead Corp.*, 533 U.S. 218 (2001);

iii) When a court has already issued a binding interpretation of the statute's clear meaning (as opposed to merely the best or likely meaning of a statute); *see Nat'l Cable & Telecomms. Ass'n v. Brand X Internet Services*, 545 U.S. 967 (2005).

Even when *Chevron* deference does not apply, the agency is still entitled to a degree of deference, based on its expertise and familiarity with the relevant issues.

V. AGENCY ACCOUNTABILITY

A. THE FREEDOM OF INFORMATION ACT (FOIA)

1. In General

Through their investigatory, rulemaking, and adjudicative actions, agencies gather and hold a vast amount of information which is generally available to the public at large. Congress enacted the Freedom of Information Act (FOIA) as a mechanism by which agencies are generally compelled to release information they hold to any person requesting it. FOIA does place limits, however, on the type of information that may be released.

FOIA mandates that agencies release information to **any person** who properly requests it; the release of information is not limited to parties of an agency action.

2. Disclosure

All federal agencies must make available for public inspection and copying:

i) Final opinions, including concurring and dissenting opinions, and orders stemming from the adjudication of cases;

ii) Statements of policy that have been adopted, but not yet published in the Federal Register;

iii) Administrative staff manuals;

iv) General instructions;

v) Copies of all records that have been released to any person, which the agency determines are likely to become the subject of subsequent requests for substantially the same records; and

vi) A general index of those records.

5 U.S.C. § 552(a)(2).

When an agency is requested to release information under FOIA, it must make a determination whether to comply with the request within **20 days**. The agency must immediately notify the information's requestor of the determination, the reasoning behind it, and instruct them of the right to appeal any adverse determination to the head of the agency. 5 U.S.C. § 552(a)(6).

3. Compelling Agency Disclosure

A person whose request is denied by the agency has the right under FOIA to challenge the denial in federal court. The agency has the burden to demonstrate why it has denied a proper request under FOIA. Courts, after *de novo* review of the matter, may compel the disclosure of the requested information.

4. Excluded Information

Not all information in an agency's possession is subject to mandatory disclosure to the public. FOIA specifically does not require the disclosure of information that is:

i) Classified by Executive Order or to be kept secret in the interest of national security or foreign policy;

ii) Related solely to internal personnel rules and practices of an agency;

iii) Specifically exempted from disclosure by statute;

iv) Trade secrets or commercial or financial information obtained from a person and privileged or confidential;

v) Inter-agency or intra-agency memoranda or letters;

vi) Files (e.g., medical records, personnel records) that would constitute a clearly unwarranted invasion of personal privacy; as well as

vii) Records and information compiled for law enforcement purposes, but only if disclosure:

    a) Could reasonably be expected to interfere with enforcement proceedings;

    b) Would deprive a person of a right to a fair trial;

    c) Constitutes an unwarranted invasion of personal privacy;

    d) Discloses the identity of a confidential source;

    e) Discloses law enforcement techniques, procedures, or guidelines that could be used to circumvent the law; or

    f) Could endanger the life or physical safety of any individual.

5 U.S.C. § 552(b).

5. Partially Excluded Information

When only a portion of the requested information is excluded from disclosure under FOIA, the agency must disclose any "reasonably segregable portion...to any person requesting such record after deletion of the portions which are exempt..." 5 U.S.C. § 552(b).

B. GOVERNMENT IN THE SUNSHINE ACT

In order to increase government accountability, the Sunshine Act requires that every portion of every meeting of a federal agency must be open to public observation. 5 U.S.C. § 552b(b).

A "meeting" is a deliberation of at least the number of individual agency members required to take action on behalf of the agency when such deliberations determine or result in the joint conduct or disposition of official agency business. 5 U.S.C. § 552b(a)(2).

For each meeting, at least one week before the meeting, the agency shall make a public announcement of the time, place, and subject matter of the meeting, and whether it is to be open or closed to the public. 5 U.S.C. § 552b(e)(1).

There are, however, a number of agency actions that are exempted from the requirements of the government in the Sunshine Act, including when the release of information may (i) violate an executive order, (ii) reveal trade secrets, (iii) threaten national security or foreign relations, (iv) involve information related solely to agency personnel and management, or (v) interfere with an agency investigation or prosecution.

C. FEDERAL STATUTES AIMED AT PROTECTING SMALL BUSINESSES

1. Regulatory Flexibility Act

The Regulatory Flexibility Act (RFA) requires federal agencies, as part of their rulemaking procedure, to "solicit the ideas and comments of small businesses, small organizations, and small governmental jurisdictions to examine the impact of proposed and existing rules on such entities, and to review the continued need for existing rules." When the rule's impact is determined to be "significant" on small entities, the agency must examine less-burdensome alternatives. 5 U.S.C. § 602.

The RFA also allows for judicial review of agency actions that fail to meet its procedural requirements. 5 U.S.C. § 611.

2. Small Business Regulatory Enforcement Fairness Act

Congress strengthened the Regulatory Flexibility Act by enacting the Small Business Regulatory Enforcement Fairness Act (SBREFA), which mandates that:

i) Federal agencies establish a policy or program that reduces and waives civil penalties for violations of a statutory or regulatory requirement by a small entity;

ii) The Small Business Administration (SBA) Administrator designates a Small Business and Agriculture Regulatory Enforcement Ombudsman to receive, investigate, and report on regulatory compliance and enforcement comments and complaints from small business owners; and

iii) The SBA Administrator appoints and designates SBA Regional Small Business Regulatory Fairness Boards to:

a) Review regulatory compliance and enforcement comments and complaints made by small business owners; and

b) Recommend regulatory improvements to the SBA Administrator and the head of affected agencies.

Federal regulatory compliance rules and guidelines must be written in plain English and readily available to small business owners.

Agency

AGENCY

Table of Contents

AGENCY

I. THE AGENCY RELATIONSHIP

A. INTRODUCTION

The law of agency addresses the legal consequences of one person (the **agent**) acting on behalf of, and subject to, the control of another person (the **principal**).

Agency relationships are anchored in contract and tort law. Under contract law, agents perform acts of negotiating and making contracts with third persons. A contract made by an agent on behalf of a principal with a third person establish certain rights and duties, depending on the agent's level of authority and how the contract is executed. On the other hand, tort law focuses on the vicarious liability that attaches to a principal for torts or crimes committed by an agent.

1. Background

Agency relationships are consensual, requiring assent by both parties. For this reason, whenever two parties with the necessary legal capacity mutually consent to a relationship in which one will act on behalf of the other and subject to the other's control, they have formed an agency relationship.

The most recognized principals are employers who control the actions of their employees (agents). A corporation or other business organization can be a principal, and the officers and other employees of the corporation are agents (just as partners are agents of a partnership).

Although agency relationships are generally based on consent, agency may be imposed by operation of law (e.g., estoppel or a state motorist statute).

2. Creation of an Agency Relationship

The most common method of creating an agency relationship is **by appointment** (oral or written). Generally, a principal's appointment of an agent need not comply with specific formalities, for example, a writing, to be effective. However, many states require an agent's appointment to be in writing when the agency relates to interests in property (e.g., a power of attorney).

The principal will generally be bound by any contract created on the principal's behalf, by an agent with the power to bind the principal, whether the power to bind is:

i) Expressed orally or in a writing;

ii) Implied by a principal's conduct; or

iii) Misinterpreted by a third party.

> **EXAM NOTE:** Partnership and corporations questions often require application of agency law. Be prepared to (i) identify the existence of agency relationships, (ii) discuss whether the principal is subject to liability for the agent's actions, (iii) articulate an agent's fiduciary duty to the principal and whether the agent has breached that duty, and (iv) determine if or when an agency relationship has terminated.

3. Determining the Existence of an Agency Relationship

An agency relationship is created when:

i) A **principal manifests assent** to an agent;

ii) The agent acts on the **principal's behalf**;

iii) The agent's actions are subject to the **principal's control**; and

iv) The **agent manifests assent** or otherwise consents.

> **EXAM NOTE:** Agency points are obtained by listing the elements that create an agency relationship and demonstrating how they are or are not present.

B. THE PRINCIPAL

1. Background

Any individual or entity (e.g., a government, organization, association) who has the legal capacity to possess rights and incur obligations can be a principal.

Principals may delegate tasks, give instructions, direct employee tasks, and monitor employee activities.

2. Principal's Control

An agent agrees to be subject to the principal's control and a principal agrees to be bound by the acts of its agent within the scope of the agent's authority. The fact that a principal lacks the right to control the full range of an agent's actions (professional judgment), or fails to exercise the right to control the agent, does not eliminate the principal's rights or affect the existence of an agency relationship.

It is sufficient that the principal has the right to control the result or the ultimate objectives of the agent's work.

> **EXAM NOTE:** Do you need to identify a principal quickly? (i) Look for the types of principals listed below when reading fact patterns, and (ii) search for examples of any person, individual, or entity that exerts control over another party. The key word is "control."

3. Types of Principals

Agency questions may arise in connection with several different types of principals.

> **EXAM NOTE:** The current Restatement (Third) of Agency reflects a change in terminology from master-servant to employer-employee relationship.

a. Individual

Any individual who has the contractual capacity and is not a minor has the legal capacity to enter into an agency relationship as a principal and to appoint an agent. Status as a principal is established by the individual's intent to delegate an act and control the way in which the act is performed by another.

b. Master or employer

A master (often referred to as an employer) is a principal who employs an agent to perform services and controls—or has a right to control—the physical conduct of the employee's performance. Restatement (Second) of Agency § 2(1) (1958). An agent who is subject to this level of control is referred to as a servant or employee.

> The more control a principal exerts over an agent's actions, the more likely the master-servant (or employer-employee) relationship exists.

Courts usually determine a principal's status as a master/employer upon the control the principal asserts over the servant/employee. Several factors contribute to this analysis, such as whether:

i) The principal exercises significant control over the details of the worker's day-to-day activities;

ii) The principal supplies the tools at the place of employment;

iii) The principal pays the worker on a structured pay period;

iv) The worker's skill level is specialized; and

v) The principal directs the work to completion.

c. Entrepreneur

Any business owner who has the legal capacity to contract with a person to represent him and conduct business on his behalf can be a principal.

> **EXAM NOTE:** Look for business owners (e.g., sole proprietors without partners) to be frequently highlighted as principals in agency and partnership fact patterns.

d. Corporation

A corporation is a legal entity created for the purpose of conducting business. A corporation must have legal existence to be considered a principal in an agency relationship. Corporations that are yet to be formed (i.e., future incorporation pending) cannot be principals.

Corporate officers, employees of the corporation, and other persons, can serve as agents of the corporation.

e. Partnership

A partnership is an association of two or more persons for the purpose of carrying on as co-owners of a business for profit. The partnership can be considered the principal in an agency relationship. Partners, employees of the partnership, and other persons, such as attorneys, can all serve as agents of the partnership.

C. THE AGENT

1. Background

Generally, any person with minimal capacity can serve as an agent. An agent is not required to have the capacity to form contracts. Therefore, minors or incompetents can serve as agents. Entities may also serve as agents. Agents may perform a variety of general or specialized tasks.

Depending on the level of the agent's authority, or the manner in which the agent conducts business with a third party, the agent may incur personal liability for acts that are unauthorized by the principal, illegal, negligent, or outside the scope of the agent's employment.

The consensual nature of the agency relationship requires an agent to:

i) Have minimal capacity;

ii) Manifest assent and consent to act on the principal's behalf; and

iii) Manifest assent to be subject to the principal's control.

2. Formalities of Agency

Creating an agency relationship is relatively easy, because:

i) An agent need not receive consideration (a gratuitous agent); and

ii) A principal's appointment of an agent generally need not be in writing or comply with other formalities.

> **EXAM NOTE:** Do you need to identify an agent quickly? (i) Look for the types of agents listed below in fact patterns, and (ii) search for persons who work on behalf of, and are subject to the control of, another person/principal.

3. Types of Agents

a. Individual

Any individual with minimal capacity (some understanding that a contract is being initiated and the general nature of its subject matter) has the requisite capacity to be an agent. Status as an agent is established by the agreement to act on behalf of, and subject to the control of, the principal.

b. Servant or employee

A servant (often referred to as an employee) is an agent who is subject to the principal's control with respect to the physical conduct of the employee's performance. Generally, employees are paid hourly or by time periods (e.g., weekly, bi-weekly, monthly). Their work is an integral part of the work of the employer, tasks are generally completed under the employer's direction, and employees are employed for long periods of time with the same employer. The more control an employer exerts over an agent's day-to-day activities, the more likely the agent qualifies as an employee.

c. Independent contractor

An agent who is not a servant/employee is referred to as an independent contractor. Courts examine several factors to determine whether an agent is an employee or an independent contractor. The most important factor is that an independent contractor is not subject to the principal's control regarding the physical conduct of the agent's performance.

An independent contractor can be identified as a person who:

    i)   Bears the risk and benefits from good management;

    ii)   Maintains a high level of independence;

    iii) Is free to work for others;

    iv) Agrees to be paid a fixed fee;

    v)   Receives payment based on results;

    vi) Is liable for work performed; and

    vii) Accepts responsibility to remedy defects at her own expense.

> **EXAM NOTE:** Questions may refer to an independent contractor as a "non-employee agent."

d. Gratuitous agent

A gratuitous agent is an agent who does not receive compensation. This does not prevent the creation of an agency relationship, but generally does prevent the formation of an enforceable contract between agent and principal due to the lack of consideration.

e. General and special agents

A general agent is an agent with broad authority over a wide variety of tasks, involving a continuity of service in a particular kind of business, without renewed authorization for each transaction or decision. General agents include store managers and purchasing agents.

Special agents generally have limited authority regarding a specific transaction or a string of repetitive acts. Common types of special agents include real estate agents, subagents, insurance agents, commission merchants, and bailees.

f. Trustee as agent

A trustee is an agent and is subject to the control of the settlor of the trust or one or more of its beneficiaries. A trustee maintains a fiduciary relationship with and holds property for the benefit of the settlor. Restatement (Third) of Agency § 1.04(10) (2006).

g. Subagents

A subagent is a person appointed by an agent to perform functions that the agent has agreed to perform on behalf of a principal. The agent is liable to the principal for the conduct of the subagent. When an appointing agent hires employees, they are presumed to be subagents of the appointing agent, acting on behalf of the appointing agent's principal.

Example: Employees of an advertising firm working on the account of a customer of the firm are presumed to be subagents of the firm.

A real estate broker who successfully markets property to a prospective buyer (i.e., a "showing broker") is treated as a subagent of the broker with whom a prospective seller has listed the property (i.e., a "listing broker").

1) Power to appoint subagent

An agent may appoint a subagent only if the agent has actual or apparent authority to do so.

2) Duties of subagent

A subagent owes a duty of loyalty to the principal as well as the appointing agent.

3) Contractual liability

a) Agent

The agent is responsible to the principal for the subagent's conduct. Thus, the agent may be liable for a loss incurred by the principal as a consequence of the subagent's misconduct.

b) Principal

A principal is bound by the subagent's acts to the same extent as if the agent had undertaken the acts. Notice received by a subagent is treated as notice to the principal; knowledge possessed by the subagent is imputed the principal. The principal is not obligated to compensate the subagent when an agreement was created between the subagent and the agent concerning compensation or other duties.

c) Agent serving co-principals

An agent has a duty of loyalty to the principal. In a situation where an agent is serving more than one principal, and there is no substantial conflict among the principals' interests or their instructions to the agent, the agent may fulfill duties owed to all principals.

If a conflict exists between the principals, the agent may not work for the conflicting principals.

4) Tort consequences

An agent who appoints a subagent may be vicariously liable for torts committed by the subagent.

D. FORMATION OF AGENCY RELATIONSHIPS

1. Capacity

To become a principal and be bound by an agent's actions, a person must have capacity both to consent to the agency relationship and to enter into the transaction to which the agent purports to bind the principal.

In contrast, virtually any person can serve as an agent. A person can serve as an agent as long as he has the physical and mental capability to do whatever he has been appointed to do.

a. Minors

A person under the age of majority does not have legal capacity to form contracts. Therefore, a minor generally may not be bound to a contract by an agent. However, a minor can serve as an agent.

b. Incompetents

A person who has a factual incapacity, such as incompetence, due to a mental condition related to medication, drugs, alcohol, or illness, does not have the legal capacity to be a principal, but may be an agent.

c. Unincorporated associations

An unincorporated association is a non-legal entity where two or more persons voluntarily associate with mutual consent or purpose. Examples of unincorporated associations include religious, literary, professional, charitable, or social associations; they each lack the capacity to form agency relationships.

2. Consent

Both the principal and the agent must consent to the agency relationship. The agent does not have to verbally consent, but may manifest assent by performing act(s) on behalf of the principal. Restatement (Third) of Agency § 1.01, cmts c, d; § 103 (2006).

Note that termination of an agency relationship may be unilateral. The principal or agent may terminate the agency without the other's consent.

3. Consideration

The parties may create an agency relationship without consideration.

Example: A and B are good friends. B has a new job starting in a week, but does not want to drive her new sports car from Ohio to California. A offers to drive B's car to California, and B offers to pay A's expenses while she is on the road. A declines the offer of payment. A (agent) is entitled to compensation for her act of driving B's (individual-principal) car to California, just as B has the obligation to compensate A. However, their prior oral agreement negates the need for compensation and the principal-agent relationship remains intact.

4. Writing Requirement

A writing is generally not necessary to create an agency relationship. In some jurisdictions, statutes require that the principal's authorization of the agent to be in writing and comply with specific requirements. This tends to occur most often when the transaction the agent enters into on the principal's behalf must be in writing and meet specific requirements. The most common example is when the agent contracts to sell or buy real property.

When a statute requires the principal's authorization to be in writing, the requirement is often referred to as the "**equal dignity rule**," i.e., the authorization must be of equal dignity to the underlying transaction. The equal dignity rule operates to protect the principal against third party actions. Therefore, a principal can raise the lack of written authorization as a defense. It does not apply in a contract action brought by a principal against a third party or in an action brought by an agent against the principal. Restatement (Third) of Agency § 3.02, cmt. b (2006).

II. LIABILITY OF THE PRINCIPAL AND AGENT TO THIRD PARTIES

A. BACKGROUND

Once an agency relationship has been created, the principal potentially can be bound to contracts by the agent and subject to vicarious liability for the agent's tortious conduct.

B. CONTRACTUAL LIABILITY OF THE PRINCIPAL

A principal is subject to liability on a contract the agent enters into on the principal's behalf if the agent has the power to bind the principal to the contract.

An agent has power to bind the principal to a contract when:

i) The agent has **actual authority** (express or implied);

ii) The agent has **apparent authority**; or

iii) The principal is **estopped** from denying the agent's authority.

In addition, even if an agent acts with no power to bind the principal, the principal can become subject to liability on the contract if the principal ratifies the contract.

1. Actual Authority

Actual authority may be either express or implied.

a. Express actual authority

Express actual authority can be created via:

i) Oral or written words;

ii) Clear, direct, and definite language; or

iii) Specific detailed terms and instructions.

> **Example:** Specific, detailed instructions such as, "Hire Nikki Jones today."

1) Objective and subjective standard of intent

In order for express (actual) authority to exist, the principal's manifestation must cause the agent to believe that the agent is doing what the **principal wants** (subjective standard) and the agent's belief must be **reasonable** (objective standard).

A principal's unexpressed subjective intent regarding an agent's authority is ineffective. Remember, it is the *manifestation of a principal's intent* (spoken/written words, instructions, statements, or any conduct by the principal) that forms the basis for actual authority. Restatement (Third) of Agency §2.01, cmt. c (2006).

2) Principal's manifestations (assent/intent)

For actual authority to exist, a principal must make a manifestation that causes the agent reasonably to believe that the agent is authorized. Silence or the failure to dissent by a principal, to the actions or words of an agent, when a reasonable person would do so, can constitute a manifestation of assent for an agent to act on the principal's behalf. A principal must give the agent **clear notice** if the principal disagrees with the agent's actions.

3) Manifestation must reach the agent

A principal's manifestation must reach the agent in order to create actual authority. The principal might communicate with the agent directly, or the manifestation might reach the agent by some other means, such as through another agent of the principal.

4) Express authority granted in error

A principal's manifestation intended for one agent and given to another agent in error can create express authority to the agent who received the manifestation by mistake. The same result occurs when a principal's manifestation concerning the subject matter is incorrect.

Example: A business owner asks A (an employee) to sign an invoice that just came over the fax machine for $400. B (also an employee), who is standing next to A says okay, picks up the invoice from the fax, and signs it.

5) Third person's knowledge of actual authority is irrelevant

In order for express actual authority to exist, the agent must believe that the agent is doing what the principal wants (subjective standard) and the agent's belief must be reasonable (objective standard). Awareness of the agent's authority by a third party does not determine the nature or extent of the authority.

b. Implied actual authority

Implied actual authority allows an agent to take whatever actions (designated or implied in the principal's manifestations) are properly necessary to achieve the principal's objectives, based on the agent's reasonable understanding of the manifestations and objectives of the principal. Restatement (Third) of Agency § 2.01, cmt. b (2006).

Example: The authority to interview is implied in the agent's authority to hire.

The authority to make purchases on behalf of the principal may create implied authority in an agent to:

i) Make payments for goods and services purchased;

ii) Accept deliveries; and

iii) Collect funds.

1) Customary implied authority

In the absence of instructions to the contrary, an agent has implied authority to act within accepted business customs or general trade usage within an industry. The agent must be aware of the normal business customs or usage before she acts.

2) Implied authority by position

A principal may manifest assent to the actions of his agent by placing the agent in a position that customarily has certain authority, such as vice president or treasurer.

3) Implied by acquiescence

Implied authority based upon acquiescence commonly results from:

i)   A principal's acceptance of the agent's acts as they occur; or

ii) The principal's failure to object to the unauthorized actions of the agent which:

   a) Affirm the agent's belief that those actions further the principal's objectives; and

   b) Support the agent's perceived authority to act in the future.

Thus, it is imperative that a principal stop, correct, and clarify any unacceptable act performed by an agent when the act takes place, so as not to grant implied authority as to the future actions of the agent.

> **Example:** A, the manager of a restaurant, has been signing the invoices for wine (without authorization) delivered to the restaurant for the last four months, since the owner of the restaurant, B, has been working on opening the outside café. B has never expressly authorized A to sign for the wine orders, but when he saw A sign for an order on two occasions, B failed to object to A's unauthorized action. A currently has implied authority by acquiescence to sign for future wine orders, and B will be liable for A's acts on his behalf.

4) Implied authority due to emergency

Agents have implied authority to take all reasonably necessary measures in cases of emergency, in the absence of the principal and/or specific instructions to act.

5) Implied authority to delegate

In general, agents are prohibited from delegating either express or implied authority to a third person without the principal's express authorization. The rationale for the rule is that the agency relationship is consensual and the principal has not agreed to a third party acting in the place of the known agent. Yet, in certain cases, a principal may be shown to have granted implied authority to the agent to delegate its duties to a third person or subagent.

a) Mechanical or ministerial acts

An agent generally has the implied authority to hire a subagent to perform mechanical acts (such as clearing debris from a work site).

b) Situation or circumstance specific

An agent has the authority to employ a subagent for a specific situation when it is required by law that an individual have a professional perform a specific task.

> **Example:** A surgeon hires the anesthesiologist and surgical nurses. The surgeon is the agent of the patient, hiring professional staff to assist as needed.

c) Custom or usage

An agent may delegate duties to a subagent to facilitate a transaction because of business or industry customs or trade usage.

Example: Lawyers hire notaries, paralegals, and legal secretaries to help administer client cases.

d) Impossibility

The agent may delegate acts that she could not perform for a variety of reasons.

Example: A wedding planner may contract with a minister to officiate at a marriage because the wedding planner (as an agent of the bride) cannot legally perform the ceremony.

2. Apparent Authority

Apparent authority derives from the **reasonable reliance of a third party** on that party's perception of the level of authority granted to the agent by the principal. The perception is based on the principal's behavior over a period of time.

> **EXAM NOTE:** The bar exam frequently tests your ability to differentiate between implied actual authority and apparent authority.
>
> **Implied authority** results when the principal's words or actions cause an *agent* to reasonably believe in the agent's authority to act.
>
> **Apparent authority** results when the principal causes a *third party* to reasonably believe agent has authority to act.
>
> To determine if a third party has a reasonable belief of apparent authority, look for a principal's manifestation that reaches the third party and could reasonably cause the third party to believe that the agent is authorized. The key is the **principal's behavior**, not the agent's, and the third party's perception which results from it.

Apparent authority, unlike estoppel, does not require the third party to establish that the third party acted in reliance on the principal's manifestations or that the third party suffered a detriment as a consequence of such reliance.

A change in position by the third party may be evidence of the third party's belief in the agent's possession of actual authority.

a. Actor/imposter agent

It is not uncommon for an individual purporting to be an agent at the time of his acts to have no agency relationship or authority delegated by a principal. This person is called an "actor" or "imposter," and a principal may be held liable for the imposter's acts when the principal negligently allows an imposter to have the appearance of actual authority to act on the principal's behalf.

b. Third party's reasonable belief

Unlike implied actual authority, which is based on the agent's reasonable belief as to the agent's authority, apparent authority focuses on the **reasonable belief of the third party**.

1) Reasonable belief factors:

To determine whether a third party's belief is reasonable, look to:

i) Past dealings between the principal and the agent of which the third party is aware;

ii) Trade customs regarding how a similar transaction is normally accomplished;

iii) Relevant industry standards;

iv) The principal's written statements of authority;

v) Transactions that do not benefit the principal; or

vi) Extraordinary or novel transactions for the principal or similar types of principals.

2) Agent's position

Information, known by a third party, that a person is an agent for an organization without knowledge of the person's position in the organization (e.g., president) is an insufficient basis to support a belief in the agent's authority to act for the organization.

However, by appointing an agent to a specific position (e.g., vice president, treasurer, general manager), the principal makes a manifestation to the public that the agent has the customary level of authority possessed by a person in the agent's position.

3. Termination of Authority

An agent's actual authority may be terminated by:

i) The principal's revocation;

ii) The principal's agreement with the agent;

iii) A change of circumstances;

iv) The passage of time;

v) The principal's death, or suspension of powers;

vi) The agent's death or suspension of powers;

vii) The principal's loss of capacity; or

viii) A statutorily mandated termination.

a. Principal's power to revoke/agent's power to renounce

1) In general

Either party to the agency relationship may revoke or renounce consent that was previously given. A revocation or renunciation is effective as soon as the other party has notice of it.

Either party has the power to terminate the agency relationship, even if they contracted not to do so. In that case, either may be liable for breach of contract. The remedy for breach is limited to damages.

2) Power coupled with an interest

A principal cannot revoke the authority of an agent if the agent's power is coupled with an interest in the subject matter of the power. For example, if a borrower conveys an interest in real property to a lender under a deed of trust, and also confers on the lender the power to sell the property in the event of default, the lender's interest is coupled with an interest in the property. Therefore, the borrower cannot revoke the lender's authority to sell.

> Termination of an agency relationship is unilateral; either party may assert the right to terminate the agreement.

b. Termination of agency agreement

The principal and agent can mutually agree to terminate the agreement that formed their agency relationship.

When an existing agreement between the agent and principal specifies the circumstances under which the agent's actual authority terminates, the occurrence of that circumstance terminates the agency, and the agent should reasonably conclude that the principal no longer would assent to the agent acting on the principal's behalf.

c. Changed circumstances

Agency relationships may end as a result of:

  i)   A change in a statute relating to the subject matter;

  ii) Insolvency of either party;

  iii) A dramatic change in business conditions;

  iv) The destruction of the subject matter of the agency relationship; or

  v)   A disaster (natural or unnatural).

The agency relationship terminates when the changed circumstance should cause the agent to reasonably believe that the principal no longer consents to the agent acting on the principal's behalf.

d. Passage of time

When the principal and agent do not specify the duration of an agent's authority, such authority terminates after a reasonable period of time.

e. Death of principal

1) In general

The traditional common law rule is that the principal's death terminates all power of the agent to act, including actual authority, regardless of whether the agent or third party has notice of the principal's death.

There is a modern judicial trend to hold that the principal's death does not terminate an agent's authority until the agent has notice of the principal's death.

2) Durable power of attorney

If a principal grants an agent authority in a durable power of attorney (*discussed below*), the principal's death may not necessarily terminate the agent's authority, depending on the circumstances under which the durable power of attorney is granted. For example, in certain cases, an agent under a durable power of attorney may order an autopsy and demand and receive medical records for the deceased principal.

3) Power coupled with an interest

The principal's death does not terminate the authority of an agent if the agent's power is coupled with an interest in the subject matter of the power.

f. Death of agent

The death of the agent *automatically* terminates the agent's actual authority. Authority does not pass to the agent's estate or heirs.

g. Principal's loss of capacity

1) In general

The common law rule is that an individual principal's loss of capacity terminates the agent's actual authority. There is a modern trend holding that actual authority does not terminate *until the agent has notice* that the principal has been adjudicated to lack capacity or that the principal's loss of capacity is permanent.

2) Durable power of attorney

A principal may override the loss of capacity rule by giving an agent a durable power of attorney in advance of incapacity. An agent's authority under a durable power of attorney continues despite the principal's lack of capacity. A durable power of attorney must be in writing, evidence the agent's appointment, and express the principal's intention that the power will not be affected by the principal's future disability or incapacity or, alternatively, will take effect upon such an event.

As long as the principal has capacity, the principal may revoke a durable power of attorney.

h. Statutorily mandated termination

The occurrence of circumstances specified by statute may affect the agency relationship and modify or terminate actual authority. For example, under the Uniform Commercial Code ("UCC"), a bank may generally pay a customer's checks for 10 days after the customer's death, despite knowledge of the death. U.C.C. § 4-405 (2007).

i. Agent's breach of fiduciary duty

The agent's authority terminates when the agent breaches his fiduciary duty to the principal.

4. Estoppel

A person who has not represented that an individual is authorized to act as an agent may be estopped from denying the existence of an agency relationship or an agent's authority with respect to a transaction entered into by the agent. Estoppel applies when a third party is justifiably induced to make a detrimental change in position because that third party believed the transaction was entered into for the principal and either the principal:

i) Intentionally or carelessly caused the belief; or

ii) Having notice of such belief and the possibility that the belief might induce others to change their positions in reliance on it, failed to take reasonable steps to notify them of the facts.

In short, a principal, or purported principal, is liable for the appearance of authority arising solely from the **principal's failure** to take reasonable steps and use ordinary care.

Example: P has two co-agents, A and B. P learns that B, acting without actual or apparent authority, is informing P's neighbors that A has the authority to sell P's ring, which P has specifically forbidden A from doing. P's next door neighbor purchases P's ring from A, in justifiable reliance on B's representation as to A's authority. P, in her suit to rescind the sale, may be estopped (prevented) from denying B's authority to make the representation as to A's authority. Restatement (Third) of Agency, § 2.05, Illustration 1 (2006).

5. Ratification

A principal can ratify an act performed by another person, whether or not the person is an actual agent of the principal. Ratification occurs when a principal affirms a prior act that was done or purported to be done on the principal's behalf. The principal's affirmation may be either express or implied (such as through conduct), and consideration is not required. In order for ratification to occur, the following elements must exist:

i) The principal must ratify the **entire act**, contract, or transaction (either by express manifestation of assent or conduct that justifies a reasonable assumption of consent);

ii) The principal must have the **legal capacity** to ratify the transaction at the time it occurs. The third party must also have the legal capacity to engage in the transaction;

iii) The principal's ratification must be **timely** (before the third party withdraws from the transaction); and

iv) The principal must have knowledge of the material facts involved in the original act.

If the principal ratifies the agent's action, the principal is bound just as if the action had been authorized at the time it occurred. This is true even if the agent acted without power to bind the principal (i.e., with no actual or apparent authority, and when estoppel does not apply).

C. PRINCIPAL'S LIABILITY TO THIRD PARTIES IN TORT FOR AGENT'S CONDUCT

A principal may be vicariously as well as directly liable to a third person who is tortiously harmed by an agent's conduct. The doctrine of vicarious liability asserts that a principal is liable for the acts of an agent, even though the principal is innocent of fault and not directly guilty of any tort or crime. Common torts include: negligence, misrepresentation, false imprisonment, and battery.

1. Principal's Vicarious Liability for Agent's Torts

a. Respondeat superior

Under the doctrine of respondeat superior, a principal may be vicariously liable for a tort committed by an agent acting **within the scope of his employment**. The principal is liable despite the absence of tortious conduct by the principal. This is also known as "derivative liability."

If the agent is not liable, the principal cannot be vicariously liable.

1) General rule

A principal is vicariously liable to a third party harmed by the agent's conduct when:

i) The agent is a servant (often referred to as an "employee"); and

ii) The agent commits a tort while acting within the scope of employment.

Note that an agent who appoints a subagent may be vicariously liable for torts committed by the subagent.

> **EXAM NOTE:** The bar exam frequently tests vicarious liability of an employer. Don't forget to use key terminology, such as acting "**within the scope of employment**" or "**scope of the employment relationship**."

2) "Servant/employee" defined

A servant or employee is an agent whose principal controls or has the right to control the manner and means of the agent's performance of work. Because of the level of control of their employers, bus drivers, food servers, and corporate officers would all be classified as employees.

When a lent employee, also known as a "borrowed servant," commits a tort, the employee's initial employer or the employer for whom the employee is currently working, or both, may be liable to a third party harmed by the lent employee's conduct. Recent court decisions have assessed liability based upon a determination as to which of the employers controlled the agent's actions at the time the harm occurred.

> **EXAM NOTE:** Remember that the key to determining liability is whether the *employer has the right to control the employee's conduct.*

3) Scope of employment

An employee acts within the scope of employment when either:

i) Performing work assigned by the employer; or

    ii)   Engaging in a course of conduct subject to the employer's control.

When an employee acts independently of any intent to serve any purpose of the employer, the employer may escape liability.

> **EXAM NOTE:** Examiners want you to establish that (i) there is an employer/employee relationship, and (ii) that the employee's harmful conduct was committed while working within the scope of employment in order to attach liability and hold the employer vicariously liable.

An employee does not act outside the scope of employment merely because he performs the work carelessly, makes a mistake in performing the work, or fails to perform assigned work. Moreover, an employee who disregards an employer's instructions or violates a generally applicable law, such as a speed limit, is not necessarily acting outside the scope of employment when the employee believes that compliance would jeopardize the employee's timely completion of his assigned task.

a) Employee's use of physical force against another

While most jobs do not include the use of physical force against another person, an employee's assigned work may contemplate the necessity of using physical force to complete the assigned task, such as a "runner" for a bail bondsperson, who tracks down individuals who have jumped bail and returns them to custody.

b) Intentional torts

Intentional torts are not automatically excluded from the scope of employment. They may fall within the scope of employment when (i) the conduct is within the space and time limits of the employment; (ii) the agent was motivated in part to act for the employer's benefit; and (iii) the act was the kind of act the employee was hired to perform.

> **Example:** A salesperson who intentionally misrepresents a product to a potential customer for the purpose of making a sale may be acting within the scope of employment. Restatement (Third) of Agency § 7.07, cmt. c (2006).

c) Work-related travel

i) Commuting

Generally, travel between work and home by an employee is not within the scope of employment. An exception exists when the employer provides the employee with a vehicle and asserts control over how the employee uses the vehicle. Restatement (Third) of Agency § 7.07, cmt. e (2006).

ii) Travel during the workday

Travel required to perform work, such a travel from an employer's office to a job site or between job sites, is generally within the scope of employment

d) Frolic and detour

i) Frolic

When an employee's personal errand involves a **significant deviation** from the path that otherwise would be taken for purposes of performing work, the errand is a frolic. Once a frolic begins, an employee is outside the scope of his employment until he resumes performance of his assigned work.

ii) Detour

Travel by an employee during the workday that involves a personal errand may be within the scope of employment when the errand is merely a detour (i.e., a *de minimis* departure from an assigned route).

b. Agent's apparent authority

A principal is vicariously liable for a tort committed by an agent with apparent authority when the agent's appearance of authority enables him to commit a tort or conceal its commission. Such torts include fraudulent and negligent misrepresentation, defamation, tortious institution of legal proceedings, and conversion of property.

1) Apparent authority

In order for apparent authority to exist, a third person must believe that the agent acted with actual authority and such belief must be *reasonable* and be *traceable to a manifestation* by the principal.

If the third party's belief in the agent's authority to make the statement is reasonable, the misrepresentation will be attributed to the principal. The third party might be able to rescind the contract and sue for damages.

Example: A principal retains a real estate agent to sell the principal's personal residence and informs a perspective buyer that the agent will answer all questions concerning the property. The agent falsely informs the buyer that the house has been rewired to comply with new regulations. The agent's statements may be attributed to the principal because of the agent's apparent authority to make such statements on the principal's behalf.

2) Effect of agent's motivation or lack of benefit to principal

The fact that an agent's conduct is not beneficial to the principal does not protect the principal from liability for such conduct.

2. Principal's Direct Liability to Third Parties

A principal is directly liable to a third person harmed by an agent's conduct if:

i) The principal authorizes or ratifies the agent's conduct;

ii) The principal is negligent in selecting, supervising, or otherwise controlling the agent; or

iii) The principal delegates to an agent performance of a non-delegable duty to use care to protect other persons or their property and the agent breaches the duty.

a. Agent with actual authority or principal's ratification

A principal is subject to liability for an agent's conduct if the principal authorizes the conduct or intends its consequences. For example, a principal who authorizes an agent to destroy a competitor's place of business is liable to the competitor.

If an agent uses means other than those the principal intended, the principal is nevertheless vicariously liable if the agent's choice of means is within the agent's actual authority.

If the agent's conduct is not tortious, the principal may still be liable if the same conduct by the principal would have rendered the principal liable.

Example: A principal has information that the agent does not, such as the nature of an object being sold. A statement by the agent about the object to a third party buyer may not support a finding of misrepresentation; however, the same statement made by the principal would constitute misrepresentation.

A principal is also liable if she ratifies an agent's conduct. Ratification requires that the principal affirm a prior act that was done or purportedly done on the principal's behalf.

b. Negligence in selecting or controlling an agent

A principal who is negligent in selecting, supervising, or otherwise controlling an agent runs the risk of liability attaching to that negligence. Basic tort requirements of duty, breach, causation, and damages must be satisfied in order for the principal to be liable.

As a general tort rule:

i) A person who conducts an activity through another person;

ii) Is liable for harm to a third party;

iii) Caused by the actor when the person fails to exercise reasonable care;

iv) With respect to the selection of the actor and the actor's performance of the activity.

A principal has a duty to a third party with respect to actions by an agent if there is a **special relationship** between a principal and the third party, such as that between a common carrier and a passenger.

c. Non-delegable duties

A principal who has a non-delegable duty cannot avoid liability by delegating the duty to another person. Generally, a duty is non-delegable when the responsibility is so important to the community that a person should not be permitted to transfer it to another person. Examples include the duty of a landlord to keep premises in a safe condition and the duty to use care in inherently dangerous activities such as the use of explosives.

D. AGENT'S LIABILITY

1. Agent's Liability in Contractual Dealings

a. Agent's liability as a party to a contract

When an agent enters into a contract on the principal's behalf and binds the principal to the contract, the agent might also become a party to (and liable on) the contract. Whether the agent becomes a party depends on the terms of the contract and the degree to which the agent discloses to the third party the existence and identity of the principal.

1) Disclosed principal

A principal is a disclosed principal if the third party has notice of both the existence and identity of the principal. Unless the agent and third party agree otherwise, an agent who enters into a contract on behalf of a disclosed principal *does not* become a party to the contract. To avoid becoming a party to the contract, the agent must:

i) Enter into the contract on behalf of the disclosed principal;

ii) Affirmatively disclose to the third party both the existence and identity of the principal; and

iii) Not agree to become a party to the contract.

2) Partially-disclosed principal

A principal is a partially disclosed principal if the third party has notice of the principal's existence, but not the principal's identity. Unless the agent and the third party agree otherwise, an agent who enters into a contract on behalf of a partially disclosed principal becomes a party to the contract.

If the agent binds the principal to the contract, or if the principal ratifies the contract, then both the principal and agent are parties to the contract with the third party.

3) Undisclosed principal

A principal is an undisclosed principal if the third party has no notice of the principal's existence. An agent who enters into a contract on behalf of an undisclosed principal becomes a party to the contract. Thus, when the agent does not inform a third party of the identity or the existence of the principal, the agent becomes liable to the third party on the contract.

If the agent binds the principal to the contract, then both the principal and the agent are parties to the contract with the third person. Once the third party discovers the existence of the principal however, the **election of remedies doctrine** requires the third party to choose to hold liable either the principal or the agent. If the third party obtains a judgment against one of them, the judgment operates as an election and the third party is precluded from seeking to hold the other liable on the contract.

Generally, a third party is liable to an undisclosed principal on a contract made with an agent on behalf the principal unless:

i) The principal or undisclosed principals are excluded by the form or terms or the contract; or

ii) The principal's existence is fraudulently concealed, i.e., the agent falsely represents to the third party that the agent does not act on behalf of the principal.

Generally, an undisclosed principal is liable to a third party if: (i) the third party is induced to make a detrimental change in position by an agent without actual authority, (ii) the principal knew of the agent's conduct and that it might induce others to change positions, and (iii) did not take reasonable steps to notify the third party of the facts. Restatement (Third) of Agency § 2.06(1).

An undisclosed principal may not rely on the fact that she gave the agent instructions that effectively reduced the agent's authority to less than what a third party would reasonably believe the agent to have if the principal had been a disclosed principal. § 2.06 (2).

b. Agent's warranty of authority

An agent or actor purporting to be an agent for a principal gives an implied warranty of authority to a third person with whom the agent enters into a contract on the principal's behalf. If the agent or actor lacks the power to bind the principal, then a breach of the implied warranty has occurred, and the agent is liable to the third party for breach.

An agent is treated as giving an implied warranty of authority when the principal is disclosed or partially disclosed, but not when the principal is undisclosed.

An agent may give an express warranty of authority in order to induce a third party to deal with the agent.

c. Fraudulent concealment

For fraudulent concealment to apply, either the principal or the agent must have notice that the third party would not have dealt with the principal. Mere suspicions or doubts about the third party's willingness to deal with a principal are insufficient to give the principal or agent notice. When the agent does not make an affirmative misrepresentation to the third party, the third party may be able to avoid the contract by establishing a unilateral mistake.

2. Agent's Tort Liability

An agent is subject to liability to a third party harmed by the agent's tortious conduct. An agent's individual tort liability extends to negligent acts and omissions as well as intentional conduct. An agent is not liable for torts committed by the principal.

III. RIGHTS AND DUTIES OF PARTIES TO AN AGENCY RELATIONSHIP

A. RIGHTS AND DUTIES OF PRINCIPALS

A principal has the legal right to require an agent to act or refrain from acting on his behalf. The agent has a corresponding obligation or duty to act or refrain from acting on behalf of the principal.

1. **Rights of Principals**

   A principal has the right to select an agent and control the agent's actions within the scope of the agency relationship.

   a. **Control of agent**

   The agency relationship is, by definition, one in which the agent acts on the principal's behalf and is subject to the principal's control. Therefore, a principal has the right to control the acts of an agent working on the principal's behalf, including third-party negotiations. However, a principal cannot require agents to perform illegal acts or acts against public policy.

   b. **Agent's duty of care**

   Principals have the right to expect an agent to follow instructions and to perform duties, tasks, and transactions with reasonable care, diligence, and judgment. Uncompensated agents are expected to perform in an acceptable manner and are *subject to the same standard of care as a compensated agent*.

   c. **Agent's duties of loyalty and obedience**

   Agency is a special relationship that gives rise to fiduciary duties on the part of the agent. A principal has the right to expect loyalty and obedience from her agent. A principal is entitled to expect the agent to avoid acts in the agent's self-interest in matters connected with the agency and to refrain from secretly profiting from transactions on behalf of the principal. The fiduciary duty owed by the agent to the principal implies that the agent will not breach the trust imposed by the agency relationship.

   An agent may be liable to a principal for breach under either contract or tort law.

   d. **Notification**

   The principal is entitled to notice from the agent of all issues relevant to the subject matter of the agency relationship. Generally, the law of agency assumes that the principal is aware of all relevant knowledge of and information provided to the agent. A core tenet of agency law is that knowledge of or notice to the agent is notice to the principal.

   e. **Accounting**

   The principal has the right to receive an accounting from the agent of all property and funds received or paid on behalf of the principal. The agent is obligated to maintain the principal's funds separate from his personal funds.

2. **Duties of Principals to Agent**

   a. **Deal fairly and in good faith**

   A principal is obligated to treat the agent fairly and in good faith, and to provide the agent with information concerning risks of physical or financial harm or loss that the principal knows or should know are present in the agent's work but unknown to the agent. In addition, while a principal does not owe an agent a duty of loyalty, a principal has a duty to refrain from conduct likely to injure an agent's business reputation or reasonable self-respect.

b. Contractual duties

A principal has a duty to act in good faith in accordance with the terms of the contract between the agent and the principal.

c. Duty to pay compensation

Whether a principal is obligated to compensate an agent depends on the terms of their agreement. To recover compensation, an agent must show that the principal expressly or impliedly agreed to pay compensation. If a principal has promised to pay compensation, the agent can maintain an action for damages if the principal fails to pay.

d. Duty not to interfere with agent's work

If a principal has agreed to furnish an agent with an opportunity for work, a principal has a duty not to interfere with the agent's completion of that work.

e. Duty to indemnify

Subject to an agreement to the contrary, a principal has a duty to indemnify the agent against pecuniary loss suffered in connection with the agency relationship and within the scope of the agent's actual authority. The principal's duty to indemnify includes expenses and other losses incurred by an agent (such as attorney's fees) in defending an action brought by a third party.

A principal is not obligated to indemnify losses that result from an agent's own negligence, illegal acts, or other wrongful conduct.

3. Principal's Remedies for Breach by Agent

A principal has the right to recover for a breach of the agent's fiduciary obligation, as well as for the agent's breach of contract and for actions of the agent that exceed the scope of employment, and for which tort law provides a remedy. A principal may pursue one or more of the following remedies against an agent who breaches a duty:

i) An injunction;

ii) A breach of contract action for monetary damages;

iii) A tort action for harm suffered, including punitive damages;

iv) Avoidance or rescission of a contract or a transaction;

v) Restitution;

vi) An accounting to principal for value of the agent's use of principal's property;

vii) Termination of agency relationship;

viii) Forfeiture of commission or other compensation paid or payable; and

ix) Disgorgement of profits earned by the agent without the principal's consent.

B. RIGHTS AND DUTIES OF AN AGENT

In general, an agent has a right to be compensated, allowed to work without interference, reimbursed for losses, provided with a safe work environment, and indemnified for working on behalf of a principal.

1. **Rights of an Agent**

   a. **Right to receive compensation**

   An agent has a right to receive compensation for the agent's services if the principal expressly or impliedly promises to compensate the agent. When no amount has been specified in the agency relationship, an agent has the right to be compensated in the customary manner of the business trade. However, a principal does not have a duty to pay compensation to subagents engaged by an agent, unless the principal agrees to do so.

   b. **Right to have principal not interfere with agent's work**

   The principal also has a duty to cooperate with the agent and assist the agent in performing the tasks associated with the objectives of the agency.

   c. **Right to indemnification and reimbursement**

   An agent has the right to indemnification for losses incurred when the agent transacted lawful business with actual authority.

   Example: If the agent, having actual authority from the principal, purchases goods from a third party and the principal refuses to pay, the third party may be able to sue the agent for damages. The principal would be responsible for compensating the agent for costs associated with the principal's breach, such as damages and attorney's fees paid by the agent.

   An agent also has the right to be reimbursed by the principal for expenses incurred by the agent in connection with the agency relationship. Generally, this right is limited to payments made or necessary expenses incurred by an agent within the scope of the agency.

   An agent does not have the right to be indemnified for losses that result from an agent's own negligence, illegal acts, or other wrongful conduct.

   d. **Right to work in a safe environment**

   The principal must provide a safe working environment, including tools, equipment, and conditions for an agent or employee.

   e. **Remedies available to agent**

   An agent might have a claim against the principal founded in contract or tort law. However, the agent is required to choose the remedy sought and to mitigate his damages prior to, and during the period that the agent seeks relief.

   In order to sue for breach of contract, the agent must establish that a right to compensation exists. This normally means that the agent must be a compensated agent, i.e. there must have been consideration to support the agency relationship.

   The agent may file a claim for compensation owed to him under the terms of the contract with the principal. Such a claim could take the form of a suit in damages to recover compensation or a lien against the principal.

2. Duties of an Agent

An agent has two basic types of duties to a principal—a duty of loyalty, which includes a fiduciary duty, and a performance-based duty which includes the duty of care.

a. Duty of loyalty

Agency is a special relationship that gives rise to fiduciary duties on the part of the agent. As a fiduciary, the agent owes the principal a duty of loyalty, which generally requires the agent to act solely for the benefit of the principal (and not for the benefit of the agent or third parties) in matters connected with the agency. This duty applies to all agents, whether they are gratuitous or compensated and can vary depending on the parties' agreement. The agent's general duty of loyalty requires the agent to do, or not to do, a number of specific things which are discussed below.

1) Duty not to deal with the principal as an adverse party

Unless the principal and agent have agreed otherwise, the agent has a duty not to deal with the principal as an adverse party in any transaction connected with the agency without the principal's knowledge. For example, an agent cannot, without the principal's knowledge, purchase goods from the principal if the principal has retained the agent to sell those goods.

2) Duty to refrain from acquiring a material benefit

The agent's duty of loyalty requires her to refrain from acquiring a material benefit in connection with transactions or other actions undertaken on the principal's behalf, unless the principal consents to the agent acquiring the benefit.

3) Duty not to usurp business opportunity

The agent's duty not to usurp a business opportunity is a component of the duty of loyalty. It arises when either the nature of an opportunity or the circumstances under which the agent learned of it require the agent to offer the opportunity to the principal.

Thus, the agent may not seek or accept monetary or beneficial gain from a third party during the course of the agency without the principal's consent. The prohibition on the agent benefitting monetarily from transactions conducted for the principal is often referred to as the "agent's duty to account for profits."

4) Duty not to compete

An agent has a duty to refrain from competing with the principal concerning the subject matter of the agency and from assisting the principal's competitors.

5) Duty to disclose—multiple principals

An agent who acts for more than one principal in a transaction between or among them owes duties of disclosure, good faith, and fair dealing to each.

6) Duty not to use principal's confidential information

An agent has a duty to refrain from using the principal's confidential information for the benefit of anyone other than the principal, including the agent. This duty survives termination of the agency relationship.

b. Performance-based duties

An agent owes performance-based duties to the principal, including a duty of obedience and a duty to perform with reasonable care.

1) Contractual duties

Although an agency relationship does not require a contract between the agent and the principal, an agent has an implied duty to act in accordance with the terms of any contract between the parties.

2) Duty of care

An agent has a duty to act with the care, competence, and diligence normally exercised by agents in similar circumstances, as reflected by local community standards. The agent's special skills and knowledge are taken into account in determining whether the agent employed due care and diligence.

3) Duty of obedience

An agent must act within the scope of the agent's actual authority and comply with a principal's lawful and reasonable instructions.

4) Duty to provide information

An agent has a duty to provide relevant information to the principal pertaining to the subject matter of the agency and that the agent knows (or should know) the principal would wish to have.

5) Duty to keep and render accounts

An agent has the duty to keep the principal's property separate from the agent's property. Also, an agent has a duty to keep and render an accounting of the principal's money and other property.

EXAM NOTE: When answering questions that require you to address the duties of an agent to the principal, make sure you state the "must have" duties:

i)   **Duty of care** to perform with *reasonable diligence and skill*;

ii) **Duty to provide information** to the principal regarding all matters relating to the agency relationship;

iii) **Duty of loyalty** to the principal and to *work only for his benefit*;

iv) **Duty of obedience** to the principal; and

v)   **Duties** not to usurp a business opportunity from the principal; not to take financial gain from the principal; to provide an accounting; and to not commingle the principal's property with that of a third party.

Civil Practice and Procedure

CIVIL PRACTICE & PROCEDURE

Table of Contents

CIVIL PRACTICE & PROCEDURE

I. SUBJECT MATTER JURISDICTION

A. IN GENERAL

1. Overview

The term "subject matter jurisdiction" refers to a court's competence to hear and determine cases of the general class and subject to which the proceedings in question belong. The five most common congressional grants of subject matter jurisdiction are (i) federal question jurisdiction, (ii) diversity jurisdiction, (iii) supplemental jurisdiction, (iv) removal jurisdiction, and (v) legislative jurisdiction.

2. Presumption

A federal court must presume an absence of jurisdiction until it determines that the matter falls within its rightful jurisdiction. The burden is on the party seeking to invoke the court's jurisdiction.

3. Waiver

Subject matter jurisdiction cannot be waived or agreed to by the parties, unlike personal jurisdiction (discussed in § II. Personal Jurisdiction, *infra*).

4. Objection to Jurisdiction

An objection to subject matter jurisdiction can be presented by any party at any stage of a proceeding, including on appeal. If, however, the issue of subject matter jurisdiction was not contested, a judgment ordinarily may not be challenged collaterally on that basis.

5. Abstention

In general, a federal court with subject matter jurisdiction is required to adjudicate the controversy despite the pendency of a similar action in a state court. A federal court may abstain from hearing a case or stay the matter pending the outcome of the state court action under the following limited circumstances:

i) Resolution of a state law issue by the state court would eliminate the need for the federal court to decide a federal constitutional issue, *R.R. Comm'n of Texas v. Pullman Co.*, 312 U.S. 496 (1941);

ii) Avoidance of federal involvement with a complex state regulatory scheme or matter of great importance to the state, *Burford v. Sun Oil Co.*, 319 U.S. 315 (1943); *Louisiana Power & Light Co. v. City of Thibodaux*, 360 U.S. 25 (1959);

iii) State action involves punishment of an individual for criminal activity or for contempt of court, or the imposition of a civil fine, and the federal court is asked to enjoin such activity, *Younger v. Harris*, 401 U.S. 37 (1971); and

iv) Parallel proceedings that go beyond mere waste of judicial resources, such as when there is a federal policy of unitary adjudication of the issues, *Colorado River Water Conservation Dist. v. United States*, 424 U.S. 800 (1976).

There are limited circumstances when federal intervention is appropriate. If a plaintiff can demonstrate unusual circumstance calling for federal equitable relief, significant and dire irreparable injury, or prosecutorial bad faith, a federal court could choose to intercede.

B. FEDERAL QUESTION JURISDICTION

1. Basis

Article III, Section 2 of the U.S. Constitution provides that federal judicial power shall extend to all cases "arising under this Constitution, the Laws of the United States, and Treaties made, or which shall be made, under their Authority." This constitutional provision authorizes Congress to give federal courts such jurisdiction. Today, the congressional grant of federal question jurisdiction is codified at 28 U.S.C. § 1331, which provides, "The district courts shall have original jurisdiction of all civil actions arising under the Constitution, laws, or treaties of the United States."

2. Concurrent versus Exclusive Jurisdiction

State and federal courts have concurrent jurisdiction of federal question claims, except when Congress expressly provides that the jurisdiction of the federal courts is exclusive, as it has with cases under the Securities and Exchange Act of 1934, patent cases, and bankruptcy proceedings. *See Charles Dowd Box Co. v. Courtney*, 368 U.S. 502, 507 (1962) ("nothing in the concept of our federal system prevents state courts from enforcing rights created by federal law").

3. Scope

There is no uniform, bright-line standard for determining whether an action arises under the Constitution, laws, or treaties of the United States. In general, if the cause of action in question is expressly created by federal law and federal law provides the underlying right, federal question jurisdiction will exist. If a right is created by federal law, and a cause of action may fairly be implied and was intended by Congress, federal jurisdiction is likely to be found. If the cause of action is neither expressly nor implicitly created by federal law, the complaint must involve a real and substantial issue of federal law, and its determination must necessarily depend on resolution of the federal issue. A federal corporation (corporate entity incorporated through an act of Congress) does not, simply by being a federal corporation, have federal jurisdiction. However, if the United States owns over 50 percent of the corporation's capital stock, the corporate entity will be considered a federal agency and may then be sued in federal court.

Federal law includes the U.S. Constitution, federal statutes, federal administrative regulations, and U.S. treaties. State laws incorporating standards of federal law are not considered laws of the United States for purposes of § 1331. *See Merrell Dow Pharmaceuticals, Inc. v. Thompson*, 478 U.S. 804 (1986). *Merrell Dow* held that when a substantive federal statute (e.g., the Food, Drug, and Cosmetic Act) does not provide a federal remedy, an alleged violation of that statute as an element of a state law complaint does not automatically establish § 1331 jurisdiction. Rather, federal courts have discretion to determine whether a federal issue or interest is important enough in a specific case to justify the exercise of jurisdiction.

4. Well-Pleaded Complaint

Federal question jurisdiction exists only when the federal law issue is presented in the plaintiff's complaint. This is the "well-pleaded complaint" rule. *See Caterpillar, Inc. v. Williams*, 482 U.S. 386 (1987).

a. Consider only elements of claim, not defenses

Under the well-pleaded complaint rule, the determination of jurisdiction must be made by considering only the necessary elements of the plaintiff's cause of action, and not potential defenses. It is not sufficient to establish jurisdiction that a plaintiff alleges some anticipated federal law defense. *Louisville & Nashville R.R. v. Mottley,* 211 U.S. 149 (1908). The federal question must appear on the face of the complaint. Thus, an action for declaratory relief, which by its nature anticipates future action or infringement of rights, cannot be brought under federal question jurisdiction unless it provides relief that is not available under state law. *See Skelly Oil Co. v. Phillips Petroleum Co.,* 339 U.S. 667 (1950).

b. Do not consider answers and counterclaims

Answers and counterclaims are not considered in determining the existence of federal question jurisdiction.

c. Original and removal jurisdiction

The well-pleaded complaint rule applies both to the original jurisdiction of the federal court and to removal jurisdiction (discussed in § I.E. Removal Jurisdiction, *infra*).

5. No Amount-in-Controversy Requirement

Unlike federal diversity jurisdiction, there is no amount-in-controversy requirement for federal question jurisdiction.

C. DIVERSITY JURISDICTION

1. Basis

Article III, section 2 of the U.S. Constitution permits Congress to extend federal judicial power to controversies "between citizens of different states ... and between a state or the citizens thereof, and foreign states, citizens or subjects." Under § 1332, Congress gave the U.S. district courts jurisdiction over actions when (i) the parties to an action are citizens of different states or citizens of a state and citizens or subjects of a foreign state and (ii) the amount in controversy in the action exceeds $75,000. In general, when these requirements are met, a federal court may exercise jurisdiction over the action, regardless of the legal subject of the controversy. This is known as diversity-of-citizenship jurisdiction or more commonly, diversity jurisdiction.

a. State law exclusions

Two areas of state law are generally excluded from diversity jurisdiction: probate matters (probate of a will or administration of an estate) and domestic relations actions (divorce, alimony, custody disputes). Note, though, that these exceptions apply only to cases that are primarily probate or marital disputes.

2. Complete Diversity

a. Rule of complete diversity

Diversity jurisdiction requires complete diversity between the parties on different sides of the case. There will be no diversity of citizenship if any plaintiff in the case is a citizen of the same state or is a citizen or subject of the same foreign country as any defendant in the case. *Strawbridge v. Curtiss,* 7 U.S. (3 Cranch) 267 (1806). Two plaintiffs in a case may be from the same state without destroying diversity, as long as no plaintiff is from the same state as any defendant in the case.

Note that under § 1332(e), the term "state" includes the District of Columbia, Puerto Rico, and the U.S. Territories.

b. Exceptions

1) Interpleader

Under 28 U.S.C. § 1335, the Federal Interpleader Act, the holder of property that is claimed by two or more persons may deposit the property with a court to determine ownership. Under the Act, there need be only two adverse claimants of diverse citizenship to establish federal jurisdiction. (*See* § VI.C.2. Federal Statutory Interpleader, *infra,* for a discussion of federal statutory interpleader, which requires complete diversity).

2) Class action lawsuits greater than $5 million

For certain class action lawsuits in which the amount at issue totals more than $5 million, diversity will be met if any member of the plaintiff class is diverse with any defendant. § 1332(d)(2)(A).

3) Multiparty, Multiforum Trial Jurisdiction Act of 2002

Under § 1369(a), for a civil action that "arises from a single accident, where at least 75 natural persons have died in the accident at a discrete location," only one plaintiff need be of diverse citizenship from one defendant in order for a federal court to have diversity jurisdiction, if:

i) A defendant resides in a state and a substantial part of the accident took place in another state or other location, regardless of whether that defendant is also a resident of the state where a substantial part of the accident took place;

ii) Any two defendants reside in different states, regardless of whether such defendants are also residents of the same state or states; or

iii) Substantial parts of the accident took place in different states.

Even if those requirements are met, however, under § 1369(b), the district court must abstain from hearing the case if:

i) The substantial majority of all plaintiffs are citizens of a single state of which the primary defendants are also citizens; and

ii) The claims asserted will be governed primarily by the laws of that state.

The Act also provides:

i) That anyone involved in the accident is permitted to intervene as a plaintiff; and

ii) Nationwide service of process.

c. "Realignment"

In evaluating whether true diversity exists, courts will look beyond the face of the pleadings to determine the "ultimate interests." If necessary, they will "arrange the parties according to their sides in the dispute." Thus, courts will not allow, for example, a party that is actually aligned with the plaintiff to be named as a defendant in order to present a false diversity. *City of Dawson v. Columbia Ave. Sav. Fund, Safe Deposit, Title, & Trust Co.,* 197 U.S. 178 (1905).

d. Date of determination of diversity

Diversity is determined at the time the case is filed. *Janzen v. Goos,* 302 F.2d 421 (8th Cir. 1962). There is no requirement that diversity exist at the time the cause of action arose. A change in citizenship after the filing of the case will not affect diversity jurisdiction that was in existence at the time of the filing. In addition, a change in the parties as a result of substitution or intervention will not affect diversity jurisdiction.

3. Citizenship of Parties

a. Individuals

To be a citizen of a state for purposes of § 1332, a person must be a citizen of the United States and a domiciliary of the state.

1) Domicile

In general, a person is a domiciliary of the state in which he or she is present and intends to reside for an indefinite period. *Janzen v. Goos,* 302 F.2d 421 (8th Cir. 1962).

a) Only one domicile

A person can have only one domicile at a time. The presumption is that a place of domicile continues until it is definitively changed, i.e., when a person:

i) Establishes presence in the new place; and

ii) Manifests intent to remain there for an indefinite period. Consequently, a compulsory change of domicile, such as for incarceration or military purposes will not result in a change in domicile.

b) When determined

Domicile is determined at the time the action is commenced. Once subject matter jurisdiction has been established, it will not be affected by a party's change of domicile.

c) Factors considered

Some factors used in determining domicile include whether a party exercises civil and political rights (e.g., registration to vote), pays taxes, owns real and personal property, and is employed in the state.

2) Aliens

Diversity jurisdiction based on alienage will be found when there are one or more citizens or subjects of a foreign country (i.e., aliens) on one side of the lawsuit, and one or more citizens of a state on the other. There is no diversity jurisdiction in an action by one foreign subject against another. Nor is there jurisdiction when an action is between a citizen of a state and an alien admitted to the United States for permanent residence who is domiciled in the same state as the citizen. § 1332(a)(2).

3) Stateless persons

Under § 1332, the presence of a stateless citizen of the United States, an alien who is present in the United States and who is not a citizen of a foreign state, or a U.S. citizen residing abroad would preclude diversity jurisdiction, as these persons are neither citizens of the United States nor citizens or subjects of a foreign country.

4) Minors, incompetents, decedents, and trusts

The legal representative of a minor, an incompetent, or an estate of a decedent will be deemed a citizen of the same state as that minor, incompetent, or decedent. § 1332(c)(2). As to trusts, the old rule was that they were deemed to be a citizen of the same state as the trustee. *See Navarro Savings Ass'n v. Lee*, 446 U.S. 458 (1980). However, this rule has been placed in doubt by *Carden v. Arkoma Assocs.*, 494 U.S. 185 (1990), which held that the citizenship of unincorporated associations is determined by the citizenship of all of its members. At least one lower federal court has recently applied the *Carden* holding to trusts, holding that *Carden* requires that diversity would be destroyed if, in a suit against a trust, any beneficiary of the trust is a citizen of the same state as a plaintiff. *See Bergeron ex rel. Ridgewood Elec. Power Trust V v. Ridgewood Elec. Power Trust V*, 2007 U.S. Dist. LEXIS 48555 (D. Mass., Jul. 5, 2007).

An unemancipated minor is generally deemed a citizen of the state in which his parents are domiciled. If a minor's parents are not citizens of the same state, the child will generally be deemed a citizen of the state of the parent with custody.

5) Class action lawsuits

Diversity in a class action lawsuit brought pursuant to Rule 23 will generally be determined by the citizenship of the named members of the class bringing the lawsuit. (*See* § VI.E. Class Actions, *infra*, for a discussion of class action lawsuits under Rule 23).

For certain class action lawsuits, however, when the amount at issue totals more than $5 million, diversity will be met if any member of the plaintiff class is diverse with any defendant. § 1332(d)(2)(A). (*See* § 5.c. Aggregation of claims, *below*.)

b. Business entities

1) Corporations

A corporation may be a party to a diversity action. Under § 1332(c), for purposes of diversity jurisdiction, "a corporation shall be deemed to be a citizen of every State and foreign state by which it has been incorporated and of the State or foreign state where it has its principal place of business." Thus, corporations, unlike individuals, may be citizens of more than one state for diversity purposes, and diversity jurisdiction will be destroyed if any opposing party is a citizen of any of the states in which the corporation has citizenship.

A pleader does not have the option of alleging that a corporation's citizenship is either its state of incorporation or the state where the principal place of business is located; both states must be listed in the pleading.

a) Incorporation

A corporation's state of incorporation is the state in which the corporate entity is legally established. Every corporation has at least one state of incorporation, and some have multiple states of incorporation. If a corporation is incorporated in more than one state or foreign country, it is considered a citizen of each state and foreign country in which it is incorporated.

b) Principal place of business

Determining where a corporation maintains its principal place of business is a question of fact more complicated than determining where a corporation is incorporated. A recent Supreme Court decision did away with looking toward where the corporation's actual physical operations were located. Instead, the Court held that principal place of business refers to the "nerve center" of the corporation. *Hertz Corp. v. Friend*, 559 U.S. ___, 130 S. Ct. 1181 (2010). The nerve center is generally the location from which the high-level officers direct, control, and coordinate the activities of the corporation. Typically, the nerve center is the corporate headquarters.

Unlike states of incorporation, a corporation has its principal place of business in only one state or foreign country.

c) Foreign corporations

A foreign corporation will be deemed a citizen of the country in which it is incorporated. In addition, if the foreign corporation also has its principal place of business in the United States, it will have citizenship in the state where the principal place of business is located.

d) Date of determination

The corporation's citizenship at the time the action is commenced determines jurisdiction.

e) Liability insurers

Under § 1332(c), a special rule applies when a plaintiff allegedly injured by an insured party brings a direct action against the liability insurer. To avoid automatic federal subject matter jurisdiction in cases in which the liability insurer is incorporated or has its principal place of business in a different state from that where the plaintiff is a citizen, § 1332(c) makes the insurer a citizen of the state or foreign country in which its insured is a citizen, in addition to the other states or foreign countries where it has citizenship.

2) Partnerships and other unincorporated associations

a) Generally

In general, unincorporated associations, like partnerships, are considered citizens of each state in which each of their partners or members is domiciled. Thus, it is possible that a partnership could be a citizen of all 50 states, if it had partners domiciled in every state. This rule holds for both general and limited partnerships; a limited partnership will therefore be a citizen of every state in which its general and limited partners are domiciled. *Carden v. Arkoma Assocs.,* 494 U.S. 185 (1990).

b) Exception

Rule 23.2 provides an exception: An unincorporated association may be treated as a class when "it appears that the representative parties will fairly and adequately protect the interests of the association and its members." In that case, the citizenship of the representative parties will control for purposes of diversity jurisdiction. Rule 23.2 may not be used merely to create diversity jurisdiction, nor may it be used if the association has the capacity under state law to sue or be sued as an entity.

4. Devices to Create or Destroy Diversity

Under § 1359, federal jurisdiction is prohibited if a party uses improper or collusive devices in order to invoke such jurisdiction.

a. Assignment of claims

When there is a legitimate assignment of a claim, the assignee becomes the real party in interest and its citizenship, as opposed to the citizenship of the assignor. Thus, the assignee's citizenship will be determinative. For example, when an insurance company pays an insured for damages caused by a third party and sues the third party in a subrogation action, the company's citizenship, and not the insured's citizenship, controls for diversity purposes.

If the assignment is being effected to manufacture or create diversity jurisdiction collusively, however, under § 1359, diversity jurisdiction will not exist. *See, e.g., Kramer v. Caribbean Mills, Inc.*, 394 U.S. 823 (1969) (assignment to nominal party having no real interest in claim found to be collusive).

b. Failure to name indispensable parties

The parties may not manufacture diversity jurisdiction by failing to join a non-diverse indispensable party. (*See* § VI.A.2. Compulsory Joinder, *infra*, regarding the standards for compulsory joinder under Rule 19.)

c. Voluntary change of state citizenship

A party may voluntarily change state citizenship after the accrual of a cause of action, but before the commencement of a lawsuit, and therefore establish or defeat diversity jurisdiction.

A party's motive for changing citizenship is irrelevant, but the change of state citizenship must be genuine in order to be recognized. In determining whether a party's change of state citizenship is genuine, a court may consider whether the party changed her domicile specifically to create or destroy diversity. *Compare Williamson v. Osenton*, 232 U.S. 619, 625 (1914) (finding that a wife separated from her husband could establish her own domicile in a new state and maintain an action based on diversity jurisdiction) *with Morris v. Gilmer*, 129 U.S. 315, 328–29 (1889) (finding that the plaintiff did not change his domicile because he only moved there to create diversity and did not intend to remain in the new state indefinitely).

d. Substitution versus replacement of parties

Sometimes there is a need to exchange parties to a lawsuit. Two processes are in place to do so depending on the circumstances. Rule 25 allows for the substitution of a party due to death or incompetence. In this case, the substituted party does not have to satisfy the diversity requirement. The original party's citizenship remains intact and controlling. A similar doctrine exists when a party must be replaced, such as when the wrong party is named in the complaint. Replacement in such instance is possible so long as the replaced party satisfies the diversity requirement.

Notice the subtle distinction between substitution and replacement. Substitution calls for the substituted party to step into the shoes of the original party, whereas replacement removes one party to the lawsuit for another party.

5. Amount in Controversy

a. Rule

Under § 1332(a), the amount in controversy must exceed the sum or value of $75,000, exclusive of interest, costs, and collateral effects of a judgment. Although interests and costs are excluded from the amount in controversy, attorney's fees may be made part of the amount in controversy if the fees are recoverable by contract or statute. Punitive damages, as well, may be permitted to be made part of the amount in controversy. The amount in controversy is determined at the time the action is commenced in federal court, or, if the action has been removed to federal court, at the time of the removal. The party seeking to invoke federal court jurisdiction must allege that the action satisfies the amount-in-controversy requirement.

In the case of injunctive relief, when it is difficult to assess a dollar amount, the court will examine either the plaintiff's viewpoint to determine the value of the harm, or the defendant's viewpoint to assess the cost of complying with the injunction. If the amount under either test exceeds $75,000, then the amount-in-controversy requirement is satisfied.

> **EXAM NOTE:** Remember that the amount in controversy must **exceed** $75,000; a claim for exactly $75,000 fails.

b. Standard of proof

1) Generally

In general, a plaintiff's good-faith assertion in the complaint that the action satisfies the amount-in-controversy requirement is sufficient, unless it appears to a legal certainty that the plaintiff cannot recover the amount alleged. *St. Paul Mercury Indem. Co. v. Red Cab Co.*, 303 U.S. 283 (1938).

If an alleged amount in controversy is challenged, the burden is on the party asserting jurisdiction merely to show that it is not a legal certainty that the claim involves less than the statutory amount.

2) Reduction of claim after filing

If events after the action has been filed reduce the amount in controversy below the statutory minimum, jurisdiction will not be lost, so long as the original claim was made in good faith. Additionally, if the plaintiff eventually recovers an amount that is less than the statutory jurisdictional amount, that fact will not render the verdict subject to challenge on appeal for lack of jurisdiction.

c. Aggregation of claims

1) By single plaintiff against single defendant

If the action involves only one plaintiff and one defendant, the total value of the plaintiff's claims is calculated in order to determine the amount in controversy.

2) By multiple plaintiffs

If the action involves multiple plaintiffs, the value of their claims may be aggregated only if the multiple plaintiffs are enforcing a single title or right, in which they have a common or undivided interest.

If multiple plaintiffs, each having separate and distinct claims, unite for convenience or economy in a single suit, each plaintiff must separately meet the amount-in-controversy requirement.

3) By single plaintiff against multiple defendants

The value of a single plaintiff's claims against each defendant may not be aggregated if the claims are separate and distinct. If the defendants are jointly liable to the plaintiff, aggregation to meet the amount-in-controversy requirement is permissible.

4) Class actions

In general, if any member of the putative class does not have a claim that meets the statutory jurisdictional amount, the amount-in-controversy requirement will not be met. *Snyder v. Harris*, 394 U.S. 332 (1969); *Zahn v. International Paper*, 414 U.S. 291 (1973).

Note, though, that the Class Action Fairness Act of 2005 amended § 1332(d) to permit aggregation of claims in certain class actions:

i)   Involving at least 100 members;

ii) In which the primary defendants are not states, state officials, or other governmental entities against whom the district court may be foreclosed from ordering relief;

iii) Do not involve certain securities-related cases, or litigation concerning the internal affairs or governance of a corporation;

iv) In which the amount in controversy exceeds the sum or value of $5,000,000, exclusive of interest and costs; and

v)   In which minimum diversity exists. Minimum diversity is satisfied when any member of a class of plaintiffs is a citizen of a state different from any defendant.

Additionally, the Supreme Court has held that when at least one plaintiff in a putative class action has a claim that meets the statutory jurisdictional amount, the other plaintiffs can be made part of the class under the doctrine of supplemental jurisdiction. *Exxon Mobil Corp. v. Allapattah Servs., Inc.*, 545 U.S. 546 (2005). (*See* § I.D. Supplemental Jurisdiction, *infra.*)

d. Counterclaims

A counterclaim by a defendant against a plaintiff is not counted for purposes of determining whether the plaintiff has met the statutory jurisdictional amount. Under some circumstances, though, the counterclaim itself will need to meet the statutory jurisdictional amount in order to be considered by the court.

1) Compulsory counterclaims

A compulsory counterclaim, which is generally a claim arising out of the same transaction or occurrence as the plaintiff's claim, does not have to meet the statutory jurisdictional amount requirement in order to be considered by the court. *See* Rule 13(a). The court will have supplemental jurisdiction over the compulsory counterclaim. (*See* § I.D. Supplemental Jurisdiction, *infra.*)

2) Permissive counterclaims

A permissive counterclaim, which is a claim arising out of a transaction that is unrelated to the plaintiff's claim (*see* Rule 13(b)), does have to meet the statutory jurisdictional amount requirement.

3) Removal based on counterclaim

a) Plaintiff

A plaintiff is not allowed to remove a case to federal court, even if the defendant is diverse and has counterclaimed for more than the federal statutory jurisdictional amount. Removal is only allowed by defendants. (*See* § I.E. Removal Jurisdiction, *infra*.)

b) Defendant—permissive counterclaim

When a diverse defendant makes a permissive counterclaim under state law for more than the federal statutory jurisdictional amount, and the plaintiff's claim is for less than the federal statutory jurisdictional amount, the defendant is not permitted to remove the case to federal court.

c) Defendant—compulsory counterclaim

When a diverse defendant makes a compulsory counterclaim under state law for more than the federal statutory jurisdictional amount, and the plaintiff's claim is for less than the federal statutory jurisdictional amount, courts are split on allowing removal by the defendant. Most, though, do not allow the defendant to remove the case to federal court.

D. SUPPLEMENTAL JURISDICTION

1. In General

A district court with jurisdiction may exercise "supplemental jurisdiction" over additional claims over which the court would not independently have subject matter jurisdiction (usually state law claims against a non-diverse defendant), but that arise out of a **"common nucleus of operative fact"** such that all claims should be tried together in a single judicial proceeding. *United Mine Workers v. Gibbs*, 383 U.S. 715 (1966).

2. Federal Question Jurisdiction Cases

When the district court's subject matter jurisdiction for a claim is based on the existence of a federal question, additional claims against the same party can be heard by the court through the exercise of supplemental jurisdiction if the "common nucleus of operative fact" test is met.

Example 1: Plaintiff sues Defendant, her corporate employer, in federal court under Title VII for sex discrimination and retaliation, matters over which the court has federal question jurisdiction. Plaintiff then seeks to sue Defendant for assault and battery under state law, a claim that arises under the same operative facts that applied to her Title VII claim. The federal court has discretion to exercise supplemental jurisdiction over the assault and battery claim.

Similarly, a district court may have supplemental jurisdiction over claims that involve the joinder or intervention of additional parties over which the court would not otherwise have jurisdiction if the claims involving the additional parties satisfy the "common nucleus of operative fact" test. Such jurisdiction is also referred to as "pendent party jurisdiction."

Example 2: Plaintiff sues Defendant 1, her corporate employer, in federal court under Title VII for sex discrimination and retaliation, matters over which the court has federal question jurisdiction. Plaintiff then seeks to sue Defendant 2, her direct supervisor, for assault and battery, a claim that arises under the same operative facts that applied to her Title VII claim against the corporate employer. The federal court could exercise supplemental jurisdiction over the assault and battery claim against the supervisor.

Dismissal of a federal claim on the merits does not preclude a federal court from exercising pendent jurisdiction over the state claim.

3. **Diversity Jurisdiction Cases**

When a district court has diversity jurisdiction over a claim, the "common nucleus of operative facts" rule also applies to determine whether the court can exercise supplemental jurisdiction over an additional claim.

a. **Permissive joinder**

Although the additional claim is not required to satisfy the amount-in–controversy requirement for purposes of supplemental jurisdiction, when the additional claim is asserted by a party seeking to join the action under Rule 20 (permissive joinder), the addition of that party cannot result in a violation of the complete diversity of citizenship requirement.

Example 1: Plaintiff 1, a citizen of Pennsylvania, brings a negligence action in federal court for $500,000 against Defendant, a citizen of New York, based on an automobile accident. Plaintiff 2, also a citizen of Pennsylvania and a passenger in Plaintiff 1's car at the time of the accident, seeks to join Plaintiff 1's action, by filing a negligence claim against Defendant for $30,000. While diversity jurisdiction does not exist for Plaintiff 2's claim because it does not satisfy the $75,000 amount in controversy requirement, the court can exercise supplemental jurisdiction over that claim because it meets the "common nucleus of operative facts" test.

Example 2: Assume for this example the same facts as those in Example 1 except that Plaintiff 2 is a citizen of New York. The federal court cannot exercise supplemental jurisdiction over Plaintiff 2's claim because the presence of Plaintiff 2 would defeat the complete diversity requirement.

b. **Counterclaims**

A counterclaim may be asserted by a defendant against a plaintiff without satisfying the jurisdictional amount when the counterclaim is compulsory. A permissive counterclaim does not qualify for supplementary jurisdiction and therefore must satisfy the jurisdictional amount and the rule of complete diversity.

c. Crossclaims

A crossclaim that arises out of the same transaction or occurrence may be asserted by one defendant against another defendant without regard to the amount in controversy or the citizenship of the parties to the crossclaim as long as the court has subject matter jurisdiction.

d. Precluded claims in diversity cases

Under § 1367(b), in actions in which the original jurisdiction of the federal court is based solely on diversity jurisdiction, supplemental jurisdiction is precluded for:

i) Claims by existing plaintiffs (but not defendants) against persons made parties under one of the following Federal Rules of Civil Procedure: Rule 14 (impleader), Rule 19 (compulsory joinder), Rule 20 (permissive joinder), or Rule 24 (intervention);

ii) Claims by persons to be joined as plaintiffs pursuant to Rule 19; and

iii) Claims by persons seeking to intervene as plaintiffs pursuant to Rule 24, when the exercise of supplemental jurisdiction over such claims would be inconsistent with the requirements for diversity jurisdiction under 28 U.S.C. § 1332.

> **Example 1:** Plaintiff, a citizen of Iowa, sues Defendant, a Nebraska corporation, in federal court under diversity jurisdiction for the wrongful death of Plaintiff's husband. Defendant then impleads Contractor, a citizen of Iowa, under Rule 14, alleging that if Defendant is liable to Plaintiff, Contractor must indemnify Defendant for any liability to Defendant. If Plaintiff then asserts a claim directly against Contractor, since they are both citizens of the same state (Iowa), supplemental jurisdiction in federal court will not apply to the claim, as it would be inconsistent with the requirements for diversity jurisdiction, pursuant to § 1367(b). Note that Defendant's claim against Contractor would fall within the federal court's supplemental jurisdiction, as it is derived from the same operative facts being considered by the court under the claim over which it has original jurisdiction and is not precluded by § 1367(b).

> **Example 2:** Plaintiff, a citizen of Arkansas, sues Defendant 1 and Defendant 2, both citizens of Oklahoma, in federal court on the basis of diversity jurisdiction, alleging negligence. Defendant 1 seeks to assert a crossclaim for negligence, under the same operative facts, pursuant to Rule 13(g), against Defendant 2. Although there would be no original jurisdiction in federal court for the crossclaim, because Defendant 1 and Defendant 2 are citizens of the same state (Oklahoma) (*see* § I.C.2. Complete Diversity, *supra*), the federal court could exercise supplemental jurisdiction over the crossclaim, as it is derived from the same operative facts being considered by the court under the claim over which it has original jurisdiction, and is not excluded under § 1367(b).

4. Discretionary Rejection of Supplemental Jurisdiction

Under § 1367(c), a district court has discretion to decline to exercise supplemental jurisdiction over a claim that would otherwise qualify for supplemental jurisdiction in each of the following circumstances:

i) The supplemental claim raises a novel or complex issue of state law;

ii) The supplemental claim substantially predominates over the claims within original federal jurisdiction;

iii) All of the claims within the court's original jurisdiction have been dismissed; or

iv) In exceptional circumstances, if there are other compelling reasons for declining jurisdiction.

E. REMOVAL JURISDICTION

1. Basis

Under § 1441(a), any civil action commenced in a state court that is within the original jurisdiction of a U.S. district court may generally be removed by the defendant to the district court for the district in which the state court action was commenced.

The right of removal is a right of the defendant only and is not available to a plaintiff defending a counterclaim that could have originally been brought in federal court. Note that removal jurisdiction is not a substitute for either federal question or diversity jurisdiction, but it is simply a mechanism by which defendants in a state action over which a federal court otherwise has subject matter jurisdiction can get the action into federal court.

2. Determination

In general, the right of removal is determined by the pleadings filed as of the time of the filing of the petition of removal. In diversity cases, however, diversity must exist at the time of filing the original action as well as at the time the notice of removal is filed, unless the plaintiff dismisses a party who would have destroyed diversity jurisdiction. In other words, removal is permitted when a party who prevents diversity jurisdiction is dismissed from an action. The federal court to which the action is removed is not precluded from hearing and determining any claim in the action because the state court from which the action was removed did not have jurisdiction over that claim. § 1441(f).

3. Other Removal Statutes

While § 1441 sets forth the general rule regarding removal, other statutes authorize removal in specific cases, including:

i) Suits against the United States, any federal agency, or federal officers for acts under color of office (§ 1442);

ii) Suits against federal employees for injuries caused from their operation of a motor vehicle within the scope of their employment (§ 2679(d)); and

iii) Actions involving international banking (12 U.S.C. § 632).

In addition, certain statutes prohibit removal for otherwise removable actions, including:

i) Actions arising under the Employers' Liability Act and under the Jones Act against a railroad or its receivers or trustees (§ 1445(a));

ii) Actions against carriers for delay, loss, or damage in shipments, when the amount in controversy does not exceed $10,000 (§ 1445(b));

iii) Actions arising under the workers' compensation laws of the state in which the action is brought (§ 1445(c)); and

iv) Actions arising under § 40302 of the Violence Against Women Act of 1994.

4. Limitation on Removal in Diversity Cases

If removal is sought solely based on diversity jurisdiction, the claim may be removed only if no defendant is a citizen of the state in which the action was filed. § 1441(b). There is no similar requirement for removal based on federal question jurisdiction.

Example: If a Texas corporation sues Illinois defendants in Illinois state court, the Illinois defendants are not permitted to remove the action to federal court based on diversity jurisdiction.

5. Removal of Separate and Independent Claims in a Federal Question Jurisdiction Case

If removal is sought on the basis of federal question jurisdiction, and the federal question claims in the state action are joined with claims that are not independently removable, the entire case may be removed. The district court must then sever and remand to the state court any claims in which state law predominates. § 1441(c).

6. Procedure

a. Notice of removal

1) Generally

Under 28 U.S.C. § 1446, a defendant who wants to remove a state court action to federal district court must file a notice of removal with the district court within 30 days after receipt by or service on that defendant of the initial pleading or summons. The notice must be:

i) Signed pursuant to Rule 11 (*see* § V.I., *infra*) and contain a short and plain statement of the grounds for removal;

ii) Filed in the district court for the district and division in which the state action is pending; and

iii) Accompanied by copies of all process, pleadings, and orders served on the defendants seeking removal.

In general, all defendants who have been properly joined and served are required to join in or consent to the removal. If the defendants are served at different times and a later-served defendant files a notice of removal, any earlier-served defendant may join in the removal even though that defendant did not previously initiate or consent to removal. § 1446(b). In cases of removal based on federal question jurisdiction, only those defendants against whom the federal claim is asserted must join in or consent to the removal. § 1441(c)(2). In addition, a class action lawsuit may be removed by any defendant without the consent of all defendants. § 1453(b).

2) Removal based on diversity

A matter cannot be removed based on diversity of citizenship more than one year after the action is commenced. This one-year rule does not apply, however, if the district court finds that the plaintiff has acted in bad faith (such as by deliberately failing to disclose the actual amount in controversy) in order to prevent a defendant from removing the action. § 1446(c).

If removal is based on diversity and the plaintiff (i) seeks nonmonetary relief, (ii) is not required under state law to demand a specific sum, or (iii) is permitted by state law to recover more than the amount demanded, then the notice of removal may assert that the amount in controversy exceeds $75,000, and the district court will have jurisdiction if it finds, by a preponderance of the evidence, that the amount does exceed $75,000.

b. Additional requirements

Promptly after the notice of removal is filed with the district court, the defendants must give written notice of the filing to all adverse parties and file a copy of the notice of removal with the clerk of the state court from which the action is sought to be removed. § 1446(d).

Once a copy of the removal notice is filed with the state court, the removal acts as a stay of the state court proceedings. The state court is not allowed to take any further action with regard to the case and can be enjoined by the federal court if it does take any action.

c. Procedure in district court following removal

Once the action is removed, procedure follows the Federal Rules of Civil Procedure. New pleadings are not required unless the court orders otherwise. Pleadings filed before removal can be amended pursuant to the federal rules.

The district court may issue all necessary orders and processes to bring before it all proper parties, regardless of whether those parties had been served by process issued by the state court. § 1447(a). If the action was removed before each defendant had been served with process, or if service of process was defective, service of process can be completed or new process issued in the same manner as in cases originally filed in district court. § 1448.

State court orders issued before removal to district court remain in effect but are subject to district court modification when necessary. § 1450.

d. Procedure for demand for jury trial

Once the action is removed to federal court, the removing party, if seeking a jury trial, must file the demand within 14 days of filing for removal or risk losing the right. Similarly, the non-removing party also has 14 days to file, but the countdown begins after service of notice of removal is received. In both cases, if the demand in not filed in a timely fashion, the right to a jury trial is waived.

There is an exception to this rule: When a party who, prior to removal, exercised his right for a jury trial, no need exists to make the same demand after removal.

7. Remand

a. For lack of subject matter jurisdiction

If at any time before final judgment it appears that the district court lacks subject matter jurisdiction, the case must be remanded to the state court from which it came. § 1447(c).

For the purposes of § 1447(c) and (d), however, when a case is remanded to a state court because the federal district court declines to exercise supplemental jurisdiction, the remand is not based on a lack of subject matter jurisdiction. *Carlsbad Tech., Inc. v. HIF Bio, Inc.*, 556 U.S. 635 (2009).

b. For other reasons

A party must make any motion to remand the case on the basis of any defect other than lack of subject matter jurisdiction within 30 days after the filing of the notice of removal. § 1447(c).

c. Burden of proof

If the propriety of the removal is challenged, the burden of establishing proper removal is on the party who removed the case.

d. Costs and attorney's fees

The district court's order remanding the case may require payment of costs, including attorney's fees, incurred as a result of the removal. § 1447(c). The Supreme Court has held that, absent unusual circumstances, federal courts may award attorney's fees under § 1447(c) only when the removing party lacked an objectively reasonable basis for seeking removal. *Martin v. Franklin Capital Corp.*, 546 U.S. 132 (2005).

e. Procedure

A certified copy of the remand order must be mailed by the district court clerk to the clerk of the state court. The state court may thereafter proceed with the case. § 1447(c).

f. Not generally appealable

Under § 1447(d), a remand order is generally not reviewable on appeal or otherwise, with the following exceptions:

i) There is statutory exception for an order remanding a civil rights case removed pursuant to § 1443; or

ii) A remand order is also appealable in a class action lawsuit, if the application for review is made to the court of appeals not less than seven days after the entry of the order.

g. Discretion to remand when proposed joinder would destroy diversity jurisdiction

Under § 1447(e), if, after removal, the plaintiff seeks to join a defendant who would destroy the federal court's diversity jurisdiction, the court has discretion to deny the joinder and proceed with the action in federal court, or to permit the joinder and remand the action to state court.

F. LEGISLATIVE JURISDICTION

In addition to the types of jurisdiction above, there are federal courts created by Congress with jurisdiction over specific types of cases. Briefly, these include:

i)   **The United States Claims Court** (formerly "the Court of Claims"), with original jurisdiction over actions brought against the United States or its officer, or concerning federal property;

ii) **The United States Court of Appeals for the Federal Circuit**, with appellate jurisdiction over claims against the federal government or its officers, etc;

iii) **The Court of International Trade**, with jurisdiction over foreign states;

iv) **United States Tax Court**, with jurisdiction over taxpayer challenges to I.R.S. deficiency determinations; and

v)   **United States Bankruptcy Court**, with jurisdiction over bankruptcy matters.

There is no amount in controversy requirement in the above cases, unless an action is brought against a party other than the United States under the Consumer Product Safety Act.

Illinois Distinction: Subject Matter Jurisdiction

Illinois Court System: Illinois has three levels of courts: the Circuit Courts, Appellate Courts, and the Supreme Court.

Circuit Courts: Circuit Courts are the trial-level courts. They have original jurisdiction over all matters not under the original jurisdiction of the Illinois Supreme Court (as discussed below), the federal courts (as discussed above), and administrative agencies.

Appellate Courts: Appellate Courts have jurisdiction over all final decisions of the Circuit Courts, except those appealable directly to the Illinois Supreme Court, and some interlocutory issues, as discussed in the section addressing Interlocutory Appeals.

Illinois Supreme Court: The Illinois Supreme Court has general authority over all other Illinois courts.

Supreme Court Jurisdiction

Original jurisdiction: The Illinois Supreme Court has original jurisdiction over actions in revenue, mandamus, prohibition, or habeas corpus. Only issues of law will be considered, and the jurisdiction is discretionary. The Illinois Supreme Court also has original mandatory jurisdiction over actions relating to redistricting of the General Assembly and the ability of the Governor to serve or resume office.

Appellate jurisdiction: Final judgments from Circuit Court cases may be appealed directly to the Illinois Supreme Court when a statute of the United States or Illinois has been held invalid or in proceedings to compel compliance with administrative orders.

Article VI, Section 4 of the Illinois State Constitution provides that appeals from criminal cases in which a death sentence has been imposed shall be appealed to the Illinois Supreme Court from the Circuit Court as a matter of right.

It is mandatory that the Illinois Supreme Court hear appeals when:

i)   An Illinois or United States statute has been found invalid;

ii) A question under the Illinois or United States Constitution arises for the first time; or

---

iii) Cases have been certified by the Illinois Appellate Court as involving an important question of law.

See Ill. Sup. Ct. R. 316–317.

The Illinois Supreme Court has discretion to grant and hear appeals by petition of a party and in cases in which the public interest requires expeditious determination.

II.   PERSONAL JURISDICTION

A.   IN GENERAL

In addition, to subject matter jurisdiction, a court must also be able to exercise judicial power over the persons or property involved in the cases or controversies before the court. This authority is broadly referred to as "personal jurisdiction" and is governed by state statutes regarding jurisdiction and the due process requirements of the U.S. Constitution.

1.   Types

There are three general types of personal jurisdiction: (i) *in personam* jurisdiction, (ii) *in rem* jurisdiction, and (iii) *quasi in rem* jurisdiction.

2.   Effect of State Jurisdictional Statutes on Personal Jurisdiction in Federal Court

In general, a federal court does not have nationwide personal jurisdiction. *Omni Capital Int'l, Ltd. v. Rudolf Wolff & Co.*, 484 U.S. 97 (1987). Under Rule 4(k)(1)(A), the service of a summons in a federal action establishes personal jurisdiction over a defendant "who is subject to the jurisdiction of a court of general jurisdiction in the state where the district court is located." A federal court must generally determine personal jurisdiction as if it were a court of the state in which it is situated. Thus, a federal court will look to state jurisdictional statutes (*see* § II.B.2.d. Long-arm statutes, *infra*) to determine if it has authority over the parties before it and will be subject to the restrictions on states imposed by the Due Process Clause of the U.S. Constitution.

a.   Exceptions

1)   Nationwide service of process

A federal court may have national personal jurisdiction for special types of statutorily created actions, such as federal statutory interpleader actions (*see* § VI.C.2.b. In personam jurisdiction, *infra*).

2)   "Bulge provision"

Under Rule 4(k)(1)(B), the so-called "bulge provision," a federal court has personal jurisdiction over a party who is served within a United States judicial district and not more than 100 miles from where the summons is issued, even if state law would otherwise not permit such service. *See Mississippi Publ'g Corp. v. Murphree*, 326 U.S. 438 (1946); *Robertson v. R.R. Labor Bd.*, 268 U.S. 619 (1925). This special rule applies to only two types of parties: a third-party defendant who is joined under Rule 14 (*see* § VI.D.4.d. In personam jurisdiction, *infra*) and a required party who is joined under Rule 19 (*see* § VI.A.2.c. In personam jurisdiction, *infra*).

3) Rule 4(k)(2)

Four conditions must be present for a federal court to have personal jurisdiction under Rule 4(k)(2):

   i)   The plaintiff's claims must be based on federal law;

   ii) No state court could exercise jurisdiction over the defendants;

   iii) The exercise of jurisdiction must be consistent with the laws of the United States; and

   iv) The exercise of jurisdiction must be consistent with the U.S. Constitution (i.e., there must be "minimum contacts," *see* § II.B.3.a. Minimum contacts, *infra*).

3. Due Process Requirements for Personal Jurisdiction

The Due Process Clause also limits a court's exercise of personal jurisdiction over the parties. A court may not exercise personal jurisdiction over a defendant unless the defendant has "minimum contacts" with the state in which the court sits (the forum state) and the exercise of jurisdiction would be fair and reasonable. A court is also required to notify a party of the commencement of an action in which his interests are at stake and provide an opportunity for the party to be heard.

4. Consent or Waiver

Unlike subject matter jurisdiction, a party may consent to personal jurisdiction. The consent may be express, implied, or by making a voluntary appearance.

An objection to a court's exercise of jurisdiction over persons and things may also be waived by a party. Under Rule 12(b), the defenses of lack of jurisdiction over the person, insufficiency of process, and insufficiency of service of process must be asserted in a responsive pleading, or by motion before a responsive pleading is submitted. A failure to object in accordance with Rule 12 waives the objection. Rule 12(h).

B. IN PERSONAM JURISDICTION

1. In General

In personam jurisdiction is the power that a court has over an individual party. It is required whenever a judgment is sought that would impose an obligation on a defendant personally. When such personal jurisdiction exists, the court has the authority to issue a judgment against the party personally, which can be satisfied by seizure of all of the party's assets. Such a judgment is entitled to full faith and credit in other states (*see* § IX.C. Full Faith and Credit, *infra*).

2. Bases for In Personam Jurisdiction

a. Voluntary presence

If a defendant is voluntarily present in the forum state and is served with process while there, the state will have personal jurisdiction over the defendant. *Burnham v. Superior Court of California*, 495 U.S. 604 (1990). However, most courts today have two exceptions to this rule. If a plaintiff fraudulently brings a defendant into the state for the purpose of serving process on him, the service will most likely be invalid. A defendant is also immune if he is merely passing through the state to attend other judiciary proceedings.

b. Domicile

If authorized by statute, a state can have jurisdiction over a person who is domiciled within the state, even if the person is temporarily absent from the state. Domicile is established when a person with capacity intends to make that state his home. Statutory authorization can be enacted retroactively to apply to a cause of action arising before the enactment of the statute. *McGee v. Int'l Life Ins. Co.*, 355 U.S. 220 (1957). Additionally, the United States has authority to subpoena a citizen of the United States living abroad to appear in court to testify. The same rules of domicile apply as are discussed in § I.C.3. Citizenship of Parties, *supra*.

c. Consent

Personal jurisdiction can be established by a party's consent. Under Rule 12(b), the defense of lack of personal jurisdiction must be asserted in a responsive pleading or by motion before a responsive pleading is submitted. The failure to timely object to a court's assertion of personal jurisdiction waives the objection. Rule 12(h).

1) Plaintiffs

Plaintiffs are said to have consented to personal jurisdiction by filing the lawsuit.

2) Defendants

a) Express consent

A defendant may agree in advance by contract to submit to the jurisdiction of the court if a lawsuit is brought by the plaintiff. Such contractual consent will not be effective if the court determines that the contract was a contract of adhesion. A defendant may also stipulate to personal jurisdiction once an action is brought. *Petrowski v. Hawkeye-Security Ins. Co.*, 350 U.S. 495 (1956). Consent is said to be given when a person authorizes an agent to accept service of process. Usually, a state will require nonresidents doing business in a heavily regulated industry to appoint an agent.

b) Implied consent

A defendant may be deemed to have consented through its conduct, such as filing a counterclaim or being party to an accident outside one's home state.

c) Voluntary appearance

Voluntary appearance of the defendant in court automatically subjects the defendant to personal jurisdiction, unless he is present to object jurisdiction.

d. Long-arm statutes

Most states have enacted statutes that authorize personal jurisdiction over non-residents who engage in some activity in the state or cause some action to occur within the state. In many states, the long-arm statute authorizes jurisdiction to the extent permissible under the Due Process Clause. Thus, a federal court in those states need only determine whether the exercise of personal jurisdiction comports with due process. A few states have enacted statutes of a more limited scope, which confer jurisdiction on the basis of specific activities undertaken in the state (e.g., owning property, committing a tort, or entering into a contract to supply goods or services in the state). These statutes, too, must comport with the Due Process Clause.

Illinois Distinction: Long-Arm Statute

The Illinois long-arm statute contains three broad bases for the Illinois courts to exercise specific personal jurisdiction over persons who may not currently be residents or domiciliaries of the state. 735 Ill. Comp. Stat. 5/2-209. The long-arm statute is applicable to authorize jurisdiction so long as the defendant's activity is constitutional under the Due Process Clause.

Specific Jurisdiction: The statute lists 14 acts that will submit a person to the jurisdiction of the Illinois courts pertaining to causes of action that arise from those specific acts:

i) Transacting business within Illinois;

ii) Committing a tortious act within Illinois;

iii) Owning, using, or possessing any real property within Illinois;

iv) Contracting to insure any person, property, or risk located in Illinois at the time of contracting;

v) With respect to actions involving the dissolution of marriage and legal separation, maintaining a marital domicile in Illinois at the time the cause of action arose, or at the time the act giving rise to the cause of action arose;

vi) With respect to actions brought under the Illinois Parentage Act, performing an act of sexual intercourse within Illinois during the possible period of conception;

vii) Making or performing any contract or promise substantially connected with Illinois;

viii) Performing sexual intercourse within Illinois that is claimed to have resulted in the conception of a child who resides in Illinois;

ix) Failing to support a child, spouse, or former spouse who has continued to reside in Illinois;

x) Acquiring ownership, possession, or control of any asset present in Illinois when ownership, possession, or control was acquired;

xi) Breaching a fiduciary duty within Illinois;

xii) Performing duties as a director or officer of a corporation organized under the laws of Illinois;

xiii) Owning an interest in any trust administered in Illinois; or

xiv) Exercising fiduciary powers granted under the authority of Illinois.

General Jurisdiction: The statute lists four bases under which a person will be subjected to general jurisdiction in Illinois due to statutory "presence" in Illinois:

i) Natural persons present in Illinois when served;

ii) Natural persons who were residing or domiciled within Illinois when the cause of action arose, the action was commenced, or process was served;

---

iii) Corporations organized under the laws of Illinois; or

iv) Natural persons or corporations doing business within Illinois.

Constitutional Basis: Under this last category, the court may exercise its jurisdiction on any basis that is in accord with the Illinois or United States Constitution.

e. Attachment

Under "Attachment Jurisdiction" (historically, a type of quasi in rem jurisdiction, *see* § II.C.2. Quasi In Rem Jurisdiction, *infra*), a plaintiff asserting a personal claim against the defendant would use attachment of the property as a device to obtain jurisdiction and satisfy the judgment, if successful. Since *Shaffer v. Heitner*, 433 U.S. 186 (1977), discussed below, when the claim is not related to the ownership of the property that has been attached, there must be minimum contacts between the defendant and the forum state in order to establish jurisdiction.

3. Due Process Requirements

In general, due process requirements are satisfied if the non-resident defendant has certain minimum contacts with the forum state such that the maintenance of the action does not offend traditional notions of fair play and substantial justice. *International Shoe Co. v. State of Washington*, 326 U.S. 310 (1945).

> **EXAM NOTE:** When analyzing a personal jurisdiction question, the focus is on (i) the contacts the defendant has or had with the forum state and (ii) whether the assertion of jurisdiction by the court would comport with fair play and substantial justice. Personal jurisdiction will depend on the facts of each case.

a. Minimum contacts

1) Required by *Shaffer*

While before *Shaffer*, it was possible to gain jurisdiction over a person merely on the basis of the presence within the state of the person or property of the person, after *Shaffer* any attempt to gain in personam jurisdiction, under whatever basis, is subject to the *International Shoe* requirement of minimum contacts.

Shaffer expressly excluded actions to enforce previous judgments by such remedies as attachment, garnishment, and sequestration from the requirement of minimum contacts with the defendant. *See Shaffer v. Heitner*, 433 U.S. at 210.

2) Purposeful availment

In order to warrant the assertion of in personam jurisdiction, a defendant's contacts with the forum state must be purposeful and substantial, such that the defendant should reasonably anticipate (foresee) being taken to court there. Foreseeability depends on whether a defendant recognizes or anticipates that by running his business, he runs the risk of being party to a suit in a particular state. *World-Wide Volkswagen Corp. v. Woodson*, 444 U.S. 286 (1980). This is the "purposeful availment" requirement.

There are situations, however, when it is difficult to discern whether purposeful availment is present. Such is the case when a product is put into the stream of commerce, not necessarily by the manufacturer, but by a party who purchased the product from the manufacturer to use in his product. The manufacturer's product is then put into the stream of commerce. The question remains, did the manufacturer avail himself of the jurisdiction's benefits and laws? The Court is split on this issue and has not been able to reach a cohesive answer. While four justices find sufficiency with the mere knowledge that the product being sold would end up in the stream of commerce, four other justices believe that the manufacturer needed to take an additional step to have availed himself of the forum. *Asahi Metal Industry Co. v. Superior Court of California*, 480 U.S. 102 (1987).

3) Specific and general jurisdiction

The scope of the contacts necessary for the assertion of personal jurisdiction depends on the relationship that the cause of action has with the forum state.

When a cause of action arises out of or closely relates to a defendant's contact with the forum state, jurisdiction may be warranted even if that contact is the defendant's only contact with the forum state. *Helicopteros Nacionales de Colombia, S.A. v. Hall*, 466 U.S. 408 (1984). This type of jurisdiction is often referred to as "specific jurisdiction."

When a cause of action does not arise out of or relate to the defendant's contacts with the forum, jurisdiction will be warranted only when the defendant's contacts with the state have been systematic and continuous. Conducting business activities in a state (e.g., keeping an office, conducting correspondence, maintaining active bank accounts, conducting meetings, and paying salaries) is sufficiently systematic and continuous to allow a court to exercise personal jurisdiction over the business for causes of action that are unrelated to the business's activities there. *Perkins v. Benguet Consol. Mining Co.*, 342 U.S. 437 (1952). This type of jurisdiction is known as "general jurisdiction."

4) Imputed contacts

Under some circumstances, the contacts of one defendant with the forum state may be imputed to another defendant for purposes of determining jurisdiction.

a) Employees/independent contractors

Contacts by a non-resident employer's agents or employees are generally imputed to the employer when the agent or employee is acting within the scope of the agency or employment. An out-of-state corporation, though, is generally not subject to personal jurisdiction solely because of contacts in the state by an independent contractor.

b) Partnerships

Each partner is generally an agent of the partnership for the purpose of its business. Accordingly, a partner's activities on behalf of the partnership can confer personal jurisdiction over the partnership entity.

Such contacts, though, may not necessarily establish personal jurisdiction over that partner or the other partners of the partnership in their individual capacities.

c) Corporations

An out-of-state corporation's contacts with the forum state will not automatically establish jurisdiction over a wholly-owned subsidiary of the corporation, and contacts by a wholly-owned subsidiary will not automatically confer jurisdiction over a corporate parent. *Cannon Mfg. Co. v. Cudahy Packing Co.,* 267 U.S. 333 (1925)). If, however, the subsidiary is the corporate parent's alter ego or is specifically acting as the corporate parent's agent, its contacts may be imputed to the corporate parent. *Id.*

b. Fair play and substantial justice

Once minimum contacts are established, a court must still examine the facts to determine if maintenance of the action would "offend traditional notions of fair play and substantial justice." *International Shoe, supra.*

Courts consider a variety of factors when making this determination, including:

   i) The interest of the forum state in adjudicating the matter;

   ii) The burden on the defendant of appearing in the case;

   iii) The interest of the judicial system in the efficient resolution of controversies; and

   iv) The shared interests of the states in promoting common social policies.

4. In Personam Jurisdiction Over Corporations

a. Resident corporations

For in personam jurisdiction purposes, a corporation will be a resident corporation only if it is incorporated in the forum state. Any action may be brought against a corporation that is incorporated in the forum state. If the corporation is not incorporated in the state, then for purposes of in personam jurisdiction it will constitute a foreign corporation.

Illinois Distinction: Resident Corporations

All resident corporations and foreign corporations authorized to transact business in Illinois must maintain a registered office in Illinois and have a registered agent who is either an individual residing in Illinois or a corporation authorized to transact business in the state. By doing so, a corporation is deemed to have consented to in personam jurisdiction in Illinois. If such an agent is not maintained, service may be made upon the Secretary of State.

---

b. Foreign corporations

The rules of minimum contacts and substantial fairness apply to a foreign corporation.

5. Internet Websites

It is generally accepted that merely having a website will not subject a defendant to process everywhere that the site can be viewed. Most courts have followed the approach of *Zippo Mfg. Co. v. Zippo Dot Com, Inc.*, 952 F. Supp. 1119 (W.D. Pa. 1997), which bases jurisdiction over a non-resident's website on the degree of interactivity between the website and the forum. The court set forth a sliding scale approach with regard to the interactivity of websites, ranging from passive sites to those that are integral to the defendant's business.

Merely making a website accessible to the public and posting information is generally considered passive on the sliding scale and should not result in personal jurisdiction. Websites that are integral to a defendant's business, however, are on the other end of the sliding scale. When a website's purpose is to assist in conducting direct business transactions, courts are more likely to find minimum contacts with a state and assert personal jurisdiction.

Example: In the *Zippo* case, the defendant was a non-resident corporation that operated an integral website that had commercial contacts with more than 3,000 Pennsylvania residents and Internet service providers. The court found a high level of interactivity with Pennsylvania and determined there was personal jurisdiction over the defendant in Pennsylvania.

Courts are struggling with how to draw the lines for sites that are interactive but that do not involve significant commercial activity. The law in this area continues to evolve.

6. Suits Based on Contract

a. Contract can be relevant to establishing minimum contacts

While the fact that one party to a contract is a resident of the forum state will not, by itself, confer personal jurisdiction over the non-resident party to the contract, the existence of the contract can be a significant factor in determining that minimum contacts exist, such that the exercise of personal jurisdiction over the non-resident is appropriate. *Burger King v. Rudzewicz*, 471 U.S. 462 (1985).

b. Choice-of-law provision

If the contract contains a choice-of-law provision indicating that the forum state's law is to be used in any action with regard to the contract, this will be a significant factor in finding jurisdiction, as it establishes that the non-resident purposefully availed herself of the benefits of the forum's laws.

c. Contracts of adhesion or procured by fraud

If the contract is adhesive or was procured through fraud, personal jurisdiction based on the contract would not be appropriate.

C.   JURISDICTION OVER THINGS

Historically, jurisdiction over property has been divided into in rem jurisdiction and quasi in rem jurisdiction.

1.   In Rem Jurisdiction

a.   Defined

In rem jurisdiction is the authority of a court to determine issues concerning rights in property, either real or personal. The court generally determines title to the property, and such determination will be conclusive as against all potential claimants in the world. Examples of in rem proceedings include admiralty, forfeiture, and eminent domain actions, when a court must be able to extinguish the interests of persons who may be outside the territory of the forum or who may be unknown. It does not include property brought into the state through fraud. Often, no parties are named and the case is known by the name of the property at issue.

b.   Due process

While in rem proceedings are commenced against property, they must still satisfy due process requirements for personal jurisdiction because they affect the rights of individuals in the property. In general, for in rem jurisdiction to exist, the property at issue must be present within the forum state. *Shaffer v. Heitner*, 433 U.S. 186 (1977).

Due process is met if the notice is "reasonably calculated, under all the circumstances, to apprise interested parties of the pendency of the action and afford them an opportunity to present their objections." *Mullane v. Central Hanover Bank & Trust Co.*, 339 U.S. 306 (1950). Thus, it is no longer sufficient to simply post the notice on the property or in a newspaper.

2.   Quasi In Rem Jurisdiction

a.   Defined

While a judgment in rem determines the interests of all persons in particular property, a quasi in rem judgment determines only the interests of the parties to the action regarding property located in the forum state. *Shaffer v. Heitner*, 433 U.S. 186, 208-209 (1977). Examples include an action to foreclose a lien and an action to quiet title. The judgment is not personally binding against the defendant, cannot be sued upon in any other court, and cannot be enforced by seizing any property of the defendant other than the property at issue in the quasi in rem action.

b.   Due process

Shaffer requires a showing of minimum contacts in every exercise of jurisdiction. In most cases, the minimum contacts requirement is apparent and thus satisfied simply because there is a close relationship between the claim and the "attached" property. Sometimes, though, disputes are unrelated to the ownership of the property, and no close relationship is formed. In these cases, in addition to having the property located in the forum state, minimum contacts must be shown to exist between the defendant and the forum state before jurisdiction will apply. Notice and an opportunity to be heard are also constitutionally required.

> Note that there is some controversy over the attachment of the defendant's property prior to the trial because some consider this to be government interference with the defendant's rights to the property. The Supreme Court has not addressed this issue.

Illinois Distinction: Due Process

Contacts: The property at issue in a quasi in rem action must in some way relate to the cause of action, or the defendant must have some other minimum contacts in the state. If the defendant appears in an Illinois court to defend an in rem or a quasi in rem action, he submits to personal jurisdiction.

Publication: Notice may be by publication in a newspaper in the county in which the action is pending if the defendant does not live in Illinois, has gone out of state, or cannot be found after diligent effort.

c. Limitation

Under Fed. R. Civ. P. 4(n)(2), quasi in rem jurisdiction can be used in a U.S. district court under the circumstances and in the manner provided by the law of the state in which the U.S. district court is located.

Illinois Distinction: Limitation

Illinois Attachment Statute: Article Four of the Illinois Code of Civil Procedure allows for the seizure of in-state property of a non-domiciliary for the purpose of obtaining quasi in rem jurisdiction.

Additionally, the Illinois Attachment Statute may be used to establish a security interest to prevent the dissipation, concealment, or fraudulent transfer of the property that is the subject of the litigation.

D. NOTICE AND OPPORTUNITY TO BE HEARD

The Due Process Clause of the U.S. Constitution requires that deprivation of property by adjudication be preceded by notice and opportunity for hearing appropriate to the nature of the case. *Mullane v. Central Hanover Bank & Trust Co.*, 339 U.S. 306 (1950).

1. Notice

a. Due process

Due process is met if the notice is "reasonably calculated, under all the circumstances, to apprise interested parties of the pendency of the action and afford them an opportunity to present their objections." *Mullane, supra.*

b. Form

If the identity and address of an interested party are known or obtainable through reasonable efforts, notice through in-person delivery, registered mail, return receipt requested, or some other means likely to notify the particular individual is required. *Mennonite Bd. of Missions v. Adams*, 462 U.S. 791 (1983). However, if the plaintiff knows that the defendant(s) did not receive notice, the plaintiff cannot proceed unless there are no other reasonable methods to notify the defendant(s).

If the identity or address of interested parties is not obtainable through reasonable efforts, other means, such as publication of notice in newspapers, may be satisfactory. The constitutional test is, generally, what is **reasonable under the circumstances**. The standards are less strict for in rem and quasi in rem cases than for in personam cases. When there are multiple defendants, each defendant must be served, but the manner of service will depend on whether their identities and addresses are known or unknown.

In situations in which an agent is appointed, either by contract or by statute, the defendant will not be subject to personal jurisdiction if the agent did not advise the defendant of service of process. This rule does not apply when the defendant selects his own agent.

c. Court rules

Satisfying due process is not the only standard for the sufficiency of notice. Both state and federal courts have procedural rules that dictate the form and service of process. While a particular form of notice may meet due process standards, it must also meet the specific procedural requirements that govern in the court where the action is to be heard. Certified mail, for example, meets due process standards, but not every court system permits it to be used.

2. Opportunity to Be Heard

In addition to requiring notice of the claim being made, due process requires that a defendant be given an opportunity to be heard whenever there is a state-sponsored interference with a defendant's property interest. The state must be an active participant in the interference for due process to apply.

E. DEFENSES TO JURISDICTIONAL CLAIMS

1. Special Appearance

A special appearance is a procedure by which a defendant appears before a court for the specific purpose of challenging personal jurisdiction. The defendant is generally not considered to have consented to jurisdiction by making the special appearance, so long as personal jurisdiction is contested in the defendant's initial pleading. If anything going to the merits of the case is raised in the pleadings, the defendant will likely be found to have made a general appearance in the case and waived any objection with regard to personal jurisdiction.

Under the Federal Rules of Civil Procedure, special appearances have been abolished, but a party may make a motion to dismiss the claim for lack of personal jurisdiction under Rule 12(b)(2), without becoming subject to jurisdiction on that basis.

2. Effect of Denial of Objection to Personal Jurisdiction

If the court overrules a defendant's objection to personal jurisdiction, most states permit the defendant to defend the case on the merits and still preserve the objection to personal jurisdiction as an issue for appeal.

3. Collateral Attack

Article IV, Section 1 of the U.S. Constitution, the Full Faith and Credit Clause, ensures that judicial decisions rendered by the courts in one state are recognized and honored in every other state (*see* § IX.C. Full Faith and Credit, *infra*). Such decisions, however, are only recognized to the extent that a valid judgment was rendered by a court that had jurisdiction over the parties, and the parties received proper notice of the action and a reasonable opportunity to be heard.

For example, if a default judgment has been entered against a defendant in an action in one state, and the plaintiff sues to enforce the judgment in another state, the defendant may collaterally attack the judgment on the basis of lack of personal jurisdiction. If, however, the defendant had both notice and an opportunity to be heard, a collateral attack on the judgment is not permitted under the doctrine of *res judicata,* (*see* § IX.D. Claim Preclusion, *infra*). *Baldwin v. Iowa State Traveling Men's Ass'n*, 283 U.S. 522 (1931).

4. Immunity

Most states provide immunity from service of process to non-residents who enter the state for the purposes of attending a trial or deposition as a witness, party, or attorney. The theory behind such immunity is that it promotes full and active participation in the judicial system.

The federal courts also generally provide immunity from federal suit under the same circumstances.

Illinois Distinction: Immunity

A person who has been subpoenaed to testify in front of an Illinois grand jury or in an Illinois criminal case, or a criminal defendant extradited to Illinois or waiving extradition is immune to service of process. In the case of a criminal defendant, the immunity only applies to civil actions arising out of the criminal activity, and lasts only until conviction.

III. VENUE

A. IN GENERAL

Sometimes a court may have the power to hear a case (subject matter jurisdiction), but it may not be the proper location to adjudicate the matter. Venue concerns which court among the courts having personal and subject matter jurisdiction is the proper forum for hearing the matter. For cases in federal court, the issue is determining the proper geographic district in which a trial should occur. Venue requirements are statutory and are intended to ensure the parties a fair and convenient forum for litigating their dispute.

B. LOCAL AND TRANSITORY ACTIONS

The common law created a distinction between local and transitory actions for purposes of venue. In general, local actions involve title to property and are required to be brought in a court where the property is located. Transitory actions involve a cause of action based on events that could have taken place anywhere. Many state venue statutes continue to apply this distinction; however, in federal court, local actions and transitory actions are now subject to the same venue provisions.

C. VENUE IN STATE COURT

The requirements of venue in state court actions are established by statute. State venue statutes vary as to what factors determine venue. In many statutes, venue will be proper in the county or judicial district where the defendant resides. Other bases for venue include the location where the cause of action arose or the location of real property on which the title is at issue.

Illinois Distinction: Venue in Illinois State Courts

Generally: Except as otherwise provided, all actions must be commenced (i) in the county of residence of any defendant joined in good faith and not just for the purpose of fixing venue, or (ii) in the county in which the transaction or some part of it occurred or the cause of action arose. If all defendants are nonresidents of Illinois, the action may be brought in any county in Illinois.

Residence: For the purposes of venue, a **corporation** is a resident of any county in which it has an office or does business. A foreign corporation not authorized to transact business in Illinois is a nonresident and venue is proper in any county as long as the corporation is the only defendant.

A **partnership** sued in its firm name is a resident of any county in which any partner resides or in which the partnership has an office or does business. If all partners are nonresidents and the partnership does not have an office or do business in Illinois, the partnership is a nonresident. If a partnership is sued in the partners' names individually, venue exists in any county in which any sued partner resides.

A **voluntary unincorporated association** sued in its own name is a resident of any county in which the association has an office or, if on due inquiry no office can be found, in which any officer of the association resides. If the association has no offices or officers in state, the association is a nonresident.

Special Rules: Actions against **public, municipal, governmental**, or **quasi-municipal** corporations must be brought in the county in which the principal office is located. If the action is to recover real estate, venue is also proper in the county in which the real estate is located.

Actions involving **real estate** must be brought in the county in which the land is located. Actions made local by a **statute** must be brought in the county designated in the statute.

In **libel** actions against a newspaper or magazine or those connected with one, venue is proper in the county in which (i) the defendant resides, (ii) the defendant has its principal office, or (iii) the article was composed or printed. If the defendant resides or the article was printed outside of Illinois, venue is proper in any county in which the libel was circulated.

Actions against **insurance companies** incorporated or doing business in Illinois may be brought in the county in which the plaintiff resides, in addition to places determined by normal rules.

Objections to Venue: Improper venue is not a ground for dismissal of an action, but should be raised in a motion to transfer to a court of proper venue. Objections to improper venue are waived by a defendant unless the motion to transfer is made on or before the date upon which a defendant is required to appear, or within any additional time frame he has to answer or draft motions. If a plaintiff moves to dismiss a defendant upon whose residence venue depends, any remaining defendant may then promptly move to transfer venue. Any determination of fact in connection with a motion to transfer does not constitute a determination of the merits of the case or any aspect thereof.

Defendants in Different Counties: When defendants reside in different counties and venue is based on residence, the overruling of the non-resident's motion to transfer venue is not grounds for reversal if she proceeds to trial on the merits. If the motion is renewed at the close of all the evidence and it appears that the defendant residing within the county was joined solely for the purpose of fixing venue in that county, there may be grounds for reversal.

Change of Venue: A change of venue in a civil action may be had when the court determines that any party may not receive a fair trial in the court in which the action is pending because the inhabitants of the county are prejudiced against that party or her attorney, or the adverse party has an undue influence over the minds of the inhabitants. Application for a change of venue should be supported by an affidavit of the applicant and at least two other reputable inhabitants of the county. Petitions for change of venue should be presented before the trial or hearing begins, and before the judge has been presented with or ruled upon any substantial issue. But, if grounds for a change of venue arise later, a petition may be filed. If granted, the venue will be changed to any convenient county where there is no valid objection.

D. VENUE IN FEDERAL COURT

Venue in federal court actions is generally governed by § 1391.

1. General Venue Rule

In general, venue is proper in only one of the following judicial districts:

i) A judicial district in which any defendant resides, if all defendants reside in the same state in which the district is located; or

ii) A judicial district in which a "substantial part of the events or omissions" on which the claim is based occurred, or where a "substantial part of the property" that is the subject of the action is located.

If there is otherwise no judicial district in which the action may be brought, venue is proper in a judicial district in which any defendant is subject to personal jurisdiction with respect to such action. § 1391.

2. Residence

a. Natural person

For venue purposes, a natural person, including an alien lawfully admitted for permanent residence in the United States, is deemed to reside in the judicial district where that person is domiciled. § 1391(c)(1).

b. Business entities

Under § 1391(c)(2), an entity with the capacity to sue and be sued, regardless of whether incorporated, is deemed to reside, if a defendant, in any judicial district in which the entity is subject to personal jurisdiction with respect to the civil action in question. If the entity is a plaintiff, it is deemed to reside only in the judicial district in which it maintains its principal place of business. In a state that contains multiple judicial districts and in which a defendant corporation is subject to personal jurisdiction at the time the action is commenced, the corporation "shall be deemed to reside in any district in that State within which its contacts would be sufficient to subject it to personal jurisdiction if that district were a separate State." If there is no such district, the corporation will be deemed to reside in the district with which it has the most significant contacts.

Example: X Corporation is incorporated in Delaware, has its principal place of business in Colorado, and maintains a regional sales office in Orlando, Florida (U.S. Middle District Court in Florida), but it conducts no activities anywhere else in Florida. If X Corporation is sued, for federal venue purposes it will reside in the District of Delaware, the District of Colorado, and the Middle District of Florida. Note that Corporation X would not be a resident for federal venue purposes of any other judicial district in Florida.

EXAM NOTE: Keep in mind that, with respect to partnerships and unincorporated associations, the "entity" approach is taken only for venue purposes. It does not apply for purposes of determining diversity jurisdiction, when a partnership or unincorporated association is considered a citizen of each state in which each of its partners or members is domiciled.

c. Nonresident of the United States

A defendant who is not a resident of the United States may be sued in any judicial district, but the joinder of such a defendant is disregarded when determining proper venue with respect to other defendants. § 1391(c)(3).

3. Special Venue Provisions

There are special rules for venue in certain types of cases.

a. Federal officials

Under § 1391(e), actions against officers or employees of the United States or its agencies acting in their official capacity or under color of legal authority may be commenced in a judicial district in which:

i) A defendant in the action resides;

ii) A substantial part of the events or omissions giving rise to the claim occurred, or a substantial part of property that is the subject of the action is situated; or

iii) The plaintiff resides, if no real property is involved in the action.

See Stafford v. Briggs, 444 U.S. 527 (1980).

b. Cases removed from state court

Under § 1441(a), in cases that are removed from state court, venue is automatically proper in the federal district court in the district where the state action was pending. It is immaterial that venue would not have been proper if the action had been brought initially in that district.

c. Cases brought under the Federal Tort Claims Act

Under § 1402(b), venue in a case brought under the Federal Tort Claims Act is proper either in the judicial district where the plaintiff resides or in the judicial district where the act or omission occurred.

4. Objection to Venue

An objection to venue, unlike an objection regarding subject matter jurisdiction, may be waived by the parties, and it will be automatically waived if not asserted in a timely manner, i.e., raised in a pre-answer motion to dismiss under Rule 12(b)(3) or in the first responsive pleading, if a motion under Rule 12(b)(3) was not filed.

E. CHANGE OF VENUE IN FEDERAL COURT

1. Change of Venue When Original Venue Is Proper

Under § 1404(a), "[f]or the convenience of parties and witnesses, in the interest of justice, a district court may transfer any civil action to any other district or division where it might have been brought or to any district or division to which all parties have consented." This transfer may be ordered upon motion of the parties or by the court on its own initiative, but it is available only when the jurisdiction and venue of the court considering the issue are proper. The burden of proof with regard to the motion rests on the party seeking the transfer.

a. Diversity cases

In diversity cases, if the motion for change of venue is granted or the court transfers the case on its own initiative, the district court to which the case is transferred must apply the law that would have been applied in the district court that transferred the case. *Ferens v. John Deere Co.*, 494 U.S. 516 (1990).

b. Federal question cases

In federal question cases when transfer is to a district court in another appellate circuit, the district court to which the case is transferred will apply the federal law as interpreted by its Court of Appeals and not the interpretation of the Court of Appeals in which the district court that transferred the matter is located.

c. Forum selection clause

When transfer is sought on the basis of a forum selection clause in a contract, the clause is generally a significant, but not determinative factor; when the contract is international, the clause is determinative, unless the party attacking venue can show that the clause's application would be unreasonable, unfair, or unjust. *M/S Bremen v. Zapata Off-Shore Co.,* 407 U.S. 1 (1972).

d. No personal jurisdiction

Even if the court lacks personal jurisdiction over the defendant, the court is not barred from transferring a case to a different venue. § 1404(a).

2. Change of Venue When Original Venue Is Improper

Under § 1406(a), if venue in a case is improper, the district court must dismiss the case, or "if it be in the interest of justice," transfer the case to any district or division in which it could have been brought. Under § 1406(b), if no timely objection is made to venue, nothing prevents the district court from maintaining jurisdiction over the case.

a. Diversity cases

In diversity cases transferred for improper venue under § 1406(a), the district court to which the case is transferred will apply the choice-of-law rules of the state in which it is located, as opposed to the state law of the district court that transferred the case.

b. Federal question cases

In federal question cases transferred for improper venue under § 1406(a), the district court to which the case is transferred will apply the interpretation of federal law in its Circuit Court of Appeals.

3. Transfer to Another Division in the Same District

Under § 1404(b), on motion or by stipulation of all parties, a case may be transferred to a different division within a judicial district at the discretion of the court.

F. FORUM NON CONVENIENS

This doctrine allows a court to dismiss an action—even if personal jurisdiction and venue are otherwise proper—if it finds that the forum would be too inconvenient for parties and witnesses and that another, more convenient, venue is available.

1. Federal Court

In the federal courts, the doctrine has had only limited application since the enactment of § 1404(a), which provides for discretionary transfer based on convenience when venue is proper. In general, the doctrine of forum non conveniens is now used in federal court only when the forum that is deemed most appropriate for the action is a state court or a foreign court, to which § 1404(a) would not apply.

2. State Courts

In state courts, the common-law doctrine continues to apply. Some of the factors that are generally considered include (i) the availability of an alternative forum, (ii) the law that will apply, and (iii) the location of the parties, witnesses, and evidence. When the doctrine of forum non conveniens is invoked, it is generally the defendant whose convenience is being respected, since the plaintiff has usually indicated his own convenience in the original choice of forum.

Illinois Distinction: *Forum Non Conveniens*

When considering a motion for *forum non conveniens*, the courts consider several factors: private factors such as the plaintiff's interest in choosing the forum and the inconvenience to the defendant, and public factors such as the public's interest in having local controversies decided locally and the unfairness of imposing trial expenses and jury duty on residents of a forum with little connection to the litigation.

Motions to dismiss or transfer under the doctrine of *forum non conveniens* must be filed no later than 90 days after the last day allowed for filing of that party's answer.

Dismissal of an action under the doctrine of *forum non conveniens* is conditional upon the following: First, if the plaintiff files the action in a court of a different venue within six months of the dismissal order, the defendant must accept service of process. Second, the defendant must waive the statute of limitations defense, if the statute of limitations has run in the other forum.

If the defendant fails to follow these conditions, the action will be reinstated in the court in which the dismissal was granted. If the other court does not accept jurisdiction, the plaintiff may, within 30 days of the final order refusing jurisdiction, reinstate the action in the original court.

Illinois Distinction: Change of Judge

A party may make an unlimited number of motions for a substitution of judge for cause. A party is entitled to one substitution of judge as of right before a judge has ruled on any substantial matter in a case. An application for substitution of judge must be timely made by motion and must be granted if presented before the judge has ruled on any substantial issues. 735 Ill. Comp. Stat. 5/2-1001.

IV. CHOICE OF LAW: THE ERIE DOCTRINE

A. IN GENERAL

When an action is commenced in U.S. district court, the court must determine the substantive law and rules of procedure that will govern the action.

1. **Federal Question Claim**

   If the action is a federal question claim, federal substantive and procedural law will control.

2. **Federal Diversity Claim**

   a. **Substantive law**

   In a diversity action, the district court is required to apply the substantive law of the state in which the district court is located. *Erie R.R. Co. v. Tompkins*, 304 U.S. 64 (1938).

   b. **Procedure**

   1) **Applicable federal law**

   With regard to procedure in a diversity action, however, if a procedural issue is addressed by a valid federal law (e.g., a statute or Federal Rule of Evidence), the federal law will be applied, even if a state rule or statute is in conflict. *Hanna v. Plumer*, 380 U.S. 460 (1965).

   2) **No applicable federal law**

   If no federal law applies, the general rule is that the district court must follow state law with regard to substance, but it can choose to ignore state law with regard to procedure, under certain circumstances.

B. **SUBSTANCE VERSUS PROCEDURE**

1. **Analytical Approach**

   It is sometimes difficult to determine if an issue involves substance or procedure for the purposes of applying the *Erie* doctrine. The following general approach is often used:

   i) The district court will start by determining whether there is a **conflict between state and federal law** with respect to the issue before the court. If no conflict exists, then the analysis does not need to proceed any further because the court can apply state and federal law harmoniously to the issue.

   ii) If, however, the applicable state and federal laws do conflict, the district court must ask whether a **valid federal statute** or Federal Rule covers the disputed issue. *Hanna, supra*.

      a) If there is a **valid federal statute** or rule of procedure on point, the district court must **apply federal law** rather than state law.

      b) If no federal statute or rule is on point, then the court must determine whether federal common law, rather than state law, should be applied. In making this determination with respect to federal common law, the district court will ask whether the **failure to apply state law will lead to different outcomes** in state and federal court. *Guar. Trust Co. v. York*, 326 U.S. 99 (1945).

         1) If the answer is no, then the district court will generally apply federal common law, rather than state law.

2) If the answer is yes, the court will apply the state law, unless affirmative countervailing federal interests are at stake that warrant application of federal law.

c) The court may also choose to examine the issue by weighing the interests of the state and federal judiciaries and apply the law whose policy is of greater importance. *Byrd v. Blue Ridge Rural Elec. Co-op, Inc.*, 356 U.S. 525 (1958).

1) If the state has a greater interest in having its rule applied, the court will apply state law.

2) Otherwise, the court will apply federal law.

d) Finally, to prevent forum shopping (selecting a court base upon where the plaintiff believes he will receive a favorable outcome), the court will follow state law if selecting state law would prevent overcrowding of the federal court system. *Hanna, supra.*

2. Substantive Law

Examples of specific areas of law that have been held to be substantive rather than procedural include:

a. Elements of a claim or defense

The elements of a claim or defense in contract or tort, for example, are considered substantive and are generally controlled by state law in a federal diversity action.

b. Statutes of limitations and tolling provisions

The Supreme Court has indicated that state statutes of limitations and the rules for tolling state statutes of limitations are substantive in nature and are thus applicable in diversity. *Guar. Trust Co. v. York*, 326 U.S. 99 (1945).

c. Burden of proof

The specification of the applicable standards of proof is considered a substantive matter and the law of the forum state will govern in a diversity case. *Bank of Am. Nat'l Trust & Sav. Ass'n v. Parnell*, 352 U.S. 29 (1956).

3. Procedural Law

Examples of specific areas of law that have been determined to be procedural, rather than substantive, include:

a. Judge-jury allocation

If there is a jury in a diversity case on a state law claim, the jury—rather than a judge—will decide all factual issues in the case, regardless of whether state law would provide otherwise. *Byrd v. Blue Ridge Rural Elec. Co-op., Inc.*, 356 U.S. 525 (1958).

b. Assessment of attorney's fees

In a diversity case on a state law claim, the federal court may properly use its inherent power to assess attorney's fees as a sanction for a defendant's bad-faith conduct during the litigation, even if the law of the forum state provides that attorney's fees may not be awarded to a successful party. *Chambers v. NASCO, Inc.*, 501 U.S. 32 (1991).

c. Equitable versus legal

Federal law usually governs whether an issue is legal or equitable. *Simler v. Conner*, 372 U.S. 221 (1963).

C. DETERMINING APPLICABLE STATE LAW

Under *Erie*, a U.S. district court with diversity jurisdiction must apply the substantive law of the state in which it is located.

Example: The U.S. District Court of Delaware will generally apply Delaware substantive law to the diversity actions over which its sits.

1. Highest State Court's Rulings on Substantive Law Control

In determining a state's substantive law, the U.S. district court will be bound by the rulings of the state's highest court.

2. Highest State Court Not Yet Ruled

If the state's highest court has not spoken on an issue, however, the federal court must try to determine how the state's highest court would rule on the issue, if it did consider it. To make this determination, the federal court will generally look to any lower state court decisions that have considered the issue and will follow a lower court's view, unless it believes that the highest state court would not follow it. If no state court has considered the issue, the federal court will have to determine how it believes the highest court in the state would rule if it looked at the issue today. Some states have procedures that allow the federal district court to certify a question of substantive law to the state supreme court for clarification.

3. Highest Court Rules After Federal Suit Complete

If, after the U.S. district court action has been completed, the state's highest court rules on an issue in a way that is different from the way the district court predicted, a federal appeals court is bound by the state court's ruling. *Vandenbark v. Owens-Illinois Glass Co.*, 311 U.S. 538 (1941).

4. Conflict of Laws

In diversity actions, a U.S. district court is bound by the conflict-of-law rules of the state in which the district court is located, but only to the extent that the state's rules are valid under the Full Faith and Credit and Due Process Clauses of the U.S. Constitution. *See Allstate Ins. Co. v. Hague*, 449 U.S. 302 (1981), *Klaxon v. Stentor Elec. Mfg. Co.*, 313 U.S. 487 (1941).

State conflict-of-law rules frequently determine whether to apply the law of the forum state or the law of a foreign jurisdiction by considering whether the law to be applied is substantive or procedural. States apply their own procedural laws and sometimes apply the substantive law of a foreign jurisdiction. Although the substance-procedure distinction arises in federal-state choice of law under *Erie*, it is not the same substance-procedure distinction in state-state choice of law under the law of conflicts under *Klaxon*.

Questions about the following issues are generally considered procedural and controlled by the law of the forum state:

i)   The proper court in which to bring an action;

ii)   The form of the action to be brought;

iii) The sufficiency of the pleadings;

iv)   The effect of splitting a cause of action;

v)   The proper or necessary parties to an action;

vi)   Whether a counterclaim may be brought;

vii) Venue;

viii) The rules of discovery;

ix)   The right to a jury trial;

x)   Service of process;

xi)   The burden of proof;

xii) Trial procedure; and

xiii) The methods of enforcing a judgment.

5.   When Venue Is Transferred

If the venue of an action is transferred under § 1404, the court to which the action is transferred must apply the law of the state of the transferor court, including that state's rules regarding conflict of law. If the transfer is made pursuant to § 1406(a), however, the court to which the case is transferred applies the conflict-of-law rules of the state in which it is located.

V.   PLEADINGS

A.   COMMENCEMENT OF PROCEEDINGS

1.   Manner

Under Rule 3, a civil action is commenced by filing a complaint with the court clerk. For the purposes of a federal diversity action, state law will apply to decide when the action commenced for purposes of the statute of limitations. *Walker v. Armco Steel Corp.*, 446 U.S. 740 (1980). Thus, if state law provides that an action is commenced by service of process on a defendant, rather than by filing with the court, the state rule will control for the purposes of diversity jurisdiction.

2.   Time Computation

a.   General rule

Rule 6 sets out guidelines for computing time limits that apply throughout the Federal Rules of Civil Procedure, unless otherwise provided. Under Rule 6(a)(1), whenever a time period is stated in days (which is the only time period discussed in this outline), the period excludes the day of the event that triggers the period, includes **every day** following, **including intervening Saturdays, Sundays, and legal holidays,** and includes the last day of the period, **except that** if the last day is a Saturday, Sunday, or legal holiday, the period is continued to the next non-weekend or holiday day. Rule 6(a)(1).

b. Motions, hearings, and affidavits

Under Rule 6(c), a written motion and notice of a hearing must be served at least 14 days prior to the hearing, unless (i) the motion can be heard ex parte, (ii) the Rules provide for it, or (iii) the court orders otherwise. An opposing affidavit must be served at least seven days before the hearing, unless otherwise ordered.

c. Additional time for responses to electronic and non-paper filings

Under Rule 6(d), when the Rules otherwise provide a time period for responding to a service or filing, and the service or filing is made electronically or otherwise non-traditionally under Rule 5(b), **three days are added** to the prescribed period.

B. SERVICE OF PROCESS

Rule 4 sets forth the procedure for service of process in a federal action, detailing the form, content, method of issuance, methods of service, and time of service of a summons and complaint. In the absence of service of process (or waiver of service by the defendant), a court ordinarily may not exercise power over a party named as a defendant in a complaint. *Murphy Bros., Inc. v. Michetti Pipe Stringing, Inc.*, 526 U.S. 344 (1999).

1. Who Must Serve

Under Rule 4(c), the plaintiff is responsible for serving the summons and complaint upon the defendant. Service may be made by any non-party who is at least 18 years old.

Illinois Distinction: Who Must Serve

Process is normally served by the sheriff, or by the coroner if the sheriff is disqualified. It is not necessary that service be made by the sheriff or coroner of the county in which service is made. The court has discretion, upon motion, to appoint a special process server.

The court may order service to be made by a private person over 18 who is not a party to the action.

---

2. Time Limit for Service

Under Rule 4(m), the plaintiff must serve the summons and complaint within 120 days after filing the complaint. If, however, the plaintiff shows "good cause" why service was not timely made, the court must extend the time for service for an appropriate period. If no such showing is made, the court, on motion or on its own after notice to the plaintiff, must dismiss the action without prejudice against that defendant or order that service be made within a specified time. Rule 4(m).

A major revision of the Federal Rules took effect in December 2009, in an effort to simplify the computation of days in a given time period. Under the new rule, a "day" is counted as any day, regardless of whether it is a weekend or holiday. Rule 6(a)(1)(B). The exclusion of the triggering day for counting purposes still stands, however.

Under Illinois Supreme Court Rule 102(b), a summons in the form provided in Ill. Sup. Ct. R. 101(d) (requiring appearance within 30 days after service) may not be served later than 30 days after its issuance date. A summons in the form provided in Ill. Sup. Ct. R. 101(b) (requiring appearance on a particular day) may not be served later than three days before the date of appearance.

3. Methods of Service

Rule 4 establishes different procedures for service of process depending on whether the defendant is an individual or a corporation, a governmental entity or subdivision, and domestic or foreign.

a. Service generally

1) In the United States

Pursuant to Rule 4(e)(2), service may be made by:

i) Personally serving the summons and complaint on the defendant;

ii) Leaving the summons and complaint at the defendant's usual place of abode with a person of suitable age and discretion who resides there; or

iii) Delivering the summons and complaint to an agent appointed by the defendant or otherwise authorized by law to receive service.

Illinois Distinction: Methods of Service

735 Ill. Comp. Stat. 5/2-203(a) also allows for serving an individual by leaving a copy of the summons with him personally, but adds restrictions to Rule 4's "abode service." Service may be made by leaving a copy of the summons at the defendant's place of abode with a family member or person residing there who is at least 13 years old. The person effecting service must inform the recipient of the contents of the summons. If service is made in this manner, the person making service must also send a copy of the summons to the defendant at the defendant's usual place of abode.

Illinois also requires that the Return, which states that service was made or attempted, include the sex, race, and approximate age of the defendant or person with whom the summons was left, as well as the place, date, and time when the summons was left.

Service by Special Order of the Court: If service upon an individual is impractical under the methods above, 735 Ill. Comp. Stat. 2-203.1 allows the plaintiff, without notice, to move the court to enter an order directing a comparable method of service. The motion must be accompanied by an affidavit including the extent of the investigation made to determine the proper place of service, a statement of why service is impractical, and a specific statement showing a diligent effort was made. The court may then direct service in any manner consistent with due process.

Service by Mailing or Publication: If a plaintiff files an affidavit that a defendant cannot be found or is concealed within Illinois, resides or has gone out of the state, or upon due inquiry cannot be found, the clerk may publish notice of the suit in a newspaper published in the county where the action is pending, or if no newspaper is published there, one that is published in an adjoining county with circulation in the county where the action is pending. The publication should contain notice of the pendency of the action, the title of the court, the title of the case, the first named defendant and plaintiff, the case number, the parties served by publication, and the date on or after which default may be entered against parties. Notice should also be mailed to each defendant's residence listed in the affidavit. Notice by publication has the same effect as out-of-state personal service on a non-resident, unless the out of state personal service is made pursuant to the state's long-arm statute.

2) Outside the United States

Pursuant to Rule 4(f), service may be effected in any manner, internationally agreed upon, which is reasonably calculated to give notice. If no international agreement exists, or if an international agreement permits service by other means, service on any competent individual outside the United States may be effected by any method permitted by the law of the foreign country; or, unless the foreign country's law prohibits it, by personal service of the summons and the complaint to the individual or by using any form of mail that the clerk addresses and sends to the individual and that requires a signed receipt; or by any other means not prohibited by international agreement, as ordered by the court.

b. Service on corporations and associations

1) Inside the United States

Pursuant to Rule 4(h), service on a corporation or association in the United States may be effected by delivering the summons and complaint to an officer, managing agent, general agent, or agent appointed or authorized by law to receive process.

If the agent is one authorized by statute and the statute so requires, the plaintiff must also mail a copy of the summons and complaint to the defendant. Rule 4(h)(1)(B).

2) Outside the United States

Service on corporations and associations outside of the United States may be made using any methods available for service on an individual outside the United States, except personal delivery under Rule 4(2)(c)(i).

Illinois Distinction: Service on Corporations and Associations

Public Corporations: Public, municipal, governmental, and quasi-municipal corporations may be served by leaving a copy of the summons with the chairperson of the county board or county clerk, if a county; the mayor or city clerk, if a city; president of the board of trustees or village clerk, if a village; supervisor or town clerk, if a town; and the president, clerk, or other corresponding officer in the case of another public, municipal, governmental, or quasi-municipal body.

Partnerships: A partnership sued in its partnership's name may be served by leaving a copy of the process with any of the partners personally or with any agent of the partnership found anywhere in the state. A partnership may also be notified by mail and publication in a like manner to individuals.

Foreign Corporations: An unregistered foreign corporation found to be doing business in Illinois may be served in the same manner as an Illinois corporation or a registered foreign corporation. In addition, the Secretary of State may be served.

---

c. Service on the United States government and its agencies and officers

1) Service on the United States government

Under Rule 4(i)(1), to serve the United States, a party must:

    i)   Deliver a copy of the summons and complaint to the U.S. attorney (or a designee) for the district where the action is brought, or send a copy by registered or certified mail to the civil-process clerk at the U.S. attorney's office;

ii) Send a copy by registered or certified mail to the U.S. Attorney General; and

iii) If the action challenges an order of a non-party agency or officer of the United States, send a copy by registered or certified mail to the agency or officer.

2) Service on U.S. agency, officer, or employee sued in an official capacity

Under Rule 4(i)(2), to serve a U.S. agency, officer, or employee only in an official capacity, a party must serve the United States and also send a copy of the summons and complaint by registered or certified mail to the agency, officer, or employee.

3) Service on U.S. officer or employee sued individually

Under Rule 4(i)(3), to serve a U.S. officer or employee in an individual capacity for an act or omission occurring in connection with duties performed on behalf of the United States, a party must serve the United States and also serve the officer or employee under the normal rules for serving an individual.

4. Waiver of Service

Pursuant to Rule 4(d), a competent individual, corporation, or association that is subject to service has a duty to avoid unnecessary expenses of serving the summons by waiving service. The plaintiff may notify such a defendant that an action has been commenced and request that the defendant waive service. The rule does not apply to government entities, infants, or incompetents.

a. Request for waiver

A plaintiff's notice and request for waiver of service must be in writing and be addressed to the individual defendant, or, for a corporation, to an officer, managing or general agent, or any other agent authorized by appointment or by law to receive service of process.

It must be accompanied by a copy of the complaint, two copies of a waiver form, and a prepaid means for returning the form, and it must give the defendant a reasonable time of at least 30 days after the request was sent (or at least 60 days if sent to a foreign defendant) to return the waiver. Rule 4(d)(1).

Illinois Distinction: Request for Waiver

A plaintiff may notify a defendant of the commencement of a lawsuit and request that the defendant waive service. The form of this notice and request can be found in Ill. Sup. Ct. R. 101(f), and it must (i) be sent to the defendant by first class U.S. mail or another reliable means, (ii) contain a copy of the complaint and identify the court, (iii) inform the defendant of the consequences of compliance and failure to comply, (iv) allow the defendant at least 30 days from the date on which the request was sent (or 60 if sent to a defendant outside the U.S.), and (v) provide the defendant with an extra copy of the notice and request, and a prepaid way in which to respond in writing.

---

b. Effect of waiver

Under Rule 4(d)(3), if a defendant timely returns a waiver of service before being served with process, the defendant does not have to serve an answer to the complaint until 60 days after the request was sent, or 90 days after it was sent to a defendant outside a judicial district of the United States. This is an incentive to waive service, because the normal time period in which an answer must be served is 21 days after service of process. Rule 12(a)(1)(A).

Rule 4(d)(5) specifically provides that waiver of service does not waive any objection to personal jurisdiction or to venue.

If the defendant agrees to waive service, the date on which the plaintiff files the waiver form with the court will be deemed the date of service. Rule 4(d)(4).

c. Failure to waive service

Under Rule 4(d)(2), if a defendant located within the United States fails, without good cause, to sign and return a waiver requested by a plaintiff located within the United States, the court must impose on the defendant the expenses that are incurred in making service and the reasonable expenses, including attorney's fees, of any motion required to collect such service expenses.

Illinois Distinction: Failure to Waive Service

If a defendant chooses not to waive service, the plaintiff must serve the defendant as otherwise provided by the Code and the Supreme Court Rules.

5. Proof of Service

Under Rule 4(l)(1), if formal service is not waived, the process server must submit proof of service to the court. Generally, this will be by an affidavit of the process server. Failure to make proof of service does not affect the validity of the service.

Illinois Distinction: Proof of Service

Under 735 Ill. Comp. Stat. 5/2-202, proof of service is called "return." Returns are generally endorsed by a sheriff or coroner on the back of the original summons. If service was made or attempted by a private person, return is by affidavit. Failure to make a return can result in a finding of contempt of court. Ill. Sup. Ct. R. 102(d) indicates that failure to make a return does not invalidate the summons or the service.

C. INJUNCTIONS

Rule 65 permits injunctions, which are a form of equitable relief that mandates or prohibits a defendant from performing a specified act. Injunctions are considered an extraordinary remedy, only to be granted in limited circumstances. *See Weinberger v. Romero-Barcelo*, 456 U.S. 305 (1982). Every order granting injunctive relief must state the reasons for its issuance, specifically state its terms, and specify the acts the defendant is restrained or required to perform. Additionally, in order to protect the adverse party against harm in the event of an erroneous grant of preliminary relief, the rule expresses a preference that the moving party posts an injunction bond. Rule 65(c), (d).

There are two types of injunctions: mandatory and prohibitory. The determining factor is the type of conduct that is affected by the injunction, if granted.

A mandatory injunction, which is a specific relief, requires a person to engage in an affirmative act that typically changes the status quo. *Yu Juan v. City of New York, et al.,*

181 Fed. Appx. 38 (2d Cir. 2006). When the injunction is directed at providing mandatory relief, as opposed to preserving the status quo, the moving party's burden is particularly heavy. *United States v. Spectro Foods Corp,* 544 F.2d 1175, 1181 (3d Cir. 1976).

A prohibitory injunction, which is a form of preventative relief, restrains or prohibits a party from engaging in a specified behavior.

Illinois Distinction: Injunctions

Each order granting injunctions and every restraining order shall (i) set forth the reasons for its entry, (ii) be specific in terms, (iii) describe in reasonable detail (not by reference to any other documents) the act sought to be restrained, and (iv) be binding only upon the parties to the action, their officers, agents, employees, and attorneys, and those who receive actual notice.

---

1. **Temporary Restraining Order**

A temporary restraining order ("TRO") preserves the *status quo* of the parties until there is an opportunity to hold a full hearing on the application for a preliminary injunction. This interlocutory injunction may remain in effect only a limited number of days, to be set by the court, and no longer than 14 days unless good cause exists or by consent of the adversary. Rule 65(b)(2).

   a. **When notice not required**

   Pursuant to Rule 65(b)(1), a TRO may issue without notice to the adverse party if:

   i) The plaintiff can establish, under written oath, that immediate and irreparable injury will result prior to hearing the adverse party's opposition; and

   ii) The plaintiff has made all reasonable efforts to provide notice and can provide the court with a reason why notice should not be required.

   b. **Contents**

   In addition to being filed with the clerk, the TRO must state the following:

   i) The date and time issued;

   ii) The irreparable harm suffered by the plaintiff; and

   iii) The reasoning behind the *ex parte* issuance.

   Rule 65(b)(2).

Illinois Distinction: Temporary Restraining Order

TROs will not be granted without notice to the adverse party unless immediate and irreparable injury, loss, or damage will result to the applicant before notice can be served. TROs granted without notice expire not more than **10 days** after issued, unless the court extends that time for good cause.

A party seeking a TRO must demonstrate a clearly ascertainable right that needs protection, that she will suffer irreparable harm without the injunction or TRO, that she has no adequate remedy at law, that she has a substantial likelihood of success on the merits, and that she will suffer greater harm without the injunction than her opponent will suffer if it is issued.

---

2. Preliminary Injunction

A preliminary injunction is a form of relief issued prior to a full hearing on the merits, but only upon notice to the defendant and a hearing on whether the injunction should issue. Should an expedited decision on the merits be appropriate, a court may order a trial on the merits to be consolidated with the preliminary injunction hearing. Rule 65(a). A plaintiff seeking a preliminary injunction must establish that:

i)   He is likely to succeed on the merits;

ii) He is likely to suffer irreparable harm in the absence of relief;

iii) The balance of equities is in his favor; and

iv) The injunction is in the best interest of the public.

Winter v. Natural Resources Defense Council, Inc., 555 U.S. 7 (2008).

Illinois Distinction: Preliminary Injunction

Unlike a TRO, a preliminary injunction will not be granted unless a previous notice of the time and place of the application has been given to the adverse party.

---

3. Permanent Injunction

A permanent injunction is a determination on the merits. Once issued, it continues until dissolved by the court, but any affected person may move for modification or dissolution. The standard for a permanent injunction is essentially the same as for a preliminary injunction except that plaintiff must show actual success on the merits. *See eBay Inc. v. MercExchange, L.L.C.,* 547 U.S. 388 (2006).

4. Limitations

When a conflict of jurisdiction occurs between state and federal courts, the federal court cannot use an injunction to prohibit pending state court proceedings unless expressly authorized by statute. Neither can a federal court grant an injunction against the collection of state taxes. In criminal law, state criminal proceedings that have not yet been instituted cannot be enjoined unless to do so would prevent irreparable harm and appellate remedies would be inadequate to provide relief.

D. COMPLAINT

1. Required Elements

a. In general

The complaint is the initial pleading in an action filed by the plaintiff and serves as notice to the opposing party.

Under Rule 8(a), a complaint (or any pleading in which a claim is made) must include:

i)   A short and plain statement of the grounds that establish the court's subject matter jurisdiction;

ii) A short and plain statement of the claim establishing entitlement to relief; and

iii) A demand for judgment for the relief sought by the pleader.

Fact Pleading: The Federal Rules allow *notice* rather than *fact* pleading. However, Illinois state courts require *fact* pleading. A plaintiff must allege all of the material, operative facts that make up the cause of action. Accordingly, all pleadings must contain a statement of facts constituting each cause of action and a prayer for relief. If damages are sought, the amount must be stated, with exceptions, which will be discussed below. Prayers for relief may be made in the alternative.

b. Subject matter jurisdiction

A complaint in federal court must contain an allegation of the subject matter jurisdiction of the court, unless the court already has jurisdiction and the claim needs no new jurisdictional support.

Caption: The Illinois Supreme Court Rules require that each complaint designate the division of the circuit court in which the proceeding shall take place, for example, "at law," "in chancery," or "in probate." However, misdesignation does not affect the jurisdiction of the court.

c. Statement of the claim

Rule 8(a)(2) requires only "a short and plain statement of the claim showing that the pleader is entitled to relief," in order to "give the defendant fair notice of what plaintiff's claim is and the grounds upon which it rests." *Conley v. Gibson*, 355 U.S. 41, 47 (1957). Detailed factual allegations are not required, but a party may not merely recite the elements of a cause of action with broad, conclusory statements. *Ashcroft v. Iqbal*, 556 U.S. 662 (2009), *Bell Atlantic Corp. v. Twombly*, 550 U.S. 544 (2007).

In Illinois, a claim is properly pleaded when every element the plaintiff is required to prove in order to recover has been alleged. However, if facts have been adequately stated in one part of a pleading, they do not need to be repeated elsewhere in that pleading, and may be incorporated by reference into that or other pleadings.

Each cause of action that would support a separate recovery must be pled in a separate count of the complaint or counterclaim and should be separately numbered. Alternative theories of recovery may but do not need to be pled in separate counts.

d. Demand for relief

The demand for judgment for the relief sought may include relief in the alternative or different types of relief (e.g., monetary damages, equitable relief, or a declaratory judgment). The demand in a contested case does not limit the nature or scope of relief that the trial court may grant. The plaintiff is entitled to whatever relief is appropriate to the claims alleged in the complaint and proved at trial. Rule 54(c).

Specific Prayer for Relief: All complaints and counterclaims must contain specific prayers for relief for each count; these may be pled in the alternative. The prayer for relief does not limit the amount the court may chose to award, though the court must prevent the other party from prejudice by reason of surprise. If relief beyond the prayer for relief is granted against a party in default, notice shall be given to the defaulted party.

Ad Damnum: Damages for personal injury may not contain an *ad damnum* (a specific amount), but may be pled to the minimum extent necessary to comply with circuit court rules (e.g. "damages in excess of").

Punitive Damages: A prayer for punitive damages may not be included in a complaint based on bodily injury or property damage based on negligence or strict liability. A plaintiff may move to amend her complaint to include punitive damages after a pretrial hearing in which she establishes a reasonable likelihood to prove facts supporting a punitive damage award at trial. Such a motion to amend the complaint must be made no later than 30 days after the close of discovery.

2. Special Matters

Rule 9 sets forth certain special rules with regard to pleading, which apply not just in the context of a complaint, but to any pleading. In certain circumstances (described below), a party is required to plead with greater detail than under the general rules. Federal courts have no power to require more specific pleading beyond the rules set forth in the Federal Rules of Civil Procedure or by statute. *See Swierkiewicz v. Sorema N.A.*, 534 U.S. 506 (2002).

a. Capacity

Under Rule 9(a), except when required to show that the court has jurisdiction, a pleading need not allege a party's capacity to sue or be sued. To challenge a party's capacity, an opposing party must make a specific denial and state any supporting facts that are peculiarly within the party's knowledge.

b. Fraud or mistake

Under Rule 9(b), a party alleging fraud or mistake must state with particularity the circumstances constituting fraud or mistake.

Malice, intent, knowledge, and other conditions of a person's mind, however, may be alleged generally.

c. Conditions precedent

Under Rule 9(c), in pleading conditions precedent in a contract action, a party may allege generally that all conditions precedent have occurred or been performed. When denying that a condition precedent has occurred or been performed, however, the party must do so with particularity.

d. Official document or act

Under Rule 9(d), in pleading an official document or official act, it is sufficient to allege that the document was legally issued or that the act was legally done.

e. Judgment

Under Rule 9(e), in pleading a judgment or decision of a domestic or foreign court, a judicial or quasi-judicial tribunal, or a board or officer, it is sufficient to plead the judgment or decision without showing any jurisdiction to render it.

f. Special damages

Under Rule 9(g), when an item of special damage is claimed, it must be specifically stated. Special damages are damages that do not normally or necessarily flow from an event.

g. Time and place

When relevant and material, facts regarding time and place must be specified in detail.

Illinois Distinction: Special Matters

Breach of Statutory Duty: If a breach of statutory duty is alleged, the plaintiff must cite the statute. Other causes of action, such as fraud, conspiracy, and existence of a fiduciary duty must be pled with specificity.

Judgment or Order: If pleading the judgment, order, or decision of any state or federal court or board, the pleading party need only state the date of entry, describe it generally, and allege generally that the judgment or decision was duly made.

Condition Precedent: A plaintiff may plead conditions precedent in a contract generally; if the allegation is denied, the defendant must allege facts in connection with the denial or failure to perform.

Verified Pleading: Pleadings are not required to be verified by oath. However, if a plaintiff files a verified complaint, every subsequent pleading must also be verified.

---

3. Time for Filing and Service

A complaint will generally be filed before service on the defendant(s), which must then generally occur within 120 days of filing. Rule 4(m). For time limits, *see* § V.B.2. Time Limit for Service, *supra*.

Illinois Distinction: Administrative Review Complaints

In General: In Illinois, specific rules apply if an affected party files a complaint in circuit court for review of an Illinois administrative decision. This procedure is governed by Article III of the Illinois Administrative Review Law, 735 Ill. Comp. Stat. 5/3-101 *et seq.* (2009). These rules apply to any decision by any administrative body with vested power to make administrative decisions. Only a decision that terminates an administrative proceeding (i.e., a final decision) can be reviewed under these rules.

Time to File the Complaint: The affected party must file the complaint in circuit court within 35 days of receiving service of his administrative decision from the administrative agency. Service constitutes either a personal delivery of the decision to the affected party or a mailing of that determination in a sealed envelope with postage prepaid, to the affected party's last known address. Filing the complaint means both filing it with the clerk of the circuit court **and** the issuance of a summons by the clerk of the circuit court to the named defendant(s). Similar to the service of an administrative decision to the affected party, service of the summons to a defendant constitutes either personal delivery to the defendant **or** a mailing of the summons to the defendant at his last known address.

Naming of Defendants: Naming as a defendant the head of an agency, in his official capacity, is sufficient to name the entire administrative agency as a defendant. In addition, the affected party may merely name the administrative agency itself on the complaint. If the court determines that a party should have been named as a defendant but was not so named, the affected party who files the complaint will be allowed 35 days to correct the error.

Exceptions: There are various exceptions to the above rules, usually involving school board or zoning cases. One important exception relates to the rules governing zoning decisions affecting jurisdictions of over 500,000 inhabitants. In this case, written notice of the proceeding must be mailed by certified mail, within two days of the commencement of the action, to every party who testified at the administrative hearing, informing them of their right to intervene in the circuit court action.

E.   MOTIONS AGAINST THE COMPLAINT

Under Rule 12, within 21 days of service of process, a defendant must respond to a complaint either by an answer or by a pre-answer motion, or she must seek additional time to answer. If a defendant does not take one of these steps, she risks a default.

1.   Rule 12(b) Motion to Dismiss

a.   Basis

Prior to filing an answer, a defendant may file a motion under Rule 12(b), raising any or all of the following defenses:

i) Lack of subject matter jurisdiction;

ii) Lack of personal jurisdiction;

iii) Improper venue;

iv) Insufficient process;

v) Insufficient service of process;

vi) Failure to state a claim upon which relief can be granted; and

vii) Failure to join a necessary or indispensable party under Rule 19.

Such motions generally seek dismissal of the claim. For the defenses of insufficient process and service of process, though, it is common to make a motion to quash the service of process or the process itself.

b.   Timing

The defense of lack of subject matter jurisdiction may be raised at any time, even on appeal. Rule 12(h)(3).

Under Rule 12(h)(1), the defenses of lack of personal jurisdiction, improper venue, insufficient process, and insufficient service of process must be raised in a pre-answer motion or, if no pre-answer motion is made, in the answer, or the defenses will be waived.

Under Rule 12(h)(2), the defenses of failure to state a claim upon which relief can be granted and failure to join a necessary or indispensable party under Rule 19 may be raised in any pleading, in a motion for judgment on the pleadings, or at trial.

Illinois Distinction: Motions Against the Complaint

A defendant may choose to file an answer, or may choose to file various motions objecting to the complaint. These Illinois motions may be made under 735 Ill. Comp. Stat. 5/2-615 (which attack defects on the face of a pleading, similar to a common law general demurrer) or 735 Ill. Comp. Stat. 5/2-619 (which request dismissal of a claim or counterclaim).

§ 2-615 Motions with Respect to Pleadings: These objections must be raised in a single motion, rather than in a responsive pleading. The motion must point out the specific defects, and request specific relief. Examples given in the Code include (i) that a pleading or portion of a pleading be stricken for insufficiency at law for lack of facts or insufficient legal conclusions, (ii) that an action be dismissed, (iii) that a pleading be made more definite or certain in a specified manner, (iv) that a designated immaterial matter be removed, (v) that necessary parties be added, or (vi) that designated misjoined parties be dismissed. This list is not intended to be exhaustive.

Motions under this section must state a specific defect and request specific relief. For example, motions to dismiss on the basis that a count is substantially insufficient at law must specify the legal insufficiency.

Upon motions based upon insufficient pleadings, the court may take into consideration substantial defects in any prior pleadings of any party.

After ruling on a 2-615 motion, the court may permit or require re-pleading or amending the complaint, or may terminate the litigation in whole or in part.

Any party may seasonably move for judgment on the pleadings.

§ 2-619 Involuntary Dismissal Based Upon Defects or Defenses: These motions aim for dismissal of a claim or defense on a wide variety of grounds, similarly to Federal Rule 12(b). These motions must be brought "within the time for pleading," meaning generally within the time allotted for answering stated within the Code or through a motion for extension of time or else they are waived. These motions cannot be filed after answering (but the defenses that can be raised herein can also be raised in alternative manners, such as in the answer, thereby avoiding waiver). Code § 2-619. If the grounds do not appear on the face of the attacked pleading the motion shall be supported by affidavit. The grounds include:

i) The court lacks subject matter jurisdiction, and transfer to another court will not remove the defect;

ii) The plaintiff lacks legal capacity to sue or the defendant lacks legal capacity to be sued;

iii) There is another action pending between the same parties for the same reason;

iv) The cause of action is barred by another judgment (i.e., collateral estoppel or res judicata);

v) The action is barred by the statute of limitations;

vi) The claim has been released, satisfied of record, or discharged in bankruptcy;

vii) The claim is unenforceable under the Statute of Frauds;

viii) The claim is unenforceable because of the defendant's minority or disability and;

ix) The claim is barred due to some affirmative defense.

If the motion is contested, the court may review affidavits and other evidence provided by the parties, and either grant or deny the motion. The court may deny the motion without prejudice, allowing the issue to be raised again in an answer, or may deny the motion on its merits.

Filing a pleading after the denial of a motion does not waive the party's right to challenge the denial on appeal.

2. **Motion to Dismiss for Failure to State a Claim Upon Which Relief Can Be Granted**

   a. **Rule 12(b)(6)**

      Under Rule 12(b)(6), a claim for relief can be dismissed if it either fails to assert a legal theory of recovery that is cognizable at law or fails to allege facts sufficient to support a cognizable claim. In deciding a motion under Rule 12(b)(6), courts treat all well-pleaded facts of the complaint as true, resolve all doubts and inferences in the plaintiff's favor, and view the pleading in the light most favorable to the plaintiff.

b. More than speculation

The U.S. Supreme Court has held that the facts alleged in the complaint must "raise a right to relief above the speculative level...on the assumption that all the allegations in the complaint are true (even if doubtful in fact)." *Bell Atl. Corp. v. Twombly*, 550 U.S. 544, 545 (2007). The complaint must state enough facts to raise a reasonable expectation that discovery will reveal evidence of the necessary element.

c. What the court may consider

In ruling on a motion to dismiss under Rule 12(b)(6), the court may consider only the allegations in the complaint, any exhibits attached to the complaint, and any matters subject to judicial notice. If a matter outside the pleadings, such as an affidavit, is presented to the court and is not excluded by the court in its review, the motion must be treated as a motion for summary judgment under Rule 56, and all parties must be given an opportunity to present all material information for the court's consideration. Rule 12(d).

d. Two-step analysis

Recently, the United States Supreme Court established a two-step analysis for adjudicating a motion to dismiss under Rule 12(b)(6). First, the court must identify and reject legal conclusions unsupported by factual allegations. This shall include mere conclusory statements and assertions devoid of facts. For example, a complaint that alleges that a defendant caused an injury, without explanation as to how it occurred, does not meet the requirements of Rule 8(a) and, as a result, cannot survive a Rule 12(b)(6) motion. Second, the court should assume the truth or veracity of well-pleaded factual allegations and should include a "context specific" analysis that "draw[s] on [the Court's] judicial experience and common sense" to determine whether the allegations "plausibly give rise to an entitlement of relief." *Ashcroft v. Iqbal*, 556 U.S. 662 (2009).

e. Outcome

1) Motion granted

If the claim is dismissed, the plaintiff may generally amend the pleading and continue the action. If the plaintiff does not wish to do so, a judgment will be entered, and the plaintiff can appeal.

2) Motion denied

If the defendant's motion to dismiss is denied, the defendant may either answer the claim or allow a default judgment to be entered and then appeal.

3. Motion for Judgment on the Pleadings

a. In general

After the pleadings are closed, a party may move for judgment on the pleadings pursuant to Rule 12(c). A motion for judgment on the pleadings allows a court to dispose of a case when the material facts are not in dispute and a judgment on the merits can be achieved based on the content of the pleadings. Motions under Rule 12(c) are not often utilized because of the availability of motions under Rule 12(b)(6) and motions for summary judgment under Rule 56.

b. Timing

A motion under Rule 12(c) must be made after an answer is filed.

c. Standard

The standard for a motion under Rule 12(c) is generally the same as that for a motion under Rule 12(b)(6). Likewise, if matters outside the pleadings are presented to the court and the court does not exclude them, the motion is to be treated as a motion for summary judgment under Rule 56.

Illinois Distinction: Motion for Judgment on the Pleadings
As mentioned above, any party may seasonably move for judgment on the pleadings.

4. Motion for a More Definite Statement

a. Vague and ambiguous

If a claim for relief is so vague or ambiguous that a party cannot reasonably draft a responsive pleading, the responding party may move for a more definite statement pursuant to Rule 12(e). The motion must specify the defects in the pleading, as well as the details sought by the party making the motion.

b. Standard

Courts are generally reluctant to grant a motion for a more definite statement, because discovery is available to get more information about an issue. The standard for granting such a motion is whether the pleading provides enough information from which the responding party can draft a responsive pleading and commence discovery. A motion for a more definite statement may be appropriate when the pleader fails to allege facts required to be specifically pleaded, such as allegations of fraud or mistake under Rule 9(b).

c. Timing

The party must make a motion for a more definite statement before filing a responsive pleading. The court may strike a failure to respond to such a motion within 14 days of the notice. Rule 12(e).

5. Motion to Strike

a. Rule 12(f)

Under Rule 12(f), if a pleading contains any insufficient defense, or redundant, immaterial, impertinent, or scandalous material, the court, upon motion or upon its own initiative, may order that such defense or material be stricken.

b. Timing

When a responsive pleading is permitted, the responding party must move to strike prior to responding to such a pleading. When no responsive pleading is permitted, the party must make a motion to strike within 21 days after service of the pleading.

Illinois Distinction: Bills of Particulars

In addition to making motions against pleadings, Illinois allows for parties to demand a bill of particulars.

If allegations against a party in a pleading are so lacking in details that party may, within the time the party is required to respond to the pleading, file and serve a notice demanding a bill of particulars. The notice shall point out specifically the defects complained of or the details desired. The pleader then has 28 days to file and serve the bill of particulars, and the party who requested it then has 28 days to plead after being served the bill.

If the pleader does not file and serve the bill of particulars within 28 days or if the bill is insufficient, the court may, on motion and in its discretion, strike the pleading, allow further time to furnish the bill of particulars, or require a more particular bill to be filed and served. If the party on whom the demand for the bill of particulars was made does not think one is required, he may move the court to deny or modify the demand.

In contract actions, if a bill of particulars containing an itemized statement of the indebtedness is verified by oath, each item is admitted unless denied in an affidavit.

F. ANSWER

An answer is a pleading by the defendant that responds to a plaintiff's complaint. A plaintiff would also file an answer if responding to a defendant's counterclaim.

1. Admissions or Denials

The answer must admit or deny the allegations of the plaintiff's complaint. Rule 8(b). If the defendant is without knowledge or information sufficient to form a belief as to the truth or falsity of an allegation, then the defendant must say so in the answer. This response has the effect of a denial, pursuant to Rule 8(b). Before pleading lack of sufficient knowledge, however, the defendant must make a reasonable investigation into whether the information exists and how difficult it would be to ascertain.

a. Specific denial

A specific denial is a denial of a particular paragraph or allegation in the complaint or other claim for relief (e.g., counterclaim, crossclaim, etc.). A party can respond to each paragraph of the complaint by either denying the allegation in the paragraph, admitting it, pleading insufficient knowledge to either admit or deny it, or admitting part of the allegation and either denying or pleading insufficient knowledge as to the rest.

b. General denial

Alternatively, a party can make a general denial, stating that he or she denies each and every allegation of the complaint. This may only be done, however, if the party, in good faith, intends to controvert all of the allegations.

A party could also make a qualified general denial, stating that he or she denies each and every allegation in the complaint, except certain specified allegations.

In Illinois, general denials are *not permitted*. However, a defendant can deny a paragraph of a complaint without restating the paragraph. Further, a defendant may admit liability and contest only the amount of damages by so stating in her responsive pleading.

c. Effect of failure to deny

An allegation, other than one relating to the amount of damages, will be deemed admitted if a responsive pleading is required and the allegation is not denied.

Illinois Distinction: Failure to Deny

In Illinois, every allegation not explicitly denied is admitted except allegations as to damages, when the party lacks knowledge sufficient to form a belief, and when there was no opportunity to deny. Additionally, a failure to deny serves as an admission to well-pleaded facts, not legal conclusions.

2. Affirmative Defenses

The answer must state any avoidance or affirmative defense that the defendant (or responding party) has, or that defense is deemed waived. Rule 8(c) lists some such affirmative defenses:

i) Accord and satisfaction;

ii) Arbitration and award;

iii) Assumption of risk;

iv) Contributory negligence;

v) Duress;

vi) Estoppel;

vii) Failure of consideration;

viii) Fraud;

ix) Illegality;

x) Injury by fellow servant;

xi) Laches;

xii) License;

xiii) Payment;

xiv) Release;

xv) *Res judicata*;

xvi) Statute of frauds;

xvii) Statute of limitations; and

xviii) Waiver.

This list is non-exclusive; thus, if there are other affirmative defenses that the party has in addition to the ones listed above (e.g., novation, qualified immunity), even if they are inconsistent, they must be raised in the answer as well.

Illinois Distinction: Affirmative Defenses

A party may plead as many defenses as he may have, and each should be separately designated and numbered. If a party is in doubt as to which of two or more statements of fact is true, he may plead them in the alternative in either separate or the same counts.

Facts of Affirmative Defenses: Facts constituting affirmative defenses, if not set forth in a previous pleading or which may take the opposing party by surprise, must be set forth in the answer or reply.

If a party fraudulently conceals a cause of action, the action may be brought within five years of the plaintiff's discovery of that cause of action. Fraudulent concealment requires more than mere silence on the part of the defendant.

3. **Counterclaims**

If a defendant has a claim against the plaintiff, the defendant may state it as a counterclaim in the answer to the complaint. Under certain circumstances, a counterclaim will be compulsory (*see* § VI.D.2. Counterclaims, *supra*) under Rule 13 and must be pleaded or it will be precluded in any future litigation.

Illinois Distinction: Counterclaims

Counterclaims should be made a part of the answer. They should be pleaded with the same particularity and in the same manner as the complaint. Counterclaims should be complete in themselves, but allegations set forth in the answer can be incorporated into the counterclaims by reference.

Illinois makes no distinction between compulsory and permissive counterclaims. Further, any claim by any defendant against any plaintiff or co-defendant, whether as a setoff, recoupment, or cross claim, whether in tort, contract, or any other relief, is considered a counterclaim. Illinois also does not require any factual or legal connection between the original claim asserted by the plaintiff and the counterclaim.

4. **Time for Filing an Answer to a Complaint**

   a. **No motion made under Rule 12**

   If no motion is made under Rule 12, then under Rule 12(a)(1)(A)(i), a defendant must serve an answer within 21 days after being served with the summons and complaint.

   If the defendant has timely waived service under Rule 4(d), the defendant must serve the answer within 60 days after the request for a waiver was sent, or within 90 days after it was sent to the defendant outside any judicial district of the United States. Rule 12(a)(1)(A)(ii).

   b. **Motion made under Rule 12**

   When a motion is made under Rule 12, a defendant will not have to file an answer while the motion is pending. If the court denies or postpones disposition of the motion until a trial on the merits, the answer must be served within 14 days after notice of the court's action. Rule 12(a)(4)(A). If the court grants a motion for a more definite statement under Rule 12(e), the answer must be served within 14 days after service of the more definite statement.

G. REPLY

1. Defined

A reply is a response by the plaintiff to a defendant's answer. It can also be a response by a defendant to a plaintiff's counterclaim answer, a third-party answer, or a crossclaim answer.

2. Court Order

A reply is made only when the court orders it. Rule 7(a)(7).

3. Timing

In general, a party must serve a reply to an answer within 21 days after being served with an order to reply, unless the order specifies a different time. Rule 12(a)(1)(C).

H. AMENDMENTS AND SUPPLEMENTAL PLEADINGS

Rule 15 provides the rules with regard to when and how pleadings can be amended or supplemented.

1. Amendments

a. By right

Rule 15(a) governing amendment as of right was revised effective December 1, 2009. Under the new Rule, a party may amend a pleading once as of right within 21 days if no responsive pleading is required, or, if a responsive pleading is required, within 21 days of service of the responsive pleading or within 21 days of being served with a motion under Rule 12(b), whichever is earlier. Thus, unlike previously, a plaintiff may amend his complaint even after being served with an answer (up to 21 days), but also is limited to 21 days to amend after being served with a 12(b) motion. A party may amend a pleading during and after a trial, if doing so will conform to the evidence and as long as the opposing party had an opportunity to prepare. Due process is required for the amended pleading.

b. By leave of the court

The court should freely give leave to amend a pleading when justice so requires. Rule 15(a)(2). Generally, a court will first determine if the proposed amendment to the pleading would be futile because it would immediately be subject to dismissal under Rule 12(b)(6). If it would not, the amendment will generally be permitted unless the amendment would result in undue prejudice to the opposing party. However, when the court has issued an order regarding the trial plan after a final pretrial conference, which may include the issues for trial, the court may modify that order only to prevent manifest injustice. Rule 16(e).

Illinois Distinction: Amendments

Illinois allows amendments to pleadings on "just and reasonable terms" at any time before final judgment. Amendments could include introducing a party, dismissing any party, or changing or adding a new cause of action or defense.

A pleading may be amended before or after judgment to conform the pleadings to the proofs. For these amendments to be allowed, the proof admitted must have been relevant to issues in the original pleadings.

---

c. Effect

An amended pleading supersedes the prior pleading.

d. Relation back

1) New claim

Under Rule 15(c)(1), an amendment to a pleading will relate back to the date of the original pleading when the amendment asserts a claim or defense that arose out of the conduct, transaction, or occurrence set out, or attempted to be set out, in the original pleading. This may be important for purposes of complying with the applicable statute of limitations. An amendment will also relate back to the date of the original pleading if the law that provides the applicable statute of limitations allows relation back.

Illinois Distinction: Relation Back

The running of a statute of limitations or contractual limitation, *does not bar* a claim, crossclaim, or defense in an amended pleading if:

i) The statute of limitations or contractual limitation had not expired before the original pleading was filed; and

ii) The added claim, crossclaim, or defense arose out of the same transaction or occurrence as the original pleading.

---

2) New party

Under Rule 15(c)(1)(C), if the amendment changes the party or the naming of the party against whom a claim is asserted, it will relate back to the date of the original pleading if:

   i) It asserts a claim or defense that arose out of the conduct, transaction, or occurrence set out, or attempted to be set out, in the original pleading;

   ii) Within 120 days after the filing of the original complaint, the party to be brought in by amendment receives notice of the action such that he will not be prejudiced in defending on the merits; and

   iii) The party to be brought in by amendment knew or should have known that the action would have been brought against him, but for a mistake concerning the proper party's identity.

The proper focus when applying the third element is on the defendant's knowledge, rather than information in the plaintiff's possession. Although the latter may be relevant, it is not dispositive. *Krupski v. Costa Croceiere*, 560 U.S. ___, 130 S. Ct. 2485 (2010).

Illinois Distinction: New Party

Illinois allows for relation back to name a defendant who would have been named originally, but the plaintiff named the incorrect party (i.e., a plaintiff sued the owner instead of the driver of a car that had injured her).

A cause of action against a person not originally named as a defendant is not barred by a statute of limitations or contractual limitation if all of the following conditions are met:

i) The original action was brought before the limitations period expired;

ii) The person, within the time the action might have been brought or the right might have been asserted against him, and with reasonable time for service:

   a) Received notice of the commencement of the action; and

   b) Knew or should have known that, but for a mistake concerning the identity of the proper party, the action would have been brought against him; and

iii) The amended claim grew out of the same transaction or occurrence in the original pleading.

---

e. Time to respond to an amended pleading

Unless the court orders otherwise, a party must respond to an amended pleading within the later of 14 days after service of the amended pleading or the time remaining for response to the original pleading. Rule 15(a)(3).

2. Supplemental Pleadings

A court has discretion under Rule 15(d) to permit supplemental pleadings that describe events occurring after the filing of an earlier pleading. The court may permit supplementation even though the original pleading is defective in stating a claim or defense. The court may also order that the opposing party respond to the supplemental pleading within a specified time. A supplemental pleading does not supersede an original pleading.

I. RULE 11

Rule 11 establishes the standards that attorneys and individual parties must meet when filing pleadings, motions, or other papers. It also provides for sanctions against parties, attorneys, and law firms for violations of the rule.

1. Signature

Under Rule 11(a), every pleading, written motion, and other paper filed with the court must be signed by at least one attorney of record, or by a party personally, if unrepresented. The paper must state the signer's address, e-mail address, and telephone number. The court must strike an unsigned paper unless the omission is promptly corrected after being called to the attention of the attorney or party.

2. Certification to the Court

Under Rule 11(b), by presenting to the court a pleading, written motion, or other paper, an attorney or unrepresented party certifies that to the best of her knowledge, information, and belief, formed after an inquiry reasonable under the circumstances:

i)   The paper is not being presented for any improper purpose, such as to harass, cause unnecessary delay, or needlessly increase the cost of litigation;

ii) The claims, defenses, and other legal contentions are warranted by existing law or by a non-frivolous argument for extending, modifying, or reversing existing law or for establishing new law;

iii) The factual contentions have evidentiary support or, if specifically so identified, will likely have evidentiary support after a reasonable opportunity for further investigation or discovery; and

iv) The denials of factual contentions are warranted on the evidence or, if specifically so identified, are reasonably based on belief or a lack of information.

"Presenting" a pleading under Rule 11 includes "signing, filing, submitting, or later advocating" a position presented in the pleading.

3. Sanctions

a. In general

Under certain circumstances, after notice and a reasonable opportunity to respond, the court may in its discretion impose sanctions on attorneys, law firms, and parties for violations of Rule 11. Absent exceptional circumstances, a law firm must be held jointly responsible for a violation committed by its partner, associate, or employee. Pursuant to Rule 11(c)(4), sanctions "must be limited to what suffices to deter repetition of the conduct or comparable conduct by others similarly situated."

b. How initiated

Sanctions can be initiated either by motion or by the court on its own initiative.

1) Motion

A motion for sanctions must be made separately from any other motion and must describe the specific conduct alleged to violate Rule 11. The motion must be served under Rule 5, but it must not be filed or presented to the court if the challenged paper, claim, defense, contention, or denial is withdrawn or appropriately corrected within 21 days after service or within any other time set by the court.

2) *Sua sponte*

On its own initiative, the court may order an attorney, law firm, or party to show cause why conduct specifically described in the order has not violated Rule 11.

c. Types of sanctions

Sanctions may include:

i) Nonmonetary directives;

ii) An order to pay a penalty into court; or

iii) If imposed on motion and warranted for effective deterrence, an order directing payment to the movant for part or the entirety of reasonable attorney's fees and other expenses directly resulting from the violation.

d. Procedure

The court cannot impose a monetary sanction on its own, unless it issued an order to show cause with regard to the matter before voluntary dismissal or settlement of the claims made by or against the party who is, or whose attorneys are, to be sanctioned.

The court also is not permitted to impose a monetary sanction against a represented party for violating the requirement that the claims, defenses, and other legal contentions of the paper be warranted by existing law or by a non-frivolous argument for extending, modifying, or reversing existing law or for establishing new law.

An order imposing a sanction under Rule 11 must describe the sanctioned conduct and explain the basis for the sanction. Rule 11(c)(6).

Illinois Distinction: Sanctions

All pleadings, motions, and other papers must be signed by a party's attorney, or the party herself, if she is not represented by an attorney. The signature of the party or attorney constitutes a certificate by her that she has read the pleading, motion, or other paper, that to the best of her knowledge it is well grounded in fact and is warranted by existing law or a good faith basis for the extension, modification, or reversal of existing law, and that it is not filed for any improper purpose, such as to harass or to cause unnecessary delay or needless increase in cost of the litigation.

If a pleading is signed in violation of the above terms, the court, upon motion or of its own initiative, may impose sanctions on the person who signed it, a represented person, or both. This sanction may include

---

an order to pay the other party or parties the amount of reasonable expenses incurred because of the filing of the paper, including reasonable attorney's fees.

Sanctions or proceedings brought for this purpose shall be brought in the same civil action in which the pleading, motion, or other paper was filed, and no alleged violation shall give rise to a separate civil suit. Motions brought for this purpose must be filed within 30 days of the entry of final judgment, or if a timely post-judgment motion is filed, within 30 days of the ruling on the post-judgment motion.

This rule applies to the State of Illinois and any of its agencies in the same manner as any other party. If the litigation involved review of a determination of an administrative agency, the court may include in its award for expenses costs incurred by a party in contesting an allegation or denial by the state without reasonable cause and found to be untrue.

When a sanction is imposed, the judge shall set forth with specificity the reasons and basis of any sanction so imposed either in the judgment itself or in a separate written order.

The Illinois Rules also allow for sanctions for violating discovery rules (see VII., *infra*).

VI. MULTIPLE PARTIES AND CLAIMS

A. JOINDER OF PARTIES

The Federal Rules of Civil Procedure provide for joining parties to existing litigation, generally for reasons of efficiency and economy. Joinder may be permissive, pursuant to Rule 20, or compulsory, pursuant to Rule 19.

1. Permissive Joinder

Rule 20 sets forth the circumstances in which a plaintiff may join other plaintiffs in an action, or defendants may be joined in the same action.

a. Plaintiffs

Pursuant to Rule 20(a)(1), persons may join in one action as plaintiffs if:

i) They assert any right to relief jointly, severally, or in the alternative with respect to or arising out of the same transaction, occurrence, or series of transactions or occurrences; and

ii) Any question of law or fact common to all plaintiffs will arise in the action.

Illinois Distinction: Joinder of Plaintiffs
Two or more plaintiffs may join to bring a single cause of action when (i) the cause of action arises out of the same transaction or series of transactions and (ii) a common question of fact or law would arise if the actions had been brought separately.
Even if joinder would have been proper, upon application, a court may order separate trials if joinder would embarrass a party or delay the trial.
Necessary plaintiffs, counterclaimants, or third-party plaintiffs who decline to join may be made defendants, cross defendants, or third-party defendants, as the case may be.

b. Defendants

Pursuant to Rule 20(a)(2), persons may be joined in one action as defendants if:

i) Any right to relief is asserted against them jointly, severally, or in the alternative with respect to or arising out of the same transaction, occurrence, or series of transactions or occurrences; and

ii) A question of law or fact common to all defendants will arise in the action.

Illinois Distinction: Joinder of Defendants

In Illinois, joinder of a defendant is permissive. Any person may be made a defendant if, jointly, severally, or in the alternative:

i) He is alleged to have an interest in the controversy or in the transaction or occurrence out of which the controversy arose;

ii) His joinder is necessary for the complete determination or settlement of a question involved; or

iii) He is alleged to be jointly, severally, or alternatively liable for one of the transactions or series of transactions, regardless of the number of causes of action joined.

Joinder in the Alternative. If a plaintiff is in doubt as to which of the defendants is liable to her and to what extent, she may join two or more defendants in the alternative.

---

c. Extent of relief

The same relief need not be demanded among the joined plaintiffs or against the joined defendants. Rule 20(a)(3).

Illinois Distinction: Extent of Relief

It is not necessary that each defendant be interested in all the relief requested, or as to every cause of action included in the proceeding.

---

d. Protective measures

To avoid unfairness or hardship to any party, the court may order separate trials on any claims joined or may make any other order to prevent delay or undue expense to any party. Rule 20(b).

Illinois Distinction: Protective Measures

The court may make any order (such as ordering separate trials) that may be just to prevent any defendant from being embarrassed or put to expense by being required to attend any proceeding in which he does not have an interest.

---

e. Jurisdiction and venue

1) Subject matter jurisdiction

A plaintiff or defendant sought to be joined must also meet the requirements of federal subject matter jurisdiction.

a) Supplemental jurisdiction

i) Joinder of defendants

Under 28 U.S.C. § 1367(b), supplemental jurisdiction does not apply to defendants sought to be joined under the permissive joinder rule in a case based exclusively on diversity jurisdiction where exercising jurisdiction would destroy diversity. Thus, if the claims are made solely on the basis of diversity jurisdiction, there must be complete diversity between the plaintiffs and the defendants, and each claim must exceed the jurisdictional amount in controversy of $75,000.

> **Example:** While driving his car, Plaintiff, a citizen of Arizona, is hit by a truck operated by Defendant 1, a citizen of New Mexico. Plaintiff is thrown from his car and is further injured by a car driven by Defendant 2, a citizen of Nevada. Plaintiff brings a negligence suit for $100,000 against Defendant 1 in federal court based on diversity jurisdiction. Plaintiff then joins Defendant 2 under Rule 20, suing for $25,000. Under § 1367(b), there is no supplemental jurisdiction against Defendant 2, and no diversity jurisdiction against Defendant 2, because the statutory jurisdictional amount is not met.

ii) Joinder of plaintiffs

If multiple plaintiffs, however, join together under Rule 20, supplemental jurisdiction is permitted for determining the statutory jurisdictional amount, but the parties must still meet the requirement of complete diversity. *Exxon Mobil Corp. v. Allapattah Servs., Inc.*, 545 U.S. 546 (2005).

> **Example:** Plaintiff 1 and Plaintiff 2, who are citizens of California, join together under Rule 20 as plaintiffs against Defendant, a citizen of Oregon, in a diversity suit for negligence. The claims arise out of the same occurrence or transaction. Plaintiff 1 claims $200,000 and Plaintiff 2 claims $25,000. There is supplemental jurisdiction, and the plaintiffs may add their claims together for the purposes of determining the statutory jurisdictional amount. If Plaintiff 2 was a citizen of Oregon, however, there would not be complete diversity, and Plaintiff 2 would have to be dropped from the federal case.

2) In personam jurisdiction

If a defendant is joined pursuant to Rule 20, the court must have in personam jurisdiction over the defendant for joinder to be proper.

3) Venue

Joinder under Rule 20 also is subject to any applicable venue requirements.

2. **Compulsory Joinder**

Rule 19 specifies circumstances in which additional parties must be joined. Note that the requirements of jurisdiction (both subject matter and personal) and venue must still be met in order for compulsory joinder to occur. Under certain circumstances, if compulsory joinder cannot occur because of jurisdictional or venue issues, Rule 19(b) may require the action to be dismissed from federal court.

a. **Necessary parties**

Under Rule 19(a), a person who is subject to service of process and whose joinder will not deprive the court of subject matter jurisdiction or destroy venue must be joined as a party if:

i) Complete relief cannot be provided to existing parties in the absence of that person; or

ii) Disposition in the absence of that person may impair the person's ability to protect his interest; or

iii) The absence of that person would leave existing parties subject to a substantial risk of multiple or inconsistent obligations.

A necessary party is therefore a person whose participation in the lawsuit is **necessary for a just adjudication**. The Supreme Court has specifically held that tortfeasors facing joint and several liability are **not** parties who must be joined under Rule 19. *Temple v. Synthes Corp.*, 498 U.S. 5 (1990).

Illinois Distinction: Necessary Parties

Parties are considered "necessary" when their presence is required (i) to protect an interest the absentee parties have in the subject of the controversy which would be materially affected by a judgment, (ii) to reach a decision that will protect the interests of those who are before the court, or (iii) to enable the court to make a complete determination of the controversy. *Burt v. Board of Education*, 477 N.E.2d 247 (Ill. App. Ct. 1985).

Actions Against Joint Debtors or Partners: All parties to a joint obligation may be sued jointly, or separate actions may be brought against one or more of them. A judgment against fewer than all parties to a joint obligation or partnership obligation does not bar an action against those not included in the judgment or not sued. The subsequently sued joint obligor will only be liable for the unsatisfied portion of the joint obligation.

---

b. **Subject matter jurisdiction**

A plaintiff or defendant to be joined under Rule 19 must meet the requirements of federal subject matter jurisdiction. Thus, if the exclusive basis for the court's subject matter jurisdiction is diversity jurisdiction and a party sought to be joined would destroy diversity, joinder is not permitted.

Note that under 28 U.S.C. § 1367(b), supplemental jurisdiction does not apply to the claims of a party sought to be joined under Rule 19 in a case based exclusively on diversity jurisdiction if the exercise of jurisdiction would be inconsistent with the diversity requirements.

c. **In personam jurisdiction**

There must be personal jurisdiction over the required party. A required party may be served within 100 miles from where the summons was issued, even if the service is outside of the state and beyond its long-arm statute jurisdiction. Rule 4(k)(1)(B).

d. Venue

Venue must be proper for joinder to occur.

e. Indispensable parties: when joinder is not feasible

Under Rule 19(b), if a necessary party cannot be joined because of jurisdictional or venue concerns, the court must determine whether, in equity and good conscience, the action should proceed among the existing parties or should be dismissed. Among the factors for the court to consider are:

i) The extent to which a judgment rendered in the person's absence might prejudice that person or the existing parties;

ii) The extent to which any prejudice could be reduced or avoided by protective provisions in the judgment, shaping the relief, or other measures;

iii) Whether a judgment rendered in the person's absence would be adequate; and

iv) Whether the plaintiff would have an adequate remedy if the action were dismissed for non-joinder.

When the court dismisses an action because of the inability to join a necessary party, the party said to be "indispensable."

Illinois Distinction: Misjoinder and Nonjoinder of Parties

An action will not be dismissed for misjoinder of parties or for failure to join a necessary party, without first affording a reasonable opportunity to add them as parties. New parties may be added and misjoined parties dropped by order of the court, at any time, as justice may require. 735 Ill. Comp. Stat. 5/2-407.

Illinois Distinction: Consolidation

A court may consolidate separate cases pending before it, in the interest of convenience, provided the consolidation would not unfairly prejudice any of the litigants.

B. INTERVENTION

Rule 24 governs the circumstances under which a non-party may join in a lawsuit. In some circumstances, the non-party may intervene as of right. In other circumstances, the non-party must have the permission of the court. Note that in either case, a motion to intervene must be timely.

Illinois Distinction: Intervention

A person desiring to intervene presents a petition setting forth the grounds for intervention accompanied by his proposed initial pleading or motion. If the intervention is by leave of court, the court should consider whether the intervention will prejudice or unduly delay the rights of the original parties. An intervenor has all the rights of an original party, except that the court may require that the intervenor be bound by judgments already entered, not raise issues that would have more properly been raised earlier in the proceeding, and other limitations.

---

1. Intervention as of Right

Under Rule 24(a)(1), a non-party has the right to intervene in an action when a federal statute confers the right and the non-party timely moves to intervene. Additionally, under Rule 24(a)(2), upon a timely motion, a non-party has the right to intervene when:

   i)   The non-party has an interest in the property or transaction that is the subject matter of the action;

   ii)   The disposition of the action may, as a practical matter, impair the non-party's interest; and

   iii)   The non-party's interest is not adequately represented by existing parties.

The criteria for intervention as of right under Rule 24(a)(2) are similar to the criteria for compulsory joinder under Rule 19(a).

The burden of proof is on the person seeking to intervene.

Illinois Distinction: Intervention as of Right

Under 735 Ill. Comp. Stat. 5/2-408(a), anyone may intervene as of right when:

i)   A statute confers an unconditional right to intervene;

ii)   An applicant's interests would not adequately be represented by existing parties and the applicant would be bound by an order or judgment; or

iii)   The applicant would be adversely affected by a distribution or disposition of property within the court's control.

---

2. Permissive Intervention

Under Rule 24(b), the court may allow intervention, upon timely motion, when either:

   i)   The movant has a conditional right to intervene under a federal statute; or

   ii)   The movant's claim or defense and the original action share a common question of law or fact.

In exercising its discretion, the court must consider whether the intervention will unduly delay or prejudice the adjudication of the rights of the original parties.

Illinois Distinction: Permissive Intervention

Upon application, a court may permit intervention if (i) a statute confers a conditional right to intervene, or (ii) an applicant's claim or defense and the main action have a question of law or fact in common.

State Intervention: The state of Illinois may intervene in cases involving the validity of a constitutional provision, statute, or regulation, by leave of court.

Municipal Intervention: A municipality or governmental subdivision may intervene in cases involving the validity of one of its ordinances or regulations and affecting the public interest, by leave of court.

---

3. Timeliness

The decision of whether the non-party timely moved to intervene is in the discretion of the trial court, considering factors such as:

i) The length of time the movant knew or reasonably should have known that its interest was threatened before moving to intervene;

ii) The prejudice to existing parties if intervention is permitted; and

iii) The prejudice to the movant if intervention is denied.

4. Subject Matter Jurisdiction

A claim of an intervenor must be supported by its own jurisdictional basis.

Pursuant to § 1367(b), supplemental jurisdiction does not apply to the claims of a person seeking to be joined under Rule 24 (either as of right or permissively) in a case based exclusively on diversity jurisdiction if the exercise of jurisdiction would be inconsistent with the requirements of diversity jurisdiction.

> **Example:** X, a citizen of Ohio, sues Y, a citizen of Michigan, in federal court under diversity jurisdiction. Z, a citizen of Michigan, seeks to intervene (as of right or permissively) pursuant to Rule 24. Z cannot intervene because she would destroy diversity jurisdiction in the action. If Z were a citizen of any state other than Michigan, she could intervene, provided the requirements for intervention under Rule 24 were established.

C. INTERPLEADER

Interpleader allows a person holding property (traditionally known as the "stakeholder") to force all potential claimants to the property into a single lawsuit to determine who has a right to the property.

1. Federal Interpleader Rule

a. Basis

Under Rule 22, persons with claims that may expose a plaintiff to double or multiple liability may be joined as defendants and required to interplead. Such joinder is proper even though the claims of the claimants, or the titles on which their claims depend, lack a common origin or are adverse and independent rather than identical; or the plaintiff denies liability in whole or in part to any or all of the claimants. A defendant who is exposed to similar liability may seek interpleader through a crossclaim or counterclaim. Rule 22(a).

The primary standard for determining the propriety of an interpleader action under Rule 22 is whether the party bringing the action legitimately fears multiple claims against the property.

b. Subject matter jurisdiction

Rule 22 does not create subject matter jurisdiction in interpleader actions. Rather, the court must already have jurisdiction over all parties. Thus, a plaintiff will need federal question jurisdiction or, for diversity jurisdiction, the citizenship of the party bringing the action must be completely diverse from that of the claimants, and the statutory amount in controversy must be met. While the stakeholder needs to be diverse from the claimants, the claimants need not be diverse among themselves.

c. In personam jurisdiction

An interpleader action is an action against the claimants, so the general requirements of in personam jurisdiction in federal court must be met.

d. Venue

Federal venue requirements must also be met in interpleader actions under Rule 22.

Illinois Distinction: Interpleader

Persons having claims against the plaintiff arising out of the same or related subject matter may be joined as defendants and required to interplead when their claims may expose the plaintiff to double (or more) liability. That the claims of the several claimants or the titles upon which the claims depend are not identical, or are adverse to or independent to one another, or the plaintiff's claim that she is not liable in whole or in part to one or more claimants, are not grounds for objection to the interpleader.

---

2. Federal Statutory Interpleader

There are some key differences in the requirements for federal statutory interpleader pursuant to § 1335.

a. Subject matter jurisdiction

For statutory interpleader, diversity jurisdiction is met if any two claimants are citizens of different states. With regard to the amount in controversy, in a statutory interpleader action the property at issue must merely exceed $500 in value, not meet the $75,000 threshold required for regular diversity matters.

b. In personam jurisdiction

Statutory interpleader provides for nationwide personal jurisdiction and service of process and permits the federal court to enjoin other federal and state proceedings that may affect the property that is subject to dispute.

c. Venue

Venue is proper in any federal judicial district where one of the claimants resides.

d. Deposit

For statutory interpleader, unlike for federal rule interpleader, the stakeholder is required to either deposit with the court the property at issue or post a bond in an appropriate amount.

D. JOINDER OF CLAIMS

1. Permissive Joinder

a. In general

Pursuant to Rule 18(a), a party asserting a claim may join with it as many independent or alternative claims of whatever nature as the party may have against the opposing party. Rule 18 permits joinder of claims, but it does not compel it. However, *res judicata* (claim preclusion) concerns will often practically require joinder, because if a claim could be raised and is not, it will generally be subject to claim preclusion. (*See* § IX.D. Claim Preclusion, *infra*.)

b. Joinder of contingent claims

Pursuant to Rule 18(b), a party may join two claims even though one of them is contingent on the disposition of the other.

Example: A plaintiff may assert both a claim for monetary damages and a claim to set aside a conveyance that was fraudulent as a result of the defendant's transfer of assets to try to frustrate enforcement of the claim for monetary damages.

c. Subject matter jurisdiction

To join a claim under Rule 18, the court must have subject matter jurisdiction over it.

If subject matter jurisdiction is based on diversity jurisdiction, the plaintiff may aggregate all claims against the defendant in order to satisfy the statutory jurisdictional amount-in-controversy requirement.

If the original claim is based on federal question jurisdiction, a non-federal claim may be joined only if diversity jurisdiction exists or if the two claims are part of the same case or controversy as the federal claim such that supplemental jurisdiction applies.

d. Venue

The venue requirements for federal court must be satisfied in order to join a claim under Rule 18.

Illinois Distinction: Joinder of Claims

Any plaintiffs may join causes of action against any defendants, and numerous legal or equitable causes of action may be brought together in a single complaint. However, joinder of causes of action is not compulsory. Actions may always be brought separately.

---

2. Counterclaims

A counterclaim is a claim for relief made against an opposing party after an original claim has been made. A counterclaim may be asserted in the answer to the complaint and the reply to a counterclaim. Rule 13 governs the requirements for bringing a counterclaim.

A party must serve an answer to a counterclaim (or crossclaim) within 21 days of service. Rule 12(a)(1)(B).

a. Compulsory

1) In general

A pleading is required to state as a counterclaim any claim that, at the time of service, the pleader has against an opposing party if the claim arises out of the same transaction or occurrence that is the subject matter of the opposing party's claim and does not require adding another party over whom the court cannot acquire jurisdiction. Rule 13(a)(1).

However, the pleader is not required to make the claim if, at the time the action was commenced, the claim was the subject of another pending action, or if the opposing party's action is in rem or quasi in rem and the party does not assert any other counterclaim in that action. Rule 13(a)(2).

2) Failure to state a compulsory counterclaim

A party that fails to assert a compulsory counterclaim waives the right to sue on the claim and is generally precluded from ever suing on the claim in federal court.

3) Subject matter jurisdiction

A federal court must have subject matter jurisdiction over the counterclaim. By definition, though, a compulsory counterclaim arises out of the same transaction or occurrence as does the original claim before the court. Thus, a compulsory counterclaim (unlike a permissive counterclaim) will likely fall under the supplemental jurisdiction of the federal court and not need independent subject matter jurisdiction from the original claim.

b. Permissive

1) In general

Under Rule 13(b), a pleading may state as a counterclaim against an opposing party any claim that is not compulsory. Thus, a party has discretion as to whether to raise the counterclaim in the action before the court or in a separate action.

2) Subject matter jurisdiction

A permissive counterclaim does not necessarily fall within the supplemental jurisdiction of the federal court, as it does not arise out of the same transaction or occurrence as the original claim. Thus, a permissive counterclaim must on its own meet the requirements for federal subject matter jurisdiction (either diversity or federal question).

c. By third parties

A third-party defendant may file a counterclaim against either an original defendant or an original plaintiff. Whether a third-party defendant's counterclaim is classified as compulsory or permissive is governed by the requirements of Rule 13(a)-(b).

Pursuant to Rule 13(h), new parties to a counterclaim may be joined so long as they meet the requirements for joinder under Rule 20. New parties must be joined if they are indispensable parties under Rule 19.

Illinois Distinction: Counterclaims and Crossclaims

Illinois makes no distinction between compulsory and permissive counterclaims—all are permissive. Further, any claim by any defendant against any plaintiff or co-defendant, whether as a set-off, recoupment, or crossclaim, whether in tort, contract, or any other relief, is considered a counterclaim. 735 Ill. Comp. Stat. 5/2-608(a). Illinois does not require any connection between the claim asserted by a plaintiff and a counterclaim. However, at its discretion, the court may order separate trials of counterclaims to avoid delay, embarrassment, or the undue complication of the trial.

Further, note that even though there are no compulsory counterclaims in Illinois, a counterclaim may still be barred by the doctrine of *res judicata* (see IX.D., *infra*). *Cabrera v. First Nat'l Bank of Wheaton*, 753 N.E.2d 1138 (Ill. App. Ct. 2001).

---

3. Crossclaims

a. In general

A crossclaim is a claim made against a co-party, as when one defendant makes a claim against another defendant.

Under Rule 13(g), a pleading may state as a crossclaim any claim by one party against a co-party that arises out of the same transaction or occurrence that is the subject matter of the original action or of a counterclaim, or if the claim relates to any property that is the subject matter of the original action. The crossclaim may include a claim that the co-party is liable to the crossclaimant for all or part of a claim asserted in the action against the crossclaimant.

b. Crossclaim not mandatory

A party is never required to assert a crossclaim against a co-party. Pursuant to Rule 13(h), new parties to a crossclaim may be joined so long as they meet the requirements for joinder under Rule 20. New parties must be joined if they meet the requirements for joinder under Rule 19.

c. Subject matter jurisdiction

A crossclaim must fall within the subject matter jurisdiction of the federal court. This is generally not a problem, since by definition, a crossclaim must arise out of the same transaction or occurrence as the subject matter of the original action or of a counterclaim or relate to the property at issue, and therefore would fall under the court's supplemental jurisdiction.

d. In personam jurisdiction and venue

Since the parties are already before the court, personal jurisdiction is satisfied. Additionally, if venue was proper over the original claim, a party cannot object to venue with regard to the crossclaim.

4. Third-Party Claims (Impleader)

a. In general

Rule 14 sets out the rules governing impleader (third-party claims). These are claims that are made by a defending party against a non-party for all or part of the defending party's liability on an original claim. Note that the impleaded claim must relate to the original claim against the defending party. The court may sever any third-party claim if justice demands it.

Illinois Distinction: Third-Party Complaints

Within the time for filing an answer or by leave of court, a defendant may bring in as a defendant a person not a party to the suit who may be liable to him for all or part of the plaintiff's claim by filing a third-party complaint. Note that this excludes liability insurance providers. Any subsequent pleadings to a third-party complaint shall be filed as in the case of a complaint and with like designation and effect.

The third-party defendant may assert any defenses he has to the third-party complaint or to which the third-party plaintiff has to the plaintiff's complaint. Further, the plaintiff may file against the third-party defendant any claim she may have had against the third-party defendant had he been joined originally.

All service rules apply to the third-party defendant as if he had been an original defendant.

The court, in its discretion, may sever the third-party complaint for a separate trial in order to avoid undue complication or prejudice.

---

b. Procedure

A defending party—including a plaintiff against whom a counterclaim has been asserted—may assert a third-party claim at any time after the complaint is filed. The defending party, referred to for impleader purposes as the third-party plaintiff, must serve a summons and third-party complaint on the non party (third-party defendant). The third-party plaintiff must obtain the court's permission if it files more than 14 days after service of the original answer. Rule 14(a)(1). There are some states, however, that do not permit a defendant to implead his own insurance company unless the company has denied coverage.

The third-party defendant may (and in some cases must) assert defenses, counterclaims, and cross-claims against any of the parties as appropriate under the Rules and may also implead another non party who is or may be liable to the third-party defendant for the claim on which he or she was impleaded. Rule 14(a)(2).

c. Subject matter jurisdiction

A third-party claim must fall within the federal court's subject matter jurisdiction. Because by definition a third-party claim will be closely related to the original claim, the court generally will have supplemental jurisdiction over the matter. If the original claims are based exclusively on diversity jurisdiction, however, under § 1367(b), supplemental jurisdiction will not apply to claims by the plaintiff against a third-party defendant brought in under Rule 14. Such claims need to meet diversity or federal question jurisdiction requirements on their own.

d. In personam jurisdiction

There must be personal jurisdiction over the third-party defendant for impleader to apply. Third parties joined by impleader may be served within 100 miles of where the summons was issued, even if the service is outside of the state and beyond its long-arm statute jurisdiction. Rule 4(k)(1)(B).

E. CLASS ACTIONS

In a class action, the court authorizes a single person or a small group of people to represent the interests of a larger group. Rule 23 and the Class Action Fairness Act of 2005 govern class actions.

1. Prerequisites

a. Basic requirements

Rule 23(a) establishes four requirements for representative members of a class to sue or be sued on behalf of all members of the class:

i) The class must be so numerous that joinder of all members is impracticable;

ii) There must be questions of law or fact that are common to the class;

iii) The claims or defenses of the representatives must be typical of the class; and

iv) The representatives must fairly and adequately protect the interests of the class.

Illinois Distinction: Class Actions

An action may become a class action and a party may sue or be sued as a member of a class only if the court finds each of the following:

i) The class is so numerous that joinder of all members is impracticable;

ii) There are questions of fact or law common to the class, and these common questions predominate over questions affecting only individual members;

iii) The representative parties will fairly and adequately protect the interests of the class; and

iv) The class action is an appropriate method for the fair and efficient adjudication of the controversy.

---

b. Three types

In addition to the requirements of Rule 23(a), before a class action can be certified, it must also fit within one of the three situations specified in Rule 23(b).

1) Risk of prejudice

Under Rule 23(b)(1), the class is maintainable if the prosecution of separate actions would create the risk that the class opponent would become subject to incompatible standards of conduct resulting from inconsistent adjudications, or if prosecution of the claims through separate actions would, as a practical matter, impair the interests of the class members.

2) Final equitable relief

Under Rule 23(b)(2), a class seeking final equitable relief may be certified if the class shares a general claim against the opposing party. The class can also seek damages, but the equitable relief must be the primary relief sought.

3) Common legal or factual questions

Under Rule 23(b)(3), a class can be certified if questions of law or fact that are common to the class members predominate over any questions affecting only individual members, and a class action is the superior method in bringing about a fair and efficient adjudication of the controversy. In making this determination, the court must consider, among other things:

i) The class members' interests in individually controlling the prosecution or defense of separate actions;

ii) The extent and nature of any litigation concerning the controversy already begun by or against class members;

iii) The desirability or undesirability of concentrating the litigation of the claims in the particular forum; and

iv) The likely difficulties in managing a class action.

c. Subject matter jurisdiction

A class action must also satisfy federal subject matter jurisdiction requirements. A class action can invoke federal question jurisdiction or diversity jurisdiction.

1) Diversity jurisdiction

If diversity jurisdiction is invoked in a class action, diversity of citizenship will be satisfied if the class representatives are diverse from the party or parties opposing the claim.

When at least one plaintiff in a putative class action has a claim that meets the statutory jurisdictional amount (generally it must exceed $75,000), the other plaintiffs can be made part of the class under the doctrine of supplemental jurisdiction. *Exxon Mobil Corp.*, 545 U.S. 546.

d. Venue

Federal venue requirements must also be satisfied for a class action. When venue is based on the residence of the class, the residences of the representative parties—not the residences of all the class members—are what matter.

e. Class actions under the Class Action Fairness Act of 2005

The Class Action Fairness Act of 2005 ("CAFA") made it easier to satisfy federal subject matter jurisdiction for certain large class actions. Subject matter jurisdiction will be met if:

i) The class action involves at least 100 members;

ii) The primary defendants are not states, state officials, or other governmental entities against whom the district court may be foreclosed from ordering relief;

iii) The action does not involve certain securities-related cases, or litigation concerning the internal affairs or governance of a corporation;

iv) The amount in controversy exceeds the sum or value of $5,000,000, exclusive of interest and costs; and

v) Minimum diversity exists. Minimum diversity is satisfied when any member of a class of plaintiffs is a citizen of a state different from any defendant.

1) Removals and exclusions

The Class Action Fairness Act allows any defendant to remove the case to federal court. If the class action claim is based only on federal securities law or corporate governance, there is no federal jurisdiction under CAFA. This exclusion also applies to primary defendants who are governmental entities.

2) Protections

The benefit to filing under CAFA is the various protections afforded to the class members. The court will generally protected members against loss in consumer class actions, ensure that the settlement is fair to the members, and ensure that the settlement is equally distributed. It will also notify federal and state officials of the proposed settlement. If no notice is given, the class member may choose not to be bound by the agreement.

3) Limitations on jurisdiction

The court is required to repudiate jurisdiction when the primary injuries were incurred in the state in which the action was filed, when more than two-thirds of the proposed plaintiffs are citizens of the state in which the case was filed, and when significant relief is sought from a defendant who is a citizen of the state in which the case was filed.

If between one-third and two-thirds of proposed plaintiffs and the primary defendants are citizens of the state in which the case was filed, the court is given discretion to decline jurisdiction.

f. Shareholder derivative suits

When a shareholder brings a cause of action on behalf of other shareholders against the corporation, he must represent the class fairly and adequately. He is bound to plead with particularity that he made a demand on the directors, when state law requires such a demand, and, if not, he is bound to state the reasons for not making the demand. He must also assert his status as a shareholder at the time the transaction occurred. Finally, he must prove to the court that the action is not a cunning enterprise to impart jurisdiction on the court.

If a corporation displays animus to the plaintiffs, it must be named on the complaint. Otherwise, the court will join the corporation as a defendant to indicate the corporation's animus. Further, the settlement or dismissal of a derivative suit must be approved by the court. In the case of a settlement, the amount awarded is measured by the damages the corporation suffered.

2. Approval of the Court

Pursuant to Rule 23(c), at an early practicable time after a person sues or is sued as a class representative, the court must determine by order whether to certify the action as a class action. The class must meet all of the above requirements to be certified. If a class is certified, the court's order must define the class and the class's claims, issues, or defenses and must appoint counsel for the class. A party may seek an appeal to the certification even though the certification is not a final judgment.

Illinois Distinction: Approval of the Court

The court determines by order whether an action may be maintained as a class action, and describes who the court considers the members of the class. The order may be conditional and may be amended before a decision on the merits.

An action may be brought or maintained as a class action with respect to particular issues, or divided into sub-classes, with each sub-class treated as a class.

---

3. **Notice of the Class Action**

Notice of the class action is required only for class actions under Rule 23(b)(3), when questions of law or fact that are common to the class members predominate over any questions affecting only individual members, and a class action is the superior method in bringing about a fair and efficient adjudication of the controversy. For all other types of class actions, notice of the action is in the court's discretion.

When notice is required for a class action, it must be the best notice that is practicable under the circumstances, including individual notice to all members who can be identified through reasonable effort. The notice must clearly and concisely state in plain, easily understood language:

i) The nature of the action;

ii) The definition of the class;

iii) The class claims, issues, or defenses;

iv) That a class member may enter an appearance through an attorney if the member so desires;

v) That the court will exclude from the class any member who requests exclusion;

vi) The time and manner for requesting exclusion; and

vii) The binding effect of a class judgment on members.

Illinois Distinction: Notice of the Class Action

Notice: Upon a determination that an action may be maintained as a class action, or at any time during the conduct of the action, the court may in its discretion order notice that it deems necessary to protect the interest of the class and the parties.

Intervention: Any class member seeking to intervene or otherwise appear in the action may do so with leave of court. Leave will be liberally granted except when the court finds that such intervention will disrupt the conduct of the action or otherwise prejudice the rights of the parties or the class.

Opting Out: Any class member seeking to be excluded from a class may request exclusion and any judgment entered in the action shall not apply to persons who properly requested to be excluded.

---

4. **Settlement**

Under Rule 23(e), the claims, issues, or defenses of the certified class may be voluntarily settled or dismissed only with the approval of the court.

a. Notice

When a proposal for settlement is made to the court, the court must direct notice in a reasonable manner to all class members who would be bound by the proposal.

b. Standard for approval

If the proposal would bind class members, the court may approve only it after a hearing and on finding that it is fair, reasonable, and adequate. The parties seeking approval must file a statement identifying any collateral agreements made in connection with the proposal.

c. Objection by class members

Any class member may object to the proposal if it requires court approval and the objection may be withdrawn only with the court's approval. Rule 23(e). They must be given an opportunity to "opt out" of the settlement and proceed on their own.

5. Judgment

For class actions certified under Rule 23(b)(1) and (2), a valid judgment binds all class members, whether or not the court has personal jurisdiction over absent members. In a class action certified under Rule 23(b)(3), however, a valid judgment in a class action binds only those class members who did not previously request exclusion from the class.

Illinois Distinction: Judgment

Judgments: Judgments entered in class action cases are binding on all class members, as the class is defined, except those who have been properly excluded.

Dismissal or Compromise: Any class action shall not be compromised or dismissed except with the approval of the court and, unless excused for good cause shown, upon notice as the court may direct.

VII. PRE-TRIAL PROCEDURE AND DISCOVERY

A. MANDATORY DISCLOSURES

Rule 26(a) requires the parties, at three different times prior to trial, to make certain disclosures: (i) initial disclosures, (ii) disclosures of expert testimony 90 days before trial, and (iii) pre-trial disclosures 30 days before trial. These disclosures are mandatory and must be made even if an opposing party does not ask for such information. Unless otherwise ordered by the court, the disclosures must be in writing, signed, and served.

Illinois Distinction: Mandatory Disclosures

Generally, there is no automatic disclosure in Illinois. Certain cases, however, are subject to automatic and limited discovery procedures (see VII.A.3., *infra*).

---

1. **Initial Disclosures**

   a. **In general**

   Under Rule 26(a)(1), unless otherwise agreed by stipulation or ordered by the court, each party must provide to the other parties:

   i) The name, and, if known, address and telephone number of each individual likely to have discoverable information, along with the subjects of that information, that the disclosing party may use to support its claims or defenses, unless the use would be solely for purposes of impeachment;

   ii) A copy, or a description by category and location, of all documents, electronically stored information, and tangible things that the disclosing party has in its possession, custody, or control and may use to support its claims or defenses, unless the use would be solely for impeachment;

   iii) A computation of each category of damages claimed by the disclosing party, who must also make available for inspection and copying the documents or other evidentiary material on which each computation is based, including materials bearing on the nature and extent of injury, unless privileged or protected from disclosure; and

   iv) For inspection and copying, any insurance agreement under which an insurance business may be liable to satisfy all or part of a possible judgment in the action or to indemnify or reimburse for payments made to satisfy the judgment.

   Pursuant to Rule 26(a)(1)(E), a party must make its initial disclosures based on the information that is then reasonably available to it. A party is not excused from making its disclosures because it has not fully investigated the case, because it challenges the sufficiency of another party's disclosures, or because another party has not made its disclosures.

   b. **Exceptions**

   Rule 26(a)(1)(B) excludes nine categories of proceedings from the initial disclosure requirements:

   i) Actions for review on an administrative record;

   ii) Forfeiture actions in rem arising from a federal statute;

   iii) Petitions for habeas corpus or any other proceeding to challenge a criminal conviction or sentence;

   iv) Actions brought without an attorney by a person in the custody of the United States, a state, or a state subdivision;

   v) Actions to enforce or quash an administrative summons or subpoena;

   vi) Actions by the United States to recover benefit payments;

   vii) Actions by the United States to collect on a student loan guaranteed by the United States;

   viii) Proceedings that are ancillary to proceedings in another court; and

   ix) Actions to enforce an arbitration award.

c. Time for initial disclosures

A party must make the initial disclosures required by Rule 26(a)(1) at or within 14 days after the parties' Rule 26(f) conference (*see* § VII.C. Discovery Conference, *infra*), unless a different time is set by stipulation or court order.

2. Disclosure of Expert Testimony

a. In general

Rule 26(a)(2) requires parties to disclose the identity of persons who may testify as expert witnesses and to produce any expert report for each such witness. The expert report must be prepared and signed by the expert and contain:

i)   A complete statement of and basis for all opinions to be expressed;

ii) The facts or data considered by the expert in forming the opinions;

iii) Any exhibits used as support for or as a summary of the opinions;

iv) The qualifications of the expert;

v)   A listing of all publications authored by the expert in the past 10 years;

vi) The expert's compensation; and

vii) A list of all other cases in which the expert has testified at trial or deposition in the past four years.

b. Time to disclose expert testimony

A party must make these disclosures at the times and in the sequence that the court orders, but absent a stipulation or court order, the disclosures must be made at least 90 days before the date set for trial or for the case to be ready for trial. If the evidence is intended solely to contradict or rebut the opposing party's expert evidence on the same subject matter, disclosure must be made within 30 days after the other party's disclosure. Rule 26(a)(2)(D).

c. Supplementing the disclosure

The parties must supplement these disclosures when required under Rule 26(e). (*See* § VII.B.7. Supplementation, *infra*.) For an expert whose report must be disclosed, the party's duty to supplement extends both to information included in the report and to information given during the expert's deposition. Any additions or changes to this information must be disclosed by the time the party's pretrial disclosures under Rule 26(a)(3) are due.

3. Pre-Trial Disclosures

a. In general

Pursuant to Rule 26(a)(3)(A), in addition to the initial and expert disclosures, the parties must make certain disclosures regarding evidence that they may present at trial other than for impeachment purposes. They must file with the court:

i)   The name and, if not previously provided, the address and telephone number of each witness, separately identifying those the party expects to present and those it may call if the need arises;

ii) The designation of those witnesses whose testimony the party expects to present by deposition and, if not taken stenographically, a transcript of the pertinent parts of the deposition; and

iii) An identification of each document or other exhibit, including summaries of other evidence, separately identifying those items the party expects to offer and those it may offer if the need arises.

b. Time for pre-trial disclosures

Under Rule 26(a)(3)(B), unless the court orders otherwise, these disclosures must be made at least 30 days before trial.

c. Objections

Within 14 days after the disclosures are made, unless the court sets a different time, a party may serve and promptly file objections to the use of the depositions at trial and to the admissibility of disclosed documents and exhibits. If an objection is not made at this point, it will be waived, unless excused by the court for good cause or unless the objection relates to relevancy, prejudice, or confusion pursuant to Rules 402 and 403 of the Federal Rules of Evidence. Rule 26(a)(3)(B).

Illinois Distinction: Mandatory Disclosure in Limited Cases

Generally, there are no automatic disclosures in Illinois. However, certain cases are subject to "limited and simplified discovery." This limited and simplified discovery applies to cases subject to mandatory arbitration, civil actions seeking money damages not more than $50,000, exclusive of interests and costs, and to cases for the collection of taxes not more than $50,000. It does not apply to small claims, ordinance violations, family or domestic disputes, or equitable relief.

Timing: The parties must make initial disclosures within 120 days after the filing of a response pleading to the complaint, counter-complaint, third party complaint or within the time prescribed by an applicable local rule, unless the parties otherwise agree, the court shortens or lengthens the time, or for good cause shown. These disclosures must be made automatically, without a discovery request from the opposing party.

Required Disclosures: Disclosures should include information and data in the possession, custody, and control of the parties, as well as information that can be ascertained, learned, or acquired by reasonable inquiry and investigation. Each party must disclose the following, in writing, to every other party:

i) The factual basis of each claim or defense;

ii) The legal theory upon which each claim or defense is based;

iii) The names and contact information of all witnesses (excluding experts) the disclosing party expects to call at trial, along with a designation of the subject matter about which each would testify;

iv) The names and contact information of all persons the party believes may have knowledge relevant to the action and the nature of that knowledge;

v) The names and contact information of all persons who have given statements, and the custodian of the copies of those statements;

vi) The identity and address of each person the disclosing party expects to call as an expert witness;

vii) A computation and measure of damages alleged, plus supporting information;

viii) The existence, location, custodian, and general description of any tangible evidence or documents the disclosing party plans to use at trial; and

ix) Copies of documents (or, in the case of voluminous documents, a list of documents) relevant to the subject matter, including documents to be used at trial.

Continuing duty: The parties have a continuing duty to disclose, supplement, and amend the above information.

Limited and Simplified Discovery Procedures: Each party may propound a total of 30 interrogatories and supplemental interrogatories in the aggregate, including subsections. No discovery deposition shall exceed three hours, absent a written agreement by the parties. Discovery depositions may be taken only of the parties, treating physicians, and opinion witnesses.

B. DISCOVERY SCOPE AND LIMITS

In addition to obtaining information under the mandatory disclosure rules, parties may use a variety of discovery methods set forth in Rules 27–36 and discussed below. Rule 26 sets forth rules establishing the scope and limitations of such discovery.

1. Scope

a. In general

Under Rule 26(b)(1), discovery is generally permitted with regard to any matter relevant to any party's claim or defense in the action that is not otherwise privileged. This includes the existence, description, nature, custody, condition, and location of any documents or other tangible things and the identity and location of persons who know of any discoverable matter.

b. Relevance

Admissibility of the evidence at trial does not matter for determining relevance for purposes of discovery. The test is whether the information sought is relevant to any party's claim or defense. Under Rule 26(b)(1), information may be discoverable if it "appears reasonably calculated to lead to the discovery of admissible evidence."

Illinois Distinction: Scope of Discovery

With some exceptions, a party may obtain full discovery of any matter relevant to the subject matter involved in the pending action, whether related to the claim or defense of the requesting party or any other party. Discovery is not limited to information that would be admissible as evidence at trial.

A party may seek information related to (including the existence and location of):

i) Any document or tangible thing (including papers, photographs, recordings, and all retrievable information in computer storage);

ii) Persons having knowledge of relevant facts;

iii) All lay witnesses, and the subjects on which the witness will testify; and

iv) All independent expert witnesses and controlled expert witnesses, the subject on which the witness will testify, and the opinions the party expects to illicit.

---

c. Privilege

Privileged information is not discoverable. In federal question cases, privileges are determined under federal common law, pursuant to Rule 501 of the Federal

Rules of Evidence. In diversity or supplemental claims in which a state's substantive laws apply, that state's law determines whether a privilege applies.

Illinois Distinction: Privilege

Anything that is privileged against disclosure at trial, including privileged communications between a party and his attorney, are privileged against disclosure through any discovery procedure.

Material prepared by or for a party in preparation for trial is subject to discovery only if it does not contain or disclose the theories, mental impressions, or litigation plans of the party's attorney.

---

2. **Limitations on Discovery**

a. **Required limitations**

On motion or on its own, the court is required to limit the frequency or extent of discovery otherwise allowed by the rules if it determines that:

i) The discovery sought is unreasonably cumulative, or can be obtained from some other source that is more convenient or less expensive;

ii) The party seeking discovery has had ample opportunity to obtain the information by discovery in the action; or

iii) The burden or expense of the proposed discovery outweighs its likely benefit, considering the needs of the case, the amount in controversy, the parties' resources, the importance of the issues at stake, and the importance of the discovery in resolving the issues.

When discovery is challenged, the court must weigh the party's interests in seeking discovery against the privacy interests of the party resisting discovery. *Eckstein Marine Serv., Inc. v. M/V Basin Pride*, 168 F.R.D. 38 (W.D. La. 1996). For example, discovery with respect to personnel records may be limited due to privacy concerns. *Gehring v. Case Corp.*, 43 F.3d 340 (7th Cir. 1994).

b. **Discretion to alter limits**

The court may alter the limits in the rules as to the number of depositions, interrogatories, or requests for admission, or on the length of oral depositions.

c. **Limitations on electronically stored information**

A party is not required to provide discovery of electronically stored information from sources that the party identifies as not reasonably accessible because of undue burden or cost. If challenged, the party will have the burden to show the undue burden and cost. Even if shown, the court may still order such discovery if the requesting party shows good cause. Rule 26(b)(2)(B). Moreover, the requesting party may specify the form in which the documents should be produced.

Illinois Distinction: Limitations on Discovery

Discovery may not be initiated until all defendants have appeared or are required to appear, except with leave of court and upon good cause shown.

A trial will not be delayed to conduct discovery unless due diligence is shown.

---

3. Trial Preparation Materials

Rule 26(b)(3) provides limited protection for otherwise discoverable trial preparation materials or the work product of attorneys. In general, a party may not discover documents and tangible things that are prepared in anticipation of litigation or for trial by or for another party or its representative.

Such materials will be subject to discovery, however, if the party shows that it has substantial need for the materials to prepare its case and cannot, without undue hardship, obtain their substantial equivalent by other means. If the court orders discovery of trial preparation materials, Rule 26(b)(3)(B) requires the court to protect against disclosure of the mental impressions, conclusions, opinions, or legal theories of a party's attorney or other representative concerning the litigation.

Illinois Distinction: Trial Preparation Materials

Attorney Work Product and Consultants: Material prepared by or for a party in preparation for trial is discoverable only if it does not disclose the theories, mental impressions, or litigation plans of the party's attorney. The court may apportion the cost involved in originally securing the discoverable material, including a reasonable attorney's fee, when appropriate.

The Illinois Supreme Court Rules define a consultant as a person retained or specially employed in anticipation of litigation or preparation for trial but who will not be called at trial. The identity, opinions, and work product of a consultant are discoverable only upon a showing of exceptional circumstances under which it is impracticable for the party seeking discovery to obtain facts or opinions on the same subject matter by other means.

---

4. Experts

Under Rule 26(b)(4)(A), a party is entitled to depose any expert witness of an opposing party whose opinions may be presented at trial.

Rule 26(b)(3) protects drafts of any expert report or disclosure required under Rule 26(a)(2). *See* § VII.A.2. Disclosure of Expert Testimony, *supra*. Any communications between the party's attorney and an expert witness who is required to provide a report are also protected, except to the extent that the communications (i) relate to the expert's compensation, (ii) identify facts or data that the party's attorney provided and that the expert considered in forming his opinion, or (iii) identify assumptions that the party's attorney provided and the expert relied upon.

If the expert was retained or specially employed by another party in anticipation of litigation or to prepare for trial but is not expected to be called as a witness, discovery is permitted only on showing exceptional circumstances under which it is impracticable for the party to obtain facts or opinions on the same subject by other means. Rule 26(b)(4)(D).

A report of an examining physician who is not expected to testify, however, can be obtained as provided under Rule 35(b).

Illinois Distinction: Experts

Expert Witnesses: Upon written interrogatory, a party must furnish the identities and contact information of:

i) **Lay Witnesses.** For each lay witness, the party must identify the subject matter on which the lay witness will testify. The party must give reasonable notice of such testimony taking into account any limitations on the party's knowledge of known facts and opinions held by the lay witness.

ii) **Independent Expert Witnesses.** An independent expert witness gives expert testimony and is not the party, the party's current employee, or the party's retained expert. For each independent expert witness, the party must identify the subjects on which the witness will testify and the opinions that the party expects to elicit. An answer must give reasonable notice of the testimony, taking into account the limitations of the party's knowledge of the facts and opinions held by the witness.

iii) **Controlled Expert Witnesses.** A controlled expert witness is a person giving testimony who is the party, the party's current employee, or the party's retained expert. For each controlled expert witness, the party must identify the subject matter on which the witness will testify, the conclusions and opinions of the witness and the bases therefore, the qualifications of the witness, and any reports prepared by the witness about the case.

Consultants: Recall that the identity, opinions, and work of consultants who are not expected to testify at trial are discoverable only upon a showing of exceptional circumstances.

5. **Claims of Privilege**

Under Rule 26(b)(5)(A), whenever a party withholds information on the basis of a privilege or the attorney work product doctrine, the party must expressly state the claim of privilege and describe the materials or communications not produced in a manner that will enable other parties to assess the applicability of the privilege or protection.

Illinois Distinction: Claims of Privilege

When a party withholds documents or information from disclosure on the basis of any statutory or common law privilege, any such claim shall be made expressly and shall be supported by a description of the nature of the documents, communications, or things not produced or disclosed and the exact privilege which is being claimed.

6. **Protective Orders**

Under Rule 26(c), the court may, for good cause, enter orders to protect parties and other persons from annoyance, embarrassment, oppression, or undue burden or expense resulting from discovery. For example, a party may seek a court order limiting the time and manner of conducting a physical examination, and a non-party who is served with a subpoena to attend a deposition may, by filing a motion to squash the subpoena, seek a court order to that effect.

Illinois Distinction: Protective Orders

Upon motion or on its own, a court may make a protective order denying, limiting, conditioning, or regulating discovery to prevent unreasonable annoyance, expense, embarrassment, disadvantage, or oppression of any person. Further, upon motion of any party or witness, on notice to all parties, a court may supervise any part of the discovery process.

7. Supplementation

Pursuant to Rule 26(e)(1)(A), if a party who has made a required disclosure or responded to an interrogatory, request for production, or request for admission learns that the disclosure or response is materially incomplete or incorrect, the party is required to supplement or correct the disclosure or response in a timely manner.

There is no duty to supplement or correct if such information has otherwise been made known to the other parties in discovery or in writing.

As to an expert whose report must be disclosed under Rule 26(a)(2)(B), the party's duty to supplement extends both to information included in the expert's report and to information given during the expert's deposition. Rule 26(e)(2).

Illinois Distinction: Supplementation

As discussed above, in cases utilizing the Limited and Simplified Discovery Procedures, there is a continuing duty to supplement and amend disclosures when a party discovers new or different information. A party also has a continuing duty to supplement or amend responses to written interrogatories and written requests to inspect, copy, photograph, or test documents, objects, or tangible things.

C. DISCOVERY CONFERENCE

1. Rule 26(f)

Under Rule 26(f), except in a proceeding exempted from the initial disclosure rules or if the court orders otherwise, the parties must confer as soon as practicable, and in any event at least 21 days before a scheduling conference is to be held or a scheduling order is due under Rule 16(b) (*see* § VII.G. Pre-Trial Conferences, *infra*) to:

   i) Consider the nature and basis of their claims and defenses and the possibilities for promptly settling or resolving the case;

   ii) Make or arrange for the automatic disclosures required by Rule 26(a)(1);

   iii) Discuss any issues about preserving discoverable information; and

   iv) Develop a proposed discovery plan.

The attorneys of record and all unrepresented parties that have appeared in the case are jointly responsible for arranging the conference, for attempting in good faith to agree on the proposed discovery plan, and for submitting to the court within 14 days after the conference a written report outlining the plan.

The discovery plan must state:

   i) The parties' views and proposals on the discovery that may be needed in the case;

   ii) The schedule for such discovery;

   iii) Any modifications and limits to the scope of the parties' required disclosures and discovery;

   iv) Any issues about electronically stored information or privilege; and

   v) Any scheduling or protective order that should be entered by the court.

The discovery plan must also indicate when the initial automatic disclosures were or are to be made.

In addition, the court may decide to hold a pretrial conference if it believes such a conference will foster a settlement and expedite the trial. An order must be entered after the pretrial conference is held.

Illinois Distinction: Initial Case Management Conference

In most cases, the court must hold a case management conference within 35 days after the parties are at issue and no more than 182 days after the filing of the complaint. At the conference, counsel familiar with the case and authorized to act shall appear and consider the following:

i) The nature, issues, and complexity of the case;

ii) The simplification of issues and any amendments to pleadings;

iii) The possibility of obtaining admissions of fact and of documents that will avoid unnecessary proof;

iv) The limitations on discovery, including the number and duration of depositions, the area of expertise and number of expert witnesses, the deadlines for disclosure of witnesses and completion of written discovery and depositions;

v) The possibility of settlement and the scheduling of a settlement conference;

vi) The advisability of alternative dispute resolution;

vii) The trial date;

viii) The advisability of holding additional case management conferences; and

ix) Any other matters which may aid in the disposition of the action.

At all case management conferences, the court will set a date for a subsequent case management conference. The court will specify any issues for trial that have not been disposed of at the conference and will choose dates for the disclosure of all witnesses and completion of all discovery, which should be no later than 60 days before the anticipated trial date, unless otherwise agreed by the parties. The court will also set a pretrial calendar.

---

2. Failure to Participate in the Framing of the Discovery Plan

Pursuant to Rule 37(f), if a party or her attorney fails to participate in good faith in the development and submission of a proposed discovery plan as required by Rule 26(f), the court may, after providing an opportunity for a hearing, order the party or attorney to pay the reasonable expenses, including attorney's fees, incurred as a result of such failure.

Illinois Distinction: Failure to Participate in the Framing of the Discovery Plan

If a party, or any person at the insistence of a party, unreasonably fails to comply with any provision of the discovery rules or an order entered pursuant to them, the court may impose sanctions on the offending party, his attorney, or both. This may include an order to pay the other party or parties the amount of reasonable expenses incurred as a result of the misconduct, including reasonable attorney's fees. When the conduct is willful, sanctions may include a monetary penalty. The court may enter further punitive orders in connection with the litigation (see § VII.F., *infra*).

D. DISCOVERY DEVICES

1. Depositions

Depositions are widely used and can take two forms: (i) oral depositions, which are common to almost all litigation in federal court, and (ii) written depositions, which are rarely used.

> **Illinois Distinction: Depositions**
>
> Illinois also makes a distinction between **discovery depositions** (which are available at trial and used only under specific circumstances) and **evidence depositions** (which may be used at trial as direct evidence if deponent is unavailable). The notice or order for taking a deposition must specify the type of deposition; if no specification is made, it will be a discovery deposition only. If a party wants both types of deposition from the same deponent, two separate depositions must be taken, unless the parties stipulate otherwise or the court orders otherwise. If the evidence deposition of a witness is to be taken within 21 days of trial, a discovery deposition will not be permitted unless the parties stipulate otherwise or the court orders otherwise.

a. Oral depositions

1) When an oral deposition may be taken

Under Rule 30, a party may take the deposition of any party or non-party witness at any time after the party has made its mandatory initial disclosures pursuant to Rule 26(a).

Without leave of the court, the plaintiffs, the defendants, and the third-party defendants, each as a group, are limited to 10 depositions by oral or written examination.

Unless the parties agree to the deposition, leave of the court must be obtained to:

i) Exceed the 10-deposition limitation;

ii) Depose a witness a second time; or

iii) Depose a person before the deposing party has complied with its initial disclosure requirements under Rule 26(a).

2) Notice of deposition

A party who seeks an oral deposition of a person must obtain a court order and give reasonable written notice, at least 21 days prior to the hearing for the order, to every other party, stating the time and place of the deposition and, if known, the deponent's name and address.

Notice of deposition is all that is needed to compel attendance by any party, even a party who is beyond the reach of the court's subpoena power. To compel attendance by a non-party, a subpoena must be served. Rule 30(b).

3) **Deposing a corporation, partnership, association, or government entity**

   When deposing a corporation, partnership, association, or governmental entity, Rule 30(b)(6) states that the notice must describe with reasonable particularity the areas of inquiry, and it must state that the named entity has the duty to designate a representative with respect to the designated areas of inquiry.

   The named entity must then designate one or more officers, directors, or managing agents, or other people who consent to testify on the entity's behalf with regard to those areas.

4) **Conducting an oral deposition**

   A deposition must be conducted before an officer appointed or designated under Rule 28 to administer oaths and take testimony, unless the parties agree otherwise.

   By stipulation of the parties or by court order, a deposition may be taken by telephonic or other remote electronic means.

   i)   Examination of the deponent may proceed as permitted at trial under the Federal Rules of Evidence except that cross-examination is not limited to matters raised on direct examination. Rule 30(c).

   ii) The deponent is to be placed under oath and the testimony is to be recorded either by stenographic or electronic means. Rule 30(b).

   iii) Any objections are to be made on the record, but the examination still proceeds. The testimony is taken subject to any objection. Rule 30(c)(2).

   iv) A person may instruct the deponent not to answer only when necessary to preserve a privilege, to enforce a limitation ordered by the court, or to present a motion to terminate or limit the examination. Rule 30(c)(2).

Under Rule 30(d)(1), a deposition is limited to one day of seven hours, unless the parties agree otherwise or the court orders otherwise. The court must allow additional time if needed to fairly examine the deponent, or if the deponent, another person, or any other circumstance impedes or delays the deposition.

Illinois Distinction: Conducting an Oral Deposition

Depositions must be taken in front of a disinterested notary public, federal court master, or other court-appointed person. That person is empowered to administer oaths and take testimony.

Scope: During oral *discovery* depositions, the deponent may be examined regarding any matter subject to discovery under the Rules. The deponent may be questioned by any party as if under cross-examination. The deponent in an oral *evidence* deposition may be examined as though the deponent was being questioned at trial (e.g., no leading questions).

Objections: Objections shall be concise, stating the exact legal nature of the objection. The following rules also apply:

i)   Objections as to notice are waived unless a written objection is promptly served upon the party giving notice.

ii) Objections as to the disqualification of the officer or person taking the deposition are waived unless made before the deposition begins or as soon thereafter, as disqualification becomes known or should have been known with reasonable diligence.

iii) Objections as to the competency of the deponent or admissibility of testimony which might have been corrected if presented during the taking of the deposition are waived by failure to make them at that time; otherwise, objections on these grounds may be made when testimony is offered in evidence.

iv) Objections to the form of questions or answers, errors and irregularities occurring in the manner of taking the deposition, in the oath or affirmation, in the conduct of any persons, and any other errors and irregularities which may be corrected if promptly presented, are waived unless a seasonable objection thereto is made at the taking of the deposition.

v)   A motion to suppress is unnecessary to preserve an objection seasonably made. A party may, but need not, obtain a ruling on an objection before trial.

vi) Errors and irregularities in the manner in which the deposition was transcribed, prepared, signed, or otherwise dealt with by the officer are waived unless a motion to suppress all or part of the deposition is made with reasonable promptness after the defect is, or should have been, ascertained.

Duration: No discovery deposition of any party or witness should exceed three hours, regardless of the number of parties in the case, except by stipulation of all parties or by order showing that good cause warrants a lengthier examination.

Remote or Electronic Depositions: Upon stipulation or court order, a deposition may be taken by telephone, videoconference, or other remote electronic means. The deponent must be in the presence of the officer administering the oath and recording the deposition, unless otherwise agreed to by the parties. Any exhibits or other demonstrative evidence to be presented to the deponent must be provided to the officer administering the oath and all other parties within a reasonable time prior to the deposition. Unless otherwise agreed, the party insisting on the remote deposition pays the costs involved.

Signature: Unless signature is waived by the deponent, the deponent is given the chance to examine the transcript of the deposition and to record changes of form and substance along with his reasons for making them. The transcript is then signed, or the refusal and reason for refusal to sign are recorded.

5) Motion to terminate or limit an oral deposition

At any time during an oral deposition, the deponent or a party may move to terminate or limit such deposition on the ground that it is being conducted in bad faith or in a manner that unreasonably annoys, embarrasses, or oppresses the deponent or party. Rule 30(d)(3)(A).

Illinois Distinction: Terminate or Limit Deposition

At any time during the taking of a deposition, the deponent or a party may move to terminate or limit the deposition on the ground that it is being conducted in bad faith or in any manner that unreasonably annoys, embarrasses, or oppresses the opponent or party. An examination terminated by order shall be resumed only upon further court order.

---

6) Failure to attend a deposition

Pursuant to Rule 30(g), if a party given notice to attend a deposition attends expecting such deposition, and the noticing party fails to attend or proceed with the deposition, the noticing party is subject to a court order requiring payment of reasonable expenses to the other parties.

Illinois Distinction: Failure to Attend a Deposition

Nonparty: A nonparty who fails to comply with a discovery order or subpoena may be held in contempt.

Party: If a party refuses to comply with any order entered pursuant to discovery rules, the court may impose sanctions on that party.

Refusal to Answer: If a deponent, whether party or non-party, refuses to answer questions, the party may move the court for an order compelling answers. If the court finds that the refusal to answer was without substantial justification, the court may order the party or deponent, or the party whose attorney advised the conduct complained of, to pay reasonable expenses incurred in obtaining the order, including reasonable attorney's fees. If the court finds that the motion was made without substantial justification, the court may order the moving party to pay reasonable expenses, including reasonable attorney's fees, incurred in opposing the motion.

---

b. Written depositions

Pursuant to Rule 31, depositions may be taken by written questions to the deponent. The same rules regarding leave of court and deposing an organization that apply to oral depositions apply to written ones. They are as follows:

i)   To take a written deposition, the deposing party must serve the questions and a notice, identifying the deponent and the officer before whom the deposition will be taken, to all other parties. Rule 31(a)(3).

ii) The other parties may then serve cross-questions, re-direct questions, and re-cross questions on all other parties. Rule 31(a)(5).

iii) The deposing party serves the notice and all questions on the officer designated in the notice. Rule 31(b).

iv) The officer asks the written questions of the deponent and records the deponent's oral responses stenographically or by electronic means. *Id.*

c. Irregularities in depositions

Certain errors and irregularities in depositions are waived if not objected to in a timely manner. There must be a written objection promptly served on the party giving notice when there are irregularities with the notice and its service. A seasonable objection must be made if there are errors in the manner of taking the deposition, while a motion to suppress is required when there are errors related to the signing, certification, and transmittal of depositions. Finally, in noting errors as to the form of the written questions, the propounding party should receive notice within five days after service of the last questions authorized.

2. Interrogatories

a. Availability

Pursuant to Rule 33(a), any party may serve no more than 25 written interrogatories on any other party. Interrogatories may not be used on non-party witnesses.

b. Scope

Pursuant to Rule 33(a)(2), interrogatories may relate to any matters permitted to be inquired into under Rule 26(b)(1) (i.e., non-privileged matters relevant to any party's claim or defense). An interrogatory is not objectionable merely because it asks for an opinion or contention that relates to fact or the application of law to fact, but the court may order that the interrogatory need not be answered until designated discovery is complete, or until a pre-trial conference or some other time.

c. Answers and objections

Under Rule 33(b)(1), the interrogatories must be answered by the party to whom they are directed, or if that party is a corporation, partnership, association, or governmental entity, by any officer or agent, who must furnish the information available to the party.

Each interrogatory must be answered fully and separately under oath, unless the responding party objects to the interrogatory. The grounds for objecting to an interrogatory must be stated with specificity. Any ground not stated in a timely objection is deemed waived, unless the court, for good cause, excuses the failure. Rule 33(b)(2), (3).

The responding party must serve its answers and any objections within 30 days after being served with the interrogatories. The court may order or the parties may stipulate to a shorter or longer time. Rule 33(b)(4).

The person who makes the answers must sign them, and the attorney who objects must sign any objections. Rule 33(b)(5).

Illinois Distinction: Answers and Objections

Responding parties must serve sworn answers or objections to the interrogatories to all parties entitled to notice within 28 days of service of the interrogatories. The response must set forth in full each interrogatory being answered immediately preceding the answer.

Sworn answers to interrogatories directed to corporations, partnerships, or associations shall be made by an officer, agent, or partner who shall furnish all information as is available to the party.

Any objection to an answer or refusal to answer shall be heard by the court upon prompt notice and motion by the party propounding the interrogatory.

---

d. Option to produce business records

Under Rule 33(d), if the answer to an interrogatory may be ascertained from the business records (including electronically stored information) or summation of the business records of the responding party, and the burden of deriving the answers is substantially the same for the party serving the interrogatories as for the responding party, the responding party may answer the interrogatory by specifying the records from which the answer may be derived and providing the party who served the interrogatories with an opportunity to examine and copy such records.

Illinois Distinction: Option to Produce Documents

When the answer to an interrogatory may be obtained from documents in the possession or control of the answering party, it is sufficient to produce the documents which respond to the interrogatory. When doing so, the responding party must comply with the requirements of Ill. Sup. Ct. R. 214 (discussed *infra*).

---

3. Requests to Produce Documents and Inspect Land

a. In general

Under Rule 34(a)(1), a party may serve on any other party a request to produce and permit the requesting party or its representative to inspect, copy, test, or sample any of the following items in the responding party's possession, custody, or control:

i) Any designated documents or electronically stored information (including writings, drawings, graphs, charts, photographs, sound recordings, images, and other data or data compilations) stored in any medium from which information can be obtained either directly or, if necessary, after translation by the responding party into a reasonably usable form; or

ii) Any designated tangible things.

A party may also serve a request to enter onto another party's land to inspect, measure, survey, photograph, test, or sample the property or a designated object or operation on the property, if relevant to the action. Rule 34(a)(2).

While these requests may be directed only to other parties, non-parties may be compelled to produce documents and other things or submit to an inspection pursuant to a subpoena served under Rule 45. Rule 34(c).

b. Contents of request

Pursuant to Rule 34(b)(1), the request:

i) Must describe with reasonable particularity each item or category of items to be inspected;

ii) Must specify a reasonable time, place, and manner for the inspection and for performing the related acts; and

iii) May specify the form or forms in which electronically stored information is to be produced.

c. Responses and objections

The party to whom the request is directed must respond in writing within 30 days after being served, unless a shorter or longer time is stipulated to by the parties or ordered by the court. If a party fails to respond to a document request or to allow inspection, or objects to a request, the propounding party may move to compel under Rule 37(a). Rule 34(b)(2)(A).

With regard to electronically stored information, if a request does not specify a form for its production, a party must produce it in a form or forms in which it is ordinarily maintained or in a reasonably usable form or forms. A party need not produce the same electronically stored information in more than one form. Rule 34(b)(2)(E).

Illinois Distinction: Requests to Produce Documents and Inspect Land

Any party may request that the other party produce for inspection, copying, reproduction, testing, or sampling specified documents, objects, or tangible things, or to permit access to real estate for the purpose of making surface or subsurface inspections, surveys, or photographs. The party may also request information calculated to lead to the discovery of any such item.

The request shall specify a reasonable time (generally not less than 28 days), place, and manner of making the inspection or performing the acts. One copy of the request shall be provided to all parties entitled to notice.

A party served with the request shall produce the requested documents as they are kept in the normal course of business, or organized, categorized, and labeled to correspond to the request, and all retrievable information in computer storage in printed form. The party served may, in the alternative, object in writing on the grounds that the request is improper in whole or in part. If an objection in part is made, the remainder of the request should be complied with. A party claiming a sought item or document is not in his possession or control, and that he has no information that would lead to its whereabouts, may be ordered to submit to examination in open court or deposition.

Parties have a duty to seasonably supplement any prior response.

4. Physical and Mental Exams

a. In general

Under Rule 35(a), if the mental or physical condition (including blood group) of a party or a person in the legal custody or control of a party is in controversy, the court may order such person to submit to a physical or mental examination by a "suitably licensed or certified examiner."

b. Procedure

Such an order may be made only upon motion, for good cause shown, and the person to be examined and all parties must be given prior notice specifying the time, place, conditions, and scope of the examination and the identity of the examiner. Rule 35(a)(2).

A "suitably licensed or certified examiner" need not be a physician and can include others licensed to report on physical or mental conditions, including psychologists and dentists.

Illinois Distinction: Physical and Mental Exams

In any action in which the physical or mental condition of a party or of a person in the party's custody or legal control is an issue, the court, upon notice and on motion made within a reasonable time before trial, may order that party to submit to a physical or mental examination by a licensed professional, whose identity should be set forth in the motion. The party requesting the examiner shall pay the fee of the examiner and compensation for any loss of earnings incurred or to be incurred by the party or person to be examined, and shall advance all reasonable expenses incurred or to be incurred by the person complying with the order.

Impartial Medical Examiner: Within a reasonable time in advance of the trial, the court may order an impartial physical or mental examination of a party whose mental or physical condition is in issue, when in the court's discretion it appears that such an examination will materially aid in the just determination of the case. The examination will be made by a member of a panel of physicians chosen by the Administrative Office of the Illinois Courts. A court may, in its discretion, order an examination during the trial. Either the party or the court may call the examining physician to testify, and that physician shall be subject to cross examination. In such a case, the physician will testify without cost to the parties.

The person to be examined has the right to have her attorney and any other person she wishes present at the examination.

c. Report of examiner

On request by the party or person examined, the party who requested the examination must provide a copy of the examiner's written report, including results of all tests, diagnoses, and conclusions, as well as any reports of earlier examinations of the same condition. If the examiner refuses to make a report, the examiner's testimony may be excluded at trial. Rule 35(b).

Illinois Distinction: Report of Examiner

Within 21 days after the completion of a mental or physical examination, the examiner shall prepare and mail or deliver to the attorney of the party requesting examination and the party examined duplicate originals of a written report of the examination, including the examiner's diagnosis and conclusions. If such mailing or delivery is not made within 21 days or within an extension granted by the court, neither the examiner's report, testimony, findings, and x-ray films, nor results of any test the examiner has made may be entered into evidence except at the insistence of the party examined or who produced the person examined. No examiner under this rule is considered a consultant

---

d. Other examinations

After delivery of the examiner's report, a party who was examined must provide the party who moved for the examination, on request, a report of all other previous or subsequent examinations of the same condition in that party's custody or control. Rule 35(b)(3).

If the party who was examined obtains the report of the examination or conducts a deposition of the examiner, the party waives any privilege it may have regarding the testimony of any other person who has examined or thereafter examines the party with respect to the same condition. Rule 35(b)(4).

5. Requests for Admission

a. In general

Under Rule 36, a party may serve upon any other party a written request for the admission of any relevant, non-privileged matters discoverable under Rule 26. The requested matters may relate to statements or opinions of fact or to the application of law to fact, including the genuineness of any documents described in the request. Rule 36(a)(1). Each matter for which an admission is requested must be set forth separately. A request to admit the genuineness of a document must be accompanied by a copy of the document unless it is, or has been, otherwise furnished or made available for inspection and copying. Rule 36(a)(2).

b. Responses and objections

A matter will be admitted unless, within 30 days after being served, the party to whom the request is directed serves on the requesting party a written answer or objection addressed to the matter and signed by the party or her attorney. Rule 36(a)(3).

If a matter is not admitted, the answer must specifically deny it or state in detail why the answering party cannot truthfully admit or deny it. A denial must fairly respond to the substance of the matter, and when good faith requires that a party qualify an answer or deny only a part of a matter, the answer must specify the part admitted and qualify or deny the rest. Rule 36(a)(4).

An answering party may assert lack of knowledge or information as a reason for failing to admit or deny only if the party states that he has made a reasonable inquiry and that the information he knows or can readily obtain is not sufficient to enable him to admit or deny. *Id.*

c. Effect of an admission

A matter admitted under Rule 36 is conclusively established unless the court, on motion, permits the admission to be withdrawn or amended. The court may permit such withdrawal or amendment if (i) doing so would promote the presentation of the merits of the action, and (ii) the court finds that it would not prejudice the requesting party in maintaining or defending the action on the merits. Rule 36(b).

An admission under Rule 36 is an admission only in the pending action and cannot be used against the party in any other proceeding. *Id.*

Illinois Distinction: Requests for Admission

A party may serve upon any other party a written request for the admission of the truth of any specified relevant fact set forth in the request, or the admission of the genuineness of any documents described in the request. A party may respond by admitting, denying all or part of the request to admit, or objecting to the request to admit. Objections should only be made to requests that seek privileged information, are irrelevant, or otherwise improper. All facts not denied under oath or objected to as improper within 28 days are deemed admitted.

Any admission made by a party pursuant to a request under this rule is for the purpose of this action only and cannot be used in any other proceeding.

Illinois Distinction: Depositions for the Purpose of Perpetuating Testimony

A person who desires to perpetuate his own testimony, or that of another person, regarding any matter cognizable in court or other proceeding may file a verified petition in the court in which the action might be brought or in which one or more of the persons to be examined resides. The petition should state the facts which he desires to establish by the proposed testimony and his reasons for desiring to perpetuate it, the names or description of the persons he expects to be adverse parties, or to be examined.

Notices should be served on all those named, and if that cannot be done, the court may order service by publication or some other way.

If the court is satisfied that the perpetuation of testimony may prevent a failure or delay of justice, it shall make an order designating or describing the persons whose depositions may be taken, specifying the subject matter of the examination and whether the depositions shall be taken upon oral examination or written questions.

If an appeal has been taken from the judgment of the trial court, or before the taking of an appeal if the time therefore has not expired, the court rendering judgment may on motion and for good cause shown allow the taking of depositions of witnesses to perpetuate their testimony for use in the event of further proceedings in that court.

E.   USE OF DISCOVERY AT TRIAL

Information gathered through the use of discovery devices is not automatically admissible as evidence at trial. In order to be admissible, the information must comply with the evidentiary rules.

1. **Use of Depositions**

   a. **At trial**

   Depositions may be used by a party to impeach the testimony of the deponent as a witness or for any other purpose permitted by the Federal Rules of Evidence. Rule 32(a)(2). Pursuant to Rule 32(a)(3), an adverse party may use for any purpose the deposition of a party or a person who, when deposed, was the party's officer, director, managing agent, or designated deponent.

   In addition, a party may use for any purpose the deposition of a witness, whether or not a party, if the court finds that:

   i) The witness is dead;

   ii) The witness is more than 100 miles from the trial or is outside the United States, unless it appears that the witness's absence was procured by the party offering the deposition;

   iii) The witness cannot attend or testify because of age, illness, infirmity, or imprisonment;

   iv) The party offering the deposition could not procure the witness's attendance by subpoena; or

   v) On motion and notice, exceptional circumstances make it desirable in the interest of justice to permit the deposition to be used.

   Rule 32(a)(4). If admissible, a deposition may generally be offered against any party who was present or represented at the deposition, or had reasonable notice of it.

   b. **Objections to the admissibility of depositions**

   Pursuant to Rule 32(b), an objection to the admission of any deposition testimony that would be inadmissible if the witness were present and testifying may generally be made at the time the deposition is offered at a hearing or trial.

Illinois Distinction: Use of Depositions

Use of Discovery Depositions: Discovery depositions may be used only:

i) To impeach the testimony of the deponent as a witness in the same manner and to the same extent as any inconsistent statement made by a witness;

ii) As an admission made by a party or by an officer or agent of a party in the same manner and to the same extent as any other admission made by that person;

iii) If otherwise admissible as an exception to the hearsay rule;

iv) For any purpose for which an affidavit may be used; or

v) If the deponent is unable to testify because of death or infirmity—if (i) reasonable notice is given to all parties, as evidence at trial or hearing against a party who appeared at the deposition or was given proper notice thereof, (ii) the court finds that the deponent is not a controlled expert witness, the deponent's evidence deposition has not been taken, and (iii) the court finds that such evidence at trial or hearing will do substantial justice between or among the parties.

Use of Evidence Depositions: The evidence deposition of a physician or surgeon may be introduced as evidence on the motion of either party, regardless of the availability of the deponent, without prejudice to the right of either party to subpoena or call as a witness the physician or surgeon for attendance at trial. All or part of other evidence depositions may be used for any purpose for which a discovery deposition may be used, and may be used by any party for any purpose if the court finds that at the time of trial:

i) The deponent is dead or unable to attend or testify because of age, sickness, infirmity, or imprisonment;

ii) The deponent is out of the country, unless it appears that the absence was procured by the party seeking to offer the deposition, provided that a party who is not a resident of Illinois may introduce his own deposition if he is out of the country; or

iii) The party offering the deposition has exercised reasonable diligence but is unable to procure the attendance of the deponent by subpoena, or finds, upon notice and motion before trial, that exceptional circumstances exist that make use of the deposition desirable.

Partial Use: If only part of a deposition is used or read at trial by a party, any other party may introduce any other part of the deposition that in fairness ought to be considered in connection with the part used.

Substitution of parties does not affect the right to use depositions previously taken.

2. Answers to Interrogatories

Under Rule 33(c), an answer to an interrogatory may be used to the extent allowed by Federal Rule of Evidence 801(d)(2), whereby a party's answer will generally constitute a party admission. An interrogatory answer could, however, constitute hearsay if offered against another party.

Illinois Distinction: Answers to Interrogatories

Answers to interrogatories may be used in the same manner as a discovery deposition. Ill. Sup. Ct. R. 213(h). Answers do not constitute judicial admissions or evidence unless they are read into evidence. Ill. Sup. Ct. R. 212.

F. ENFORCEMENT

1. Motion to Compel

a. In general

Under Rule 37, if a party fails to make the automatic disclosures required by Rule 26(a) or fails to respond to discovery that has been properly served, the party seeking the information may move to compel such disclosure or discovery.

An evasive or incomplete disclosure, answer, or response is treated as a failure to disclose, answer, or respond. Generally, making a motion to compel is a prerequisite to obtaining any sanctions under Rule 37 (*see* § VII.F.2. Sanctions, *below*).

b. Procedure

A motion to compel must be served on all parties and be accompanied by a certificate that the movant has in good faith conferred or attempted to confer with the opposing party in an effort to obtain the disclosure or secure the information or material without court action. Rule 37(a)(1).

If the subject of the motion to compel is a party, the motion must be filed with the court where the action is pending. If the subject of the motion is a non-party who was subpoenaed under Rule 45, the motion must be filed in the court that issued the subpoena. Rule 37(a)(2).

c. Fees and expenses

1) If motion is granted

A successful movant is entitled to recover her reasonable expenses incurred in connection with the motion, including reasonable attorney's fees. The court may order the opposing party, his attorney who advised the refusal of disclosure or discovery, or both, to pay the expenses. Rule 37(a)(5)(A).

Expenses cannot be awarded if:

i) The movant failed to make a good-faith effort to secure the information before filing the motion;

ii) The opposing party demonstrates that his nondisclosure, response, or objection was substantially justified; or

iii) Other circumstances render unjust an award of expenses.

2) If motion is denied

If the motion to compel is denied and the court determines that the motion was made without substantial justification, the court must, after providing an opportunity to be heard, require the movant, the attorney filing the motion, or both, to pay the party or deponent who opposed the motion her reasonable expenses incurred in opposing the motion, including attorney's fees. Rule 37(a)(5)(B).

3) If motion is granted in part and denied in part

If the motion is granted in part and denied in part, the court may apportion fees in its discretion, after providing an opportunity for the parties to be heard. Rule 37(a)(5)(C).

2. Sanctions

a. Failure to comply with a court order

If a party fails to obey a court order regarding discovery, the court may impose any of the following sanctions pursuant to Rule 37(b)(2):

i) Directing that the matters addressed in the order or other facts be taken as established for purposes of the action;

ii) Prohibiting the disobedient party from supporting or opposing designated claims or defenses, or from introducing designated matters in evidence;

iii) Striking pleadings in whole or in part;

iv) Staying further proceedings until the order is obeyed;

v) Dismissing the action in whole or in part;

vi) Rendering a default judgment against the disobedient party; and

vii) Treating as contempt of court the failure to obey any order, except an order to submit to a physical or mental examination.

Note that the mere failure to respond to discovery or disclosure obligations is not subject to sanctions under Rule 37; there must be a violation of a court order.

The list of sanctions in Rule 37(b)(2) is not exhaustive. The court may order any sanction that is "just." Instead of, or in addition to, such sanctions, the court may also require the disobedient party, his attorney, or both to pay the movant's reasonable expenses, including attorney's fees incurred as a result of the failure to comply, except when the failure was substantially justified or imposition of fees would be unjust. Rule 37(b)(2)(C).

b. Failure to make automatic disclosures

Under Rule 37(c)(1), if a party fails to make or supplement its automatic disclosures as required by Rules 26(a) and (e), the party will not be permitted to use the documents or witnesses that were not disclosed unless the non-disclosure was substantially justified or was harmless.

This rule applies to the use of such evidence at trial and for motions and hearings, but it does not apply to the use of such evidence for impeachment purposes, since Rule 26(a) does not require disclosure of impeachment evidence or witnesses.

c. Failure to admit under Rule 36

Pursuant to Rule 37(c)(2), when a party fails to admit a matter requested under Rule 36 and another party proves the matter to be true at trial, the party proving the matter can move for the award of reasonable expenses, including reasonable attorney's fees, incurred in proving the matter.

d. Failure of party to attend her own deposition, serve answers to interrogatories, or respond to a request for inspection

Under Rule 37(d)(1)(A)(i), if a party fails to appear at her own deposition after being properly noticed, the court may impose sanctions. A failure to appear will not be excused on the ground that the discovery sought was objectionable, unless the party failing to act has a pending motion for a protective order.

The court may also impose sanctions if a party fails to answer or object to properly served interrogatories under Rule 33 or fails to serve a written response to a properly served request for the production of documents or other things under Rule 34. Rule 37(d)(1)(A)(ii). A party moving for sanctions under such circumstances must certify that she conferred with or attempted to confer with the opposing party in good faith in an effort to obtain a response without court action. Rule 37(d)(1)(B).

e. Electronically stored information

Under Rule 37(e), absent exceptional circumstances, a court may not impose sanctions on a party for failing to provide electronically stored information lost as a result of the routine, good-faith operation of an electronic information system.

f. "Abuse of discretion" review standard

Sanctions are subject to review under the "abuse of discretion" standard. Generally, the harshest sanctions—dismissal of the action and entry of a default judgment—are reserved for misconduct that is serious, repeated, contumacious, extreme, or inexcusable. Usually, a court should impose lesser sanctions before meting out more severe ones. *See Bachier-Ortiz v. Colon-Mendoza*, 331 F.3d 193 (1st Cir. 2003).

Illinois Distinctions: Sanctions

Refusal to Answer or Comply: If a party or other deponent refuses to answer any question or comply with any discovery request, the proponent of the discovery may move the court to order compliance. Failure to timely comply or improperly denying the genuineness of a document can result in the offending party paying costs of delay, including reasonable attorney's fees.

Failure to Comply with Order or Rules: If a party unreasonably fails to comply with any provision of the discovery rules or orders, the court may impose sanctions. In addition to an order to pay other parties' reasonable expenses incurred as a result of misconduct, these sanctions could include:

i) That further proceedings be stayed until compliance with the order or rule;

ii) That the offending party be barred from filing any other pleading related to any issue to which the refusal or failure relates;

iii) That the offending party be barred from maintaining any particular claim, counterclaim, third-party complaint, or defense related to that issue;

iv) That a witness be barred from testifying concerning that issue;

v) That a judgment by default be entered against the offending party as to claims or defenses asserted in any pleading to which that issue is material, or that the party's action be dismissed with or without prejudice;

vi) That any portion of the offending party's pleadings related to that issue be stricken and, if thereby made appropriate, judgment be entered on the issue; or

vii) That in cases when a money judgment is entered against a party subject to sanctions, order the offending party to pay interest at the rate provided by law for any period of pretrial delay caused by the conduct.

Abuse of Discovery Procedures: The court may order that information obtained through abuse of discovery procedures be suppressed. In cases of willful attempt to obtain information improperly, the court may enter any order provided for in section (c) of Ill. Sup. Ct. Rule 219.

G.   PRE-TRIAL CONFERENCES

Under Rule 16(a), the court may direct counsel and unrepresented parties to appear for pre-trial conferences for such purposes as expediting disposition of the action, effective case management, and facilitating settlement. The court may require that a party or its representative be present or reasonably available by other means to consider possible settlement. If counsel or a party fails to appear, fails to participate in good faith, or fails to obey a pre-trial conference order, the court may generally impose the same sanctions as those permitted for failure of a party to comply with a discovery order, including contempt of court or dismissal of an action (*see* § VII.F.2. Sanctions, *supra*). Dismissal of an action is a severe sanction, and generally is appropriate only when a party's conduct is serious, repeated, extreme, and otherwise inexcusable.

H. ADJUDICATION WITHOUT TRIAL

1. Dismissal

Rule 41 sets forth the procedure for obtaining dismissal of a complaint, counterclaim, cross-claim, or third-party claim. Dismissal can be voluntary or involuntary under the rule.

a. Voluntary

1) By the plaintiff or by stipulation of the parties

Pursuant to Rule 41(a)(1)(A), a plaintiff may dismiss an action without leave of the court by filing a notice of dismissal at any time before the opposing party serves either an answer or a motion for summary judgment or by filing a stipulation of dismissal signed by all parties who have appeared in the action.

Unless otherwise stated in the notice or stipulation, the voluntary dismissal will be without prejudice. If, however, a plaintiff had dismissed a prior action based on the same claim, the dismissal is to be with prejudice. Rule 41(a)(1)(B).

2) By court order

Except as provided above, an action may be dismissed at the plaintiff's request only by court order, on terms that the court considers proper. Any voluntary dismissal by court order is without prejudice, unless the order states otherwise. Rule 41(a)(2).

3) Counterclaim, cross-claim, or third-party claim

A voluntary dismissal of a counterclaim, cross-claim, or third-party claim must be made before a responsive pleading is served, or, if there is no responsive pleading, before evidence is introduced at a hearing or trial.

A party may refile a cause of action that was voluntarily dismissed within one year of the dismissal or the running of the statute of limitations, whichever is longer.

b. Involuntary

Under Rule 41(b), if the plaintiff fails to prosecute or to comply with the Rules or a court order, a defendant may move to dismiss the action or any claim against him.

Unless the court's dismissal order specifies otherwise, a dismissal under Rule 41(b) is with prejudice and operates as an adjudication on the merits. A dismissal based on a lack of jurisdiction, improper venue, or failure to join an indispensable party under Rule 19, however, will not operate as an adjudication on the merits.

Illinois Distinction: Involuntary Dismissal

Unless the order or dismissal or another Illinois statute otherwise specifies, an involuntary dismissal of an action other than for lack of jurisdiction, improper venue, or failure to join an indispensible party, operates as an adjudication on the merits. Ill. Sup. Ct. R. 273.

2. Default and Default Judgment

a. Standard

When a party has failed to plead or otherwise defend an action, and that failure is shown by affidavit or otherwise, the clerk must enter the party's default. Rule 55(a). Once a default is entered against a party, the plaintiff may seek a default judgment, which must be entered before the plaintiff can collect the amount sought in the underlying action. Rule 55(b). Defaults and default judgments, however, are considered drastic remedies, and are strongly disfavored by the courts. *See, e.g., Hughes v. Holland,* 320 F.2d 781 (D.C. Cir. 1963).

b. Appeal

Under Rule 55(c), an entry of default or default judgment may be set aside for good cause. Courts have interpreted this standard broadly. The three factors the courts generally consider are: (i) whether the movant's failure to act (in the underlying action) was willful, (ii) whether setting the default aside would prejudice the non-moving party, and (iii) whether the movant has presented a meritorious claim. *See Lacy v. Sitel Corp.,* 227 F.3d 290, 292 (5th Cir. 2000), *Berthelsen v. Kane,* 907 F.2d 617, 620 (6th Cir. 1990).

Illinois Distinction: Default Judgment

A default judgment may be entered for want of an appearance, or for failure to plead, but the court may in either case require proof of the allegations of the pleadings upon which relief is sought. Upon entry of default judgment, the attorney for the party moving for default judgment should immediately give notice to each party who has appeared, and to the party against whom default was entered or his attorney of record. Failure to do so does not impair the entry of judgment. Upon motion filed within 30 days of the entry of judgment or final default judgment, the court may set aside any order or judgment upon reasonable terms and conditions.

3. Summary Judgment

a. Standard

Under Rule 56, a motion for summary judgment is applicable to all civil actions and should be granted if the pleadings, the discovery and disclosure materials on file, and any affidavits show that there is no genuine issue as to any material fact and that the movant is entitled to judgment as a matter of law. A genuine issue of material fact exists when a reasonable jury could return a verdict in favor of the non-moving party. *Anderson v. Liberty Lobby, Inc.*, 477 U.S. 242 (1986). In ruling on a motion for summary judgment, the court is to construe all evidence in the light most favorable to the non-moving party and resolve all doubts in favor of the non-moving party.

Illinois Distinction: Summary Judgment

Much like in federal court, a motion for summary judgment is granted if the pleadings, depositions, and admissions on file, in addition to any affidavits, show that there is no genuine issue as to any material fact and that the moving party is entitled to a judgment as a matter of law.

---

b. Burden of proof

The movant has the burden of persuasion on a motion for summary judgment. Once the movant makes a prima facie showing that summary judgment is appropriate, the burden of proof shifts to the opposing party to set forth specific evidence showing the existence of a genuine issue of fact for trial. *Celotex Corp. v. Catrett*, 477 U.S. 317 (1986). "When opposing parties tell two different stories, one of which is blatantly contradicted by the record, so that no reasonable jury could believe it, a court should not adopt that version of the facts for purposes of ruling on a motion for summary judgment." *Scott v. Harris*, 550 U.S. 372, 380 (2007).

c. Evidence

In deciding a motion for summary judgment, the court must consider the materials cited by the parties—affidavits, documents, electronically stored information, pleadings, deposition transcripts, interrogatory answers, admissions, and stipulations filed by the party, even if not presented in a form that is admissible at trial, so long as the facts contained in the submissions are admissible at trial. *Stinnett v. Iron Works Gym/Executive Health Spa, Inc.*, 301 F.3d 610, 613 (7th Cir. 2002). However, the court is not limited to these materials—it may also consider other materials in the record. Supporting and opposing affidavits must be made on personal knowledge, must set out facts that would be admissible in evidence, and must establish the affiant's competency to testify on the matters stated.

If a motion for summary judgment is properly made and supported, an opposing party may not rely merely on allegations or denials in her own pleading, but she must set out specific facts showing a genuine issue for trial. If the opposing party does not so respond, summary judgment, if appropriate, will be entered against that party. Rule 56(e).

d. Partial summary judgment

Pursuant to Rule 56(g), if the court does not grant all the relief requested by the motion, it may enter an order stating any material fact—including an item of damages or other relief—that is not genuinely in dispute and treating the fact as established in the case.

e. Time for making motion

Unless a different time is set by local rule, under Rule 56(b) a party may file a motion for summary judgment at any time until 30 days after the close of all discovery.

f. Appeal

In general, an order denying summary judgment is not subject to immediate appeal. A grant of full summary judgment is a final disposition on the merits and is subject to appeal.

However, if a party fails to properly support an assertion of fact or fails to properly address another party's assertion of fact as required by Rule 56(c), the court may (i) give an opportunity to properly support or address the fact, (ii) consider the fact undisputed for the purposes of the motion, (iii) grant summary judgment if the motion and supporting materials show that the movant is entitled to it, or (iv) issue any other appropriate order. Rule 56(e).

4. Declaratory Judgment

A declaratory judgment is a ruling in which the court tells the parties to a dispute what their rights, responsibilities, or obligations are, without awarding damages or ordering the parties to do (or refrain from doing) anything. Parties generally seek a declaratory judgment in order to resolve uncertainty and avoid the possibility of a future lawsuit. Under the federal Declaratory Judgment Act, 28 U.S.C. § 2201, a federal court may award declaratory relief in actions within the court's original jurisdiction, with the exception of certain actions concerning taxes, bankruptcy, free trade, or drug patents. Most states have enacted statutes permitting their courts to issue declaratory judgments.

Illinois Distinction: Declaratory Judgment

A plaintiff may request, in his prayer for relief, a binding declaration of rights, having the force of a final judgment, either with or without consequential relief. This could include the construction of any statute, municipal ordinance, or other governmental regulation; or of any deed, will, contract, or other written instrument; or a declaration of the rights of the interested parties.

A court will not enter a declaratory judgment if it appears that the judgment will not terminate all or part of the controversy giving rise to the proceedings. Nor will the court enter a declaratory judgment against a state officer whose election is provided for in the constitution involving a "political question."

A declaration of rights may be obtained by a pleading seeking only that, or in a complaint, counterclaim, or other pleading seeking other additional relief.

If a declaratory judgment action involves the determination of issues of fact triable by a jury, they shall be tried and determined in the same manner as issues of fact are tried and determined in other civil trials.

VIII. TRIAL PROCEDURE

A. JURY TRIAL

1. Right to Jury Trial

Rule 38 provides that the right of trial by jury as declared by the Seventh Amendment to the U.S. Constitution, or as provided by a federal statute, is preserved to the parties inviolate. In general, an action at law will be tried on demand to a jury, but an action in equity (e.g., an action for injunction) will not. If a new cause of action that was unknown at common law is created, the court must look to the remedy sought and will generally allow a jury if the relief sought is legal rather than equitable.

The right to trial by jury is evaluated for each claim. If an action involves both legal and equitable claims, the jury normally determines the legal claims first, and the court then determines the equitable claims, but the court is bound by the jury's findings on the legal claims. *Beacon Theatres, Inc. v. Westover*, 359 U.S. 500 (1959).

With regard to state law claims in diversity actions, federal law will determine whether there is a right to a jury trial. However, federal courts will apply state law when taking into account a motion for a new trial based on excessiveness of the verdict. Federal law will usually govern whether an issue is legal or equitable. *Simler v. Conner*, 372 U.S. 221 (1963). *See* § IV.A.3.c. Equitable versus legal, *supra*.

Illinois Distinction: Right to Jury Trial

The right to a trial in civil cases in Illinois is specified in the constitution, Ill. Const. Art. I. § 13, and conferred by statutes. A constitutional right to a jury in Illinois is determined by the type of relief sought, whether legal or equitable. A court has discretion to direct issues to be tried by a jury in an action seeking equitable relief as opposed to legal (monetary) relief in which the party has the right to a jury trial.

When matters are treated as a single equitable cause of action, they should be heard and determined by courts of equity. When legal and equitable matters that may be asserted separately are properly joined, the court will determine if matters are severable and, if so, whether they should be tried together or separately and in what order.

If the court determines the matters are severable, the issues formed on the law counts shall be tried before a jury when a jury has been properly demanded, or by the court when a jury has not been properly demanded. The equitable issues shall be heard and determined by courts of equity.

---

2. Jury Demand and Waiver

Under Rule 38(b), any party may make a demand for trial by jury. The demand must be in writing and may be made in a pleading. It must be served within 14 days after service of the last pleading directed to the issue that is sought to be tried by a jury. A party waives a jury trial unless her demand is properly served and filed.

Illinois Distinction: Jury Demand and Waiver

If a party fails to timely file a demand for trial by jury, he will be deemed to have waived his right to a jury trial. A plaintiff must demand a jury trial when the action is commenced. A defendant seeking a jury trial must file a demand not later than the filing of her answer.

If a court enters an order stating that a party in an action seeking equitable relief is entitled to a trial by jury, the plaintiff has three days from the entry of such an order to file a jury demand, and the defendant has six days.

If a plaintiff files for jury demand and thereafter waives the jury, any defendant may file a jury demand. Similarly, if a defendant waives the jury, a co-defendant may file a jury demand.

---

3. Jury Size

Under Rule 48, a jury must initially have at least six and no more than 12 members. Each juror must participate in the verdict unless excused for good cause under Rule 47(c).

Illinois Distinction: Jury Size

All cases in which the claim for damages is $50,000 or less shall be tried by a jury of six, unless either party demands a jury of 12. Further, the court has the discretion to impanel alternate jurors.

---

4. Jury Deliberations and Verdicts

a. Deliberations

One of the duties of a juror is to listen to the evidence presented in court and weigh that evidence fairly when reaching a verdict. Jurors may take their notes and all papers or exhibits presented during the trial into the deliberation room.

Jurors cannot consider other matters not formally admitted into evidence, nor are they permitted to discuss the facts of the case with any non-jurors.

b. Verdicts

A verdict is formal decision issued by a jury on the issues of fact that were presented at trial. The trial court will instruct the jury to use one of three types of verdicts. Unless the parties stipulate otherwise, the verdict must be unanimous and must be returned by a jury of at least six members. Rule 48(b).

1) Special

A special verdict is a form of a special written finding on each issue of fact. In a special verdict, the facts of the case are put on the record, and the law is submitted to the judges. Thus, a court will submit written questions to the jury correlating to each ultimate fact of the case and ask the jury to make a finding on each fact. Rule 49(a).

2) General

A general verdict is the one we are most accustomed to knowing. It is the usual form of verdict when a jury's decision in a civil case is in favor of one or the other party.

3) General with special interrogatories

This type of verdict is an ordinary general verdict coupled with special findings of fact, similar to a special verdict. This type of verdict is used to ensure that the jury independently considered the material facts of the case.

4) Verdicts in error

When a party believes that the jury has returned an erroneous verdict that can be corrected, he must raise this issue with the court. The court will ask the jury to re-deliberate. The verdict may be set aside if the court believes that the jury did not follow its instructions properly.

Illinois Distinction: Verdicts

Unless the nature of the case requires otherwise, a jury renders a general verdict, which is read in open court and entered immediately.

If there are several counts in a complaint, counterclaim, or third-party complaint based on different claims for separate recovery, the jury must—upon request—find a separate verdict on each demand. If several grounds of recovery are pleaded in support of the same claim, an entire verdict rendered for that claim shall not be set aside or reversed if any ground is defective, unless before submitted to the jury, a motion was made to withdraw that ground from the jury on account of insufficient evidence and it appears that denial of the motion was prejudicial.

Special Interrogatories: The jury may be required by the court, and must be required at the request of any party, to find specially upon any material questions of fact submitted to the jury in writing. Submitting or refusing to submit a question of fact to the jury may be reviewable on appeal. When a special finding of fact is inconsistent with the general verdict, the special finding controls the general verdict, and the court may enter judgment accordingly.

---

5. Polling

The jury must be polled on a party's request, and any lack of unanimity or assent will result in continued deliberations or a new trial. Rule 48(c).

6. Selection

Under Rule 47(a), the court may permit the parties or their attorneys to examine prospective jurors or may do so itself. If the court examines the jurors, it must permit the parties or their attorneys to make any further inquiry it considers proper, or must itself ask any of their additional questions that it considers proper.

a. Peremptory challenges

Peremptory challenges may not be made for racial- or gender-based reasons. *Edmonson v. Leesville Concrete Co.*, 500 U.S. 614 (1991); *J.E.B. v. Alabama*, 511 U.S. 127 (1994). Rule 47(b) requires the court to allow the number of peremptory challenges provided by 28 U.S.C. § 1870, which is three for each party in civil cases. Several defendants or several plaintiffs may be considered as a single party for the purposes of making such challenges, or the court may allow additional peremptory challenges and permit them to be exercised separately or jointly.

b. Challenges for cause

Each party is entitled to an unlimited number of challenges for cause, such as bias or a personal relationship with a litigant. The court rules on such challenges. 28 U.S.C. § 1870.

Illinois Distinction: Selection

Voir Dire: The court must conduct the *voir dire* examination of prospective jurors as to their qualifications. In its discretion, the court may permit the parties to submit additional questions for further inquiry, including by direct inquiry.

Challenges for Cause: Each party may challenge jurors for cause, and each party has an unlimited number of challenges for cause. If a prospective juror has a physical impairment, the court shall consider that prospective juror's ability to perceive and appreciate the evidence when considering a challenge for cause.

Peremptory Challenges: Each side has five peremptory challenges. If there is more than one party on either side, the court may allow each side additional peremptory challenges, not to exceed three per additional party on the side having the greatest number of parties as long as each side is entitled to the same number of peremptory challenges. If the parties on a side are unable to agree on an allocation of challenges among themselves, the court must allocate the challenges.

Alternate Jurors: If the court directs the impaneling of alternate jurors, each side is entitled to one additional peremptory challenge, regardless of the number of alternates, to be used only against alternate jurors. Unused original peremptory challenges may also be used against prospective alternates.

---

7. Jury Instructions

Under Rule 51, at the close of evidence or at such earlier time as directed by the court, parties may file and serve proposed instructions for the court to give the jury. The court is required to inform the parties of any instructions it proposes to give and of its actions with respect to the parties' requested jury instructions prior to the parties' closing arguments to the jury. The parties are then entitled to an opportunity to object on the record and out of the jury's presence before the instructions and arguments are delivered. The court may instruct the jury on the applicable law in the case either before or after closing arguments.

Illinois Distinctions: Jury Instructions

Submission of Instructions: The court must give the jury written instructions, unless the parties agree on oral instructions. These instructions must be limited to the applicable law. After the instructions are given, they may be modified, clarified, or explained only in writing, unless otherwise agreed by the parties.

At the close of evidence or earlier at the direction of the court, any party may tender instructions. They must be reasonable in number or length, or they will be modified. Instructions asked by any party must be tendered to the court, numbered, and labeled. Copies of the instructions given on the court's own motion or modified by the court shall be so identified. The court may also, before or during trial, direct counsel to prepare designated instructions to be marked by counsel as "Court's Instruction."

If the court refuses to give requested instructions, the court must write "refused" on the margin of the original and copy and write "given" on the original and copy of those given. The court must hold a conference with counsel to settle the instructions and inform counsel of the court's proposed action prior to argument to the jury. The court may approve further instructions, if necessary.

Objections to Instructions: Counsel may object at the conference to any instruction prepared at the court's discretion, regardless of who prepared it, and the court must rule on these objections as well as objections to other instructions. On appeal, no party may raise the failure to give a jury instruction unless the party tendered the objection before the conference.

Giving Jury Instructions and Other Papers: The jury instructions and any modifications, and explanations must be in writing, unless otherwise agreed to by the parties. The written instructions are given by the court to the jury to take into the jury room, and should be returned by the jury with the verdict. Papers received in evidence, other than evidence depositions, are also taken into the jury room.

Illinois Pattern Jury Instructions: Applicable Illinois Pattern Jury Instructions must be used unless, after consideration of the facts and the prevailing law, the court determines that the pattern jury instruction does not accurately state the law. Any instructions given should be brief, simple, impartial, and free from argument.

Other Jury Instructions: Before opening statements, the court may orally instruct the jury on cautionary or preliminary matters, such as the burden of proof, the believability of witnesses, and the receipt of evidence for a particular purpose, or on the substantive law applicable to the case, such as elements of a claim or affirmative defense. The court may also give any appropriate instruction to the jury during the course of the trial, in its discretion.

---

8. Jury Misconduct

Misconduct occurs when a juror conceals facts relating to his qualifications or gives false testimony during voir dire. If the juror violates the confidentiality of deliberations, is improperly influenced by non-jurors, or takes it upon himself to investigate facts outside of those presented at trial, a new trial will be ordered.

B. TRIAL BY THE COURT

A case will be tried by the court without a jury if no right to a jury trial exists (or if it has been waived). The court is the finder of fact; it must find the facts specially and state its conclusions of law separately. The court may also consolidate common actions or separate different claims when called for.

On appeal, a court's finding of facts will be set aside only if clearly erroneous, and the reviewing court must give due regard to the trial court's opportunity to judge the witnesses' credibility.

Illinois Distinction: Trial by the Court

In all cases tried without a jury, at the close of a plaintiff's case, a defendant may move for a finding or judgment in his favor. In ruling on the motion, the court weighs the evidence, considering the credibility of witnesses and the weight and quality of the evidence. If the ruling on the motion is favorable to the defendant, the court shall enter a judgment dismissing the action. If not, the defendant may proceed to present his case. If the motion is granted and later the order granting the motion is reversed on appeal, the case is remanded with directions to proceed as if the motion had been denied by the trial court or waived.

Post-trial motions in nonjury cases shall be filed within 30 days of entry of judgment. Failure to file or the filing of a post-judgment motion does not limit the scope of review.

C. PREJUDGMENT ATTACHMENT

At the commencement and through the course of an action, a plaintiff may file a motion for prejudgment attachment as allowed by the state where the court is located. A prejudgment attachment provides for seizing a person or property to secure satisfaction of a potential judgment. Federal statute governs the extent to which the state statute may be applied, and remedies include arrest, attachment, garnishment, replevin, sequestration, and other equivalent remedies.

In addition to filing the motion, the plaintiff must also give the defendant notice and an opportunity to be heard by preparing a writ of attachment in addition to a summons and complaint. A court will only grant a prejudgment attachment if the plaintiff shows that there is a likelihood of success of recovering an amount equal to the amount being sought to attach. Rule 64.

D. JUDGMENT AS A MATTER OF LAW (DIRECTED VERDICT)

Under Rule 50(a), once a party has been fully heard on an issue at a jury trial, the court may grant a motion for judgment as a matter of law resolving the issue against a party if the court finds that there is insufficient evidence for a jury reasonably to find for that party. The court may also grant such a motion against the party on any claim or defense that is dependent on a favorable finding on that issue.

1. Standard

The court must view the evidence in the light most favorable to the opposing party and draw all reasonable inferences from the evidence in favor of the opposing party. It may not consider the credibility of witnesses or evaluate the weight of the evidence, and it must disregard all evidence favorable to the moving party that the jury is not required to believe. *Reeves v. Sanderson Plumbing Prods., Inc.*, 530 U.S. 133 (2000). If reasonable persons can draw different inferences, then the issue is for the jury to decide, and the motion cannot be granted.

2. Procedure and Timing

A motion for judgment as a matter of law may be made at any time before the case is submitted to the jury. The motion must specify the judgment sought and the law and facts that entitle the movant to the judgment. If a party moves for a directed verdict after the close of the plaintiff's case and the motion is denied, the party may be unable to pursue a renewed motion for judgment as a matter of law after entry of judgment unless the party also moves for a directed verdict after the presentation of all evidence. There is a dispute among the circuit courts as to whether the second motion is always mandatory or is unnecessary when the defendant's evidence could not have caused the court to grant the motion. *Compare Mid-America Tablewares, Inc. v. Mogi Trading Co.*, 100 F.3d 1353 (7th Cir. 1996) (second motion required) *with BE & K Constr. Co. v. United Bhd. of Carpenters & Joiners*, 90 F.3d 1318 (8th Cir. 1996) (second motion not required).

Illinois Distinction: Judgment as a Matter of Law (Directed Verdict)

At the close of evidence and before the case is submitted to the jury any party may move for a directed verdict and the court may grant the motion, deny the motion, or reserve its ruling and submit the case to the jury. If the court grants the motion, it is effective without assent of the jury. If the court denies the motion or reserves its ruling, the motion is waived unless the request is renewed in the post-trial motion. However, a motion for directed verdict may be made as part of the post-trial motion in the form of a motion for judgment not withstanding an adverse jury verdict, even if not made before the verdict.

Standard for Directed Verdict or Judgment Not Withstanding the Verdict: Under Illinois law, a directed verdict or JNOV is appropriate when "all of the evidence, when viewed in its aspect most favorable to the opponent [to the directed verdict or JNOV motion], so overwhelmingly favors the movant that no contrary verdict based on that evidence could ever stand." *Pedrick v. Peoria & E. R.R. Co.*, 229 N.E.2d 504 (Ill. 1967). Note that this standard "does not require a complete absence of evidence supporting the side against whom the verdict is directed; however there must be a substantial factual dispute before a jury trial is required." *Cincinnati Ins. Co. v. City of Taylorville*, 818 F.2d 1345 (7th Cir. 1987).

E. RENEWED MOTION FOR JUDGMENT AS A MATTER OF LAW ("JNOV")

Under Rule 50(b), if the court does not grant a motion for judgment as a matter of law, the court is considered to have submitted the action to the jury subject to the court's later deciding the legal questions raised by the motion. The movant may file a renewed motion for judgment as a matter of law no later than 28 days after the entry of judgment. If the motion addresses a jury issue not decided by a verdict, the renewed motion must be filed no later than 28 days after the jury was discharged.

In ruling on the renewed motion, the court may (i) allow judgment on the verdict if the jury returned a verdict, (ii) order a new trial, or (iii) or direct the entry of judgment as a matter of law. The same standards apply to the entry of the renewed motion as applied to the initial motion.

Under Rule 50(c), if the renewed motion for judgment as a matter of law is granted and the party had alternatively moved for a new trial, the court must also determine whether the motion for a new trial should be granted if the judgment is reversed or vacated on appeal.

F. MOTION FOR A NEW TRIAL

1. Grounds

Under Rule 59(a), the court may, on motion, grant a new trial on all issues or with respect only to certain issues or parties. Rule 59 does not specifically list the grounds that will justify a new trial, but it does state that for actions that have been tried to a jury, a new trial may be granted for any of the reasons for which new trials have traditionally been granted in actions at law in federal courts. In non-jury trial actions, the court may grant a new trial for any of the reasons for which re-hearings have traditionally been granted in suits in equity in federal courts. Some of the reasons that have been held to justify a new trial include:

i) Error at trial that renders the judgment unfair;

ii) Newly discovered evidence that existed at the time of trial was excusably overlooked and would likely have altered the outcome of the trial;

iii) Prejudicial misconduct of counsel, a party, the judge, or a juror;

iv) The verdict is against the clear weight of the evidence;

v) The verdict is based on false evidence such that a new trial is necessary to prevent injustice; or

vi) The verdict is excessive or inadequate.

In general, whether a new trial is warranted rests within the sound discretion of the trial court. *Montgomery Ward & Co. v. Duncan,* 311 U.S. 243 (1940). Under Rule 61, the court must disregard all errors and defects that do not affect any party's substantial rights. This is the "harmless error" rule.

After giving the parties notice and an opportunity to be heard, the court may grant a timely motion for a new trial for a reason not stated in a party's motion. The court must specify the reasons in its order.

A court will not grant a new trial on the ground that a verdict is against the clear weight of the evidence unless the record shows that a jury's verdict resulted in a miscarriage of justice. *See Tennant v. Peoria & Pekin Union Ry. Co.,* 321 U.S. 29 (1944).

Illinois Distinction: Motion for JNOV; Motion for a New Trial; Single Post-Trial Motion

Any relief desired after trial in jury cases, sought by reserved motions for directed verdict or motions for judgment notwithstanding the verdict ("JNOV"), in arrest of judgment, or for a new trial must be brought in a single, written, post-trial motion. A party may not urge as error on review of the ruling on the party's post-trial motion any point not specified in the motion.

Relief sought in post-trial motions may be in the alternative or may be conditioned upon the denial of other relief asked. Any party who fails to seek a new trial in his post-trial motion waives the right to apply for a new trial, except in cases in which the jury has failed to reach a verdict.

The court must rule upon all relief sought in all post-trial motions. Although the ruling on a portion of the relief sought renders unnecessary a ruling on the other relief sought, the court may rule conditionally on the other relief sought by determining whether it should be granted if the unconditional rulings are thereafter reversed, set aside, or vacated. The reviewing court, if it determines to reverse an unconditional ruling of the trial court on a post-trial motion, may review and determine any conditional rulings made by the trial court on other questions raised by the motion. No cross-appeal is required.

2. **Remittitur**

If the court determines that a verdict was excessive, the court may offer a reduction of the verdict, known as a remittitur, and grant a new trial on the condition that the remittitur is not accepted. *See Hetzel v. Prince William County.,* 523 U.S. 208 (1998). If the court determines that the verdict was inadequate, the court only has the option of ordering a new trial. An additur (enhanced judgment) is not permitted.

Consenting to a remittitur as a condition to the denial of a new trial does not preclude the consenting party from asserting on appeal that the amount of the verdict was proper. A cross-appeal is not required.

It does not appear that Illinois courts allow additur.

3. Timing

Pursuant to Rule 59(b), a motion for a new trial must be filed no later than 28 days after the entry of judgment.

When the motion is based on affidavits, those affidavits must be filed with the motion. The opposing party then has 14 days after being served to file opposing affidavits. The court may permit reply affidavits. Rule 59(c).

Illinois Distinction: Timing

Post-trial motions must be filed within 30 days after the entry of judgment or the discharge of the jury, if no verdict is reached, or within any further time the court may allow within the 30 days or any extensions thereof. A party against whom judgment is entered pursuant to a post-trial motion shall have like time after the entry of the judgment to file a post-trial motion.

4. Order by the Court on Its Own Initiative

Pursuant to Rule 59(d), no later than 28 days after the entry of judgment, the court, on its own, may order a new trial for any reason that would justify granting one on the motion of a party. The court must specify the reasons in its order.

IX. POST-TRIAL PROCEDURE

A. ALTERATION OF OR RELIEF FROM JUDGMENT

1. Rule 60(a): Correction of a Judgment

Rule 60(a) allows a court to correct a clerical or other mistake resulting from oversight or omission whenever one is found in a judgment, order, or other part of the record. Fed. R. Civ. P. 60(a). An example of such a mistake would be when a court meant to enter a judgment for the plaintiff for $100,000, and it appeared in the written judgment as "$10,000." The court may make such a correction on its own initiative, with or without notice. However, once an appeal from the judgment or order has been docketed in the appellate court, such a correction can only be made with leave of the appellate court. *Id.*

2. Rule 60(b): Relief from a Judgment or Order

Rule 60(b) allows a court to relieve a party from a final judgment:

i) Within a reasonable time, and **no later than one year following the entry of the judgment** for mistake, inadvertence, surprise, excusable neglect, newly discovered evidence that could not have been earlier discovered with reasonable diligence, fraud (intrinsic or extrinsic), misrepresentation, or misconduct by an opposing party;

ii) Within a reasonable time, with no definite limiting period, on the grounds that: a judgment is void; a judgment has been satisfied, released, or discharged; a judgment was based on a judgment that was reversed or vacated; applying the judgment prospectively is no longer equitable; or for any other reason that justifies relief.

In sum, Rule 60(b) allows a court to exercise its equitable jurisdiction to relieve a party from a judgment in any case in which enforcing the judgment would work injustice, and the party seeking relief or its counsel was not guilty of misconduct or gross negligence. If a motion for relief is made, but the court lacks the authority to rule because of the pendency of an appeal, the court may (i) defer, (ii) deny the motion, or (iii) state that it would grant the motion upon remand. Rule 62.1.

The court may provide any relief that it believes to be appropriate based on the evidence, and it is not harnessed by the relief requested on the pleadings.

B. APPEALS

1. Final Judgment Rule

Under 28 U.S.C. § 1291, the federal courts of appeals have jurisdiction over appeals from the final judgments of the district courts. A final judgment is a decision by the court on the merits that leaves nothing for the court to do but execute the judgment. *Catlin v. United States*, 324 U.S. 229, 223 (1945). Judicial economy alone is insufficient grounds to expand a court's jurisdiction to include non-final judgments. Parties must demonstrate that review of the non-final judgment together with the appealable order will assist the court in reviewing the appealable order. *Swint v Chambers County Comm'n.*, 514 U.S. 35 (1995).

Pursuant to Rule 54(b), if more than one claim is presented in a case, or if there are multiple parties, the district court may direct entry of a final judgment as to one or more issues or parties, but only if the court "expressly determines that there is no just reason for delay." This modifies the rule's default position that any order or other decision, however designated, that adjudicates fewer than all of the claims or the rights and liabilities of fewer than all of the parties will not end the action as to any of the claims or parties, and may be revised at any time before the entry of a judgment adjudicating all of the claims and all of the parties' rights and liabilities.

Under the Federal Rules of Appellate Procedure, the notice of appeal required in a civil case must be filed with the district clerk within 30 days after the judgment or order appealed from is entered.

> **Illinois Distinction: Final Judgment Rule**
>
> A final judgment is the court's order on the merits of the case. More than one final judgment can be entered in an action with more than one party or claim. Generally, only final judgments can be appealed, and as a matter of right, final judgments in circuit court civil actions may be appealed. However, there are now many exceptions to the Illinois final judgment rule.

2. Appeal of Interlocutory Orders

While most interlocutory orders, such as the denial of a summary judgment motion or a motion to dismiss, are not immediately appealable, 28 U.S.C. § 1292(a) makes certain equitable orders reviewable immediately as a matter of right, including:

i) An order granting, modifying, refusing, or dissolving an injunction;

ii) An order appointing or refusing to appoint a receiver; and

iii) A decree determining the rights and liabilities of the parties to admiralty cases in which appeals from final decrees are allowed.

In addition, under 28 U.S.C. § 1292(b), if a district court certifies that an order involves a controlling question of law as to which there is substantial ground for difference of opinion and that an immediate appeal from the order may materially advance the ultimate termination of the litigation, a court of appeals has discretion to permit an appeal to be taken from such order if application is made to it within ten days after the entry of the order.

Illinois Distinction: Appeal or Interlocutory Orders

As of Right: Within 30 days of entry of an interlocutory order, a party may appeal such order:

i)   Granting, modifying, refusing, dissolving, or refusing to dissolve or modify an injunction;

ii) Appointing or refusing to appoint a receiver or sequestrator;

iii) Giving or refusing to give other or further powers or property to a receiver or sequestrator already appointed;

iv) Placing or refusing to place a mortgagee in possession of mortgaged premises;

v)   Appointing or refusing to appoint a receiver, liquidator, rehabilitator, or other similar officer for a bank, savings and loan association, currency exchange, insurance company, or other financial institution, or granting or refusing to grant custody of the institution or requiring turnover of any of its assets;

vi) Terminating parental rights or granting, denying, or revoking temporary commitment in adoption cases; or

vii) Determining issues raised in proceedings pursuant to the Eminent Domain Act.

With Permission: An immediate appeal may be sought from an interlocutory order not otherwise appealable if the trial court finds that the order involves a question of law as to which there is substantial ground for a difference of opinion *and* that an immediate appeal from the order may materially advance the ultimate termination of the litigation. Leave to appeal should be filed with the Appellate Court within 14 days after the entry of the order in the trial court.

---

3. Collateral Order Rule

Under the so-called **collateral order rule**, a court of appeals has discretion to hear and rule on an issue if it is distinct from the merits of the case, involves a serious and unsettled legal question, and would be effectively unreviewable if the court waited until final judgment to hear the claim or issue. *See, e.g., Mohawk Indus., Inc. v. Carpenter*, 558 U.S. ___, 130 S. Ct. 599 (2009) (holding that a disclosure order whose enforcement would allegedly violate attorney-client privilege did not qualify for review under the collateral order rule).

4. Mandamus Review

Under mandamus review, a court of appeals can immediately review an order that is an abuse of judicial authority, such as an order beyond the trial court's jurisdiction or an order that violates a mandatory duty of the trial court, but such review does not extend to all orders that constitute an error of law. *See Kerr v. U.S. Dist. Court*, 426 U.S. 394 (1976).

The following judgments and orders are appealable without a court's special finding that that there is no just reason for delaying enforcement, appeal, or both. These are:

i)   A judgment or order entered in the administration of an estate, guardianship, or similar proceeding which finally determines a right or status of a party;

ii) Most judgments or orders entered in the administration of a receivership, rehabilitation, liquidation, or other similar proceeding which finally determine a right or status of a party;

iii) A judgment or order granting or denying any of the relief prayed in a petition under § 2-1401 of the Code of Civil Procedure (a final judgment or decree);

iv) A final judgment or order entered in a proceeding under § 2-1402 of the Code of Civil Procedure (collecting from judgment debtors); and

v)   An order finding a person or entity in contempt of court which imposes a monetary or other penalty.

A notice of appeal must be filed within 30 days after the entry of final judgment appealed from, or if a post-trial motion is filed disposing of the entire case, within 30 days of the entry of the order disposing of the motion.

A party may also petition for leave to appeal to the Appellate Court from the following orders of the trial court:

i)   From an order of the circuit court granting a new trial;

ii) From an order of the circuit court allowing or denying a motion to dismiss on the grounds of *forum non conveniens*, or from an order of the circuit court allowing or denying a motion to transfer a case to another county within Illinois on such grounds;

iii) From an order of the circuit court denying a motion to dismiss on the grounds that the defendant has done nothing which would subject defendant to the jurisdiction of the Illinois courts;

iv) From an order of the circuit court granting or denying a motion for a transfer of venue based on the assertion that the defendant is not a resident of the county in which the action was commenced, and no other legitimate basis for venue in that county has been offered by the plaintiff;

v)   From interlocutory orders affecting the care and custody of unemancipated minors, if the appeal of such orders is not otherwise specifically provided for elsewhere in the Illinois Supreme Court Rules;

vi) From an order of the circuit court which remands the proceeding for a hearing *de novo* before an administrative agency;

vii) From an order of the circuit court granting a motion to disqualify the attorney for any party; or

viii) From an order of the circuit court granting or denying class certification.

These petitions must be filed within 30 days after the issuance of the order that is in question, and the non-petitioning party may file an answer within 21 days thereafter.

5. Class Action Certification

Under Rule 23(f), a court of appeals may permit an appeal from an order granting or denying class action certification if a petition for permission to appeal is filed with the circuit clerk within 14 days after the order is entered. The court of appeals has discretion to deny the appeal. If an appeal is permitted, it will not stay proceedings in the district court unless the district court or the court of appeals so orders.

6. Standards for Reversal

a. Review of a district court's factual findings

Under Rule 52(a), a district court's findings of fact may not be set aside unless "clearly erroneous," and "due regard shall be given to the opportunity of the trial court to judge of the credibility of the witnesses." A finding is clearly erroneous when, although there is evidence to support it, the court of appeals, based on the entirety of the evidence, is left with the definite and firm conviction that a mistake has been committed. *United States v. U.S. Gypsum Co.*, 333 U.S. 364 (1948).

b. Review of legal rulings

In general, appellate review of legal rulings is de novo. The appeals court will use the trial court's record, but reviews the evidence and law without deference to the trial court's rulings. Thus, the appellate court may reach its own independent conclusions on an issue.

c. Review of factual findings by a jury

A factual finding by the jury that is reasonable and supported by sufficient evidence must be affirmed even if it is against the weight of the evidence. *Lavender v. Kurn*, 327 U.S. 645 (1946). A district court, however, has discretion to grant a motion for a new trial if it believes that the verdict is against the weight of the evidence.

C. FULL FAITH AND CREDIT

1. State to State

Article IV, Section 1 of the Constitution provides that "Full Faith and Credit shall be given in each State to the public Acts, Records, and judicial Proceedings of every other State." The clause is invoked primarily to enforce the judgment of one state court in another state.

If a valid judgment is rendered by a court that has jurisdiction over the parties, and the parties receive proper notice of the action and a reasonable opportunity to be heard, the Full Faith and Credit Clause requires that the judgment receive the same effect in other states as in the state where it was rendered. Thus, a party who obtains a judgment in one state may petition the court in another state to enforce the judgment. In general, the issues are not re-litigated, and the court in the state in which enforcement is sought must honor the judgment of the other state's court.

The same principle applies to challenges based on an alleged lack of personal or subject matter jurisdiction; a party against whom enforcement is sought may collaterally challenge the original state judgment based on lack of personal jurisdiction or subject matter jurisdiction **only** if the jurisdictional issues were not litigated or waived in the original action. *Durfee v. Duke*, 375 U.S. 106 (1963).

The requirement of full faith and credit extends to the *res judicata* effect of the original state court judgment. Thus, if the original state court judgment would bar a subsequent action in the original state, it acts to bar a subsequent action in any other state. This is the case even if the subsequent action would otherwise be permitted in that state. (*See* § IX.D. Claim Preclusion, *infra*, for a discussion of *res judicata* generally.)

2. Federal to State

Under 28 U.S.C. § 1738, federal courts must also give full faith and credit to state court judgments. The same rules as discussed above for states apply with respect to a federal court.

3. State to Federal in Diversity Cases

If a federal court with diversity jurisdiction over an action issues a judgment, then a state court must give such judgment the same, but no greater, claim preclusion (*res judicata*) effect that the judgment would have been given by the courts of the state where the federal court was located. *Semtek Int'l Inc. v. Lockheed Martin Corp.*, 531 U.S. 497 (2001).

D. CLAIM PRECLUSION (*RES JUDICATA*)

1. In General

The doctrine of claim preclusion (*res judicata*) provides that a final judgment on the merits of an action precludes the parties from successive litigation of an identical **claim** in a subsequent action. *New Hampshire v. Maine,* 532 U.S. 742, 748 (2001).

2. Requirements

a. Valid final judgment on the merits

1) Valid

The judgment must be valid, meaning that the court had both personal and subject matter jurisdiction, and the defendant had proper notice and an opportunity to be heard.

2) Final

The judgment must also be final, meaning that there is nothing further for the court to do but to order entry of judgment.

3) On the merits

The decision must have been made in consideration of the merits of the claim or defense, rather than on technical grounds. A claim or defense does not actually have to have been raised in the earlier action to be barred in the later action. If the claim or defense could have been raised in the earlier action, it will be precluded in the later action. A judgment on the merits includes judgment entered after a full trial, summary judgment, judgment as a matter of law, and default judgment where the court has jurisdiction over the subject matter and personal jurisdiction over the parties.

4) Voluntary dismissal without prejudice

A voluntary dismissal "without prejudice" expressly reserves the right to sue again on the same claim in the same court so long as the statute of limitations has not expired. Unless the notice of dismissal states otherwise, a voluntary dismissal will be "without prejudice." Rule 41(a)(1)(B).

5) Voluntary dismissal with prejudice

A voluntary dismissal "with prejudice" is treated as a judgment on the merits and will have a preclusive effect in the court that issued the order of dismissal. A dismissal on the merits under Rule 41(b) will bar a plaintiff from re-filing the claim only in the same federal court, not in state court. *Semtek*, *supra*.

6) Involuntary dismissal

Unless otherwise provided by the order of dismissal, an involuntary dismissal on non-jurisdictional grounds will constitute an adjudication on the merits. Rule 41(b). While such an involuntary dismissal will bar re-filing of the claim in the same federal court, it does not preclude re-filing of the claim in state court. *Semtek*, *supra*.

7) Dismissal for lack of jurisdiction

Under Rule 41(b), a dismissal on jurisdictional grounds, or for lack of venue or failure to join a party under Rule 19, is without prejudice, because a court that has no jurisdiction cannot adjudicate a matter on the merits.

8) Diversity jurisdiction

If a federal court with diversity jurisdiction over an action issues a judgment, a state court must give such judgment the same claim preclusion effect that the judgment would have been given by the courts of the state where the federal court was located. *Semtek*, *supra*.

9) Family law decisions

A divorce decree must generally be given a preclusive effect so long as the court had jurisdiction, which usually requires only a long-term connection of the plaintiff-spouse with the forum state rather than *in personam* jurisdiction over the defendant-spouse. However, a decision involving property rights, including alimony or child custody, is not entitled to a preclusive effect unless the court had *in personam* jurisdiction over the defendant-spouse. *Estin v. Estin*, 334 U.S. 541 (1948).

b. Sufficiently identical causes of action

The original and later-filed causes of action must be sufficiently identical to be barred under claim preclusion. Federal courts apply a transactional approach under which they bar a subsequent claim with respect to all or any part of the transaction, or series of connected transactions, out of which the action arose.

Factors that are considered in determining what constitutes a transaction or series of transactions include:

i)   Whether the facts are related in time, space, origin, or motivation;

ii) Whether the facts form a convenient trial unit; and

iii) Whether treating the facts as a unit conforms to the parties' expectations.

Illinois Distinction: Sufficiently Identical Causes of Action

Transactional Test: For the doctrine of *res judicata* to apply, it is necessary that (i) there was a final judgment on the merits rendered by a court of competent jurisdiction, (ii) there is an identity of parties or their privies, and (iii) there is an identity of causes of action. *See River Park, Inc. v. The City of Highland Park*, 184 Ill. 2d 290, 302 (1998).

Illinois does employ the common "transactional test." An Illinois court will consider whether the facts occurred within a short time frame, whether the facts have a common origin, whether the facts are more conveniently tried together, and whether a joint trial of all facts would conform to the parties' expectations or common business practices.

Remember that, even though all counterclaims in Illinois are permissive, *res judicata* can prevent a party from asserting a claim that could have been brought as a counterclaim, if the three elements are met (see § VI.D.2., *supra*).

---

c. **Sufficiently identical parties**

For claim preclusion to apply, the claimant and the defendant must be the same (and in the same roles) in both the original action and the subsequently filed action. Note that claim preclusion is limited to the parties (or their privies). Thus, a similar action by a different party would not be precluded.

E. **ISSUE PRECLUSION (COLLATERAL ESTOPPEL)**

1. **In General**

The doctrine of issue preclusion, often called collateral estoppel, precludes the re-litigation of issues of fact or law that have already been necessarily determined by a judge or jury as part of an earlier claim. Unlike claim preclusion, issue preclusion does not require strict mutuality of parties, but only that the party against whom the issue is to be precluded (or one in privity with that party) must have been a party to the original action. Thus, "offensive" use of collateral estoppel is permitted. *Parklane Hosiery Co. v. Shore*, 439 U.S. 322 (1979). Issue preclusion applies to findings of jurisdiction that are fully litigated. *Stoll v. Gottlieb*, 305 U.S. 165 (1938).

Illinois Distinction: Issue Preclusion (Collateral Estoppel)

If two parties undergo a full and fair trial that results in a final judgment, neither party may seek a different result upon the same facts and issues in a subsequent lawsuit. *Kessinger v. Grefco, Inc.*, 173 Ill. 2d 447, 460 (1996).

"Offensive" collateral estoppel occurs when a plaintiff seeks to foreclose a defendant from litigating an issue the defendant has previously litigated unsuccessfully in another action. *In re Owens*, 125 Ill. 2d 390, 397 (1988). "Defensive" collateral estoppel occurs when a defendant attempts to stop a plaintiff from asserting a claim the plaintiff lost in a prior lawsuit. *Talarico v. Dunlap*, 177 Ill. 2d 185, 191 (1997).

> **Illinois Distinction: Issue Preclusion (Collateral Estoppel) (cont'd.)**
>
> Illinois does not require "mutuality of parties." An Illinois court may allow a non-party to assert collateral estoppel if the minimum elements of the doctrine are satisfied (i.e., identical issue, decided on the merits, and the party against whom estoppel is being asserted was a party in the first case) and it is clear that no fundamental unfairness will result to the party being estopped. *See Kessinger*, 173 Ill. 2d at 461.

2. Requirements

a. Same issue

The issue sought to be precluded must be the same as that involved in the prior action. The facts relevant to the particular issue and the applicable law must be identical in order for issue preclusion to apply. *Comm'r of Internal Revenue v. Sunnen*, 333 U.S. 591 (1948).

b. Actually litigated

The issue must have been actually litigated in the prior action in order for issue preclusion to apply.

c. Final, valid judgment

The issue must have been determined by a valid and binding final judgment. Generally, this requires that the first determination of the issue was within the authority of the court that decided it, and that the determination was made in a final decision on the merits.

d. Essential to the judgment

The determination of the issue must have been essential to the prior judgment. Generally, an issue that constitutes a necessary component of the decision reached will be considered essential to the judgment.

3. Equitable Issues

Issues decided under a court's equitable power, such as a bankruptcy court's avoidance of preferential transfers, can be precluded from relitigation just as can be legal issues, if all the requirements for collateral estoppel are met. *See Katchen v. Landy,* 382 U.S. 323 (1966).

Commercial Paper

COMMERCIAL PAPER

Table of Contents

COMMERCIAL PAPER

I. INTRODUCTION

The purpose of Article 3 of the Uniform Commercial Code ("UCC") is the creation of uniform rules for the payment of obligations in forms other than cash. These non-cash forms of payment, known as **negotiable instruments** or **commercial paper**, have unique characteristics that convey rights from one party to another while creating legally enforceable obligations.

A. TYPES OF COMMERCIAL PAPER

Article 3 applies to two types of commercial paper: **notes** and **drafts**.

1. Note

A note is a two-party instrument in which the **maker** promises to pay the **payee** a sum of money. This promissory instrument is generally used to evidence an extension of credit. §§ 3-103(a)(5), 3-104(e). (All citations are to the UCC unless otherwise indicated.)

> Notes contain **promises**: "I, Mark, promise to pay to the order of Paula the sum of $1000."

A **certificate of deposit** ("CD") is also a two-party instrument, particular to banks, in which a bank (i) acknowledges that it has received an amount of money, and (ii) promises to repay that amount. § 3-104(j). A CD is an Article 3 instrument only if it is negotiable; most CDs are not.

2. Draft

A draft (or "bill of exchange") is a three-party commercial paper in which the **drawer** orders the second party (**drawee** or **payor**) to pay a sum of money to a third party **payee**. § 3-104(e).

> Drafts contain **orders**: "To National Bank, pay to the order of Paula the sum of $1000, signed, Mark."

a. Check

One type of draft is a check, which is drawn upon a bank and payable on demand. This is true even if the paper is described as something else (e.g., a money order). § 3-104(f).

b. Traveler's check

Another type of draft is the traveler's check, which must be **countersigned** by a person whose "specimen signature" appears on the traveler's check. § 3-104(i).

c. Cashier's check

A cashier's check is a draft with respect to which the drawer and the drawee are the same bank. § 3-104(g).

d. Teller's check

A teller's check is a draft drawn by a bank on another bank or payable at or through a bank. § 3-104(h).

3. Contradictory Terms

When conflicting or contradictory terms exist within an instrument, handwritten terms take precedence over typewritten terms, typewritten terms over printed terms, and words over numbers. § 3-114.

II. FORMAL REQUIREMENTS OF "NEGOTIABILITY"

Article 3 applies only to **negotiable** instruments. An instrument's negotiability depends on whether it meets specific technical form requirements. To be negotiable, an instrument must be:

i)   A **writing**, **signed** by the maker/drawer;

ii)   Containing an **unconditional promise or order**;

iii) To pay a **fixed** amount of money;

iv)   To **order or bearer**;

v)   Payable **on demand** or at a **definite time**; and

vi)   Without stating any **additional undertaking or instruction**.

§ 3-104.

A. WRITING SIGNED BY MAKER/DRAWER

To be negotiable, the instrument must be a writing signed by the maker (in the case of a note) or drawer (in the case of a draft). A signature may be manual or by machine, including any mark intended as a signature. The signature need not appear at the end of the instrument, but may be in its body. The UCC is liberal in its interpretation of what constitutes a signature. §§ 3-401; 3-402. It also should be noted that anything in tangible form can qualify as a writing; it does not have to be a piece of paper. § 1-201(43).

B. UNCONDITIONAL PROMISE OR ORDER

As the purpose of Article 3 is to establish a convenient substitute for currency that can be freely exchanged, any limitations or conditions on an instrument may destroy its negotiability. If the instrument (together with any documents referenced in it) limits payment, then it is not a negotiable instrument. § 3-106.

1. Conditional Promises and Orders: Non-Negotiable

a. Express conditions to payment

If a promise or order contains an express condition to payment, it is not a negotiable instrument. § 3-106(a).

Example: "I promise to pay if I win the lottery" is a conditional promise; the instrument is not a negotiable instrument.

b. Subject to another writing

If the promise or order is made subject to or governed by another writing, it is not a negotiable instrument. § 3-106(b).

> **Example:** "Payment is subject to the written contract between the parties executed on January 1, 2010." This instrument is subject to another writing and as such is not negotiable.

2. Unconditional Promises and Orders: Negotiable

a. Reference to other documents

If the promise or order refers to another document for a statement of rights regarding collateral, prepayment, down payment, or acceleration, the instrument is still unconditional. § 3-106(b).

> **Example:** "This check is made as a down payment on a contract for the purchase of a 1970 Mustang." The statement simply refers to another document and is not subject to it. This qualifies as an unconditional order and does not render the instrument non-negotiable.

b. Payment from a particular fund

A provision that payment must be from an identified fund does not render the promise conditional. § 3-106(b).

> **Example:** "I will pay from the proceeds of the sale of my household furniture." This qualifies as an unconditional promise; the instrument is negotiable. However, a statement that the maker will pay "if she sells her household furniture" would render the promise conditional and the note would, therefore not be negotiable.

c. Countersignature required

The requirement of a countersignature, as in a traveler's check, does not render an instrument non-negotiable. § 3-106(c).

C. TO PAY A FIXED AMOUNT OF MONEY

The principal amount to be paid must be a fixed amount of money. §§ 3-104(a), 3-112, cmt. 1.

1. Money Defined

A negotiable instrument must be payable only in **money** (which includes "currency" and "currency funds"). An instrument that calls for payment in any form other than money (e.g., gold) or allows for payment in the alternative (e.g., "money or gold") is *not* a negotiable instrument under Article 3. § 1-201(24).

A negotiable instrument can instruct payment in foreign money/currency. Unless otherwise indicated, it can be paid in that currency or in the equivalent amount of U.S. currency. § 3-107.

2. Interest

While the amount of the principal must be fixed, negotiable instruments may accrue interest. Unless stated, an instrument does not automatically convey an interest payment. § 3-112(a).

a. Fixed or variable rate

Interest may be at a fixed or variable rate, and may be determined by reference to other documents or information (e.g., "Rate shall be at 4% above the interest on U.S. Government Treasury Bills"). § 3-112(b).

b. Unspecified rate

If the instrument specifies only that interest will be paid, the rate is the established judgment rate in the jurisdiction of the place of payment of the instrument at the time interest first accrues. § 3-112(b).

D. PAYABLE TO ORDER OR TO BEARER

A negotiable instrument must be either an order or a bearer instrument. An **order instrument** is payable only to the person named or to his order. The term "order" must appear. A **bearer instrument**, however, is payable to anyone who possesses the instrument.

1. Order Instrument

An instrument is payable to order if it identifies a person, (e.g., "Pay to the order of Joe Smith") or order ("Pay Joe Smith or his order"). More than one payee may be named. § 3-109(b).

To be negotiated, order paper must be **delivered** (i.e., transfer of possession) and properly **indorsed** by the holder. § 3-201.

2. Bearer Instrument

An instrument is payable to bearer (i.e., any person in possession of it) if:

i)   It is payable to "bearer" or "order of bearer";

ii) No payee is identified; or

iii) It is made "payable to cash."

If an instrument names a specific person, but also includes "bearer" (e.g., "payable to the order of Joe Smith or bearer"), it is payable to bearer. § 3-109.

A bearer instrument only requires **delivery** (not indorsement) to be negotiated.

3. Instruments Payable with Words of Description

An instrument payable to a trust or estate is payable to the representative. An instrument payable to an agent or other representative is payable to the representative or the person being represented. § 3-110(c).

E.   PAYABLE "ON DEMAND" OR AT A "DEFINITE TIME"

A negotiable instrument must be payable either **on demand**, or **at a definite time**.

1.   On Demand

An instrument is payable on demand if (i) it states that it is payable "on demand," or "at sight," or is otherwise payable at the will of the holder, or (ii) does not state a time for payment. § 3-108(a).

2.   At a Definite Time

An instrument is payable at a definite time if it is payable (i) on a **fixed date**, (ii) at the end of a **definite period** after sight or acceptance, or (iii) at a time **readily ascertainable** when the instrument is issued. § 3-108(b).

a.   Acceleration and extension clauses

The instrument is payable at a definite time even if it is subject to an acceleration clause. Extensions, conditioned on the option of the maker or on the happening of an event, do not destroy negotiability when the extension is to a further definite time. If no such time is specified, the instrument is not negotiable. The holder of the instrument, however, may freely extend the time for payment.

b.   "Readily ascertainable"

Events that will undoubtedly occur, but are not ascertainable as to a specific time are not "readily ascertainable."

Example: An instrument states, "Payable upon the death of my father." It is not negotiable because the father's death, although inevitable, is not definite as to time.

F.   NO ADDITIONAL UNDERTAKING OR INSTRUCTIONS

Article 3 generally prohibits negotiable instruments from including additional undertakings or instructions given by the maker or drawer. The following three types of undertakings, however, can be included in an instrument:

i)   An undertaking or power to give, maintain, or protect collateral;

ii)   An authorization or power to the holder to confess judgment or realize on or dispose of collateral; and

iii)   A waiver of any legal benefit intended for the advantage of the obligor (e.g., a waiver of a homestead exemption).

§ 3-104(a)(3). Note that an additional agreement that is entered into by the parties as part of the same transaction for which the instrument is issued does not affect negotiability if the agreement is neither included as part, nor referenced by, the instrument. However, subject to the parol evidence rule, such an agreement may give rise to personal defenses with respect to enforcement of the instrument. § 3-117.

III. HOLDER IN DUE COURSE

The primary purpose of Article 3 is to establish a secure alternative to the use of cash in financial transactions. In order for a transferee to be fully protected by Article 3, one must obtain the status of a **holder in due course** ("**HDC**"). To become the HDC of a negotiable instrument, one must:

i) Take the instrument as a **holder**;

ii) For **value**;

iii) In **good faith**; and

iv) **Without notice** of certain infirmities of the instrument or the transaction out of which the instrument arose.

§ 3-302(a)(2). In addition, a holder cannot be an HDC if the instrument, when negotiated to the holder, has apparent evidence of forgery or alteration or is otherwise so incomplete or irregular as to call its authenticity into question.

A. TAKING THE INSTRUMENT AS A HOLDER

A person can become a holder in two ways: through **issuance** or through **negotiation**.

1. Issuance

An instrument is issued when it is **delivered**, by the maker or the drawer to either a holder or non-holder, for the purpose of giving rights in the instrument to any other person. § 3-105(a). "Delivery" means the transfer of possession.

2. Negotiation

Negotiation is the delivery, regardless of voluntariness, by a person other than the maker or drawer to any other person who, as a consequence, becomes the holder of the instrument. As a holder of the instrument, a person is entitled to enforce it. §§ 3-201(a), 3-301.

a. Bearer instrument

If the instrument is payable to bearer, negotiation occurs upon the **transfer of possession**. It does not have to be voluntary. Accordingly, a thief or finder of the bearer instrument becomes a holder, even though transfer of possession was involuntary. § 3-201(b).

b. Order instrument

If the instrument is payable to order, in addition to the transfer of possession, the instrument must be indorsed by the holder in order to be negotiated. § 3-201(b).

If a bank receives an instrument from a customer for deposit that the customer fails to indorse, the bank is deemed a holder if the customer was a holder at the time of deposit despite the lack of an indorsement. § 4-205(1), incl. cmt.

1) Indorsement

An indorsement is a signature on the instrument by someone other than the maker, drawer, or acceptor that is typically made for the purpose of negotiating the instrument. § 3-204(a).

To effect a negotiation, the indorsement must be authorized and valid. A forged or unauthorized indorsement is generally ineffective. No transferee after the forged or unauthorized indorsement can become a holder.

Compare Forged Maker or Drawer's Signature: Since the signature of a maker or drawer on an instrument is not an indorsement, forgery of the maker or drawer's signature *does not* prevent transferees of the instrument from being holders. §§ 3-201, 3-204(a), 3-403(a).

a) Special indorsement

A "special indorsement" names an identified person as indorsee. The indorsee must sign in order for the instrument to be further negotiated. § 3-205(a).

b) Blank indorsement

A "blank indorsement" is a signature that is not accompanied by the naming of a specific indorsee. A blank indorsement of an order instrument creates a bearer instrument. § 3-205(b).

EXAM NOTE: It is important to recognize the status of an instrument as either order paper or bearer paper. An instrument may contain several indorsements, making it difficult to determine whether it is currently order or bearer paper. In these instances, look to the *most recent indorsement*. Order paper can become bearer paper with a blank indorsement, while bearer paper can likewise convert to order paper with a special indorsement.

c) Qualified indorsements

An indorser may, in addition to signing the instrument, include words that disclaim liability (e.g., "without recourse"). By qualifying the indorsement, the indorser is not liable to pay the instrument if it is dishonored. § 3-415(b).

d) Restrictive indorsements

An indorser may add words seeking to impose a restriction (e.g., "Pay James Smith *only*") or condition (e.g., "Pay James Smith if he finishes painting my house") on the payment of the instrument. While such restrictive words are generally ineffective as a limitation on transfer, words that require bank collection such as "for deposit" or "for collection" are valid. § 3-415(b).

e) Anomalous indorsements

Indorsement by a person who is not a holder of the instrument is sometimes done for the purpose of accommodation. The person signing becomes liable on the instrument, and the instrument may be further negotiated. § 3-205(d).

2) Multiple payees

An instrument payable to more than one payee is payable to them **jointly** or **severally**. When there is an ambiguity as to whether the instrument is payable jointly or severally, it is payable severally. § 3-110(d).

a) Jointly

An order instrument that is payable jointly (e.g., "Pay to the order of James Smith and Joan Doe") must be *indorsed by all payees*.

b) Severally

An order instrument that is payable severally (e.g. "Pay to the order of James Smith or Joan Doe) may be *indorsed by any payee*.

c) No split of instrument

An attempt to split an instrument (i.e., transfer less than the entire instrument or its amount) does not constitute a negotiation and the transferee does not qualify as a holder. The transferee does not have Article 3 rights, but merely the contractual rights of a partial assignee. § 3-203(d).

> **Example:** A holder indorses a note "Pay B and C each one half." Neither B nor C becomes a holder of the note.

c. Remitter transaction

A remitter is a person who purchases an instrument, usually a cashier's check or a teller's check, from its issuer in which the instrument is payable to an identified person other than the purchaser (e.g., a person selling goods to the remitter). Transfer of the instrument by the remitter to the person named in the instrument constitutes a negotiation. §§ 3-103(a)(11), 3-201.

B. TAKING THE INSTRUMENT FOR VALUE

A holder must establish HDC status by showing that the transfer occurred for value, in good faith, and without notice of certain proscribed facts.

1. Types of Value

Any of the following constitutes value:

i) Agreed performance is completed (an executory promise is not value);

> ***Contrast with Contract Law:*** Under Article 3, if the consideration is not yet completed, no value is given. For example, if B promise's to paint A's house in exchange for A's promise to deliver a $500 note, there is no value given until B completes the paint job. In contract law, however, B's promise to paint is sufficient consideration to support a bilateral contract.

ii) The transferee acquires a valid lien or security interest (but not as the result of judicial action);

iii) The instrument was acquired as the result of a payment or security for an antecedent debt;

> ***Contrast with Contract Law:*** Value exists despite the fact that the transfer was on account of a pre-existing debt. Under general contract principles, a pre-existing debt cannot serve as consideration for a contract. For Article 3 purposes, however, payment for such a debt is "giving value."

iv) Exchanging a negotiable instrument for another instrument; or

v) Exchanging the instrument for an irrevocable debt obligation to a third person by the person taking the instrument.

§ 3-303(a).

2. Equivalent Value not Required

Value given in exchange for an instrument need not be equivalent to the face amount of the instrument.

> **Example:** A pays $1000 for a $1500 note. As long as A pays the $1000, she has given value for Article 3 purposes.

3. Partial Value

When the holder agrees to provide consideration in exchange for the negotiable instrument, but has only partially performed that consideration, the holder is treated as having given value only to the extent of the consideration performed. § 3-302(d).

> **Example 1:** Ann agrees to pay $1500 for a note with a face value of $1500. Ann pays $750 and receives the note. Ann has given value with respect to the note to the extent of her $750 payment.

When the agreed upon consideration is less than the face value of the negotiable instrument, a holder who has partially performed the consideration is treated as having given value in an amount equal to the face value of the instrument times the ratio of the value of the consideration performed to the total value of the consideration agreed upon.

> **Example 2:** Alan agrees to pay $1000 for a note with a face value of $1500. Alan pays $500 and receives the note. Alan is treated as having given value with respect to $750 of the note ($1500 x ($500/$1000)).

4. When Value Given

The date that value is given determines whether a person takes an instrument in good faith and without notice, unless the date of negotiation is later, in which case that date is used.

5. Bank Customer's Deposit

A bank does not give value by crediting a customer's account for the amount of the instrument deposited. Instead, the bank gives value only when the customer withdraws the credited amount from her account or the bank applies the credited amount. In determining when a credited amount is withdrawn, the first-in, first-out (FIFO) accounting method is used. A withdrawal is deemed made from the earliest deposit first and then from subsequent deposits in the order in which the deposits were made. §§ 4-210, -211.

C. TAKING THE INSTRUMENT IN GOOD FAITH

Good faith amounts to honesty-in-fact and the observance of reasonable commercial standards of fair dealing. § 1-201(20).

1. Honesty-in-Fact

Honesty-in-fact is judged by a *subjective* standard as to what the holder actually believed, not what a reasonable person did or should have believed.

2. Fair Dealing

Reasonable commercial standards of fair dealing are judged by an objective standard as to whether the holder was attempting to take advantage of the obligor or otherwise acting unfairly (not whether the holder was merely negligent in his actions).

D. TAKING THE INSTRUMENT WITHOUT NOTICE

The holder cannot be an HDC if he has notice of (i) infirmities in the instrument itself, or (ii) infirmities in any underlying transaction in which the instrument was issued or negotiated. § 1-202.

1. Notice

Notice may be obtained by actual knowledge, receipt of notification, or the existence of a reason to know.

a. Actual knowledge

If a holder has actual knowledge of an infirmity, he cannot be an HDC. § 1-202(a).

b. Notification

A holder receives notification of an infirmity when it (i) comes to his attention, or (ii) is delivered to any place held out by him as a place to receive notice. § 1-202(e).

c. Reason to know

A holder has notice if, from all of the facts and circumstances known to him at the time in question, he had reason to know of the infirmity. § 1-202(a)(3). According to some courts, a holder has reason to know of an infirmity if, under the circumstances, reasonable diligence would have uncovered the infirmity. *E. Bierhaus & Sons, Inc. v. Bowling*, 486 N.E.2d 598 (Ind. Ct. App. 1985).

2. Types of Infirmities

Upon the following, HDC status is not conferred:

a. Claim or defense

HDC status is not conferred if a holder has notice of a claim to the instrument, claim in recoupment, or any defense. §§ 3-302(a)(2), 3-305, 3-306.

However, disqualifying notice *is not* obtained as a result of: (i) a public filing or recording (e.g., a filed financing statement); (ii) an executory (future) promise; (iii) a purchase at a reasonable discount; (iv) the instrument being postdated, antedated, or undated; (v) the instrument having been negotiated by a fiduciary (unless there is notice of a breach of fiduciary duty); (vi) a default in the payment of interest; or (vii) the discharge of a party. § 3-302.

1) Notice of breach of fiduciary duty

Notice of breach of a fiduciary duty by an agent or other fiduciary constitutes notice of the claim of the represented person (e.g., principal). In order for the taker to have notice of breach of a fiduciary duty with respect to an instrument, the taker must, in addition to having knowledge of the fiduciary status of the fiduciary, know that the fiduciary is personally benefiting, such as by crediting an agent's personal account for the amount of a check or taking a check in payment of a personal debt of the agent. § 3-307.

b. Apparent forged, altered, or otherwise irregular instrument

HDC status is not conferred if a reasonable person can determine that the negotiated instrument has apparent evidence of forgery or alteration or is otherwise so irregular or incomplete as to call into question its validity. § 3-302(a)(1).

c. Overdue or dishonored instrument

A purchaser cannot be an HDC if he has notice that the instrument is overdue or was previously dishonored. § 3-302(a)(2)(iii).

1) Checks

A check is overdue 90 days after its stated date or the day after demand for payment is made, whichever is earlier. § 3-304.

2) Other demand instruments

Any other instrument payable on demand is overdue at the earlier of (i) the day after demand is made, or (ii) after an unreasonable period of time, measured by the nature of the instrument and usage of the trade. § 3-304(a)(1),(3).

3) Time instruments

If an instrument is payable at a definite time (i.e., a "time instrument"), it generally becomes overdue on the day after the due date. § 3-304(b)(2).

a) Acceleration

An accelerated instrument becomes overdue the day after the accelerated due date. § 3-304(b)(3).

b) Installment

A time instrument payable in installments becomes overdue upon default, and remains overdue until the default is cured. A time instrument does not become overdue if there is a default in payment of interest, but no default in payment of principal. § 3-304(b)(1), (c).

3. Timing of Notice

Effective notice is measured in terms of reasonableness for the recipient to have an opportunity to respond. § 3-302(f).

E. SPECIAL LIMITS ON HDC STATUS

Certain holders are subject to special limits on HDC status.

1. Excluded Acquisitions

A person *cannot* become an HDC if the instrument is:

i) Acquired as a successor in interest to an estate or other organization;

ii) Purchased in an execution, bankruptcy, or creditor's sale, or under legal process; or

iii) Purchased in a bulk transaction, not in the regular course of the transferor's business.

However, such a person may have the rights of an HDC if the transferor or predecessor in interest held the instrument as an HDC. § 3-302(c).

2. Consumer Notes

In regulations adopted by the Federal Trade Commission, the ability of a purchaser of a consumer note to take free of the consumer's defenses is curtailed by the mandated inclusion of language that subjects the holder or transferee of the instrument to the claims and defenses that the issuer could assert against the original payee of the note. § 3-302(g); 16 C.F.R. Part 433.

3. Payee

While a payee may be an HDC, this tends to be the exception rather than the rule. A payee generally is not an HDC because the payee was involved in the initial transaction that resulted in the instrument. Since a payee typically has had dealings with the maker or drawer, a payee usually has notice of the defenses that the maker or drawer can raise. § 3-302, cmt. 4. Even if the payee were to qualify as an HDC, it would nevertheless take the instrument subject to the claims and defenses of the person with whom it dealt. § 3-305(b).

IV. DEFENSES AND CLAIMS ON NEGOTIABLE INSTRUMENTS

A non-HDC holder may recover from an obligor in the absence of a claim to the instrument, a defense, a claim in recoupment, or a discharge. However, if the obligor has grounds to deny payment, the holder (or a person with the rights of a holder) may be able to recover from the obligor depending upon (i) whether the holder is an HDC, and (ii) the ground on which the obligor seeks to refuse payment. If the holder is not an HDC, the obligor may assert any defense available under ordinary contract principles. If the holder is an HDC, the obligor can assert only the so-called **real defenses**. § 3-305.

A. REAL DEFENSES

The following are the *only defenses* available to an obligor against the HDC of a negotiable instrument.

1. Infancy

An obligor's infancy is available as a defense against an HDC to the same extent it is a defense to a simple contract under non-Code law. Infancy may be defense whether it makes the contract void or merely voidable. § 3-305(a)(1)(i).

2. Incapacity

If the applicable state non-Code law makes a contract void (not merely voidable) for any legal incapacity other than infancy, the incapacity is a real defense. Incapacity may include incompetence, guardianship, or other statutory incapacity, such as an ultra vires act by a corporation. § 3-305(a)(1)(ii), incl. cmt. 1.

3. Duress

As with incapacity, if the applicable state non-Code law makes a contract void (not merely voidable) for duress, duress is a real defense. An obligation obtained under physical harm or a threat of immediate physical harm is void and, therefore, such duress is a real defense. Whether other types of harm (e.g., economic harm) or threats of harm constitute duress depends on state law. § 3-305(a)(1)(ii), incl. cmt. 1.

4. Illegality

An obligor may raise illegality of the underlying transaction as a defense against an HDC only in rare circumstances when illegality makes the transaction void, not voidable. § 3-305(a)(1)(ii).

5. Fraud

An obligor may raise the defense of **fraud in the factum** against an HDC if the obligor was induced to sign the instrument without knowledge or reasonable opportunity to obtain knowledge of the instrument's "character or essential terms." § 3-305(a)(1)(iii).

Example 1: A person with only an elementary school education and a limited understanding of English seeks work through an employment agency. She signs an instrument, which she cannot comprehend, after being told that it is a job application form. She can assert fraud in the factum as a real defense against holder in due course of the instrument.

An obligor may not raise the personal defense of **fraud in the inducement** against an HDC. In other words, if there was knowledge that a negotiable instrument was being executed, the obligor may not assert fraud as a defense.

> **Example 2:** A person knowingly signs a check to pay for jewelry. He is led to believe the jewelry is gold, but in fact it is not. He cannot assert fraud in the factum, only fraud in the inducement, which is not a real defense that can be used against a holder in due course.

6. Discharge in Insolvency Proceedings

An obligor may raise the defense of discharge in an insolvency proceeding against an HDC. An insolvency proceeding includes a bankruptcy, even if the debtor is not insolvent. § 3-305(a)(1)(iv).

7. Alteration and Forgery

When an alteration of the terms of an instrument occurs, an obligor may assert it as a defense against an HDC in some limited circumstances. *See* § IX., "Unauthorized Signatures and Alterations," *infra*.

8. Statute of Limitations

The statute of limitations serves as a defense against an action by any holder, including an HDC.

A **three-year limit** applies to the following types of actions:

i)   Actions on unaccepted drafts, which must be brought within three years of the date of dishonor or within ten years of the date of the draft, whichever is earlier;

ii) Actions against an acceptor of a certified check or the issuer of a teller's, cashier's, or traveler's check, which must be brought within three years after demand for payment;

iii) Actions for conversion, which must be brought within three years of accrual;

iv) Actions for breach of warranty, which must be brought within three years of accrual; and

v)   All other actions under Articles 3 and 4, which must be brought within three years of accrual.

A **six-year limit** applies to the following types of actions:

i)   Actions on notes payable at a definite time, which must be brought within six years of the due date, or "on demand," which must be brought within six years after the demand; and

ii) Actions on certificate of deposits, which must be brought within six years of the later of the demand for payment or the due date.

§ 3-118.

9. Accommodation Party

An HDC is generally not subject to an accommodation party's personal defenses, even if the HDC has notice that a party is an accommodation party. However, when an HDC is aware of a party's status as an accommodation party when he takes the instrument, the HDC takes subject to the accommodation party's suretyship defenses. (*See* § X.B.6., "Discharge of Indorsers and Accommodation Parties," *infra*.) § 3-605.

B. PERSONAL DEFENSES

A person without the rights of an HDC takes subject to any defense provided for under Article 3, including a defense of an obligor that would be available against a person enforcing a right to payment under a simple contract. In contrast to the real defenses to which an HDC as well as a non-HDC are subject, these defenses are termed "**personal defenses**." § 3-305(a)(2).

1. Issuance

A non-HDC takes subject to the Article 3 defenses that the instrument was not issued, was conditionally issued, or was issued for a special purpose. §§ 3-105(b), 3-305 (a)(2), incl. cmt. 2.

2. Any Contract Defense

A non-HDC takes subject to all contract defenses, including but not limited to lack of consideration, failure of consideration, non-occurrence of a condition precedent, mistake, impossibility, fraud, duress, incapacity, infancy, illegality, and usury. §§ 3-303(b), 3-305(a)(2), incl. cmt. 2.

3. Claims in Recoupment

A non-HDC takes subject to a claim in recoupment (i.e., an offset against an amount owed on an instrument, such as a warranty claim). The claim must arise from the transaction that gave rise to the instrument and is limited to the amount owed on the instrument at the time that the action is brought. § 3-305(a)(3), (b).

4. Defenses and Claims in Recoupment of Other Persons

An obligor may generally raise only his own defenses. He cannot rely on the defenses or claims in recoupment of any other person. However, with regard to a claim to the instrument, there is an exception to this rule. If the obligor knows that a non-HDC is in wrongful possession of a lost or stolen instrument, the obligor is not obliged to pay the instrument. If the obligor pays the instrument with knowledge that it was stolen, the obligation on the instrument will not be discharged. §§ 3-305(c), incl. cmt. 4; 3-602(b)(2).

5. Claims to the Instrument

A non-HDC takes subject to all valid claims of a property or possessory interest in the instrument or its proceeds. § 3-306.

V. TRANSFER OF INSTRUMENT AND LIABILITY OF THE PARTIES

A. TRANSFER OF INSTRUMENT

1. Rights Obtained by Transferee

A **transfer** is the delivery of an instrument by a person, *other than the maker or drawer*, for the purpose of giving the person receiving it the right to enforce the instrument. With the transfer or delivery of an instrument, all of the transferor's rights vest in the transferee. In other words, the transferee is "sheltered" by the transferor, even if the transferee's rights in the instrument would otherwise be less than those of the transferor. § 3-203.

2. Right to Transferor's Indorsement

When an instrument is transferred for value and the transferor fails to provide a necessary indorsement, a transferee is entitled to specific performance to obtain the transferor's indorsement. § 3-203.

3. The Shelter Rule

Under the shelter rule, a person to whom an HDC transfers an instrument usually acquires the rights of the HDC, even if the transferee herself does not qualify as an HDC. Since the transferee's HDC rights are derivative, the transferee does take the instrument subject to the real defenses that may be asserted against the **transferor** by the obligor. §§ 3-203(b), 3-305(b).

> **Example:** A issues a check to B for repairing a car, which A discovers the next day was done improperly. B negotiates the check to C who takes it as an HDC. C gives the check as a gift to her daughter, D. Even though D is not an HDC because she did not give value, D can enjoy C's rights as an HDC and enforce the instrument, despite A's personal defense against B.

> **EXAM NOTE:** The shelter rule confers the rights of a prior HDC on all subsequent persons to whom the instrument is transferred since each transferee takes the rights of the previous transferee.

4. Exception to the Shelter Rule

No transferee who has engaged in fraud or illegality affecting the instrument can acquire the rights of an HDC through transfer, directly or indirectly, from an HDC. However, a transferee who is merely aware of an earlier fraud perpetrated by another may enjoy the rights of a previous HDC. § 3-203(b), incl. cmt. 2, 4.

> **Example 1:** A fraudulently induces B to issue a note to A. A negotiates the note to C, who takes the note as holder in due course. C sells the note back to A. A does not enjoy C's rights as an HDC due to A's prior fraud with respect to the note.
>
> **Example 2:** Assume the same facts as Example 1, except that C instead transfers the note to D. D is aware of A's fraud because A told him about it after the fact. D enjoys C's rights as an HDC and is not subject to A's fraud in the inducement defense (through the shelter rule), even though D was aware of A's fraud at the time that he took the note and therefore could not himself be an HDC.

B. NATURE OF LIABILITY OF PARTIES ON INSTRUMENTS

When a person signs her name on a negotiable instrument, her liability to pay depends on the **capacity** in which she signs.

1. Liability of Issuer of Note or Cashier's Check

The maker of a note, who upon issuance of the note becomes an "**issuer**," promises to pay usually according to the instrument's terms at the time it was issued. The issuer's liability to pay the instrument is **primary**. The issuer must generally pay the note upon presentment if a demand note, or otherwise on the date payment is due, without imposing other conditions. The issuer may, of course, refuse to pay based on a defense.

The drawer of a cashier's check (i.e., a check with respect to which the drawer and drawee are the same bank) has the same liability as the maker of a note. § 3-412.

2. Liability of Drawer

A drawer of an unaccepted draft is secondarily liable on the instrument. If the draft is dishonored, the drawer has promised to pay the unaccepted draft according to its terms when issued. The drawer is only liable upon dishonor, but his liability is not conditioned upon notice of dishonor. If the draft is paid instead of being dishonored, or if it is accepted by a bank, the drawer is completely discharged. If a draft is accepted by a non-bank, the drawer is treated as an indorser. § 3-414(b)-(d).

Except with respect to a check, a drawer may disclaim liability by writing on a draft the words "without recourse." § 3-414(e).

3. Liability of Drawee

The drawee is the person ordered by the drawer to pay the draft. While normally a holder or other person entitled to enforce the draft seeks payment of it from the drawee, the drawee is generally not liable on the instrument to such person for failure to do so. This conclusion follows from the rule that only those who sign an instrument are liable on the instrument. §§ 3-401; 3-408. The drawee may be liable on the draft if the drawee accepts the draft (*see* V.B.4., "Liability of Acceptor," *infra*). § 3-408.

If the drawee is a bank, the bank's obligation with regard to the payment of a check is determined by its agreement with its customer (i.e., the drawer).

a. Drawee bank

If the drawee is a bank, the bank's obligation with regard to the payment of a check is determined by its agreement with its customer (i.e., the drawer).

1) "Properly payable" rule

Generally, a bank can only charge a customer's account for checks that are properly payable.

a) Sufficient funds

The bank must honor a customer's check if there are sufficient funds to cover the check. If there are insufficient funds, the bank may choose to honor the check, but the customer is liable to the bank for the overdraft unless the customer did not sign the check or benefit from its proceeds, such as a joint account holder. §§ 4-401(a), (b); 4-402(a), (c).

b) Customer's authorization

Generally, in order to be properly payable, the check must have been authorized by the customer.

1) Forged signature

A check that contains a forged drawer's signature or a forged indorsement (e.g., payee's signature) is generally not properly payable. In the case of a forged drawer's signature, there has not been an order to pay made by the customer. In the case of a forged indorsement, the person that the customer ordered the bank to pay has not been paid. § 4-401(a), incl. cmt. 1.

ii) Altered amount

If the amount of the check has been altered by someone other than the customer, the bank may charge the customer's account only for the original amount of the check. If the check has been completed by someone other than the customer, the bank may charge the customer's account for the completed amount of the check unless the bank has notice that the completion was improper. § 4-401(d).

iii) Time for payment

If a check has been dated a future day (i.e., postdated), the bank may properly pay the check prior to the stated date unless the customer gives the bank notice of the postdating. § 4-401(c). If a check other than a certified check is presented for payment more than six months after its date, the bank may, but is not required to, pay the check. § 4-404.

2) Wrongful dishonor

If the bank wrongfully dishonors a check (i.e., dishonors a check that is properly payable), the customer may sue for damages proximately caused by the wrongful dishonor, which may include consequential damages, such as those resulting from the arrest or prosecution of the customer. § 4-402(b).

b. Duties of customer to bank

A customer, upon receipt of his bank statement, must exercise reasonable care and promptness to discover any unauthorized payments resulting from a forged drawer's signature or alteration, and promptly notify the bank. § 4-406. The failure of the customer to meet these duties gives the bank the right to refuse to re-credit his account for the unauthorized payments if the bank suffered a loss due to the customer's failure. §4-406(d).

c. Death of customer

The death of its customer does not automatically revoke the bank's authority to pay a check unless (i) the bank knows of the death, and (ii) it has a reasonable opportunity to act on that knowledge. Despite such knowledge, however, the bank may continue to pay checks for 10 days after the date of death, unless ordered to stop by a person claiming an interest in the account. § 4-405.

d. Stop payment orders

A customer may order the bank to stop payment of a check, except for a certified check. The bank must be given a reasonable opportunity to act on the stop payment order. § 4-403(a), incl. cmt. 4.

1) Period of effectiveness

A written stop payment order is binding on the bank for 6 months. A verbal stop payment order is valid for 14 days unless confirmed in writing during that period. § 4-403(b).

2) Violation of order

It is no defense that a bank's violation of a stop payment order was due to mistake or inadvertence. The burden is on the customer to prove loss in the event of payment by the bank despite a valid stop payment order. Once the drawee-bank has paid a check, it is subrogated to the rights of any HDC, payee or other holder on a check against the drawer. Consequently, where there is an HDC with respect to a check, the customer cannot prove loss because the HDC could have demanded payment from the customer-drawer even if the bank complied with the stop payment order. §§ 4-403(3), incl. cmt. 7; 4-407, incl. cmt. 1.

4. Liability of Acceptor

Acceptance is the drawee's agreement to pay a draft as presented. The acceptance is usually manifested by the drawee's signature on the draft. As acceptor, the drawee promises to pay the draft according to its terms at the time of its acceptance. On acceptance, the acceptor becomes primarily liable to pay the draft. § 3-409(a).

a. Variance

An acceptor may change the terms of a draft, subject to a holder's right to either assent to the variance or treat the draft as dishonored. § 3-410(a), (c).

b. Check certification

The certification of a check is the functional equivalent of an acceptance of a check by the bank on which it is drawn. § 3-409(d). Absent a contractual agreement, a bank is not required to certify a check.

c. Refusal to pay

If the acceptor of a certified, check or the issuer of a teller's or cashier's check wrongfully refuses to pay, the person attempting to enforce the instrument may recover interest, expenses, and under some circumstances, consequential damages. § 3-411(b).

5. Liability of Indorser

An indorser promises that, if an instrument is dishonored, she will pay the amount of the instrument according to its terms at the time of indorsement. An indorser may be liable to the person entitled to enforce the instrument, or to any subsequent indorser who pays the instrument. § 3-415(a).

a. Secondary liability

Unlike a maker, drawer, or an acceptor, each of whom is primarily liable on an instrument, an indorser is secondarily liable. In order for an indorser to be required to pay an instrument, the instrument must first be **dishonored**, and, unless excused, the indorser must receive **notice of dishonor**. Absent notice of dishonor, the indorser is discharged. In addition, if a check is not presented for payment within 30 days after indorsement, the indorser is discharged. §§ 3-415(c), (e); 3-503(a).

b. Disclaimer of liability

An indorser may disclaim liability by including language such as "without recourse" along with her signature. § 3-415(b).

6. Liability of Persons Signing Jointly

When parties sign an instrument jointly, they are jointly and severally liable on the instrument. Either one, or both, may be sued for the entire amount. If one party pays more than his individual share, he is entitled to contribution from the jointly liable party. Indorsers usually do not indorse jointly and, therefore, do not have joint and several liability. Rather, an earlier indorser has liability to a later indorser. § 3-116.

VI. PRESENTMENT, DISHONOR, NOTICE OF DISHONOR

A. PRESENTMENT

Presentment is generally a demand for payment made to the maker of a note or the drawee of a draft by a person entitled to enforce the instrument. Presentment may be made by any commercially reasonable means. The person from whom payment is demanded may request that the person making presentment exhibit the instrument provide reasonable identification and surrender the instrument if full payment is made. § 3-501(a), (b)(1)-(2).

1. Excused Presentment

Presentment is excused when:

i) It cannot be made by the exercise of reasonable diligence (e.g., presenter cannot locate the party to whom presentment must be made);

ii) The maker or acceptor has repudiated the obligation to pay, is dead, or is in insolvency proceedings;

iii) The terms of the instrument make it unnecessary;

iv) The drawer or indorser has waived it (as is usually the case with a note) or is estopped from requiring it; and

v) The drawer has instructed the drawee not to pay the instrument (e.g., a stop payment order on a check).

§§ 3-502, cmt. 2; 3-504(a).

2. Presentment Warranties

Presentment warranties are made by any person who obtains payment or acceptance and by any prior transferor, and are made to any person who in good faith pays or accepts. They cannot be disclaimed with respect to a check. § 3-417.

a. Presentment warranties on unaccepted drafts

If a draft is presented to the drawee for payment or acceptance and the drawee pays or accepts the draft, the person obtaining payment or acceptance, at the time of presentment, and any previous transferor of the draft, at the time of transfer, warrant to the drawee in good faith that:

i) The warrantor is, or was, at the time the warrantor transferred the draft, a person entitled to enforce the draft or authorized to obtain payment or acceptance of the draft on behalf of a person entitled to enforce the draft;

ii) The draft has not been altered; and

iii) The warrantor has no knowledge that the signature of the drawer of the draft is unauthorized.

§§ 3-417(a)(1)-(3); 4-208(a)(1)-(3).

The warranty that the warrantor is a person entitled to enforce the instrument is not breached by a forged drawer's signature, but is generally breached by the forgery of a necessary indorsement (e.g., a payee's signature). This places the burden of determining the validity of the drawer's signature on the drawee.

b. Other presentment warranties

If (i) a dishonored draft is presented for payment to the drawer or an indorser, or (ii) any other instrument is presented for payment to a party obliged to pay the instrument, and (iii) payment is received, the person obtaining payment and a prior transferor of the instrument warrants to the person making payment in good faith that the warrantor is, or was at the time the warrantor transferred the instrument, a person entitled to enforce the instrument. The person making payment may recover from *any warrantor* for breach of warranty an amount equal to the amount paid, plus expenses and loss of interest resulting from the breach. §§ 3-417(d); 4-208(d).

B. DISHONOR

Dishonor occurs when the drawee of a draft or maker of a note does not pay within the required time after presentment.

1. Time of Dishonor

a. Time instrument

A note that is payable on a particular day and is payable at or through a bank is generally dishonored if it is not paid on the day it becomes payable or the day of presentment, whichever is later. If a note is a time instrument that is not payable at or through a bank, the note is generally dishonored if it is not paid on the day it becomes payable. §§ 3-502(a)(3).

A draft that is payable on a date stated in the draft is generally dishonored if it is not paid on the day it becomes payable or the day of presentment, whichever is later. § 3-502(b)(3).

b. Demand instrument

A note or draft that is payable on demand is generally dishonored if it is not paid on the day of presentment. §§ 3-501(a)(1), 3-502(b)(2). However, if a check is not taken for immediate payment over the counter, the check is dishonored if the bank returns the check or sends written notice of dishonor before either final payment or the bank's midnight deadline. A bank that has taken a check for deposit generally has until midnight of the banking day after the check is presented to make final payment. Before that midnight deadline, the bank can reverse any provisional credit made to the customer's account for the check if, for instance, the payor bank dishonors the check. §§ 3-502(b)(1), 4-104(a)(10), 4-105(2), (3), 4-215, 4-301.

C. NOTICE OF DISHONOR

An indorser is not liable on an instrument unless given timely notice of dishonor. Such notice may be given by any person and may be given by any reasonable commercial means. § 3-503(a), (b).

1. Timing of Notice

Notice of dishonor must ordinarily be given within 30 days after dishonor occurs. If the instrument was taken by a bank for collection, notice of dishonor must be given by the bank before the bank's midnight deadline. For such an instrument, any other person must give notice of dishonor within 30 days after the day on which the person receives notice of dishonor. § 3-503(c).

2. Excused Notice

Notice of dishonor is excused if waived, either by the terms of the instrument or the person entitled to such notice. Delay in giving notice of dishonor is excused if it was the result of circumstances beyond the control of the notifier, provided the notifier exercises reasonable diligence in giving such notice after the circumstances cease to exist. § 3-504(b), (c).

VII. TRANSFER WARRANTIES

There are six transfer warranties associated with an instrument. The transferor warrants that:

i) The transferor is entitled to enforce the instrument;

ii) All signatures are authentic;

iii) All signatures are authorized;

iv) The instrument has not been altered;

v) There are no defenses or claims that can be asserted against the transferor; and

vi) The maker, acceptor, or drawer is not, to his knowledge, subject to insolvency proceedings.

§§ 3-416(a); 4-207(a).

Unlike the presentment warranty, the transfer warranty is breached by a forged drawer's signature, as well as the forgery of a necessary indorsement (e.g., a payee's signature).

A. REQUIREMENTS

1. Transfer of Instrument

In order for the transfer warranties to apply, the transferor must transfer (i.e., deliver, rather than issue) the instrument to another person for the purpose of giving that person the right to enforce the instrument. A maker or drawer who issues the instrument, as well as the person who presents the instrument for payment, are not transferors. §§ 3-203(a), 3-416(a).

2. Consideration

The transferor must transfer the instrument for consideration. Any consideration sufficient to support a simple contract is adequate. § 3-416(a), incl. cmt 1.

3. Irrelevant Acts

Presentment, dishonor, and notice of dishonor are irrelevant to liability under these warranties.

B. BENEFICIARIES OF WARRANTIES

A transferee who indorses the instrument makes the transfer warranties to *all* subsequent transferees. One who does not indorse the instrument makes these warranties only to his *immediate transferee*. § 3-416(a).

C. DAMAGES FOR BREACH

A beneficiary of the transfer warranties who took the instrument in good faith may recover damages for breach of warranty. The damages are based on the loss suffered as a consequence of the breach, but are limited to the amount of the instrument, plus expenses and loss of interest due to the breach. In addition, any loss to the warrantor caused by the beneficiary's delay in giving notice of a breach (which is required within 30 days after the beneficiary has reason to know of the breach and the identity of the warrantor) cannot be recovered. § 3-416(b), (c).

D. DISCLAIMER OF WARRANTIES

Transfer warranties may be disclaimed unless the instrument is a check. Disclaimer may be by agreement between immediate parties. Otherwise, for an indorser, words such as "without warranties" must be used in conjunction with the indorsement to disclaim these warranties. § 3-416(c), incl. cmt. 5.

VIII. ACCOMMODATION PARTIES AND AGENTS

A. ACCOMMODATION PARTIES

An accommodation party is a type of **surety**, or one who guarantees the debt of another. § 3-419(a). In order to be an accommodation party, a person cannot have received a direct benefit from the instrument. However, an accommodation party is liable on the instrument in whatever capacity he has signed—indorser, maker, acceptor, or drawer. § 3-419.

If the accommodation party pays the instrument, he has a right to be reimbursed by the accommodated party and may enforce that right. § 3-419(d).

1. Both the Surety and the Debtor must Sign

A person is an accommodation party only when both he and the debtor sign the instrument. § 3-419(a). If the surety does not sign the same instrument as the debtor, he is a surety, but his rights and obligations are governed by the general law of suretyship rather than Article 3.

2. Liability of Accommodation Party

An accommodation party is liable in whatever capacity he has signed the instrument, usually as a co-maker or an anomalous indorser. § 3-419(b), incl. cmts. 1, 4. For example, an accommodation party who signs as a co-maker is primarily liable to a holder of the instrument; the holder may seek payment of the instrument solely from the accommodation party.

Generally, an accommodation party is not liable for breach of a transfer warranty, as the accommodation party usually does not transfer the instrument.

3. Collection Guaranteed

When "collection guaranteed" or similar words added to a signature unambiguously indicate an intention to guarantee collection only, the signer guarantees only collection rather than payment. In other words, the accommodation party is liable on the instrument only if (i) the person entitled to enforce the instrument has reduced his claim to judgment against the other party and execution is returned unsatisfied, (ii) the other party has become insolvent, (iii) the other party cannot be served with process, or (iv) it appears useless to proceed against the other party. § 3-419(d).

4. Defenses of an Accommodation Party

An accommodation party may raise his own defenses, except for the defense of lack of consideration. In addition, an accommodation party may raise any of the accommodated party's defenses or claims in recoupment except for the defenses of discharge in insolvency proceedings, infancy, or lack of capacity. For special defenses that an accommodation party may raise, *see* § X.B., Discharge of Indorsers and Accommodation Parties, *infra*. §§ 3-305(d), 3-419(b).

B. EFFECT OF SIGNATURE BY AGENT

Liability on an instrument generally requires a signature of the person to be bound. When an instrument is signed by the representative of a person (i.e., a fiduciary, such as an agent), the represented person (i.e., principal) may be bound, even though the principal did not sign the instrument himself, and the agent who did sign the instrument may not be. § 3-401(a).

1. Liability of the Principal

Whether a principal is liable on an instrument signed by an agent turns in part on whether the agent had **authority**. If the agent is authorized, the principal is liable whether the agent signed the principal's name, the agent's own name, or both. § 3-402(a). If the agent is not authorized, the principal generally will not be liable; the law of agency, however, recognizes two sets of circumstances under which the principal may nonetheless be bound: ratification and estoppel.

a. Ratification

If the principal **knowingly adopts** the signature of the unauthorized representative, or **fails to deny** its validity with knowledge that his silence may mislead others, the principal ratifies the signature and is bound on the instrument. § 3-403(a), incl. cmt. 3.

b. Estoppel

If the principle **negligently contributed** to the making of the unauthorized signature by the agent, including a forgery, the principal may be estopped from denying liability against an HDC or one who pays in good faith pursuant to reasonable commercial standards.

2. Liability of the Agent

a. Unauthorized signature

If an agent is not authorized to sign or exceeds his authority, the signature will operate as the signature of the agent *personally*. The agent will be liable in the capacity in which she signs to a person who pays the instrument in good faith or takes it for value. § 3-403(a), incl. cmt. 2.

b. Authorized signature

1) Principal's name only

An authorized agent who signs only the principal's name is not personally liable. § 3-401(a).

2) Agent's name and capacity

An agent whose signature shows unambiguously that it is made in his capacity as an agent and identifies the principal is not personally liable. § 3-402(b)(1).

Example: A, treasurer of X, Inc., signs a note payable to the corporation "X, Inc., by A, Treasurer." A is not liable on the note.

3) Agent's name only or failure to indicate capacity

An authorized agent who signs his own name but does not unambiguously indicate that the signature is made in a representative capacity, or who does not identify the principal in the instrument, is personally liable to an HDC who takes without notice that the parties never intended for the agent to be personally liable. § 3-402(b)(2).

Example 1: A, an authorized agent of P, signs "A" on a note payable to P. A may be liable on the note to an HDC.

The agent is not liable to a non-HDC if he can establish that the parties never intended for him to be personally liable. § 3-402(b)(2).

Example 2: A, an authorized agent of P, signs "A, agent" on a note payable to P. A may not be liable on the note to a non-HDC.

4) Signature on principal's check

An authorized agent who signs his own name as drawer on a check of the principal is not personally liable if the check is drawn on the principal's account and identifies the principal. § 3-402(c).

Example: A, treasurer of X, Inc., signs "A" as drawer of a corporate check. A is not liable on the check.

IX. UNAUTHORIZED SIGNATURES AND ALTERATIONS

Generally, an unauthorized signature is ineffective as the signature of the person whose name is signed. Such a signature may be a forgery or the signature of an agent that exceeds the agent's authority. However, an unauthorized signature is effective as the signature of the unauthorized signer in favor of a person who, in good faith, pays the instrument or takes it for value. §§ 3-401(a), 3-403(a).

In limited circumstances, an unauthorized signature will be treated as though it was authorized. Those circumstances include the issuance of an instrument to an imposter or a fictitious payee, an employee's violation of an employer's trust, negligence that contributes to an alteration or forgery, and the failure of a bank customer to examine his bank statement and report any alteration or forgery.

A. FRAUDULENT PAYEES AND EMPLOYEES

1. Imposters

Drawers and makers must take care when they issue instruments. If an impostor induces a person to issue an instrument to the impostor or to a person acting in concert with the impostor by impersonating the payee of the instrument, an indorsement of the instrument by any person in the name of the payee may be effective as the indorsement of the payee. § 3-404(a).

Example 1: A convinces B that he is, in fact, C. B makes out a check to C and gives it to A. A signs the check "C" as payee. A's signature can be effective as an indorsement.

This rule also applies to persons who, without authorization, misrepresent themselves as agents of the payee.

Once the drawer or maker issues the instrument to the imposter, *anyone* may indorse the instrument as payee.

Example 2: Assume the same facts as in Example 1, except that A loses the check before signing it. E finds the check and signs it "C" as payee. E then transfers the check to D for value. E's signature can be effective as an indorsement.

2. Fictitious or Unintended Payee

If a person whose intent determines to whom an instrument is payable (e.g., a drawer or maker) does not intend the person identified as payee to have any interest in the instrument, or the person identified as payee of an instrument is a fictitious person, the following rules apply:

i)   Any person in possession of the instrument is its holder; and

ii) An indorsement by any person in the name of the payee stated in the instrument may be effective as the indorsement of the payee.

§ 3-404(b).

> **Example 1:** A is authorized to draw checks on behalf of B. A writes a check to "C," as payee. C does not exist. A takes the check and signs "C" as payee. A's signature can be effective as an indorsement.
>
> **Example 2:** A is authorized to draw checks on behalf of B. A writes a check to "C," as payee. C does exist, but A intends to cash the check himself. A takes the check, signs "C" as payee. A's signature can be effective as an indorsement.

The indorsement need not be exactly the same as the named payee so long as it is substantially similar to the payee's name. § 3-404(c).

3. Employer's Liability for Employee's Fraudulent Indorsement

If an employer entrusts an employee with responsibility for the instrument, and the employee or a person acting in concert with the employee makes a fraudulent indorsement of the instrument, the indorsement may be effective as the indorsement of the person to whom the instrument is payable if it is made in the name of that person. § 3-405(a), (b).

> **Example:** A is authorized to deal with checks on behalf of B. A steals a check payable to B and signs B's name as payee. A's signature of B's name can be effective as an indorsement.

If an employer has hired an independent contractor who has responsibility for an instrument, the employer may also be liable for the independent contractor's fraudulent indorsement. § 3-405(a)(1).

4. Benefited Parties

With respect to a fraudulent indorsement by an impostor or employee or on behalf of a fictitious or unintended payee, the fraudulent indorsement is effective in favor of a person who, in good faith, pays the instrument or takes it for value or for collection. However, if that person fails to exercise ordinary care in paying or taking the instrument, and that failure substantially contributes to loss resulting from payment of the instrument, the person bearing the loss may recover from the person failing to exercise ordinary care to the extent the failure to exercise ordinary care contributed to the loss. §§ 3-404(c), (d); 3-405(b), (c).

The indorsement need not be exactly the same as the named indorsee so long as it is substantially similar to the indorsee's name. §§ 3-404(c), 3-405(c).

B. NEGLIGENCE CONTRIBUTING TO FORGED SIGNATURE OR ALTERATION

A person whose failure to exercise ordinary care **substantially contributes** to an alteration of an instrument, or to the making of a forged signature on an instrument, is precluded from asserting the alteration or the forgery against a person who, in good faith, pays the instrument or takes it for value or for collection. § 3-406(a).

1. Lack of Ordinary Care

The traditional tort test for negligence applies. Common instances of negligence include (i) delivery of check to a third person under circumstances when forgery is foreseeable, (ii) mailing a check to a person with a similar name, (iii) failing to protect check forms, and (iv) leaving open spaces on the instrument.

2. Person Asserting Preclusion

The person asserting preclusion has the burden of proving the failure to exercise ordinary care. If the person asserting the preclusion fails to exercise ordinary care in paying or taking the instrument and that failure substantially contributes to loss, the loss is allocated between the person precluded and the person asserting the preclusion according to the extent to which the failure of each to exercise ordinary care contributed to the loss. § 3-406(b), (c).

C. ALTERATIONS AND INCOMPLETE INSTRUMENTS

An **alteration** is the unauthorized modification of an instrument, including the addition of words or numbers that, if given effect, alters a party's obligation. § 3-407(a).

1. Fraudulent Alterations

A fraudulent alteration generally discharges a party whose obligation is affected by the alteration, unless that party assents or is precluded from asserting the alteration. A payor bank or drawee paying a fraudulently altered instrument, or a person taking it for value in good faith and without notice of the alteration (an HDC), may enforce the instrument (i) according to its original terms, or (ii) in the case of an incomplete instrument that is altered by unauthorized completion, according to its terms as completed. § 3-407(b).

2. Incomplete Instrument

When the signer intends that the instrument be completed after signing by the addition of words or numbers, the instrument is termed an "**incomplete instrument**." If the completion is authorized, the instrument may be enforced as completed. § 3-115(a), (b). If the completion is unauthorized, the obligor is generally discharged, but a payor bank or HDC can enforce the instrument as completed. The burden of establishing the lack of authority is on the person asserting the lack of authority. § 3-407.

X. PAYMENT AND DISCHARGE

A. PAYMENT

An instrument is paid to the extent payment is made by or on behalf of a party obliged to pay the instrument and to a person entitled to enforce the instrument. The person entitled to enforce the instrument must generally be in possession of the instrument (i.e., a holder). §§ 3-301, 3-309, 3-602(a).

1. Final Payment

Payment of a negotiable instrument cannot be recovered if made to a person who took the instrument in good faith and for value or to a person who in good faith changed position in reliance on the payment or acceptance. However, the payor may recover from the party paid if the party breached a presentment warranty. § 3-418(c).

2. Payment or Acceptance by Mistake

Unless payment is made to a person who took the instrument in good faith and for value or to a person who in good faith changed position in reliance on the payment, if the drawee of a draft pays or accepts the draft and the drawee acted on the mistaken belief that (i) payment of the draft had not been stopped, or (ii) the signature of the drawer of the draft was authorized, then the drawee may recover the amount of the draft from the person to whom or for whose benefit payment was made or, in the case of acceptance, may revoke the acceptance. The rights of the drawee are not affected by the failure of the drawee to exercise ordinary care in paying or accepting the draft. § 418(a).

In all other cases when an instrument has been paid or accepted by mistake (e.g., insufficient funds in the drawer's account), the person paying or accepting may recover the payment from the person to whom or for whose benefit payment was made or, in the case of acceptance, may revoke acceptance to the extent permitted by the law governing mistake and restitution. § 3-418(a).

B. DISCHARGE

1. Effect on Instrument

"**Discharge**" refers to the discharge of a party's personal obligation. The instrument itself is not discharged. It is better to think of discharge as a personal defense because it may or may not be effective, depending on whether the person entitled to enforce the instrument is an HDC.

A discharge is not effective against an HDC who did not have notice of the discharge. § 3-601.

2. Effect on Underlying Obligation

a. Suspension of obligation

Unless otherwise agreed, if a note or a check (other than a certified, cashier's, or teller's check) is taken for an obligation, the obligation is suspended to the same extent the obligation would be discharged if an amount of money equal to the amount of the instrument were taken. § 3-310(b).

1) Length of suspension

a) Uncertified check

In the case of an uncertified check, suspension of the obligation continues until dishonor of the check or until it is paid or certified. Payment or certification of the check results in discharge of the obligation to the extent of the amount of the check. § 3-310(b)(1).

b) Note

In the case of a note, suspension of the obligation continues until dishonor of the note or until it is paid. Payment of the note results in discharge of the obligation to the extent of the payment. § 3-310(b)(2).

2) Effect of dishonor

If a check or note is dishonored and the obligee is the person entitled to enforce the instrument, the obligee may enforce either the instrument or the obligation for which the instrument was taken. In the case of an instrument of a third person that is negotiated to the obligee by the obligor, discharge of the obligor on the instrument also discharges the obligation. § 3-310(b)(3).

3) Instrument not in hands of obligee

If the person entitled to enforce the instrument taken for an obligation is a person other than the obligee, the obligee may not enforce the obligation to the extent the obligation is suspended. § 3-310(b)(4).

4) Lost, stolen, or destroyed instruments

If the obligee is the person entitled to enforce the instrument, but no longer has possession of it because it was lost, stolen, or destroyed, the obligation may not be enforced to the extent of the amount payable on the instrument, and to that extent the obligee's rights against the obligor are limited to enforcement of the instrument. § 3-310(b)(4).

b. Discharge—certified, cashier's, and teller's checks

Unless the parties agree otherwise, if a certified check, cashier's check, or teller's check is taken for an obligation, the obligation is discharged to the same extent discharge would result if an amount of money equal to the amount of the instrument were taken in payment of the obligation. Discharge of the obligation does not affect any liability that the obligor may have as an indorser of the instrument. § 3-310(a).

3. Discharge by Payment

a. In general

The obligation of the party obliged to pay an instrument is generally discharged to the extent that payment is made by or on behalf of that party to a person entitled to enforce the instrument (e.g., a holder). The obligation may be discharged, even though payment is made with knowledge of a claim to the instrument by another person. § 3-602(a).

b. Exceptions

The obligation is not discharged if the person with a claim to the instrument has obtained an **injunction** against payment, and payment is nevertheless made with knowledge that such payment violates an injunction. Similarly, with respect to an instrument other than a certified, casher's, or teller's check, the obligation is not discharged if the obligor is **indemnified** by a person with a claim to the instrument against loss resulting from refusal to pay a person entitled to enforce the instrument, and the obligor pays despite the indemnification. In addition, the obligation is not discharged if the person making payment knows that the instrument is a **stolen instrument** and pays a person who he knows is in wrongful possession of the instrument. § 3-602(b).

4. **Discharge by Tender of Payment**

If tender of payment of an obligation is made to a person entitled to enforce the instrument, the effect of tender is governed by principles of law applicable to tender of payment under a simple contract. § 3-603(a).

a. **Interest payments**

If tender of payment of an amount due on an instrument is made, the obligation of the obligor to pay interest after the due date on the amount tendered is discharged. § 3-603(c).

b. **Tender refused**

If tender of payment of an obligation to pay an instrument is made and refused, there is discharge to the extent of the amount of the tender of the obligation of an indorser or accommodation party having a right of recourse with respect to the obligation to which the tender relates. § 3-603(b).

5. **Discharge by Cancellation or Renunciation**

A person entitled to enforce an instrument may discharge the obligation of a party to pay the instrument by:

i) An intentional **voluntary act**, such as surrender of the instrument to the party, destruction, mutilation, or cancellation of the instrument, cancellation or striking out of the party's signature, or the addition of words to the instrument indicating discharge; or

ii) By **agreeing not to sue** or otherwise renouncing rights against the party in a separate, signed writing.

The discharge may be done gratuitously or for consideration. The striking out or canceling of an indorsement does not affect the rights of a party derived from the indorsement. § 3-604(a), (b).

The cancellation or renunciation does not affect the rights of an HDC who takes the instrument without notice of the discharge. § 3-601(b).

6. **Discharge of Indorsers and Accommodation Parties**

Special discharge rules apply to an indorser or accommodation party who has recourse against another party to the instrument (e.g., a principal obligor). § 3-605.

a. **Effect of discharge**

The discharge of the obligation of a party to pay an instrument generally *does not* discharge the obligation of an indorser or accommodation party who has a right of recourse against the discharged party. § 3-605(b).

b. Effect of extension of due date and material modifications

If a person entitled to enforce the instrument agrees to an extension of the due date of the obligation of a party to pay the instrument, the extension discharges an indorser or accommodation party having a right of recourse against the obligated party to the extent it proves that the extension caused a loss. § 3-605(c).

In cases of other material modifications agreed to by a person entitled to enforce an instrument, the loss suffered by the indorser or accommodation party as a result of the modification is equal to the amount of the right of recourse unless the person enforcing the instrument proves that no loss was caused by the modification or that the loss was less than the amount of the right of recourse. § 3-605(d).

c. Impairment of collateral

If a party's obligation to pay an instrument is secured by an interest in collateral and the person entitled to enforce the instrument impairs the value of the interest in collateral, the obligations of an indorser or accommodation party are discharged to the extent of the impairment. The burden of proving the collateral's impairment is on the party asserting discharge. § 3-605(e).

Impairing value of an interest in collateral includes:

i) Failure to obtain or maintain perfection or recordation of the interest in collateral;

ii) Release of collateral without substitution of collateral of equal value;

iii) Failure to perform a duty to preserve the value of collateral owed to a debtor or surety or other person secondarily liable; or

iv) Failure to comply with applicable law in disposing collateral.

d. Limitations on discharge

A party is not discharged if the party (i) consents to the event or conduct that is the basis of the discharge, or (ii) the instrument or separate agreement of the party provides for waiver of discharge. § 3-605(i).

An accommodation party is not discharged unless the person entitled to enforce the instrument *knows of the accommodation* or has notice that the instrument was signed for accommodation. § 3-605(h).

7. Discharge by Reacquisition

When a former holder reacquires an instrument, he may cancel any subsequent indorsements occurring after his prior possession. Any cancellation discharges those indorsers, even as against any subsequent holder, including an HDC. § 3-207.

8. Other Methods of Discharge

A discharge may be achieved by any act or agreement that would discharge an obligation to pay money under a simple contract. § 3-601(a). Other ways in which a party's obligation on an instrument may be discharged include:

i) Acceptance of a draft by a bank—the drawer is discharged;

ii) Acceptance of a draft by a bank after indorsement—the indorser is discharged;

iii) Notice of dishonor is not given when required—the indorser is discharged;

iv) Failure to present a check for payment within 30 days after the date of indorsement—the indorser is discharged; and

v) A fraudulent alteration—generally, any party whose obligation is affected by the alteration is discharged.

§ 3-415(c)-(e).

9. Accord and Satisfaction

If a claim is unliquidated or otherwise subject to dispute, the claim can be discharged if the person against whom the claim is asserted in good faith tenders an instrument that contains a conspicuous statement to the effect that the instrument was tendered as full satisfaction of the claim (e.g., "Payment in full"), and the claimant obtains payment of the instrument. § 3-311(a), (b).

When the claimant is an organization, the discharge will not be effective if the instrument is not tendered to a person, place, or office designated by the organization. If no such designation is made, or if the claimant is not an organization, the discharge will not be effective if the claimant returns the payment within 90 days. However, regardless of the type of claimant, these exceptions do not apply and the claim is discharged when the claimant, or the claimant's agent who has direct responsibility with respect to the disputed obligation, knew, within a reasonable time before collection was initiated, that the instrument was tendered in full satisfaction of the claim. The burden to establish such knowledge is on party seeking discharge. § 3-311(c).

XI. PROCEEDINGS WITH RESPECT TO AN INSTRUMENT

Article 3 provides procedural rules in cases involving disputes over negotiable instruments.

A. PRIMA FACIE CASE

A plaintiff seeking enforcement must prove that (i) the plaintiff is a person entitled to enforce the instrument; and (ii) the signatures are valid. § 3-308(b).

1. Person Entitled to Enforce

In order to be able to enforce an instrument, a person must be a:

i) Holder;

ii) Non-holder in possession of the instrument who has the rights of a holder (e.g., rights acquired through subrogation), such as when a person takes possession of an order instrument through a valid transfer (e.g., a gift) from a holder who fails to indorse the instrument; or

iii) Person not in possession of the instrument, but a person who has the right to enforce it, such as when the instrument has been lost, stolen, or destroyed.

§ 3-301, incl. comment.

2. Validity of Signatures

In an action with respect to an instrument, the authenticity of and authority to make each signature on the instrument is admitted unless specifically denied in the pleadings. If the validity of a signature is denied in the pleadings, the burden of establishing validity is on the person claiming validity. However, the signature is rebuttably presumed to be authentic and authorized, unless the action is to enforce the liability of the purported signer and the signer is dead or incompetent at the time of trial. Consequently, the party challenging the validity of a signature generally has the burden of production on the issue; that party must introduce some evidence that calls into question the validity of the signature. The party claiming the validity of the signature then has the burden of persuasion by a preponderance of the evidence. § 3-308(a), incl. cmt 1.

3. Undisclosed Principal as Defendant

If an action to enforce the instrument is brought against a person as the undisclosed principal of a person who signed the instrument as a party to the instrument, the plaintiff has the burden of establishing that the defendant is liable on the instrument as a represented person. § 3-308(a).

B. DEFENSES

Once the plaintiff establishes a prima facie case, the defendant may escape paying the instrument by proving a defense or claim in recoupment. If the defendant establishes a defense or claim in recoupment, the plaintiff must re-establish the right to payment by proving that she is an HDC who is not subject to the defense or claim. § 3-308(b).

C. LOST, DESTROYED, OR STOLEN INSTRUMENT

1. Ability to Enforce

If an instrument has been lost, destroyed, or stolen, a person is entitled to enforce the instrument if the person was in possession of the instrument and entitled to enforce the instrument when the loss of possession occurred. The loss cannot have been the result of a transfer by such person or a lawful seizure. § 3-309(a).

2. Procedure

A person seeking enforcement of a lost, destroyed, or stolen instrument must prove the terms of the instrument and the person's right to enforce the instrument.

The court may not enter judgment in favor of the person seeking enforcement unless it finds that the person required to pay the instrument is adequately protected against loss that might occur by reason of a claim by another person to enforce the instrument (e.g., an HDC). Adequate protection may be provided by any reasonable means, such as a security bond. § 3-309(b).

3. Missing Certified, Cashier's, or Teller's Check

In lieu of proceeding via a court action, a person who claims the right to receive the amount of a certified check as drawer or payee, or who is the remitter or payee of a cashier's or teller's check that was lost, destroyed, or stolen may file a claim with the obligated bank (i.e., the issuer of the cashier's or teller's check or the acceptor of the certified check). The claim, which must be written and made under penalty of perjury, must describe the check with reasonable certainty, contain a declaration of loss, and request payment of the amount of the check. § 3-312(a), (b).

a. Time for enforcement of claim

The claim becomes enforceable at the later of (i) the time the claim is asserted, or (ii) the 90th day following the date of the check, in the case of a cashier's check or teller's check, or the 90th day following the date of the acceptance, in the case of a certified check. Until the claim becomes enforceable, it has no legal effect, and the obligated bank may pay the check or, in the case of a teller's check, may permit the drawee to pay the check. Payment discharges all liability of the obligated bank with respect to the check. § 3-312(b).

b. Enforcement of claim

When the claim becomes enforceable, the obligated bank becomes obliged to pay the amount of the check to the claimant if payment of the check has not been made. Payment to the claimant discharges all liability of the obligated bank with respect to the check. § 3-312(b).

c. Subsequent presentment of check

If the claim becomes enforceable before the check is presented for payment, the obligated bank is not obliged to pay the check. However, if an HDC subsequently presents the check for payment, the claimant must refund its payment to the obligated bank if the bank pays the check, or the claimant must pay the HDC if the check is dishonored. § 3-312(b),(c).

D. CONVERSION

The law applicable to conversion of personal property applies to instruments. An instrument is converted if it is taken by a transfer, other than a negotiation, from a person not entitled to enforce the instrument, or a depository or payor bank makes or obtains payment with respect to the instrument for a person not entitled to enforce the instrument or obtain payment. A collecting bank has no conversion liability beyond the amount of any proceeds that it has not paid out. § 3-420.

1. Conversion Action Plaintiffs

Generally, a person entitled to enforce an instrument (e.g., its true owner) may bring a conversion action. An action for conversion of an instrument *may not* be brought by (i) the issuer or acceptor of the instrument, or (ii) a payee or indorsee who did not receive delivery of the instrument, either directly or through delivery to an agent or a co-payee. § 3-420(a).

2. Recovery Amount

The measure of recovery is presumed to be the amount payable on the instrument, but recovery is limited to the amount of the plaintiff's interest in the instrument. § 3-420(b).

Conflict of Laws

CONFLICT OF LAWS

Table of Contents

CONFLICT OF LAWS

Editor's Note
Transactions or events that give rise to legal disputes can have connections to two or more different legal jurisdictions. The laws of such jurisdictions may differ with regard to the resolution of such disputes. Courts have developed legal doctrines and rules to determine what effect may be given to the fact that a case may have a significant relationship to more than one legal jurisdiction. This outline covers the basic doctrines that are used in different jurisdictions to address these conflicts of law. When Illinois law differs from the majority rules, or requires clarification, that law is set out in shaded boxes such as this one.

I.   DOMICILE

Domicile is a legal concept that can be significant for both choice of law determinations and jurisdictional purposes. If a person is domiciled in a particular state, the person will be subject to personal jurisdiction in that state's courts whether or not the person can be found and personally served process. *Milliken v. Meyer*, 311 U.S. 457 (1940). In the conflict of laws context, domicile will be considered an important contact in jurisdictions that apply a "contacts" approach to choice of law. *See* § II.B.2 (Most Significant Relationship Approach), *infra*. Ordinarily, the determination of a person's domicile is a question of fact.

A.   DOMICILE OF INDIVIDUALS

Individuals can have more than one residence at a time, but they can have only one domicile at a time, which can be acquired either by choice or by operation of law.

1.   Domicile by Choice

If a person has legal capacity, the person's domicile is the location where he has chosen to establish domicile. In general, domicile will be where the person is present with the intent to remain for an unlimited time, and abandons any prior domicile. Thus, courts will look at the person's physical presence and intent to determine a person's domicile.

a.   Physical presence

Actual physical presence in the location is required to establish the location as the person's domicile. The person, though, need not be present for any specific amount of time in order to establish domicile, so long as the amount of time is coupled with the intent to establish domicile.

b.   Intent

To establish a location as the domicile, a person must demonstrate, in addition to physical presence in a location, the intent to make the location his home for the time being, or the absence of an intent to go elsewhere. Presence under compulsion, such as a person in prison, will not establish domicile by choice.

Permanency is not required, but the intent to remain must be bona fide. In general, the person's actions and statements are used to establish intent. Ownership of real estate, voting, payment of taxes, having a bank account, or registration of an automobile are all factors that could be used to establish intent; however, none of these factors is conclusive.

c. Potential problem of multiple states claiming domicile

A forum state will apply its own law in determining questions of domicile. Although a person may have only one domicile, two states could theoretically conclude that the person is domiciled within its jurisdiction.

2. Domicile by Operation of Law

Domicile by operation of law occurs when an individual does not have the legal capacity to choose his domicile, as in the case of infants and incompetents. Historically, a married woman's domicile was that of her husband, although today married women may choose their states of domicile.

a. Infants

Infants (i.e., minor children) are domiciled where their custodial parents are domiciled. If a child is emancipated, the child may establish his or her own domicile.

b. Incompetents

A person lacking the mental legal capacity to choose a domicile will retain his or her parents' domicile. If the person once had legal capacity, chose a domicile, and then lost legal capacity, his domicile remains the place where he was domiciled before losing capacity.

B. DOMICILE OF CORPORATIONS

A corporation's domicile is always the state where it is incorporated.

C. CONTINUITY OF DOMICILE

Once established, a domicile is presumed to continue until a new domicile is acquired. The burden of showing a change in domicile is on the party that asserts it. Temporary or even prolonged absences will not, by themselves, result in a change of domicile. Thus, a domiciliary of one state can live in another state for years and retain his domicile in the original state, so long as he or she intends to return to that state. An old domicile by choice continues even though a new residence is established until there is the intention to create a new domicile.

D. CHANGE OF DOMICILE

A change of domicile takes place when a person with capacity to change his or her domicile is physically present in a place and intends to make that place home, at least for the time being. The physical presence and the intent must concur.

> **EXAM NOTE:** Before addressing choice of law, a court must have proper jurisdiction over a matter. This subject is discussed fully in the Civil Procedure outline. Keep in mind that once you have determined that a particular court has jurisdiction over a case, that court still may refuse to hear the case if it believes venue should be somewhere else. Once you have determined jurisdiction, if the transactions or events giving rise to the dispute involve more than one state, you generally need to determine which state's law governs the different issues in the case.

II. CHOICE OF LAW

When a cause of action involves contacts with more than one state, the forum court must determine which state's law is to be applied to decide the issues in the case. State choice-of-law rules generally have three sources: (i) specific choice-of-law statutes, (ii) contractual choice-of-law agreements, and (iii) general choice-of-law rules governed by forum state common law. Choice-of-law issues are possible whenever a lawsuit involves a foreign element, such as a non-resident party or an event outside the forum state.

A. LIMITATIONS ON CHOICE OF LAW

Both the U.S. Constitution and state and federal statutes can limit a court's power to apply a particular choice-of-law rule. In certain circumstances, an agreement between the parties can also require the application of a particular choice of law in court.

1. Constitutional Limitations

The U.S. Constitution can limit a state court's ability to apply its own substantive law to litigation having multistate issues.

a. Due process

Under the Due Process Clause of the Fourteenth Amendment, the U.S. Supreme Court has held that a forum state may apply its own law to a particular case only if it has a significant contact or significant aggregation of contacts with the state such that a choice of its law is neither arbitrary nor fundamentally unfair. *Allstate Ins. Co. v. Hague*, 449 U.S. 302 (1981). If the forum state's only contact is the fact that the cause of action was brought in its courts or the fact that the plaintiff once lived there, application of the substantive law of the forum state will violate due process. *Home Ins. Co. v. Dick*, 281 U.S. 397 (1930).

b. Full faith and credit

Under Article IV, § 1 of the U.S. Constitution, "[f]ull faith and credit shall be given in each State to the public acts, records and judicial proceedings of every other State." The Supreme Court has held that the term "public acts" includes both a state's statutes and its substantive case law. *Carroll v. Lanza*, 349 U.S. 408 (1955). The Full Faith and Credit Clause requires a forum state to apply the law of another state when the forum has no contacts with or interest in the controversy, but does not prevent the forum state from applying its own law when the forum has such contacts or interest in the controversy. *Allstate Ins. Co. v. Hague*, 449 U.S. 302 (1981). In addition, the Full Faith and Credit Clause does not require a state to apply another state's law in violation of its own legitimate public policy. *Franchise Tax Bd. of California v. Hyatt*, 538 U.S. 488 (2003).

2. Statutory Limitations

a. State statutes

Some states have statutes requiring certain choice of law rules to be applied in particular cases. For example, the Uniform Commercial Code ("UCC") contains choice-of-law provisions that require a forum state to apply the UCC if the state has a reasonable relationship to the transaction.

b. Federal statutes

Certain federal statutes may preempt a state from claiming jurisdiction over certain cases. For example, federal courts are given exclusive jurisdiction in patent, anti-trust, and bankruptcy matters.

3. Party-Controlled Choice of Law

Most courts will enforce a contractual choice-of-law provision if it is:

i) A valid agreement with an effective choice-of-law clause;

ii) Applicable to the lawsuit under the terms of the contract;

iii) Reasonably related to the lawsuit (i.e., the law to be applied is from a state with connections to the parties or the contract); and

iv) Not in violation of the public policy of the forum state or another interested state.

Illinois Distinction: Party-Controlled Choice of Law

A choice-of-law provision will be given full effect in Illinois if it does not contravene Illinois public policy and there is some relationship between the chosen forum and the parties or the transaction. Note that despite a choice-of-law provision by the parties, Illinois holds that the law of the forum will control statute of limitations matters because statutes of limitations are procedural.

Note that a state's legislature may restrict the power of contracting parties to choose a governing law.

B. APPROACHES TO CHOICE OF LAW—IN GENERAL

So long as there is no constitutional mandate or statutory directive dictating which law applies, courts generally approach choice-of-law questions using one of three different approaches. These approaches are: (i) the "vested rights" approach of the First Restatement of Conflicts, (ii) the "most significant relationship" approach of the Second Restatement of Conflicts, and (iii) the "governmental interests" approach.

Note that a state may use different choice-of-law approaches for different substantive areas of the law. Thus, a state might use the vested rights approach for contract cases, while applying the most significant relationship approach for tort matters.

1. Vested Rights Approach

This approach, used in the First Restatement of Conflicts, is a territorial approach. It looks to the jurisdiction where the parties' rights are vested, meaning where the act or relationship that gives rise to the cause of action occurred or was created. Generally, this approach looks for the place where the last liable event took place.

a. Characterization

In determining where vesting occurred, the forum court will first characterize the issues in the cause of action. Initially, this involves a determination of whether the issue is substantive or procedural. If the issue is procedural, the forum court will apply its own procedural rules. If the issue is substantive, the court must identify the substantive area of the law involved. In general, the forum court will apply its own state law to determine whether an issue is one of tort, contract, property, domestic relations, etc. Note that in characterizing an issue in a particular way (e.g., as contract rather than tort or as substantive rather than procedural), a court may be able to avoid the application of a particular foreign law in favor of its own state's law, or vice versa.

b. Determination of the choice-of-law rule to be applied

After characterizing the issue in the cause of action, the forum court will then determine what the forum state's choice-of-law rules require with regard to the characterized issue. For example, if the issue has been characterized as a tort, the law of the forum state may require that the law of the place of the injury apply.

2. Most Significant Relationship Approach

While the First Restatement's vested rights approach offered certainty, ease of application, and predictability of results, many courts and commentators criticized it for often resulting in the application of a jurisdiction's law that was only applied because the jurisdiction had a fortuitous or attenuated connection to the events giving rise to the case.

Attempting to fix these problems, the Second Restatement of Conflicts applies the law of the state with the **most significant relationship** to the issue in question. This approach is also sometimes referred to as the "center of gravity" approach or the "grouping of contacts" approach. It focuses on the policy objectives behind competing laws of different states.

Illinois Distinction: Most Significant Relationship Approach

In general, with regard to tort and contract matters, Illinois applies the Second Restatement's **most significant contacts** approach to conflicts of law. Thus, the law of the state with the most significant contacts controls substantive matters.

A choice-of-law analysis begins by isolating the issue and defining the conflict. A choice-of-law determination is required only when a difference in law will make a difference in the outcome.

When determining which state has the most significant relationship, the forum court generally considers the "connecting facts" or contacts that link each jurisdiction to the case, as well as the seven policy principles that are set forth in the Second Restatement. The seven principles are:

i) **The needs of the interstate or international system**: This is designed to achieve judicial efficiency and facilitate agreement between the two competing jurisdictions involved in the case.

ii) **The relevant policies of the forum:** The forum state must determine how its policies relate to the issues at hand for a particular case in a specific area of the law.

iii) **Policies of interested states:** The forum state evaluates its own laws as well as those of interested states in order to determine which laws should apply.

iv) **Party expectations:** The court will look to see if the parties have any justified expectations that should be protected. This principle *only* applies to planned transactions, such as contracts.

v) **Policies underlying the substantive areas of law:** The court must consider how the application of a particular law in a particular substantive area will affect basic policies relating to that area of the law.

vi) **Certainty, predictability, and uniformity:** The court will strive to achieve these goals and ultimately discourage forum shopping.

vii) **Ease of future application:** In the interest of making the final application of law easy, the court evaluates how difficult the application of the second jurisdiction's law would be to the case at hand. The court then decides if it should be used.

The list is not exclusive, and the particular factors will vary in importance according to the type of case at issue.

The forum court will: (i) isolate the precise legal issue that results in a conflict between the competing states, (ii) identify the policy objectives that each state's law seeks to achieve with respect to such issue, and (iii) determine each state's interest in view of its policy objectives, to determine which state has a superior connection with the dispute. The contacts with each interested state are analyzed and their relative importance is considered, recognizing that different choices of law may be made with regard to different issues in a single case.

> **EXAM NOTE:** Note that the Second Restatement includes specific presumptive rules for several different substantive areas of the law. *See* § II.C (Rules for Specific Areas of Substantive Law), *infra*. Nonetheless, the forum court must still examine the seven principles listed above to determine if the presumptive rule should not be applied because another state has a more significant relationship under the seven principles.

3. **Governmental Interest Approach**

Under the governmental interest approach, it is presumed that the forum state will apply its own law, but the parties may request that another state's law be applied. If a party makes such a request, then that party must identify the policies of competing laws.

If there is a false conflict (i.e., the forum has no interest in the litigation) the court applies the law of the state that does have an interest in the case. If there is a true conflict (i.e., the forum state and another state each have an interest in the litigation) the forum state will review its own policies to determine which law should apply. If the conflict cannot be resolved, the law of the forum state is applied.

However, if the forum state has no interest in applying its own laws (i.e., is a "disinterested forum"), and the doctrine of *forum non conveniens* is available, then the forum court should dismiss the case. The doctrine of *forum non conveniens* allows a court to dismiss an action even if personal jurisdiction and venue are otherwise proper, if it finds that the forum would be too inconvenient for parties and witnesses, and that a more convenient venue is available. Some of the factors that are generally considered include: (i) the availability of an alternative forum, (ii) the law that will apply, and (iii) the location of the parties, witnesses, and evidence. If forum non conveniens is not available, then the forum state may either make its own determination as to which law is better to use, or apply the law that most closely matches its own state law. If no state has an interest, then the forum law generally prevails.

States have an interest in applying their conduct-regulating laws (i.e., laws designed to regulate conduct) when the wrongful conduct occurs within their territory, or when a state domiciliary is injured. States have an interest in applying its loss-shifting laws (i.e., immunize people from liability) when doing so would benefit a state domiciliary.

4. **Conflict-of-Law Rules in Federal Diversity Cases**

Under *Klaxon Co. v. Stentor Electric Mfg. Co.*, 313 U.S. 487 (1941), in federal diversity cases the federal district court is generally required to apply the conflict-of-law rules of the state in which it sits. However, such application of a state's conflict-of-interest rules are only required to the extent the state's rules are valid under the Full Faith and Credit and Due Process Clauses of the U.S. Constitution. *Allstate Ins. Co. v. Hague*, 449 U.S. 302 (1981). If a diversity case was transferred from a federal court in another state under federal venue law, 28 U.S.C. § 1404(a), the first state's choice-of-law rules will be applied. *Van Dusen v. Barrack*, 376 U.S. 612 (1946).

5. *Depeçage*

Under the traditional approach to choice of law, the forum court is required to analyze a case in its entirety, applying only one state's law to all of the issues in the case. Modern approaches to choice of law require the forum court to consider separately which state's law should govern for each substantive issue if the issue would be resolved differently under the law of two or more potentially interested jurisdictions. This approach, which can allow the law of one state to govern one or more particular issues while still other issues are controlled by the law of one or more other states, is known as "*depeçage.*"

> **Illinois Distinction: Depeçage**
>
> Illinois courts apply the doctrine of depeçage, separately considering which state's law governs each substantive issue if the issue would be resolved differently under the law of two or more potentially interested jurisdictions.

6. *Renvoi*

a. **Doctrine**

The doctrine of *renvoi* requires that a forum court applying the law of another state to decide a matter also apply that foreign state's conflict of laws rules. Such rules might require the forum state to refer to its own law (this is known as remission) or to the laws of another state (this is known as transmission). Theoretically, this could result in a vicious circle with no state's internal laws being able to be applied.

b. **Rejection**

Most states generally reject the application of renvoi either by choosing not to apply the whole law of the foreign state or by accepting the reference back to its own law and applying only that law to the case. The governmental interests approach wholly rejects the application of renvoi. The Second Restatement generally rejects the application of renvoi, but does require that a state look to the whole law of the foreign state in determining title or succession to land.

c. Federal Tort Claims Act

The Federal Tort Claims Act, 28 U.S.C. § 1346(b), requires application of the whole law, including the conflict rules, of the place where the act or omission occurred. *See Richards v. United States*, 369 U.S. 1 (1962). Thus, the forum will refer to the place where the act or omission occurred and then apply the conflict-of-laws rules of that state.

C. RULES FOR SPECIFIC AREAS OF SUBSTANTIVE LAW

1. Torts

a. Vested rights approach

Under the First Restatement's vested rights approach, a tort case will be governed by the law of the place where the wrong was committed (i.e., *lex loci delicti*). This means the place where the last event necessary to make the actor liable for the tort took place (generally the place where the person or thing that is injured is situated at the time of the wrong). The place of injury will generally govern whether the plaintiff has sustained a legal injury, what conduct creates liability, the standard of care to be applied, defenses, and damages.

b. Most significant relationship approach

Under the most significant relationship approach of the Second Restatement, the seven policy principles discussed at § II.B.2 (Most Significant Relationship Approach), *supra*, are applied to determine the applicable substantive rules of law. In tort matters, the default rule under the Second Restatement approach is that the place of injury controls, unless another state has a more significant relationship to the parties or to the occurrence of the tort.

c. Governmental interest approach

Under the governmental interest approach, the forum state generally looks to its own law, so long as that state has a legitimate interest in applying its own law. Another state's law would be applied if a party makes a request for such application and the forum court determines that the other state's law should apply in accordance with the forum state's policies. *See* § II.B.3 (Governmental Interests Approach), *supra*.

Illinois Distinction: Torts

Illinois follows the most significant contacts approach in tort cases, applying the local law of the place of the injury unless Illinois has a more significant relationship with the occurrence and with the parties. If Illinois has the more significant relationship, the law of Illinois should apply. Contacts that should be evaluated include: the place where the injury occurred; the place where the conduct causing the injury occurred; the domicile, residence, place of incorporation, and place of business of the parties; and the place where the relationship between the parties, if any, is centered.

In conducting the significant contacts analysis, Illinois courts do not merely count the contacts. Instead, they apply an "interest analysis" process, under which they:

i)   Isolate the issue presented;

ii)   Identify the relevant policies embraced in the laws in conflict; and

---

iii) Examine the contacts and determine which jurisdiction has a superior interest in having its policy applied.

2. Contracts

a. Express choice of law of the parties

If there is an express choice-of-law provision in the contract, then that law will govern unless:

i) It is contrary to public policy;

ii) There is no reasonable basis for the parties' choice; or

iii) There was fraud or mistake and true consent was not given.

If there is no express choice of law provision in the contract, the forum court will apply the vested rights approach, the most significant relationship approach, or the governmental interest approach, depending on the choice-of-law rules applicable in the forum state.

Illinois Distinction: Contracts

For contracts governed by the UCC, as applicable in Illinois, when a transaction bears a reasonable relation to Illinois and also to another state, the parties may agree that either the law of Illinois or of the other state will govern their rights and duties. If the parties do not come to an agreement as to choice of law, Illinois's version of the UCC will apply to transactions bearing an appropriate relationship to Illinois.

The parties may not choose the law that will govern if the UCC specifies the applicable law. In that case, the Illinois UCC provision governs and a contrary agreement is effective only to the extent permitted by the Illinois UCC, including its conflict-of-laws rules. 810 Ill. Comp. Stat. 5/1-301(2).

Illinois Distinction: Illinois Choice of Law and Forum Act

Under 735 Ill. Comp. Stat. 105/5-5, the parties to any contract for $250,000 or more (including contracts that would otherwise fall under the above rule of the UCC), may agree that Illinois law will govern their contract, in whole or in part, regardless of whether the contract is reasonably related to Illinois. This rule does not apply to any contract, agreement, or undertaking for labor or personal services or relating to any transaction for personal, family, or household services.

---

b. Vested rights approach

Under the vested rights approach of the First Restatement, certain contractual issues are deemed to "vest" in the location where the contract was executed, while others are deemed to "vest" in the location where the contract was to be performed.

1) Location where the contract is executed

a) Validity of the contract

In general, the place of execution governs issues regarding the validity of the contract, including the capacity to contract, formalities of the contract (e.g., whether there must be a writing and whether it must be signed), and consideration for the contract.

b) Defenses to formation of the contract

Generally, issues regarding whether there are defenses to the formation of the contract are governed by the law of the place of the execution of the contract. This can include defenses such as misrepresentation, fraud, and illegality.

c) Interpretation of the contract

The interpretation of a contract is governed by the law of the place of execution.

2) Location where the contract was to be performed

a) Details of performance

The details of performance are governed by the law of the place of performance. Such details can include:

i) The time and manner of performance;

ii) The person who is obligated to perform and the person to whom performance is to be made;

iii) The sufficiency of performance; and

iv) Any excuse for non-performance.

c. Most significant relationship approach

1) In general

Under the most significant relationship approach of the Second Restatement, the seven policy factors (discussed at § II.B.2 (Most Significant Relationship Approach), *supra*) are considered, as are the following:

i) The location of the contracting, negotiation, and performance;

ii) The place where the contract's subject matter is located; and

iii) The location of the parties' domiciles, residences, nationalities, places of incorporation, and places of business.

Generally, when the location of negotiation and performance are the same, the forum court will apply the law of that state.

2) Default rules

Under the Second Restatement approach, there are also default rules that apply to certain kinds of contracts. These default rules will generally apply **unless** another state is found to have a more significant relationship with regard to the issue.

i) **Land contracts** are controlled by the law of the state of the situs of the land;

ii) **Personalty contracts** are controlled by the law of the state where the place of delivery is located;

iii) **Life insurance contracts** are controlled by the law of the state where the insured is domiciled (*see* § I (Domicile), *supra*, for a discussion of the rules regarding domicile);

iv) **Casualty insurance contracts** are controlled by the law of the state where the insured risk is located;

v) **Loans** are controlled by the law of the state where repayment is required;

vi) **Suretyship contracts** are controlled by the law of the state governing the principal obligation; and

vii) **Transportation contracts** (covering both persons and goods) are controlled by the law of the state where the place of departure is located.

> **EXAM NOTE:** Remember, the most significant relationship still prevails and the default rules relating to these specific kinds of contracts are subject to exception if there are other factors showing a more significant relationship to another state.

d. Governmental interest approach

The governmental interest approach does not change based on substantive areas of law. *See* § II.B.3, *supra*, for the rules governing the governmental interest approach.

3. Property

Property can be classified as real or personal. The law of the place where the property is situated generally determines whether it is real or personal. Note that the law can change when property is removed from one state to another. Thus, the character of the same property, whether personal or real, may vary according to its location.

a. Tangible personal property

1) UCC

The UCC generally governs most issues involving the sale of (or security interests in) tangible personal property. Under the UCC, the parties may stipulate to the applicable law that will govern the transaction or, in the absence of such stipulation, the forum state will apply its version of the UCC "to transactions bearing an appropriate relation to" the forum state. UCC § 1-301. If a particular code provision specifies the applicable law, a contrary agreement is effective only to the extent permitted by the law (including the conflict-of-law rules) so specified. UCC § 1-301(c).

Under the UCC, the law governing the perfection, non-perfection, and priority of security interests in tangible and intangible collateral is generally the law of the state in which the debtor is located. UCC § 9-301. In general, this means the principal residence of an individual, the place of business of an organization, and the chief executive office of an organization with more than one place of business. UCC § 9-307(b). Registered organizations (i.e., corporations, limited partnerships, and other entities requiring registration under state law), however, are located in their state of registration, rather than the state of their principal place of business. UCC § 9-307(e). If the debtor or the collateral moves to another state, the secured party generally has a fixed period of time to perfect his or her security interest there or it will become unperfected and will be deemed never to have been perfected as against a previous or subsequent purchaser of the collateral for value. The period of time is generally four months in the case of the debtor and one year in the case of collateral. UCC § 9-316.

While the law of the debtor's location governs perfection of non-possessory security interests in negotiable documents, goods, instruments, money, or tangible chattel paper, the law of the situs of the property will apply to issues of priority or the effect of perfection. UCC § 9-301. If a possessory security interest is at issue, the controlling law will be the state where the collateral is located. UCC § 9-301(2). The law of the situs also controls with regard to perfection and priority in fixtures and timber that is to be cut. UCC § 9-301(3).

2) Transactions not covered by the UCC

For transactions not covered by the UCC, one of the following approaches will generally be followed by the forum court:

a) Vested rights approach

Under the vested rights approach of the First Restatement, the creation and transfer of interests in tangible personal property are governed by the law of the state in which the property was located at the time of the transaction at issue. This rule controls even where the property at issue may have been taken to another state without the permission of the owner.

b) Most significant relationship approach

Under the most significant relationship approach of the Second Restatement, the law of the situs of the tangible personal property at the time the relevant transaction took place generally determines the choice of law. However, if it is determined that another state has a more significant relationship to the transaction, then that state's law will apply.

c) Governmental interest approach

The governmental interest approach does not change based on substantive areas of law. *See* § II.B.3, *supra*, for the rules governing the governmental interest approach.

b. Intangible property

1) UCC

As noted above (*see* § II.C.2, *supra*), under the UCC, the law governing the perfection, non-perfection, and priority of security interests in intangible collateral is generally the law of the state in which the debtor is located. UCC § 9-301. This means the principal residence of an individual, the place of business of an organization, or the chief executive office of an organization with more than one place of business. UCC § 9-307(b). Registered organizations (i.e., corporations, limited partnerships, and other entities requiring registration under state law), however, are located in their state of registration, rather than the state of their principal place of business. UCC § 9-307(e). If the debtor moves to another state, the secured party has four months to perfect his or her security interest there or it will become unperfected and will be deemed never to have been perfected as against a previous or subsequent purchaser of the collateral for value. UCC § 9-316.

For non-possessory security interests in negotiable documents, goods, instruments, money, or tangible chattel paper, the debtor's location governs the issue of perfection, but questions of priority and the effect of perfection are governed by the law of the state of the situs of the property. UCC § 9-301(3).

For issues involving corporate securities, the law of the issuer's state of incorporation generally controls. UCC § 8-110.

2) Transactions not covered by the UCC

a) Vested rights approach

An intangible (e.g., a claim, a share of stock, a promissory note) has no physical situs. Under the vested rights approach of the First Restatement, such intangibles are governed by the law of the state in which the intangible was created.

b) Most significant relationship approach

Under the most significant relationship approach of the Second Restatement, the transfer of intangible property is governed by the law of the state to which the transaction is most significantly related. *See* § II.B.2 (Most Significant Relationship Approach), *supra*, for the seven factors that are generally used to determine the most significant relationship.

c) Governmental interest approach

The governmental interest approach does not change based on substantive areas of law. *See* § II.B.3 (Governmental Interests Approach), *supra*, for the rules governing the governmental interest approach.

c. Real property

1) Vested rights approach

Under the vested rights approach of the First Restatement, the law of the situs of the real property governs legal issues concerning the title and disposition of real property and whether any interests in the property can be gained or lost. Such issues can include the formalities required for instruments affecting the title to real property and the validity of transfers and mortgages of the property. The forum state will refer to the law of the situs state even with regard to the choice-of-law rules.

2) Most significant relationship approach

Under the most significant relationship approach of the Second Restatement, the law of the situs of the real property is generally presumed to be most significant. *See* § II.B.2 (Most Significant Relationship Approach), *supra*, for the seven factors that are generally used to determine the most significant relationship.

3) Governmental interest approach

The governmental interest approach does not change based on substantive areas of law. *See* § II.B.3, *supra*, for the rules governing the governmental interest approach. Note, though, that under the governmental interest approach, less importance is placed on the situs than under the other two major choice-of-law approaches. If another state has a more significant relationship to the case, its law will prevail.

4) Equitable conversion

Some states apply the doctrine of equitable conversion, under which as soon as a valid contract is made for the sale of real property, the buyer is deemed the owner of the land and the seller is deemed a trustee for the buyer. At the same time, the seller is deemed the owner of the money, while the buyer is deemed a trustee for the seller. Whether the doctrine of equitable conversion will apply to a transaction is governed by the law of the state in which the land at issue is located.

Example: Alice is domiciled in state 1 and contracts with Bill to sell him land in state 2. Under state 1's law, a purchaser has equitable title to land under a contract of sale. Under state 2's law, Bill has no equitable interest in the land. Because the land is located in state 2, the doctrine of equitable conversion is inapplicable and Bill has no equitable interest in the land.

Illinois Distinction: Real Property

Generally, Illinois courts apply the law of the state in which the real property is located when dealing with issues involving title to and the acquisition and disposition of real property, including the formalities required for instruments affecting the title to real property and the validity of transfers and mortgages of the property. The forum state will refer to the law of the situs state even with regard to the choice-of-law rules.

d. Trust property and trust administration

Transfers of trust property are governed by the appropriate rules indicated above for the particular type of property. A property question that involves the administration of a trust, however, is usually governed by the law of the place where the trust is administered.

4. Inheritance

There are many questions that may arise when determining the law that governs inheritance. These questions include the validity of the will, the rights of non-marital or adopted children to inherit property, and the marital rights of the surviving spouse. Which state's laws will govern these issues will depend upon the type of property at issue.

a. Personal property

Questions regarding the transfer of personal property from someone who dies intestate or who has a will are governed by **the law of the deceased's domicile** at the time of death.

b. Real property

Questions regarding the transfer of real property from someone who dies intestate or who has a will are governed by **the law of the situs**.

> **EXAM NOTE:** Note that for the decedent's personal property, the question of whether a person has died testate or intestate is determined by the law of the decedent's domicile, but for the decedent's real estate, this question is decided by the law of the place where the real estate is situated.

c. Equitable conversion

As noted above (*see* § II.C.3.c, *supra*), the application of the doctrine of equitable conversion is governed by the law of the state in which the land at issue is located. The doctrine of equitable conversion can also apply to testamentary directions to sell real property and distribute the proceeds. If the directions are absolute and leave the executor with no discretion, the real estate is turned into personalty under the doctrine of equitable conversion as soon as the will takes effect. Thus, if a will instructs an executor to sell real property, the doctrine of equitable conversion may be applicable and the interest in real property may be treated as an interest in personalty if the will is valid under the law of the state where the real property is located.

5. Corporations

Under the vested rights approach of the First Restatement, the law of the state of incorporation governs questions regarding the existence of the corporation (creation and dissolution), and issues about its structure, the rights of shareholders, and other internal corporate affairs. The Second Restatement concurs in concluding that the law of the state of incorporation decides such questions. *See* § II.B.3, *supra*, for the rules governing the governmental interest approach.

6. Family Law

a. Marriage

1) In general

In general, marriages are valid where they took place and are recognized in all other states. This also holds true for voided marriages. If a marriage violates a particularly strong public policy of the domicile of either party, however, it will be invalid. Such policies can include bigamy and incest.

2) Violation of prohibitory rule

A marriage that is valid in the state where it took place, but violates a prohibitory rule of the domicile of one of the parties will be void in the state where the marriage would have been prohibited if the parties immediately return to that state and become domiciled there. A prohibitory rule is a rule that expresses the strong public policy of a state, such as rules against bigamy, incest, or marriage below a minimum age. Even though one state may refuse to recognize such a marriage, other states are not required to respect such policy and may choose to recognize the marriage.

Illinois Distinction: Marriage

By statute in Illinois, if any Illinois resident who is prohibited from contracting into marriage under Illinois law goes to another state or country and enters into a marriage that is prohibited and declared void by Illinois law, the marriage will be null and void for all purposes in Illinois with the same effect as though such prohibited marriage had been entered into in Illinois.

---

3) Annulment

In cases of annulment, the court will generally look to the jurisdiction where the ceremony took place to determine whether the law permits the annulment.

4) Same-sex marriage

Same-sex marriages are not afforded full faith and credit. States are not required to recognize marriages of same-sex partners that take place in one state but violate another state's laws. *See* The Defense of Marriage Act, 28 U.S.C. § 1738C.

b. Divorce and marital property

Questions of law relating to the grounds for divorce are controlled by the law of the plaintiff's domicile in a divorce matter. Thus, the forum court will look only to its own law to determine if grounds for the divorce exist.

For issues regarding marital property already owned by either spouse at the time of the marriage, the law of the situs will control with regard to real property, while the law of the domicile will control with respect to personal property. For personal property acquired during marriage, the law that controls is the law of the domicile of the parties at the time of the acquisition. For real property acquired during marriage, the law that controls is the law of the situs of the real property. Note, though, that if marital funds or property are used by one spouse to acquire land in another state, the land that is acquired has the same character as the funds or property used to acquire it. Thus, if a wife in a community property state purchases a house in a separate property state using community funds, the house will be community property and not separate property.

In determining the enforceability of a premarital agreement, most states apply the law of the state with the most significant relationship to the matter at hand. *See* Restatement (Second) of Conflict of Laws § 188.

c. Legitimacy

Legitimacy is the legal kinship between a child and its parent(s). The status of a child's legitimacy at birth is governed by the law of the domicile of the parent whose relationship to the child is in question.

d. Legitimation

A child who was born illegitimate may, by force of law, become legitimate through the marriage of his or her parents or if the child's parent acknowledges the child as his own. A child will usually be legitimate if this would be the child's status under the local law of the state where either (i) the parent was domiciled when the child's status of legitimacy is claimed to have been created, or (ii) where the child was domiciled when the parent acknowledged the child as his own.

e. Adoption

The forum court will apply its own state law to determine whether to grant an adoption.

7. Workers' Compensation

Workers' compensation is governed by state statutes and administered by state agencies. Conflicts between state laws can develop, though, particularly with regard to which state can award benefits.

a. Jurisdiction

1) In general

Any state with a "legitimate interest" in an injury and its consequences may apply its workers' compensation act. *Alaska Packers Ass'n. v. Indus. Accident Comm'n*, 294 U.S. 532 (1935). In general (and this can vary depending on the state's statute), a state will have a legitimate interest if it is the state where: (i) the employment relationship was entered into by the worker and the employer, (ii) the injury to the employee occurred, (iii) the employment relationship principally occurred (even if the injury did not occur there), or (iv) the employee or the employee's dependents reside. *See Pac. Employers Ins. Co. v. Indus. Accident Comm'n*, 306 U.S. 493 (1939); Restatement (Second) of Conflict of Laws § 181 (1971).

> Note that issues that arise with regard to workers' compensation are not always a choice of law between one state and another. Rather, the forum court decides whether its state's interests are sufficient to permit a recovery under its own workers' compensation statute. If the forum court determines that it does not have sufficient interest to apply its statute, the case will likely be dismissed without prejudice. The forum court will not choose to apply another jurisdiction's workers' compensation act.

2) Contractual choice of law provision

An employer and employee may agree as part of the employment contract that a certain state's workers' compensation laws will govern. Such agreement will generally be upheld so long as it is reasonable and does not violate the public policy of another state that has a legitimate interest.

b. Recovery in more than one state

If more than one state is involved and has a legitimate interest, each state's workers' compensation statutes should be compared before determining which law governs. For example, if one state bars an independent tort action or limits such an action under its workers' compensation statute (see discussion below), while another does not, that can significantly affect the decision of which state the worker will want to file a compensation claim.

A subsequent workers' compensation award in another state is barred only if there is "unmistakable language by a state legislature or judiciary" barring such recovery. *Industrial Commission of Wis. v. McCartin*, 330 U.S. 622 (1947). Amounts paid under a prior award must be credited against any subsequent recovery in another state in order to avoid a double recovery.

c. Immunity

The law is currently unclear as to whether an employee is permitted to bring a tort or wrongful death action against an employer from whom the employee has already been awarded damages in a workers' compensation action in another state if the workers' compensation statute of the other state grants the employer immunity from tort liability. A plurality of the U.S. Supreme Court has held that a state may grant supplemental workers' compensation benefits to an employee who previously received such benefits against the same person under another state's workers' compensation statute. *See Thomas v. Washington Gas Light*, 448 U.S. 261 (1980). As noted above, the second state is required to credit the amount awarded by the first state in order to avoid a double recovery.

Immunity is generally only given to the employer under a state's workers' compensation act. Thus, other parties, such as manufacturers of defective equipment, could be liable in tort despite the workers' compensation award. *See Carroll v. Lanza*, 349 U.S. 408 (1955). A third party that is held liable in tort will generally not be permitted to seek indemnification from the injured employee's employer who has complied with the state's workers' compensation statute.

D. DEFENSES AGAINST APPLICATION OF FOREIGN LAW

There are generally three arguments against the application of foreign law, that the law to be applied is:

i)   Procedural, rather than substantive;

ii) Against public policy; or

iii) A penal law.

1. Substance/Procedure Distinction

If the foreign law sought to be applied is procedural, the forum state's law will always govern. The forum state's law is applied to determine whether a law is substantive or procedural, so long as the result is not arbitrary or so unreasonable as to constitute a denial of due process or full faith and credit.

a. Procedural

Questions about the following are generally considered procedural and controlled by the law of the forum state:

i)   The proper court in which to bring an action;

ii) The form of the action to be brought;

iii)   The sufficiency of the pleadings;

iv)   The effect of splitting a cause of action;

v)   The proper or necessary parties to an action;

vi)   Whether a counterclaim may be brought;

vii)   Venue;

viii)   The rules of discovery;

ix)   The right to a jury trial;

x)   Service of process;

xi)   The burden of proof;

xii)   Trial procedure; and

xiii)   The methods of enforcing a judgment.

b. Evidence and privileges

1) Admissibility of evidence

Questions regarding the admissibility of evidence are usually considered procedural and controlled by the law of the forum state.

2) Existence or validity of privilege

Issues relating to the existence of a privilege are treated differently than other evidentiary issues depending on the choice-of-law approach applicable in the forum. Under the vested rights approach of the First Restatement, the existence and validity of a privilege is considered procedural and governed by the law of the forum state. Under the most significant relationship approach of the Second Restatement, the law of the state with the most significant relationship to the privileged communication will control. Under the governmental interest approach, the underlying interests of the competing states are weighed to determine whether a particular privilege should apply.

3) Parol evidence rule

Questions regarding the application of the parol evidence rule are considered substantive and controlled by the law of the state that governs the validity of the contract. *See* § II.C.2 (Contracts), *supra*.

c. Statute of limitations

Statutes of limitations are usually considered procedural, with the law of the forum state controlling. The theory for such treatment is that the statute of limitations bars the remedy, but does not extinguish the underlying substantive right. However, there are several exceptions to this general rule.

1) Right vs. remedy

If the statute of limitations limits a statutory right, as opposed to simply limiting a remedy, it will be substantive, rather than procedural. Generally, a limitation period in a statute that creates a right, such as a wrongful death act, will be treated as substantive.

2) Prescription or adverse possession

If the statute of limitations vests as a result of prescription or adverse possession, it will be treated as substantive.

3) Borrowing statutes

Most states have adopted "borrowing statutes," which bar suits on foreign causes of action that are precluded under the shorter of the forum state's statute of limitations or the statute of limitations of the place where the cause of action arose (for tort cases, the place of the wrong; for contract cases, generally the place where the contract was to be performed).

Illinois Distinction: Statute of Limitations

Borrowing Statute: Illinois law provides that an action arising in another state that is barred by that state's statute of limitations will be barred in Illinois. This rule is applied when none of the parties are Illinois residents and the foreign statute of limitations is shorter than that of Illinois.

---

4) Second Restatement approach

The Second Restatement's most significant relationship approach applies to statute of limitations issues. *See* § II.B.2 (Most Significant Relationship Approach), *supra*. Under this approach, the forum will apply its own state's statute of limitations barring the claim, unless: (i) maintenance of the claim would serve no substantial interest of the forum, and (ii) the claim would be barred under the statute of limitations of a state having a more significant relationship to the parties and the occurrence. Restatement (Second) of Conflict of Laws § 142 (1988 Revision).

d. Statute of repose

Statutes of repose limit the time within which an action may be brought, regardless of whether an injury has occurred or been discovered. It cuts off the right to a cause of action before it accrues. It is considered substantive, rather than procedural, and is controlled by the law of the state that governs the action under its choice of law rules.

e. Statute of Frauds

A Statute of Frauds is considered substantive, rather than procedural. Questions regarding the Statute of Frauds are controlled by the law of the state that governs the validity of the contract. *See* § II.C.2 (Contracts), *supra*.

f. Survival of actions

The issue of whether a tort action survives the death of the plaintiff is treated as substantive, and is controlled by the law of the state that governs the action under its choice-of-law rules.

g. Damages

States are split as to whether the measure of damages is procedural or substantive. The majority rule is that damages are substantive and measured by the law that governs the subject matter from which the damages arise.

h. Federal diversity cases

Under the *Erie* Doctrine, in diversity jurisdiction cases, federal district courts must apply the substantive law of the state where the court sits. *Erie R. Co. v. Tompkins*, 304 U.S. 64 (1938). The *Erie* Doctrine does not require that the state's procedural laws be applied, however, and if a Federal Rule of Civil Procedure addresses the procedural issue at hand, that rule will be applied. If no federal rule applies, the district court must follow state law with regard to substance, but can choose to ignore state law with regard to procedure, under certain circumstances. To determine whether a given law is substantive or procedural, the court considers whether the failure to apply state law would lead to different outcomes in state and federal court. If the answer is yes, the court will generally apply state law.

2. Laws Against Public Policy

Both the First Restatement and the Second Restatement provide that if a foreign law violates the public policy of the forum state, the forum court may refuse to apply that law. If the public policy exception is applicable, the court dismisses the action without prejudice. Public policy concerns must be fundamental and strongly held and the mere variance between the foreign law and forum law is not enough to deny the application of the foreign law. The forum court must closely scrutinize the foreign law and the forum state's public policy. Under the governmental interest approach this defense is not incorporated. Instead, the forum state will apply its public policy affirmatively in reaching a decision to apply its own law.

3. Penal Laws

Both the First and Second Restatements provide that a forum state will not enforce another state's penal laws. For penal laws, only an actual criminal prosecution is prohibited, not a civil action involving monetary sanctions, which might otherwise be considered a "penalty." The Second Restatement specifically excludes wrongful death actions and cases based on the statutory liability of officers, directors, and shareholders of corporations for debts from being considered penal in nature.

E. PROOF OF FOREIGN LAW

Historically, the laws of another state were not considered law at all, but were treated as facts to be proven in court. If the law that controlled was not forum law, the parties were required to carefully comply with the forum's rules for pleading and proving foreign law. Such rules were procedural and governed by forum law. If neither party raised the applicability of foreign law in its pleadings, forum law would generally be applied.

Most states today allow their courts to take judicial notice of the laws of other states and federal laws and treat them as law rather than fact. Some states allow judicial notice of the laws of a foreign country. Others require that it be proved as fact. By federal common law, federal courts must take judicial notice of the laws of all states. *Lamar v. Micou*, 114 U.S. 218 (1885). Federal law requires pleading and proof of foreign country law. *See* Fed. R. Civ. P. 44.1.

Illinois has adopted the Uniform Judicial Notice of Foreign Law Act, 735 Ill. Comp. Stat. 5/8-1003, under which every state court must take judicial notice of the common law and statutes of every state, territory, and other jurisdiction of the United States.

If the parties fail to provide information as to applicable foreign law, the forum court will decide the case in accordance with its own local law.

III. RECOGNITION OF FOREIGN JUDGMENTS

A. FULL FAITH AND CREDIT JUDGMENTS

Article IV, § 1 of the U.S. Constitution, the Full Faith and Credit Clause, provides that "Full Faith and Credit shall be given in each State to the public Acts, Records, and judicial Proceedings of every other State." The clause is invoked primarily to enforce the judgment of one state court in another state. If a valid judgment is rendered by a court that has jurisdiction over the parties, and the parties receive proper notice of the action and a reasonable opportunity to be heard, the Full Faith and Credit Clause requires that the judgment receive the same effect in other states as it receives in the state where it was rendered.

Thus, a party who obtains a judgment in one state may petition the court in another state to enforce the judgment. The issues are not re-litigated and the court in the state where enforcement is sought must honor the judgment of the other state's court. Note, though, that the party against whom enforcement is sought may collaterally challenge the original state judgment based on lack of personal jurisdiction, or subject matter jurisdiction, if the jurisdictional issues were not litigated or waived in the original action. *Durfee v. Duke*, 375 U.S. 106 (1963).

The requirement of full faith and credit extends to the res judicata effect of the original state court judgment. Thus, if the original state court judgment would bar a subsequent action in the original state, it acts to bar a subsequent action in any other state. This is the case even if the subsequent action would otherwise be permitted in that state.

1. Requirements

In order for a judgment to meet the full faith and credit requirements, it must:

i)   Have been brought in the proper jurisdiction;

Note that if the question of jurisdiction was fully and fairly litigated in the original case, such determination will itself be entitled to full faith and credit, even if it was wrong.

ii) Be finalized, with no appeals outstanding; and

iii) Be "on the merits," meaning the substantive issues were decided by a court, rather than the matter being resolved by procedural issues such as improper jurisdiction, venue, or the statute of limitations.

A judgment on the merits would include a judgment entered after full trial, a summary judgment, a judgment as a matter of law, and a default judgment.

A determination of whether the full faith and credit requirements have been met is made by looking to the law of the state that rendered the judgment. If a valid, final judgment is inconsistent with another valid, final judgment, the most recent judgment is entitled to full faith and credit.

2. Defenses to Full Faith and Credit of Judgments

a. Penal judgment

Penal judgments (cases where the judgment is punishment for an offense against the public) do not have to be enforced.

b. Equitable defenses

Equitable defenses such as extrinsic fraud do not have to be enforced. Note that only extrinsic fraud cases, such as a misrepresentation of facts by a party or a party's attorney that does not allow the case to be tried fully with all of the evidence, fall under this defense. Intrinsic fraud, such as perjured testimony, would not constitute a valid defense.

c. Inconsistent judgments

If there are inconsistent judgments between the same parties with regard to the same cause of action, courts resolve this problem by recognizing the last judgment that was rendered.

d. Erroneous proceedings—no defense

A state may not refuse to recognize the judgment of another state because the other state made a mistake of fact or law. Such mistakes must generally be attacked on direct appeal of the original judgment.

3. Res Judicata Effects

If all of the Full Faith and Credit requirements are met, then the judgment is entitled to res judicata in other states as well as the original state that decided the judgment. These effects include merger and bar.

a. Merger

If the judgment is final and the plaintiff won, a merger of the plaintiff's cause of action into the plaintiff's judgment occurs. As a result, the defendant is prohibited from re-litigating on the merits of the case.

b. Bar

If a judgment has been rendered and the final judgment is in favor of the defendant, the plaintiff may not file another suit for that same cause of action in another state.

4. Collateral Estoppel

Collateral estoppel eliminates the opportunity for parties to litigate an issue again in a subsequent suit. Collateral estoppel applies when:

i) The substantive issue of the case at hand was previously litigated;

ii) The issue was necessary to supporting the judgment in the initial proceeding; and

iii) The party against whom collateral estoppel will be applied was either a party in the original suit, or had access to information from the original proceeding, and had a "full and fair" opportunity to litigate the issue in the original suit.

5. Enforcement

Judgments determined to be entitled to full faith and credit must be enforced. This is true even if the judgment was granted erroneously, as long as it is not barred by one of the defenses discussed above (merger and bar). The law of the state that is recognizing the judgment governs the method of enforcement.

6. Federal Court Judgments

a. Federal to state recognition

Under 28 U.S.C. § 1738, federal courts must also give full faith and credit to state court judgments. The same rules as discussed above for states apply with respect to a federal court. A federal court will not give greater effect to a state court judgment than the state itself would give.

b. State to federal recognition for diversity cases

If a federal court with diversity jurisdiction over an action issues a judgment, a state court must give such judgment the same res judicata effect that the judgment would have been given by the courts of the state where the federal court was located. *Semtek Int'l Inc. v. Lockheed Martin Corp.*, 531 U.S. 497 (2001).

B. RECOGNITION OF JUDGMENTS FROM FOREIGN COUNTRIES

1. Comity

Comity is the voluntary agreement to recognize a foreign judgment. In most cases, full faith and credit is not extended to cases decided in foreign countries, except in cases where there are treaties agreeing to recognize certain judgments. United States courts have discretion to decide whether to recognize foreign country judgments. In deciding whether to recognize such judgments, the forum court will consider whether the foreign court had jurisdiction over the matter, and whether the foreign court used fair procedures in deciding the case. If recognition of a foreign country judgment is granted, the law of the state that is recognizing the judgment governs the method of enforcement.

2. Uniform Foreign Money Judgment Recognition Act

Many states have adopted the Uniform Foreign Money Judgments Recognition Act. The act covers foreign judgments that grant or deny specific lump sums of money, but excludes judgments for taxes, judgments for alimony or child support, and penal judgments.

C. RECOGNITION OF DIVORCE JUDGMENTS

Divorce decrees from other states are entitled to full faith and credit as long as the original state had jurisdiction to issue the decree and the decree is valid in the original state. Decrees have proper jurisdiction if at least one person resides where the decree was issued.

1. Bilateral Divorce

If the court has personal jurisdiction over both spouses and at least one spouse is domiciled in the state, the divorce judgment will be a valid bilateral divorce and will be entitled to full faith and credit.

2. Ex Parte Divorce

An ex parte divorce is a divorce based on the domicile of only one of the spouses. For an ex parte divorce to be afforded full faith and credit, it must adhere to the subject matter jurisdiction rules, namely that at least one person must reside in the state. Personal jurisdiction must exist over one spouse. The difference between a bilateral divorce and ex parte divorce is that in an ex parte divorce, full faith and credit is **not** given to other marital agreements such as property rights, alimony, and child custody. However, a divorce order dealing with property rights, alimony, or custody will be binding if the non-domiciled spouse agrees. A bilateral divorce decree will generally receive full faith and credit with regard to such matters.

3. Estoppel Against Collateral Attack

Anyone who has an interest in a case may collaterally attack the validity of another state's decrees. However, where the third party is in privity with one of the parties to the divorce, the third party may be estopped from making an attack based on that party's relationship to the initial proceedings. The spouse who brought the proceeding in the original court is estopped from challenging its validity.

4. Child Custody

There is a reciprocal statute in all 50 states that governs child custody: the Uniform Child Custody Jurisdiction and Enforcement Act ("UCCJEA"). Under the UCCJEA a court can make initial custody decisions if it is in the child's home state, and all other states must give full faith and credit to such decisions. Other states cannot modify these custody decrees unless the original court has no significant connection to the child or parents anymore (i.e., neither the child nor parents resides in that state anymore).

5. Property and Alimony

Bilateral divorces usually include all issues related to property and alimony. Full faith and credit are given to these provisions in a divorce. In ex parte divorces, however, the parties must settle issues related to property and alimony in a court that has personal jurisdiction over both parties.

6. Divorce Judgments from Foreign Countries

Courts will generally extend comity to foreign divorce judgments, as long as the requirements of domicile are met. With respect to other divorce-related agreements such as alimony, property, and child custody, the rules are usually followed the same as if the judgment came from another state.

Corporations

CORPORATIONS

Table of Contents

CORPORATIONS

I. FORMATION

A. PRE-INCORPORATION TRANSACTIONS

1. Promoters

Prior to the formation of a corporation, a promoter engages in activities, such as procuring capital and entering into contracts, in order to bring the corporation into existence as a business entity.

a. Liability for pre-incorporation agreements

A promoter is personally liable for acting on behalf of a corporation before incorporation, and is jointly and severally liable for all liabilities created while so acting, even after the corporation comes into existence, unless a subsequent novation releases the promoter from liability. An express adoption of the contract by the corporation or use of the benefits from the contract also may relieve the promoter of liability. Revised Model Business Corporation Act ("RMBCA") § 2.04. However, if a party who contracts with a promoter knows that the corporation has not yet been formed and agrees to look only to the corporation for performance, the promoter is not liable.

> **EXAM NOTE:** Promoter liability is often tested in the context of pre-incorporation agreements. Remember that promoters are liable to third parties for pre-incorporation agreements even after incorporation, unless the corporation specifically relieves the promoter of liability.

b. Fiduciary duty to the corporation

A promoter stands in a fiduciary relationship with the pre-incorporated corporation. The promoter can be liable to the corporation for violating a fiduciary duty, such as failing to disclose a commission on a pre-incorporation transaction.

c. Right to reimbursement

While a promoter can seek compensation for pre-incorporation activities undertaken on the corporation's behalf and reimbursement for related expenses, the promoter cannot compel the corporation to make such payments, as the promoter's acts, while done to benefit the corporation, are not undertaken at the corporation's direction.

2. Corporation's Liability for Pre-Incorporation Transactions

a. General rule—no liability

A corporation is not liable for pre-incorporation transactions entered into by a promoter. The fact that the promoter entered in a transaction to benefit a future corporation is not sufficient to hold the corporation liable.

> Because a corporation is not necessarily in existence during a pre-incorporation transaction, a principal-agent relationship does not exist between the corporation and the promoter.

b. Exception—liability upon contract adoption

The corporation can be liable when the corporation adopts the contract. Adoption of a contract can be express or implied. Adoption takes place when the corporation accepts the benefits of the transaction or gives an express acceptance of liability for the debt, such as through board resolution after incorporation.

3. Incorporator Liability

An incorporator is a person who signs and files the articles of incorporation with the state. By performing such acts, an incorporator does not engender liability for a contract entered into by a promoter of the corporation.

Illinois Point of Law: Incorporator Liability

In Illinois, corporations may have one or more incorporators. Incorporators may be foreign or domestic corporations, or natural persons at least 18 years old. Unless provided otherwise in the articles of incorporation, any actions taken by the incorporators may be taken without a meeting as long as all the incorporators give written consent. 805 Ill. Comp. Stat. 5/2.05.

B. INCORPORATION

1. Procedures

In order to form a corporation, a document, referred to as the "articles of incorporation" or "charter," must be filed with the state.

a. Articles of incorporation

The articles of incorporation must include certain basic information about the corporation, such as its name, the number of shares that the corporation is authorized to issue, the name and address of the corporation's registered agent, and the name and address of each incorporator. RMBCA § 2.02(a).

1) Corporate name

The corporation's name must contain the word "corporation," "company," "incorporated," "limited," or an abbreviation thereof.

2) Corporate purpose

The articles of incorporation must include a statement of the corporation's purposes. A broad statement of such purpose, such as "to engage in any lawful activity," is acceptable. The RMBCA presumes that each corporation has the broadest lawful purpose unless a more limited purpose is defined in the articles of incorporation. RMBCA § 3.01.

3) Corporate powers

In addition to specifying purposes, the articles of incorporation may also enumerate powers that the corporation possesses. Most states automatically grant all corporations broad powers, such as the powers to buy and sell property and to sue and be sued. RMBCA § 3.02. Some states place restrictions on various corporate actions, including corporate loans to officers and directors. For a corporation with stock listed on a national securities exchange, federal law prohibits the corporation from making personal loans to a director or executive officer of the corporation. 15 U.S.C. § 78m.

4) Corporate duration

Although a corporation can have perpetual existence, it may instead choose to limit its duration. RMBCA § 3.02.

b. Filing requirements

The articles of incorporation must be filed with a state official, usually with the secretary of state, and a filing fee paid.

Once the requirements are met, some states treat the corporation as having been formed as of the date of the filing, while other states consider the corporation a legal entity only when the state has accepted the articles of incorporation. RMBCA §§ 1.23, 2.03.

Illinois Point of Law: Filing Requirements

Required reports, such as the articles of incorporation, must be filed with the Secretary of State's office. Any incorporators must sign the articles of incorporation. 805 Ill. Comp. Stat. 5/1.10.

After the Secretary of State files the articles of incorporation, the corporate existence begins, and the filing constitutes conclusive evidence (except as against the state) that the incorporators have complied with all required conditions precedent. 805 Ill. Comp. Stat. 5/2.15.

---

2. Ultra Vires Actions

When a corporation that has stated a narrow business purpose in its articles of incorporation subsequently engages in activities outside that stated purpose, the corporation has engaged in an ultra vires act. When a third party enters into a transaction with the corporation that constitutes an ultra vires act for the corporation, the third party generally cannot assert that the corporation has acted outside those powers in order to escape liability.

a. Challenges to ultra vires acts

An ultra vires act can be challenged in only the following three situations:

　　i) A shareholder can file suit to enjoin the corporation's ultra vires action;

ii) The corporation can take action against a director, officer, or employee of the corporation who engages in such action; or

iii) The state can initiate a proceeding against the corporation to enjoin its ultra vires action.

RMBCA § 3.04(b).

> **Illinois Distinction: Challenges to Ultra Vires Acts**
>
> Illinois also allows an ultra vires act to be challenged in a proceeding by the state to dissolve the corporation. 805 Ill. Comp. Stat. 5/3.15.

b. Enjoining an ultra vires act

An ultra vires act will only be enjoined if it is equitable to do so.

3. Effect of Incorporation—"De Jure" Corporation

When all of the statutory requirements for incorporation have been satisfied, a de jure corporation is created. Consequently, the corporation, rather than persons associated with the corporation (i.e., shareholders, directors, officers, and other employees), is liable for activities undertaken by the corporation.

4. Defective Incorporation

a. Lack of good faith effort to incorporate

When a person conducts business as a corporation without attempting to comply with the statutory incorporation requirements, that person is liable for any obligations incurred in the name of the nonexistent corporation. RMBCA § 2.04.

b. Good faith effort to incorporate

When a person makes an unsuccessful effort to comply with the incorporation requirements, that person may be able to escape personal liability under either the de facto corporation or corporation by estoppel doctrines.

1) De facto corporation

The owner must make a good-faith effort to comply with the incorporation requirements and must operate the business as a corporation without knowing that these requirements have not been met. If the owner has done so, the business entity is treated as a de facto corporation and the owner, as a de facto shareholder, is not personally liable for obligations incurred in the purported corporation's name.

2) Corporation by estoppel

A person who deals with an entity as if it were a corporation is estopped from denying its existence and is thereby prevented from seeking the personal liability of the business owner. This doctrine is limited to contractual agreements. In addition, the business owner must have made a good-faith effort to comply with incorporation requirements and must lack knowledge that the requirements were not met.

II. STOCK AND OTHER CORPORATE SECURITIES

A. TYPES

Traditionally, there are two broad types of securities by which a corporation secures financing for its endeavors—stocks, which carry ownership and control interests in the corporation, and debt securities, which do not. Over time, many securities have been created that blur this distinction. However, every corporation is required to have stock that is entitled to vote on matters of corporate governance (e.g., the election of directors to the board) and stock that represents the basic ownership interest in a corporation. RMBCA § 6.01(b). Stocks that possess these two characteristics are referred to as "common stock." Stocks having preference over other stock to such items as distributions are referred to as "preferred stock."

> In general, upon liquidation, a secured creditor of the corporation will generally take precedence over a preferred shareholder with regard to the corporation's funds and a preferred shareholder will take precedence over a common shareholder. Preferred shareholders generally take precedence to common shareholders with regard to distributions by the corporation.

B. ISSUANCE OF STOCK

When a corporation sells or trades its stock to an investor, the transaction from the corporation's perspective requires the issuance of stock. The corporation may issue such stock provided the articles of incorporation authorize the issuance. RMBCA § 6.03(a).

1. Authorization

In general, the issuance of stock must be authorized by the board of directors. RMBCA § 6.21(b). Many states also permit the shareholders to authorize the issuance of stock if the articles of incorporation so provide. RMBCA § 6.21(a).

> **Illinois Point of Law: Authorization**
>
> Illinois law gives corporations the power to create and issue the number of shares stated in the articles of incorporation. 805 Ill. Comp. Stat. 5/6.05.

2. Consideration

a. Types of consideration

The RMBCA removed restrictions on the types of consideration that can be accepted by a corporation in payment for its stock. Acceptable consideration includes money, tangible or intangible property, and services rendered to the corporation. RMBCA § 6.21(b).

b. Payment of consideration

When the corporation receives consideration for stock, the stock is deemed fully paid and non-assessable. RMBCA § 6.21(d). A shareholder who fails to pay the consideration is liable to the corporation and any issued stock may be canceled. If stock has not been fully paid, the corporation or a creditor of the corporation may be able to recover the unpaid amount from the shareholder. RMBCA § 6.22(a).

c. Valuation of consideration

Under the RMBCA, the board of directors must merely determine that the consideration received for the stock is adequate. Moreover, once the board makes such a determination, the adequacy of the consideration is not subject to challenge. RMBCA § 6.21(c).

1) Par value stock

A corporation may, but is not required to, issue par value stock. For such stock, the corporation is required to receive at least the value assigned to that stock (i.e., par value), which need not be its market value, and which even can be a nominal amount.

2) Watered stock

Because stock is deemed validly issued, paid in full, and non-assessable once the corporation receives adequate consideration (as determined by the board of directors), the RMBCA does not recognize or address the issue of "watered stock," i.e., stock that is issued for consideration less than par value.

Illinois Distinction: Valuation of Consideration

Shares may issue: (i) through an action by the board which establishes a price in cash, other consideration, or both, (ii) a minimum price, or (iii) a general formula or method to determine the price. 805 Ill. Comp. Stat. 5/6.25.

---

3. Stock Subscriptions

Prior to incorporation, persons may subscribe to purchase stock from the corporation when it comes into existence.

a. Revocability

Unless the subscription agreement provides otherwise, a pre-incorporation subscription is irrevocable for six months from the date of the subscription, but a revocation can happen if all subscribers agree to it. RMBCA § 6.20(a).

b. Nonpayment by subscriber

A corporation can pursue normal collection methods when a subscriber fails to pay the subscription amount. In addition, the corporation can sell the stock to someone else, provided that the corporation has made a written demand for payment and given the subscriber at least twenty days to comply with the demand. RMBCA § 6.20(d).

Illinois Distinction: Stock Subscriptions

Shareholder and Subscriber Liability: A shareholder or subscriber is under no obligation to the corporation or its creditors with respect to its shares other than the obligation to pay the corporation full consideration for the issued shares. 805 Ill. Comp. Stat. 5/6.40.

Subscribers Become Shareholders: In Illinois, once the articles of incorporation are filed with the Secretary of State, all existing subscriptions to its shares are deemed accepted and all subscribers for such shares, or their assigns, are deemed shareholders of the corporation. 805 Ill. Comp. Stat. 5/6.20.

---

4. Stock Rights, Options, and Warrants

In addition to stock, a corporation may issue rights, options, or warrants to buy its stock. Generally, the board of directors has the authority to issue these instruments and to dictate their terms. RMBCA § 6.24.

5. Shareholder's Preemptive Rights

When the board of directors decides to issue new shares, the rights of shareholders to purchase those shares in order to maintain their proportional ownership share in the corporation are known as "preemptive rights." Shareholders automatically had such rights at common law, but the RMBCA explicitly precludes preemptive rights unless the articles of incorporation provide otherwise. RMBCA § 6.30(a).

Example: A and B, the only shareholders of Corporation X, each own 50 shares of stock. The board of directors of Corporation X authorizes the issuance of another 20 shares. With preemptive rights, A and B would each be entitled to purchase 10 additional shares of stock and would retain a 50% ownership interest in the corporation. Without such rights, A or B could become the controlling owner of Corporation X by purchasing at least 11 additional shares of the new stock offering.

Illinois Point of Law: Shareholder's Preemptive Rights

Illinois follows the general rule that shareholders have no preemptive rights to acquire unissued shares unless that right is provided in the articles of incorporation. Additionally, unless the articles provide otherwise, and as long as two-thirds of the voting shareholders or board of directors approve, any corporation having preemptive rights may issue and sell its shares to employees or a subsidiary without first offering the option to its shareholders. 805 Ill. Comp. Stat. 5/6.50.

a. Waiver

If the corporation does elect to have preemptive rights, a shareholder may waive that right. A waiver evidenced by a writing is **irrevocable,** regardless of whether it is supported by consideration. RMBCA § 6.30(b)(2).

b. Exceptions

Preemptive rights do not apply to shares that are:

i) Issued as compensation to directors, officers, agents, or employees of the corporation;

ii) Authorized in the articles of incorporation and issued within six months from the effective date of incorporation; or

iii) Sold for payment other than money (e.g., property).

RMBCA § 6.30(b)(3).

6. Federal Restrictions—Registration of Securities

Under the Federal Securities Act of 1933, a corporation that issues stock or other securities may be required to register the security with the Securities Exchange Commission (SEC). In addition to filing the required registration statement with the SEC, which involves significant disclosures about the company offering the security, the issuer is also required to provide the buyer of the security with a prospectus.

The prospectus represents the main part of the registration statement, and includes information about the company, its business, and its financial performance.

a. Public offerings

In general, registration is only required for public offerings of stocks or other securities that are considered public offerings. Offerings that are considered private, called "private placements," are exempt from the registration requirements. Private placements include stock sold by a corporation to institutional investors, sophisticated investors, and companies with annual sales of less than $1 million.

b. Civil liabilities

The purchaser of a security from a corporation that has not complied with the registration requirements may sue the corporation to rescind the transaction. In addition, the purchaser can sue for compensatory damages caused by a material misrepresentation or omission in the registration statement. The purchaser need not have relied on the error or omission, but she cannot have purchased with knowledge of the error or omission. Any of the following individuals may be liable:

i) The issuer;

ii) Any other signer of the registration statement (generally senior executives of the issuer);

iii) A director of the issuer at the time the statement is filed;

iv) An expert whose opinion is used in the registration statement; or

v) The underwriter of the issue.

The issuer is strictly liable, but the other defendants may defend on the basis of the reasonableness of their actions. This is referred to as a "due diligence" defense.

C. DISTRIBUTIONS

A distribution is the transfer of cash or other property from a corporation to one or more of its shareholders. The most common form of a distribution is a dividend, which is normally a cash payment made to shareholders. Other forms of distribution include a distribution of indebtedness or a corporation's purchase of its own stock. RMBCA § 1.40(6).

1. Authorization by Board of Directors

The power to authorize a distribution rests with the board of directors. RMBCA § 6.40. Having authorized a distribution and set sufficient parameters, the board may delegate to a board committee or corporate officer the power to fix the amount and other terms of the distribution.

In general, a shareholder cannot compel the board of directors to authorize a distribution, as that decision is usually discretionary. However, when a board acts in bad faith and abuses its discretion by refusing to declare a distribution, a court may order the board to authorize a distribution. *Dodge v. Ford Motor Co.*, 170 N.W. 668 (Mich. 1919).

2. Limitations on Distributions

A corporation may not make a distribution if it is insolvent or the distribution would cause the corporation to be insolvent. RMBCA § 6.40(c).

a. Insolvency determination

A corporation must pass two tests in order to be deemed solvent and, as such, capable of making a distribution: an equity test and a balance sheet test.

1) Equity test

Under the equity test, a corporation must be able to pay off its debts as they come due in the usual course of business. RMBCA § 6.40(c)(1).

2) Balance sheet test

Under the balance sheet test, a corporation's total assets must exceed its total liabilities plus liquidation preferences of senior securities. RMBCA § 6.40(c)(1).

b. Time of measurement

In the case of a dividend, a corporation's solvency is measured on the date the dividend is declared; in the case of a stock purchase, it is the date the purchase price is paid. RMBCA § 6.40(e).

Illinois Distinction: Time of Measurement

In Illinois, a corporation's solvency is measured as of the earlier of the following:

i)   The date the distribution is authorized, if payment occurs within 120 days;

ii) The payment date, if payment occurs more than 120 days after the authorization date; or

iii) If the distribution is by purchase, redemption, or other acquisition of corporate shares, the earlier of the date money or property is transferred or debt incurred or the date shareholders cease to be shareholders.

805 Ill. Comp. Stat. 5/9.10.

---

3. Director's Liability for Unlawful Distributions

A director who votes for or assents to an unlawful distribution, in violation of the director's duties of care and loyalty, is personally liable to the corporation for the amount of the distribution in excess of the lawful amount.

a. Contribution from directors

A director is entitled to contribution from any other director who also is liable for the unlawful distribution. RMBCA § 8.33(b)(1).

b. Recoupment from shareholders

If a shareholder knowingly accepts an unlawful distribution, a director is entitled to recoupment from that shareholder's pro rata portion of the unlawful distribution. RMBCA § 8.33(b)(2).

> **Illinois Distinction: Director's Liability for Unlawful Distributions**
>
> **Joint and Several Liability:** Directors who vote for or assent to any unlawful distribution are jointly and severally liable to the corporation for the distribution amount. However, if a director relied and acted in good faith on corporate financial statements, he will not be liable. 805 Ill. Comp. Stat. 5/8.65.

4. Dividend Distributions

Dividends are distributed to persons who are shareholders on the record date set by the board of directors. If the board does not set a date, the dividend is payable to persons who are shareholders on the date that the board authorized the dividend. RMBCA § 6.40(b).

5. Suit to Compel a Dividend Distribution

A shareholder can sue to enforce her individual right; this is not the same as a derivative lawsuit that the shareholders bring on behalf of the corporation. *See, generally, Doherty v. Mutual Warehouse Co.,* 245 F.2d 609 (5th Cir. 1957); *Knapp v. Bankers Securities Corp.,* 230 F.2d 717 (3d Cir. 1956) (the right to compel a dividend is a primary and a personal right of the shareholder).

To prevail in a suit to compel a dividend distribution, a shareholder must prove the existence of (i) funds legally available for the payment of a dividend and (ii) bad faith on the part of the directors in their refusal to pay. *See Gay v. Gay's Super Markets, Inc.,* 343 A.2d 577 (Me. 1975).

6. Shares Reacquired by Corporation

Stock authorized and issued by the corporation is known as "outstanding stock." Such stock may be reacquired by the corporation through purchase or redemption (i.e., stock acquired by a forced sale). Upon repurchase or redemption, that stock constitutes authorized but unissued shares. If the articles of incorporation prohibit the reissuance of stock, the number of authorized shares is automatically reduced by the number of shares purchased. RMBCA § 6.31.

> **Illinois Distinction: Shares Reacquired by Corporation**
>
> An Illinois corporation's reacquired shares are considered **treasury shares** until canceled. To cancel treasury shares, the board must past a cancelation resolution that converts the treasury shares into authorized but unissued shares, unless the articles state otherwise. The number of authorized shares will then be reduced by the number of canceled shares. Treasury shares may not be voted at any meeting. Shares converted or exchanged for other shares are not deemed treasury shares. 805 Ill. Comp. Stat. 5/1.80; 5/9.05.

7. Debt Distribution

Distribution of indebtedness of a corporation, such as bonds or promissory notes, is subject to the same requirements as other distributions. When indebtedness is to be repaid over time (i.e., on an installment basis), the lawfulness of the distribution is tested as of the date of distribution. RMBCA § 6.40(e). Corporate indebtedness received as a lawful distribution is on par with a corporation's general unsecured creditors. RMBCA § 6.40(f).

8. **Stock Dividends—Not a Distribution**

A corporation may issue its own stock to current shareholders without charge in lieu of making a distribution of cash or other property. Commonly referred to as stock dividends or stock splits, these transactions do not alter the corporation's assets or liabilities, nor do they constitute a distribution. RMBCA § 6.23.

D. SALE OF SECURITIES

Generally, a shareholder is free to sell his stock to anyone at any time or price. Such freedom is subject to two significant restrictions—limitations imposed on shareholders of closely-held corporations, and penalties imposed on transactions that violate federal securities law.

1. **Private Restrictions on Sale**

Restrictions on the transfer of stock are generally found in closely-held corporations. This is because owners of a closely-held corporation often seek to maintain control over the corporation's business and profits by limiting the number of shareholders in a corporation. This limitation can be accomplished through restrictions on the transferability of shares.

a. **Conspicuously noted**

If the corporation issuing the shares imposes a restriction on transferability, the stock certificate must contain either a full and conspicuous statement of the restriction or a statement that the corporation will provide a shareholder with information about the restriction upon request and without charge. RMBCA § 6.27(b).

b. **Enforceability**

A restriction in the transfer of a security, even if otherwise lawful, may be ineffective against a person without knowledge of the restriction. Unless the security is certified and the restriction is conspicuously noted on the security certificate, that restriction is not enforceable against a person without knowledge of it. RMBCA § 6.27(b).

c. **Form of restrictions**

Restrictions on the transfer of stocks can take various forms, including:

i) Outright prohibition on transfers;

ii) Transfers requiring consent from the corporation or its shareholders;

iii) Options to buy the stock held by the corporation or its shareholders;

iv) Right of first refusal (i.e., stock must be offered to the corporation or its shareholders before selling it to another person);

v) Corporation requires or has the right to buy back the stock; or

vi) Buy-sell agreement with either the corporation or its shareholders being obligated to buy the stock.

When a restricted transfer is permitted, the transfer itself may be required upon the occurrence of a specific event, such as retirement, death, or divorce of the shareholder. RMBCA § 6.27(d).

d. Challenge to restrictions

Stock transfer restrictions have been subject to challenge as unreasonable restraints on alienation. Of the various forms noted above, the outright prohibition on transfer and the need for prior consent are the most susceptible to attack. However, since the test is one of reasonableness, even these two forms may be justified in particular circumstances, such as when a corporation seeks to preserve its status because it is dependent on the number or identity of its shareholders. RMBCA § 6.27(c).

Since many of these restrictions are created through contractual arrangements, they may be subject to contractual defenses. In addition, the restrictions may be narrowly interpreted and subject to equitable challenges such as abandonment, waiver, or estoppel.

e. Persons bound by restrictions

Parties to an agreement that restricts stock transfers are bound by the terms of the contract. Other parties are not subject to a transfer restriction unless they are aware of it. If the restriction is noted on the face of the stock certificate, the buyer may be treated as having had constructive notice of the restriction.

A transfer restriction imposed through an amendment of the articles of incorporation or corporate bylaws raises the question as to whether persons who were shareholders before the restriction was imposed are subject to it. The RMBCA does not subject such shareholders to a restriction unless the shareholders voted in favor of the restriction or were parties to the restriction agreement. RMBCA § 6.27(a).

Illinois Distinction: Private Restrictions on Sales

Illinois law permits restrictions on the transfer of securities if the restriction:

i) Obligates the holder of the restricted securities to offer to the corporation, other shareholders, or any other person the prior opportunity to acquire the restricted securities;

ii) Obligates the corporation, any shareholder, or any other person to purchase the securities that are the subject of an agreement about the purchase and sale of the restricted securities;

iii) Requires the corporation or shareholders to consent to any proposed transfer of the restricted securities or to approve the proposed transferee; or

iv) Prohibits the transfer of the restricted securities to designated persons as long as the designation is not manifestly unreasonable.

Additionally, to be valid, the restriction must be conspicuously written on either the transfer of the security or its registration, or, if inconspicuously noted on the transfer, the shareholder must have actual knowledge of the restriction at the time of becoming a shareholder. 805 Ill. Comp. Stat. 5/6.55.

---

2. Sale of Control in a Closely Held Corporation

A shareholder with a controlling interest in a corporation that sells to an outsider may have a fiduciary obligation to the other shareholders. See § IV.E.2., Controlling Shareholder's Fiduciary Obligation, *infra*.

3. **Federal Causes of Action**

Violations of 17 C.F.R. § 240.10b-5 ("**Rule 10b-5**") and Section 16(b) of the Securities Exchange Act of 1934, 15 U.S.C. § 78p, ("**Section 16(b)**"), which are based on the purchase and sale of stock and other securities, are federal causes of action and must be pursued in federal court. Because each involves a federal claim, diversity of citizenship is not needed.

The SEC also may enforce these provisions through civil penalties and criminal prosecution.

a. **Rule 10b-5 action**

The fraudulent purchase or sale of any stock or other security (e.g., bonds, stock options, and warrants) can give rise to a Rule 10b-5 action. In order for a private person to pursue a Rule 10b-5 action, **each** of the following requirements must be met:

i) The plaintiff purchased or sold a security;

ii) The transaction involved the use of interstate commerce;

iii) The defendant engaged in fraudulent or deceptive conduct;

iv) The conduct related to material information;

v) The defendant acted with scienter, i.e., with intent or recklessness;

vi) The plaintiff relied on the defendant's conduct; and

vii) The plaintiff suffered harm because of the defendant's conduct.

1) **Plaintiff's purchase or sale of security**

In order to maintain a Rule 10b-5 action, the plaintiff must have either bought or sold a security. A person who refrains from buying or selling a security because of the defendant's conduct cannot bring a Rule 10b-5 action for damages. *Blue Chip Stamps v. Manor Drug Stores*, 421 U.S. 723 (1975). (Note: Courts are split as to whether private action for injunctive relief is possible by someone who did not buy or sell stock. However, the SEC can bring such an action).

The defendant is not required to be a participant in the transaction. Only the plaintiff must be a buyer or seller.

a) **Forced sale doctrine**

Under the forced sale doctrine, the forced exchange of shares in a merger or similar transaction constitutes a sale.

2) **Use of interstate commerce**

Interstate commerce must be used in connection with the transaction. Use of a telephone, mail, or email to make the transaction satisfies this requirement, as does the use of a national securities exchange.

An in-person transaction may not necessarily satisfy the interstate commerce requirement.

3) Fraudulent or deceptive conduct

A Rule 10b-5 action requires fraudulent or deceptive conduct by the defendant in connection with the sale or purchase of a security. The defendant can engage in such conduct by (i) making an untrue statement of a material fact or (ii) failing to state a material fact that is necessary to prevent statements already made from being misleading.

a) Opinions and predictions

Generally, an opinion or a prediction is not false merely because it does not purport to be factual. However, such a statement may be fraudulent if the defendant made the statement without a reasonable basis or did not make the statement in good faith. See Securities Exchange Act Rule 3b-6.

i) "Bespeaks caution" doctrine

Under the "bespeaks caution" doctrine, a statement of opinion or prediction accompanied by adequate cautionary language does not constitute a false or misleading statement. Securities Exchange Act Rule 21E.

b) Nondisclosure and insider trading

The mere possession of material information that is not public knowledge does not give rise to Rule 10b-5 liability; a person who has such insider knowledge does not incur liability **unless he also trades stock or other securities on the basis of such knowledge**. This is often referred to as the "disclose or abstain" rule.

i) Possession as use of information

In establishing that a person has traded on the basis of nonpublic information, a person is presumed to have traded on the basis of the information that he possessed at the time of the trade. An exception exists for trades made in accordance with a pre-existing written plan. Securities Exchange Act Rule 10b-5-1.

ii) Affected traders

There are four types of traders who may be liable for failure to disclose information: (i) insiders, (ii) constructive insiders, (iii) tippees, and (iv) misappropriators.

(a) Insiders

An insider is a director, officer, or other employee of the corporation who uses nonpublic information for personal gain.

(b) Constructive insiders

A constructive insider is a person who has a relationship with the corporation that gives that person access to corporate information not available to the general public. Such individuals include lawyers, accountants, consultants, and other independent contractors.

(c) Tippees

A tippee is a person who is given information by an insider or constructive insider (the "tipper") with the expectation that the information will be used to trade the stock or other securities. The tipper must receive a personal benefit from the disclosure or intend to make a gift to the tippee.

In order to be liable, the tippee must have known (or should have known) that the information was provided to him in violation of the insider's duty to the corporation. *Dirks v. SEC*, 463 U.S. 646 (1983).

(d) Misappropriators

A misappropriator is a person who uses confidential information in order to trade stock or other securities in violation of the duty of confidentiality owed to the corporation. *United States v. O'Hagan*, 521 U.S. 642 (1997).

4) Materiality

A defendant's conduct must involve the misuse of material information. A fact is material if a reasonable investor would find the fact important in deciding whether to purchase or sell a security. *Basic, Inc. v. Levinson*, 485 U.S. 224 (1988).

5) Scienter

A defendant is not strictly liable for making a false or misleading statement or for negligently making such a statement. Instead, the defendant must make the statement intentionally or recklessly. This fault requirement is also known as scienter. *Ernst & Ernst v. Hochfelder*, 425 U.S. 185 (1976).

6) Plaintiff's reliance

In order to maintain a Rule 10b-5 action, a plaintiff must establish that he relied on the defendant's fraudulent conduct. However, when the defendant's fraudulent conduct is not aimed directly at the plaintiff, such as if the defendant issues a press release, courts have permitted the plaintiff to establish reliance by finding that the defendant's conduct constituted a fraud on the market. *Basic Inc. v. Levinson*, 485 U.S. 224 (1988).

a) Justifiable reliance

A plaintiff must not only rely on the defendant's fraudulent conduct; the reliance must be justifiable. In ascertaining whether the plaintiff's reliance is justifiable, mere negligence by the plaintiff is not sufficient to prevent the plaintiff's recovery.

7) Harm to plaintiff

The plaintiff must establish that he suffered harm caused by the defendant's fraudulent conduct.

a) Damages

Generally, a plaintiff is entitled to recoup his "out-of-pocket" loss, which is the difference between the stock's value at the time of the fraud and the price that the plaintiff paid or received for the stock. In determining the stock's value at the time of the fraud, the value cannot exceed the mean average market price of the stock during the ninety-day period after disclosure of such fraud. Securities Exchange Act Rule 21D(e). Punitive damages are not allowed.

b) Rescission

Rescission may be permitted if the defendant was involved in the transaction as a seller or buyer.

c) Defendant's liability

When a defendant has engaged in a knowing violation, she is jointly and severally liable for the damages. If a defendant's violation results from reckless behavior, her liability is proportionally limited to the damages for which she is responsible. Securities Exchange Act Rule 21D(f).

b. Section 16(b) action

A corporate insider can be forced to return short-swing profits to the corporation through a Section 16(b) action. An insider's reasons for trading are immaterial. Even an insider who does not possess nonpublic material information must return short-swing profits.

The following four elements are necessary for a Section 16(b) cause of action:

1) Applicable corporations

Only the following publicly traded corporations are protected by Section 16(b): (i) corporations that have securities traded on a national securities exchange or (ii) corporations that have assets of more than $10 million and more than 500 shareholders of any class of stock or other equity security.

2) Corporate insiders

Only corporate directors, officers (e.g., president, vice-president, secretary, treasurer, or comptroller), and shareholders who hold more than ten percent of any class of stock are subject to a Section 16(b) action. Generally, transactions made before becoming a corporate insider are not considered in determining short-swing profits. However, transactions made after ceasing to be a corporate insider are considered in determining short-swing profits.

3) Short-swing profits

During any six-month period, a corporate insider who both buys and sells his corporation's stock is liable to the corporation for any profits made. Profits are computed by matching the highest sale price with the lowest purchase price, then the next highest sale price with the next lowest purchase price, and so on, during the six month period. Any loss is not taken into account and all shares are matched with other shares only once.

> **Example:** On January 1, President sells 200 shares of ABC Corporation's stock for $500 each that she had purchased several years before for $100 each. On May 1, President purchases 200 shares of stock for $400 each. President has a short-swing profit of $20,000 (i.e., the sale of 200 shares at $500 each, less purchase of 200 shares at $400 each).

4) Reporting

A corporate insider is required to report a change in his stock ownership to the SEC in order to encourage compliance with the short-swing profits rule.

4. State Cause of Action

The primary state cause of action available to persons who have traded stock is the tort of fraud.

5. Tender Offer

A tender offer is an offer to shareholders of a publicly traded corporation to purchase their stock for a fixed price, which is usually higher than the market price. It is frequently used to effect a hostile takeover of a corporation (i.e., a takeover that is opposed by the current management of the corporation).

a. For more than five percent

A person who acquires more than five percent of any class of stock must file a statement with the SEC that reveals his ownership interest, the source of his funding, and his purpose in acquiring the stock.

b. Persons subject to disclosure rules

A tender offer made by a person subject to the disclosure rules must also provide specific shareholder rights. Securities Exchange Act Rule 14(d)(g).

III. GOVERNANCE

A. INSTRUMENTS

1. Articles of Incorporation

The articles of incorporation must be filed in order to incorporate, but need not spell out the manner in which the corporation is to be governed. RMBCA § 2.02(b).

a. Articles of correction

If the articles of incorporation contain an inaccuracy or were defectively executed, articles of correction may be filed with the state to correct the inaccuracy or defect. RMBCA § 1.24.

b. Amendment of articles

The corporation can amend its articles with any lawful provision. The procedure for securing approval to amend the articles of incorporation varies depending on whether the corporation has issued stock. Once the necessary approval is obtained, articles of amendment must be filed with the state.

Illinois Point of Law: Amendment of Articles

An Illinois corporation may amend its articles to add, change, or remove provisions as long as the amended articles contain provisions that are required or permitted in the original articles. Additionally, if its period of duration has expired, a corporation may amend its articles any time within five years after the date of expiration, thereby reviving its articles. 805 Ill. Comp. Stat. 5/10.05.

---

1) No stock issued

If the corporation has not issued stock, the board of directors—or, if the board does not exist, the incorporators—may amend the articles of incorporation. RMBCA § 10.02.

Illinois Distinction: No Stock Issued

If no stock has been issued, an amendment may be passed by a majority of incorporators or by a majority of directors. 805 Ill. Comp. Stat. 5/10.10.

---

2) Stock issued

If stock has been issued, corporations generally must follow a two-step approval process:

  i)   The board of directors must adopt the amendment to the articles of incorporation; and

  ii) The board must submit the amendment to the shareholders for their approval by majority vote.

RMBCA § 10.03(a)–(b).

Illinois Distinction: Stock Issued

In addition to the two steps noted above, Illinois requires that written notice setting forth the proposed amendment be sent to each record shareholder. To pass, unless otherwise noted in the articles of incorporation, the proposed amendment must receive at least two-thirds of the shares entitled to vote on such amendment. 805 Ill. Comp. Stat. 5/10.20.

Illinois Distinction: Class Voting on Amendments

Any class of shareholders has the right to vote as a class on a proposed amendment if the articles so provide or if the amendment would:

i)   Increase or decrease the aggregate number of authorized class shares;

ii)   Effect an exchange, reclassification, or cancelation of all or part of the class shares;

iii) Change the designations, preferences, qualifications, limitations, restrictions, or special or relative rights of the class shares;

---

iv) In the case of a preferred or special class of shares, divide the shares of such class into series and fix or authorize the board of directors to fix the variations in the relative rights and preferences between the shares of such series;

v) Change the class shares into the same or a different number of shares of the same or another class;

vi) Create a right of exchange of all or part of another class's shares into the shares of such class;

vii) Create a new class of shares;

viii) Limit or deny existing preemptive rights of the class shares;

ix) Cancel or affect dividends on the class shares that had accumulated but not declared; or

x) Limit or deny the class shares' voting rights.

805 Ill. Comp. Stat. 5/10.25.

2. Bylaws

The bylaws contain any lawful provision for the management of the corporation's business or the regulation of its affairs that is not inconsistent with the articles of incorporation. When there is a conflict between the articles of incorporation and the bylaws, the articles of incorporation control. RMBCA § 2.06(b).

Generally, the board of directors adopts the initial bylaws. RMBCA § 2.06(a). However, a majority vote by either the directors or the shareholders can adopt, amend, or repeal a bylaw. RMBCA § 10.20.

Illinois Distinction: Bylaws

If the power to make, alter, amend, or repeal a bylaw is reserved to the shareholders by the articles of incorporation, the board of directors may not make, alter, amend, or repeal such bylaw. 805 Ill. Comp. Stat. 5/2.25.

B. ORGANIZATIONAL MEETING

Once the articles of incorporation are filed, an organizational meeting is held at which the appointment of officers, adoption of bylaws, and approval of contracts may take place. When the incorporators hold the meeting, election of the board of directors also takes place. RMBCA § 2.05.

Illinois Distinction: Organizational Meeting

If there are no pre-incorporation subscribers and if initial directors are not named in the articles of incorporation, a meeting of the incorporators shall be held at the call of a majority of the incorporators to name initial directors. If there are pre-incorporation subscribers and if the initial directors are not named in the articles, the first shareholder meeting shall be held after the articles are filed at the call of a majority of the incorporators to:

i) Elect initial directors;

ii) Adopt bylaws if the articles require or the shareholders decide to do so; and

iii) Take care of any other matters as stated in the meeting notice.

Shareholder action may also be taken by consent in writing. 805 Ill. Comp. Stat. 5/2.20.

IV. SHAREHOLDERS

A. MEETING REQUIREMENTS

There are two basic types of shareholder meetings—annual and special. In addition, shareholders may express their collective will through written consent.

1. Annual Meeting

A corporation is required to hold a shareholders' meeting each year. Generally, the time and place of the meeting are specified in the corporate bylaws. The primary purpose of the annual meeting is to elect directors, but any business that is subject to shareholder control may be addressed. RMBCA § 7.01.

2. Special Meeting

A corporation may also hold a special meeting, the purpose of which must be specified in the notice of the meeting. Generally, a special meeting may be called by the board of directors or shareholders who own at least ten percent of the shares entitled to vote at the meeting. RMBCA §§ 7.02, .05(c).

Illinois Distinction: Special Meeting

In Illinois, the president, the board of directors, anyone designated in the articles or bylaws, or the shareholders of not less than one-fifth of all outstanding shares entitled to vote on the matter may call a special meeting. 805 Ill. Comp. Stat. 5/7.05.

---

3. Notice of Meeting

Shareholders must be given notice of either type of meeting. In order to properly call a meeting, the corporation must notify all shareholders entitled to a vote at the special meeting in a timely manner. A shareholder may waive notice either in writing or by attending the meeting. Usually, notice must be given no less than 10 days and no more than 60 days before the meeting date. The notice must include the time, date, and place of the meeting. RMBCA §§ 7.05, .06.

Illinois Distinction: Notice of Meeting

Notice must be in writing, and, in the case of a special meeting, must include the purpose for which the meeting is called. 805 Ill. Comp. Stat. 5/7.15.

---

4. Failure to Hold

The failure to hold the annual meeting does not affect the existence of the corporation or invalidate any business conducted by the corporation. RMBCA § 7.01(c). A shareholder may seek a court order compelling the corporation to hold an annual or special meeting. RMBCA § 7.03.

Illinois Point of Law: Failure to Hold

If the annual meeting is not held within the earlier of six months after the end of the corporation's fiscal year or 15 months after the last annual meeting, a shareholder may send a written request to the corporation's president requesting an annual meeting. If notice of the meeting is not given within 60 days of such request, a shareholder entitled to vote at an annual meeting may seek a court order compelling the corporation to hold an annual meeting. 805 Ill. Comp. Stat. 5/7.05.

---

5. Action by Unanimous Written Consent

Instead of voting at a meeting, all shareholders may take any action by unanimous written consent that could have been undertaken at a meeting.

Illinois Distinction: Action by Unanimous Written Consent

Shareholders' Informal Action: Unless provided otherwise in the articles or bylaws, instead of voting at a meeting, any action may be taken without a meeting and vote, as long as written consent setting forth the action is signed by either:

i) The outstanding shareholders having not less than the minimum number of votes that would be necessary to authorize the action at a meeting; or

ii) All of the shareholders entitled to vote on the subject matter.

If not all shareholders consent to the action, notice must be given to those who have not consented. 805 Ill. Comp. Stat. 5/7.10.

B. VOTING REQUIREMENTS

1. Voting Eligibility

Typically, ownership of stock entitles the shareholder to vote. There are two basic issues regarding shareholder voting—who the owner of the stock is and when such ownership is measured.

a. Ownership issues

Generally, a corporation maintains a list of shareholders who are entitled to vote (i.e., record owners). RMBCA § 7.20(a). A beneficial owner is not entitled to vote at a meeting of shareholders. A person who is not a record owner may nevertheless be entitled to vote. For example, a beneficial owner of the stock may compel the record owner to recognize the beneficial owner's right to vote. See RMBCA § 7.23. Similarly, a guardian for an incompetent or a personal representative of a decedent's estate may compel the corporation to allow her to vote in lieu of the record owner. Voting rights issues may also arise when stock is jointly held.

1) Unpaid stock

When stock has been subscribed to but not fully paid for, the subscriber's right to vote such stock may be limited or denied.

2) Corporation's stock

A corporation is generally not entitled to vote its stock. Stock that has been authorized but not issued by a corporation cannot be voted by the corporation. Similarly, stock that has been authorized and issued by a corporation and then reacquired by the corporation (i.e., treasury stock) cannot be voted.

3) Stock in another corporation

A corporation that owns stock in another corporation generally can vote such stock as any other shareholder can.

b. Transfer issue—record date

When stock is sold or otherwise transferred, an issue may arise as to whether the transferor or the transferee of the stock is entitled to vote at a subsequent shareholders' meeting. Typically, the record date is fixed by the board of directors, although the date can be set by reference to the articles of incorporation or the corporate bylaws and, failing corporate guidance, by statute. The owner of the stock at the close of business on the record date has the right to vote the stock at the upcoming meeting. A transferee of shares after the record date who wants to vote at a scheduled shareholder meeting should obtain a proxy to vote the shares from his her transferor. RMBCA § 7.07.

2. Shareholder Voting

The primary issue upon which shareholders are entitled to vote is the selection of the board of directors. Shareholder approval is also required for fundamental corporate changes such as changes to the articles of incorporation or structural changes to the corporation.

Illinois Point of Law: Transfer Issue—Record Date

Time Limit: The record date may not be more than 60 days and not fewer than 10 days immediately preceding the shareholders' meeting. 805 Ill. Comp. Stat. 5/7.25.

---

3. Voting Power

Typically, each share of stock is entitled to one vote. However, a corporation, through its articles of incorporation, can create classes of stock that have greater voting power (e.g., each share is entitled to five votes) or that cannot vote (i.e., nonvoting stock). RMBCA § 7.21(a).

4. Quorum Requirements

In order for a decision made at a shareholders' meeting to be valid, there must be a quorum of the shares eligible to vote present at the meeting. Usually, the required quorum is a majority of votes entitled to be cast on a matter. A share that is present for any purpose at a meeting is deemed present for quorum purposes. RMBCA § 7.25.

Illinois Point of Law: Quorum Requirements

Unless provided otherwise by the articles, a majority of votes of shares entitled to vote on a matter constitutes a quorum. A quorum is not reached if less than one-third of the votes of the shares entitled to vote are present. 805 Ill. Comp. Stat. 5/7.60.

---

5. Approval Requirements

While approval of the shares entitled to vote on an issue is the generally accepted standard, when there are classes of shares, each class of stock may be required to approve the issue separately. RMBCA § 7.26.

a. Level of approval

The requisite level of shareholder approval is a majority, but approval by a plurality may be permissible, especially if the issue is the election of directors. RMBCA §§ 7.25(c), 7.28(a). A plurality vote requirement for directors means that the individuals with the largest number of votes are elected as directors up to the maximum number of directors to be chosen at the election.

b. Basis for determining level

Usually, the level of shareholder approval is based on the number of votes cast. For some issues, such as fundamental changes, the level of shareholder approval is based on the number of votes eligible to be cast.

6. Special Voting For Directors

Corporations may choose directors by cumulative voting if so provided in the articles of incorporation.

a. Cumulative voting

When more than one director is to be elected, corporations can allow shareholders to cumulate their votes and cast all those votes for only one (or more than one) of the candidates. The effect of cumulative voting is to allow minority shareholders to elect representatives to the board.

> **Example:** A owns 30 shares of X, Inc. stock. B owns the remaining 70 shares. X, Inc. has three directors. Without cumulative voting, A is unable to elect any of the three directors because B owns a majority of the shares. With cumulative voting, A can elect at least one director by casting all of her 90 votes (i.e., 30 votes per director x three directors) for one director.

b. Staggered terms

Typically, all directors of the corporation are elected annually. However, some corporations provide for the election of fewer than all of the directors, thereby staggering the terms of the directors, which provides for some continuity on the board from election to election. The main purpose for staggered terms is to limit the impact of cumulative voting.

7. Proxy Voting

A shareholder may vote in person or by proxy. A proxy vote must be executed in writing and delivered to the corporation or its agent. A proxy is valid for 11 months unless otherwise specified. A proxy is revocable unless it expressly provides that it is irrevocable and the appointment of the proxy is coupled with an interest. Any act by the shareholder that is inconsistent with a proxy, such as attending a shareholder meeting and voting the shares, revokes the proxy. RMBCA § 7.22. In the case of multiple proxies given, the last given revokes all previous proxies.

Whether a proxy is coupled with an interest depends on whether the proxy holder has (i) a property right in the shares, or (ii) a security interest given to him to protect him for any obligations he incurred or money advanced. Typically, proxy holders who have a property interest in the shares or a security interest are those who have purchased the shares or otherwise have a business arrangement with the corporation (such as a creditor or employee of the corporation).

> **Illinois Distinction: Proxy Voting**
>
> Illinois requires a shareholder to appoint a proxy by delivering a signed valid "**proxy appointment form**" to the appointed person or proxy solicitation firm. 805 Ill. Comp. Stat. 5/7.50.

8. Voting Together With Other Shareholders

a. Voting pool—retention of legal ownership

Shareholders may enter into a binding voting agreement, also known as a voting pool, which provides for the manner in which they will vote their shares. Under such an agreement, shareholders retain ownership of their stock. Such an agreement is a contract that may be specifically enforced. It does not need to be filed with the corporation and there is no time limit. RMBCA § 7.31.

b. Voting trust—transfer of legal ownership

A voting trust constitutes a separate legal entity to which the shareholders' stock is transferred. While the shareholders retain beneficial ownership of their shares, legal ownership is transferred to the trustee who votes the shares and distributes the dividends in accord with the terms of the trust. The trustee owes a fiduciary duty to the trust and the beneficial owners of the stock. A voting trust must be in writing, is limited to 10 years, and the trust instrument must be filed with the corporation. RMBCA § 7.30.

c. Management agreements

Generally, shareholders may agree to alter the way in which a corporation is managed even though the agreement is inconsistent with statutory provisions. Among the matters on which shareholders may agree are:

i) Elimination of the board of directors or restrictions on the discretion or powers of the board of directors;

ii) Authorization or making of distributions;

iii) Determination of who is a member of the board of directors, the manner of selection or removal of directors, and the terms of office of directors;

iv) The exercise or division of voting power by or between the shareholders and directors or by or among any of them, including director proxies;

v) A transfer to one or more shareholders or other persons all or part of the authority to exercise corporate powers or to manage the business and affairs of the corporation; and

vi) The manner or means by which the exercise of corporate powers or the management of the business and affairs of the corporation is affected.

RMBCA § 7.32(a).

1) Form of agreement

The agreement must be set forth either (i) in the articles of incorporation or the corporate bylaws and approved by all persons who are shareholders at the time of the agreement, or (ii) in a written agreement that is signed by all persons who are shareholders at the time of the agreement and is made known to the corporation. The agreement may be amended only by persons who are shareholders at the time of amendment. RMBCA § 7.32(b).

2) Length of agreement

Unless otherwise fixed in the agreement, the agreement is valid for 10 years. RMBCA § 7.32(b).

3) Rescission of agreement

A person who purchases stock in a corporation with a management agreement without knowledge of the agreement can rescind the purchase agreement. RMBCA § 7.32(c).

4) Limitation on type of corporation

Such an agreement cannot be entered into with respect to a corporation the shares of which are listed on a national securities exchange, and ceases to be effective for a corporation when its shares are listed on such an exchange. RMBCA § 7.32(d).

5) Effect on liability

If the agreement limits the discretion or powers of the board of directors, the directors are relieved of liability for acts or omissions to the extent of the limitation, and the persons in whom such discretion or powers are vested are subject to liability. The existence of the agreement is not a ground for imposing personal liability on shareholders for corporate acts or debts, even though the shareholders, by virtue of the agreement, fail to observe the corporate formalities. RMBCA § 7.32(e)–(f).

C. INSPECTION OF CORPORATE RECORDS RIGHTS

A shareholder has a right to inspect and copy corporate records, books, papers, etc., upon five days' written notice stating a proper purpose. As a litigant against the corporation, the shareholder also has a right to discovery.

1. Shareholders with Inspection Rights

Generally, not only a shareholder of record, but also a beneficial owner of the shares enjoys inspection rights. RMBCA § 16.02. Some states can restrict access to corporate records to shareholders who own stock for a limited amount of time and/or own a minimum amount of stock.

2. Records Subject to Inspection

Generally, a shareholder can inspect any corporate records, but the inspection may be limited to specified records, such as excerpts from the minutes of a board meeting. RMBCA § 16.02(b).

Illinois Distinction: Records Subject to Inspection

Illinois does not limit the corporate records a shareholder may inspect, as long as a proper purpose is stated. 805 Ill. Comp. Stat. 5/7.75.

3. Time and Place Limits on Inspection

The inspection right is usually restricted to normal business hours at the corporation's principal place of business. Five days' advance written notice is required. RMBCA § 16.02.

Illinois Distinction: Time and Place Limits on Inspection

In Illinois, instead of five days' advance notice, written demand must be made upon the corporation, and any shareholder of record may examine the records at any reasonable time. 805 Ill. Comp. Stat. 5/7.75.

4. Purpose Limitation on Inspection

A shareholder's inspection right is conditional on having a proper purpose. RMBCA § 16.02(c). A proper purpose is one that relates to the shareholder's interest in the corporation, such as determining the value of one's shares in a closely-held corporation even though the shareholder does not plan to sell the shares. Improper purposes may include harassment of corporate officials or acquiring corporate secrets.

5. Enforcement of Right

Some states enforce a shareholder's inspection right indirectly by imposing fines on the corporate official who improperly refuses a shareholder access to the corporate records. Under the RMBCA, direct enforcement of a shareholder's inspection right is recognized via an expedited court proceeding, under which the shareholder can secure access to the corporate records and reimbursement for litigation costs. RMBCA § 16.04.

Illinois Distinction: Enforcement of Right

If the **corporation** refuses inspection, a shareholder may file a suit in court to compel such examination. If any **officer, agent, or corporation** refuses inspection after a proper purpose is stated, such person or entity will be liable to the shareholder in a penalty of up to ten percent of the value of the shares owned by the shareholder, for any other damages owed, or for any lawful remedies. 805 Ill. Comp. Stat. 5/7.75.

6. Disclosure of Financial Statement

Under the SEC, publicly held corporations that have issued securities are required to supply shareholders with an annual audited financial statement. Securities Exchange Act of 1934 Rule 14(a); Securities Exchange Act of 1964 Rule 14(c). Likewise, the RMBCA requires all corporations to furnish shareholders with an annual financial statement. RMBCA § 16.20.

D. SUITS BY SHAREHOLDERS

A shareholder may bring a direct or a derivative action against the corporation in which the shareholder owns stock. How the action is characterized will affect the requirements for bringing suit and to whom any recovery is paid.

1. Direct Actions

A shareholder may pursue two basic types of direct actions: (i) an action to enforce shareholder rights or (ii) a non-shareholder action, the recovery from which is to the benefit of the indirect shareholder.

a. Action to enforce shareholder rights

A shareholder may sue the corporation for breach of a fiduciary duty owed to the shareholder by a director or an officer. Typical actions are based on the denial or interference with a shareholder's voting rights, the board's failure to declare a dividend, or the board's approval or failure to approve a merger.

b. Non-shareholder actions

A shareholder may sue the corporation on grounds that do not arise from the shareholder's status as a shareholder.

Example: A shareholder who is struck by a vehicle owned by the corporation and driven by a corporate employee may pursue a negligence claim against the corporation as the injured party of the corporation's tortious conduct.

2. Derivative Actions

In a derivative action, a shareholder is suing on behalf of the corporation for a harm suffered by the corporation. While the shareholder also may have suffered harm, recovery generally goes to the corporation. For example, a shareholder may bring a derivative action to force a director to disgorge a secret profit earned by the director on a transaction with the corporation.

a. Who may bring suit

Generally, only a person who is a shareholder at the time of the act or omission (or one who receives the shares via transfer from such shareholder) may bring a derivative action. RMBCA § 7.41.

Excluded as plaintiff: A creditor of a corporation cannot bring a derivative action.

b. Standing

A shareholder must have standing in order to bring a derivative action. To have standing, a shareholder must have been a shareholder (i) at the time of the wrong or (ii) at the time that the action is filed and, regardless of when one became a shareholder, he must continue to be a shareholder during litigation. Lastly, the shareholder must fairly and adequately represent the interests of the corporation. RMBCA § 7.41(2).

Illinois Distinction: Standing
The plaintiff in a derivative action must be a shareholder of record at the time of the wrong. A plaintiff who was not a shareholder of record may still sue as long as the court determines that the plaintiff acquired the shares before there was disclosure to the public or the plaintiff of the relevant wrongdoing. 805 Ill. Comp. Stat. 5/7.80.

c. Demand upon board

The plaintiff in a derivative action must make a written demand upon the board of directors in order to take action. A derivative action may not commence until 90 days have passed from the date of demand.

Illinois Distinction: Demand Upon Board
Illinois does not restrict the commencement of a derivative action for 90 days. Instead, if a corporation is investigating a demand, the court may stay the suit for 30 days or until the investigation is completed, whichever occurs first. 805 Ill. Comp. Stat. 5/7.80.

1) Futility exception

A demand upon the board is not required if the demand would be futile. Factors for determining futility include whether the directors are disinterested and independent, and whether the transaction was the product of a valid exercise of business judgment. *Marx v. Akers*, 666 N.E.2d 1034 (1996).

2) Irreparable injury excuse

The plaintiff may be excused from waiting a reasonable time for the board to respond to the demand if the delay would result in irreparable injury to the corporation. RMBCA § 7.42(2).

3) Effect of board rejection of demand

If the board specifically rejects the demand, the rejection is tested against the business judgment rule. If there is a business justification for the rejection, the plaintiff must establish that the board's rejection was due to a lack of care, loyalty, or good faith in order to persuade the court to override the board's refusal. *Findley v. Garrett*, 240 P.2d 421 (Cal. 1952).

d. Litigation expenses

Although the plaintiff-shareholder is usually not entitled to share in a recovery, she can seek reimbursement from the corporation for reasonable litigation expenses, including attorney's fees, if the lawsuit has resulted in a substantial benefit to the corporation. If the court finds the proceeding was commenced or maintained without a reasonable cause or for an improper purpose, it may order the plaintiff-shareholder to pay the defendant's litigation expenses. RMBCA § 7.46.

E.   LIABILITY

One reason the corporate form is favorable is that the investors in a corporation are subject to limited liability for corporate acts, and are only at risk to the extent of their investment. This principle of limited liability is subject to challenge, primarily with respect to shareholders of closely held corporations.

1.   Piercing the Corporate Veil

If a plaintiff is able to "pierce the corporate veil," a corporation's existence is ignored, and the shareholders of the corporation are held personally liable.

Although courts are reluctant to hold a director or active shareholder liable for actions that are legally the responsibility of the corporation (even if the corporation has a single shareholder), they will sometimes do so if the corporation was markedly noncompliant, or if holding only the corporation liable would be singularly unfair to the plaintiff.

a.   Totality of circumstances

In most jurisdictions, no bright-line rule exists for piercing the corporate veil, and courts look at the "totality of circumstances." Courts generally look to whether the corporation is being used as a "façade" for a dominant shareholder's personal dealings (i.e., whether the corporation is an "alter ego" of the shareholder). Additionally, courts look to whether there is "unity of interest and ownership" between the entity and the members, that the corporation in fact did not have an existence independent of the members.

In general, a plaintiff must prove that the incorporation was merely a formality and that the corporation neglected corporate formalities and protocols, such as voting to approve major corporate actions in the context of a duly authorized corporate meeting. This is often the case when a corporation facing legal liability transfers its assets to another corporation with the same management and shareholders. It also happens most often with single-person or small, closely held corporations that are managed in a haphazard manner.

b.   Factors to consider

Factors considered by the courts when piercing the corporate veil include:

i)   Undercapitalization of the corporation at the time of its formation;

ii)   Disregard of corporate formalities;

iii)   Use of corporate assets as shareholder's own assets;

iv)   Self-dealing with the corporation;

v)   Siphoning of corporate funds or stripping of corporate assets;

vi)   Use of corporate form to avoid existing statutory requirements or other legal obligations;

vii)   Shareholder's impermissible control or domination over the corporation; and

viii)   Wrongful, misleading, or fraudulent dealings with a corporate creditor.

Not all of the above factors need to be met in order for the court to pierce the corporate veil. Some courts might find that one factor is so compelling in a particular case that it will find the shareholders personally liable.

The failure of a shareholder to respect the corporate entity is insufficient by itself to justify piercing the corporate veil; such failure must also adversely affect the third party's ability to recover from the corporation.

2. Controlling Shareholder's Fiduciary Obligation

When one shareholder—or a group of shareholders acting in concert—holds a high enough percentage of ownership in a company to enact changes at the highest level, the shareholder or group is a "controlling shareholder." Anyone controlling 50% of a corporation's shares, plus one, is automatically a controlling shareholder. A much smaller interest, whether owned individually or by a group in combination, can be controlling if the remaining shares are widely dispersed (as in a large, publicly traded corporation) and not actively voted. Additionally, a corporation that requires a two-thirds super-majority of shares to vote in favor of a motion can effectively grant control to a minority shareholder or block of shareholders that own just more than one-third of the shares of the corporation. Thus, in some cases, a shareholder can essentially maintain control of a corporation with only 33.4% of the outstanding shares.

Generally, shareholders do not owe fiduciary duties to the corporation or to each other. However, a fiduciary duty to the minority shareholders may arise if the controlling shareholder is (i) selling that interest to an outsider, (ii) seeking to eliminate other shareholders from the corporation, or (iii) receiving a distribution denied to the other shareholders. A controlling shareholder has a duty to disclose to the minority shareholder any information that it knew or should have known if it is information that a reasonable person would consider important in deciding how to vote on a transaction. A controlling shareholder breaches its fiduciary duty to the minority shareholder if nondisclosure causes a loss to the minority shareholders. A loss includes being deprived of a state remedy that would otherwise have been available. Furthermore, when a majority shareholder purchases the interest of the minority, it has a fiduciary duty of fair dealing. The controlling shareholder bears the burden of demonstrating that the process it employed was fair and the price it selected was fair. *Weinberger v. UOP, Inc.*, 457 A.2d 701 (Del. 1983).

V. BOARD OF DIRECTORS

The board of directors manages and directs the management of the corporation's business and affairs. The board also authorizes the officers and other corporate employees to exercise the powers possessed by the corporation. RMBCA § 8.01.

A. COMPOSITION REQUIREMENTS

1. Number of Directors

Traditionally, a board needed three or more directors, but today a board can have as few as one director, regardless of the number of shareholders. In its articles of incorporation or bylaws, a corporation may permit the board to vary the number of directors. RMBCA § 8.03.

2. Qualifications of Directors

A corporation cannot serve as the director of another corporation; a director must be a natural person. Unless required by the articles of incorporation or the bylaws, a director need not be a shareholder of the corporation or resident of a particular state. RMBCA §§ 8.02, 8.03.

B. SELECTION OF DIRECTORS

Directors are selected by the shareholders at the annual shareholders' meeting and may be elected by straight or cumulative voting, and by one or more classes of stock. RMBCA §§ 7.28, 8.03.

C. TERM OF DIRECTORS

1. Annual Terms

Typically, a director serves for a one-year term that expires at the first annual meeting after the director's election. RMBCA § 8.05.

2. Staggered Terms

A director may serve for longer than one year if the terms are staggered. With staggered terms, each year some directors are elected for multi-year terms. The main purpose of staggered terms is to limit the impact of cumulative voting. RMBCA §§ 8.05, 8.06.

3. Holdover Director

A director whose term has expired may continue to serve until a replacement is selected. RMBCA § 8.05(e).

4. Resignation of Director

A director may resign at any time by delivering a written notice to the board, its chair, or the corporation. RMBCA § 8.07.

5. Removal of Director

At common law, shareholders had the inherent power to remove a director. However, because directors were deemed to have an entitlement to their offices, they could only be removed for cause based on substantial grounds (such as breach of fiduciary duty, fraud, criminal conduct, etc.).

The current trend in most states and the RMBCA is to allow shareholders to remove a director with or without cause, unless the articles of incorporation provide otherwise.

a. Meeting requirements

A director may be removed only at a meeting called for the purpose of removing the director and the meeting notice must state that removal is at least one of the purposes of the meeting. RMBCA § 8.08(d).

b. Voting requirements

A director who was elected by a particular voting class of stock can only be removed by that same class (or by court proceeding). RMBCA § 8.08(b).

If cumulative voting is not authorized, a shareholder vote removes a director if the number of votes for removal exceeds the number of votes against removal. RMBCA § 8.08(c).

If cumulative voting is authorized, a director may be removed only if the votes sufficient to elect the director are cast against the director's removal. RMBCA § 8.08.

Notwithstanding the foregoing, a director can be removed by court proceeding.

Illinois Distinction: Removal of Director

Illinois generally allows directors to be removed with or without cause at a shareholder meeting by the affirmative vote of the holders of a majority of the outstanding shares so entitled to vote. In addition to the exceptions noted above, the following restrictions also apply:

i) No director may be removed unless the meeting notice states that a purpose of the meeting is to vote on the removal of the specified director; and

ii) Directors of a corporation with six or more directors who are separated into two or three classes for purposes of creating staggered terms may only be removed for cause if the articles of incorporation so provide.

805 Ill. Comp. Stat. 5/8.35.

---

6. Replacement or New Director

When there is a vacancy on the board or an increase in the number of directors, either the shareholders or the directors may fill the vacancy. When the vacancy leaves the board without a quorum, the directors remaining can elect a replacement director by a majority vote. RMBCA § 8.10(a).

D. COMPENSATION OF DIRECTORS

Directors of a corporation may receive compensation for serving as directors. RMBCA § 8.11.

Illinois Point of Law: Compensation of Directors

In Illinois, directors may set up reasonable compensation for themselves as long as a majority of disinterested directors approves the action. 805 Ill. Comp. Stat. 5/8.05.

E. MEETING REQUIREMENTS

1. Types of Meetings

The board of directors may hold regular or special meetings. A director is only entitled to notice of a special meeting. A director may waive notice of a meeting at any time by a signed written waiver. In addition, a director's attendance waives notice of that meeting unless the director promptly objects to lack of notice. RMBCA §§ 8.20–.23.

2. Presence at Meetings

A director is not required to be physically present at a meeting. A meeting may be conducted via conference call or any other means that allows each director to hear the other directors during the meeting. RMBCA § 8.20(b).

3. Action Without Meeting

The board of directors may act without holding a meeting by unanimous written consent to the action. RMBCA § 8.21.

> **Illinois Point of Law: Action Without Meeting**
>
> Any unanimous consent signed by all the directors or members of a committee constitutes approval of an action by a unanimous vote. 805 Ill. Comp. Stat. 5/8.45.

F. VOTING REQUIREMENTS

1. Quorum Rules

In order for the board of directors' acts at a meeting to be valid, a quorum of directors must be present at the meeting. RMBCA § 8.24(a).

a. Number of directors

A majority of all directors in office constitutes a quorum, unless a higher or lower number is required by the articles of incorporation or bylaws. RMBCA § 8.24.

b. Presence of directors

Unlike shareholders, a director must be present at the time that the vote is taken in order to be counted for quorum purposes. RMBCA § 8.24. Presence includes appearances made via communications equipment that allows all persons participating in the meeting to hear and speak to one another.

2. Passage Level

Typically, the assent of a majority of the directors present at the time the vote takes place is necessary for board approval. However, the articles of incorporation or bylaws may specify a higher level of approval. RMBCA § 8.24(c).

3. Director Dissent

A director may incur liability for illegal or improper action taken by the board at a meeting at which the director is present, even though the director does not vote in favor of the action.

In order to forestall such liability, the director must:

i) Promptly object to the holding of the meeting;

ii) Ensure that his dissent or abstention from the specific action is noted in the minutes of the meeting; or

iii) Not vote in favor of the action and deliver written notice of his dissent to the presiding officer of the meeting before its adjournment or to the corporation immediately afterwards.

RMBCA § 8.24(d).

Illinois Distinction: Director Dissent

A director is conclusively presumed to have assented to an action at a meeting unless:

i) His dissent is entered into the meeting's minutes;

ii) He files a written dissent to the action with the corporation's secretary before the meeting's adjournment; or

iii) He forwards his dissent by registered or certified mail to the corporation's secretary immediately after the meeting's adjournment.

805 Ill. Comp. Stat. 5/8.65.

---

4. Voting Agreements

Generally, an agreement between directors as to how to vote (i.e., a pooling agreement) is unenforceable. Each director is expected to exercise independent judgment. A director also may not vote by proxy.

G. COMMITTEES

The board of directors may take action through one or more committees. RMBCA § 8.25.

1. Composition of Committee

A committee may consist of two or more directors. RMBCA § 8.25.

Illinois Distinction: Composition of Committee

In Illinois, a committee may consist of one or more board members. 805 Ill. Comp. Stat. 5/8.40(a).

---

2. Selection of Committee Members

Generally, a majority of the directors must vote for the creation of a committee and the appointment of a director to a committee. RMBCA § 8.25(b).

3. Committee's Powers

A committee may generally exercise whatever powers are granted to it by the board, the articles of incorporation, or the bylaws. RMBCA § 8.25(d)–(e).

A committee may not:

i) Declare distributions, except within limits set by the board;

ii) Recommend actions that require shareholder approval;

iii) Fill vacancies on the board or its committees; or

iv) Adopt, amend, or repeal bylaws.

Illinois Distinction: Committee's Powers

In addition to the aforementioned, in Illinois, a committee may not:

i)   Elect or remove officers or fix the compensation of any committee member;

ii) Approve a plan of merger requiring shareholder approval;

iii) Authorize or approve the reacquisition of shares that do not follow a general formula or method prescribed by the board;

iv) Authorize or approve the issuance or sale of shares unless the board so directs; or

v)   Amend, alter, repeal, or take action inconsistent with a board resolution or action that provides that a committee may not so act.

805 Ill. Comp. Stat. 5/8.40.

---

4. Type of Committees—Sarbanes-Oxley Act

Typically, the board of a publicly held corporation has an audit committee, a compensation committee, and a nominating committee. A corporation with stock listed on a national securities exchange or a national securities association must have an audit committee that has direct responsibility for selecting, compensating, and overseeing the corporation's outside auditors. The members of the audit committee must be independent directors (i.e., not otherwise employed or compensated by corporation).

Outside auditors cannot otherwise be employed by the corporation. Sarbanes-Oxley Act 301.

H. DUTIES

A director owes two basic duties to the corporation, (i) a duty of care and (ii) a duty of loyalty. In discharging these duties, a director is required to act in good faith and in a manner the director reasonably believes to be in the best interest of the corporation. RMBCA § 8.30.

1. Duty of Care

a. Prudent person

Directors have a duty to act with the care of an **ordinarily prudent person in a like position and similar circumstances**. As an objective standard, the director is presumed to have the knowledge and skills of an ordinarily prudent person. In deciding how to act, the director is also required to use any additional knowledge or special skills that he possesses.

b. Reliance protection

A director is entitled to rely on the performance of, as well as information, reports, and opinions supplied by the following persons if the director reasonably believes them to be reliable and competent:

i)   Officers and other employees of the corporation;

ii) Outside attorneys, accountants, or other skilled or expert individuals retained by the corporation; and

iii) A committee of the board of which the director is not a member.

RMBCA § 8.30(e).

c. Business judgment rule

The business judgment rule is a rebuttable presumption that a director reasonably believed his actions were in the best interest of the corporation. The exercise of managerial powers by a director is generally subject to the business judgment rule. A typical decision protected by the business judgment rule includes whether to declare a dividend and the amount of any dividend.

1) Overcoming the rule

In order to overcome the business judgment rule, it must be shown that:

i) The director did not act in good faith (e.g., intense hostility of the controlling faction against the minority; exclusion of the minority from employment by the corporation; high salaries, or bonuses or corporate loans made to the officers in control; and the existence of a desire by the controlling directors to acquire the minority stock interests as cheaply as possible);

ii) The director was not informed to the extent the director reasonably believed was necessary before making a decision;

iii) The director did not show objectivity or independence from the director's relation to or control by another having material interest in the challenged conduct;

iv) There was a sustained failure by the director to devote attention to an ongoing oversight of the business and affairs of the corporation;

v) The director failed to timely investigate a matter of significant material concern after being alerted in a manner that would have caused a reasonably attentive director to do so; or

vi) The director received a financial benefit to which he was not entitled, or any other breach of his duties to the corporation.

RMBCA § 8.31(a).

d. Exculpatory provisions in the articles of incorporation

A corporation's articles of incorporation may include an exculpatory provision shielding its directors from liability for money damages for failure to exercise adequate care in the performance of their duties as directors. Typically, exculpatory provisions do not protect directors from liability for any breach of the duty of loyalty, for acts or omissions that are not in good faith, or for any transactions from which the director received an improper personal benefit. *See* Del. Gen. Corp. Law § 102(b)(7); Model Bus. Corp. Act § 2.02(b)(4).

2. Duty of Loyalty

The duty of loyalty requires a director to act in a manner that the director reasonably believes is in the best interest of the corporation. RMBCA § 8.60. Typically, a director breaches this duty by placing his own interests before those of the corporation.

a. Conflict-of-interest transaction—self-dealing

A director who engages in a conflict-of-interest transaction with his own corporation, also known as self-dealing, has violated his duty of loyalty unless the transaction is protected under the safe harbor rule. The business judgment rule does not apply when a director engages in a conflict-of-interest transaction with his corporation. In addition, a director must not profit at the corporation's expense.

1) Type of transactions

A conflict-of-interest transaction is any transaction between a director and his corporation that would normally require approval of the board of directors and that is of such financial significance to the director that it would reasonably be expected to influence the director's vote on the transaction. RMBCA § 8.60(1)–(2).

2) Related persons

Corporate dealings with persons who are related to the director are also subject to conflict-of-interest rules. Related individuals include the director's immediate family, parents, siblings, and grandchildren, including the spouses of these individuals, as well as a trust or estate of which any of those individuals is a substantial beneficiary or the director is a fiduciary.

In addition, the conflict-of-interest rules can apply to transactions between the corporation and another entity with which the director is associated, such as another corporation of which the director is a director, employee, or agent or a partnership of which the director is a general partner, employee, or agent. RMBCA § 8.60(1), (3).

3) Safe harbor rules

a) Standards for upholding transactions

There are three safe harbors by which a conflict-of-interest transaction may enjoy protection:

i) Disclosure of all material facts to, and approval by a majority of, the board of directors without a conflicting interest;

ii) Disclosure of all material facts to, and approval by a majority of, the votes entitled to be cast by the shareholders without a conflicting interest; and

iii) Fairness of the transaction to the corporation at the time of commencement.

RMBCA § 8.61.

b) Fairness of transaction

The fairness test looks at the substance of the transaction to see if the corporation received something of comparable value in exchange for what it gave to the director. RMBCA §§ 8.60(5), 8.61(b)(3). Interested directors who were on both sides of transactions in question have the burden of establishing the fairness of the transactions. *HMG/Courtland Properties, Inc. v. Gray*, 749 A.2d 94, 115 (Del. Ch. 1999).

c) Effect of safe harbor provisions

Satisfaction of the safe harbor defenses is not necessarily a complete defense, and some states instead hold that the burden of proof shifts to the party challenging the transaction to establish that the transaction was unfair to the corporation. *Kahn v. Lynch Communication System*, 638 A.2d 1110 (Del. 1994).

Illinois Distinction: Safe Harbor Rules

Burden of Proof: In a proceeding contesting the validity of the conflict-of-interest transaction, the person asserting the validity has the burden of proving fairness, unless the safe harbor defenses apply. 805 Ill. Comp. Stat. 5/8.60.

---

4) Remedies

A conflict-of-interest transaction that is found to be in violation of the safe harbor provisions may be enjoined or rescinded. In addition, the corporation may seek damages from the director. RMBCA § 8.61.

5) Business judgment rule

Approval of a conflict-of-interest transaction by fully informed disinterested directors triggers the business judgment rule and limits judicial review to issues of gift or waste, with the burden of proof upon the party attacking the transaction. *See* Del. Gen. Corp. Law § 144(a)(1); *Marciano v. Nakash*, 535 A.2d 400, 405 n.3 (Del. 1987).

b. Usurpation of corporate opportunity

In addition to a conflict-of-interest transaction, a director may violate his duty of loyalty by usurping a corporate opportunity rather than first offering the opportunity to the corporation. RMBCA § 8.70.

1) Corporate opportunity

In determining whether the opportunity is one that must first be offered to the corporation, courts have applied the "interest or expectancy" test or the "line of business" test.

a) "Interest or expectancy" test

Under the "interest or expectancy" test, the key is whether the corporation has an existing interest (e.g., an option to buy) or an expectancy arising from an existing right (e.g., purchase of property currently leased) in the opportunity. An expectancy can also exist when the corporation is actively seeking a similar opportunity.

b) "Line of business" test

Under the broader "line of business" test, the key is whether the opportunity is within the corporation's current or prospective line of business. Whether an opportunity satisfies this test frequently turns on how expansively the corporation's line of business is characterized.

c) Other factors

Courts look at additional factors in determining whether an opportunity belongs to the corporation. These factors include: (i) the relationship between the person offering the opportunity and the director and corporation, (ii) how and when the director acquired knowledge of the opportunity, and (iii) the relationship of the director to the corporation.

c. Competition with corporation

A director who engages in a business venture that competes with the corporation has breached his duty of loyalty to the corporation. However, a director may engage in unrelated business that does not compete with the corporation. Note that corporate officers and other employees more frequently engage in this kind of breach than directors do.

3. Indemnification and Insurance

When a director is involved in a legal action as a consequence of her role as director, she may seek indemnification for expenses incurred as well as for any judgment or award declared against her. Indemnification may be (i) mandatory, (ii) prohibited, or (iii) permissive. RMBCA §§ 8.50–8.59.

a. Mandatory indemnification

A corporation is **required** to indemnify a director for any reasonable expense, including court costs and attorney's fees, incurred in the **successful** defense of a proceeding against the director in his role as a director. In addition, a corporation must indemnify a director when ordered by the court. RMBCA §§ 8.52, 8.56.

b. Prohibited indemnification

A corporation is prohibited from indemnifying a director against liability due to the receipt of an improper personal benefit. RMBCA § 8.51(d)(2).

c. Permissive indemnification

A corporation **may** indemnify a director in the unsuccessful defense of a suit when:

i) The director acted in good faith with the reasonable belief that his conduct was in the best interests of the corporation, or that his conduct was at least not opposed to the best interests of the corporation; and

ii) In the case of a criminal proceeding, the director did not have reasonable cause to believe that his conduct was unlawful.

Indemnification can extend to liability as well as expenses when the action is brought by a third party, but only to expenses if the action is brought by or on behalf of the corporation. RMBCA § 8.51(a)(1), (d)(1).

The authorization for permissive indemnification requires the approval of a disinterested majority of directors or shareholders or an independent attorney chosen by disinterested directors. RMBCA § 8.55.

Illinois Distinction: Indemnification and Insurance

Unlike other voting requirements, in order to indemnify a director or officer, the approval of a disinterested majority of directors may be sufficient, even though less than a quorum exists. 805 Ill. Comp. Stat. 5/8.75.

---

d. Advance of expenses

A corporation may, upon a petition by the director, advance litigation expenses to the director. Upon termination of the action, the director must repay such expense if the director is not entitled to indemnification for them. RMBCA § 8.53.

e. Liability insurance

A corporation may acquire insurance to indemnify directors for actions arising from service as a director. The insurance can cover all awards against a director as well as expenses incurred by him, even though the corporation could not otherwise indemnify the director for such amounts. RMBCA § 8.55.

f. Applicability to officers

An officer of a corporation is entitled to indemnification on the same basis and subject to the same restrictions as a director. RMBCA § 8.56.

I. INSPECTION RIGHTS OF DIRECTORS

A director is entitled to inspect and copy corporate books, records, and other documents for any purpose related to the performance of his duty as a director. When the corporation refuses to grant the director access to these items, the director can seek a court order to enforce this right. RMBCA § 16.05.

VI. OFFICERS AND OTHER EMPLOYEES

A. TYPES

Typically, a corporation's officers are composed of a president, secretary, and treasurer. An individual may hold more than one office, but some states prohibit a person from serving dual roles when such officers serve as a check on each other. The RMBCA does not specify which officers a corporation must have, but simply indicates that the corporate bylaws are responsible for delineating the officers of the corporation. RMBCA § 8.40.

Illinois Point of Law: Types

Dual Roles: In Illinois, the same person may hold two or more offices, so long as the bylaws provide for it. 805 Ill. Comp. Stat. 5/8.50.

B. SELECTION

The primary officers of a corporation are elected by the board of directors. These officers may in turn be empowered by the board of directors or the bylaws to select other corporate officers and employees. RMBCA § 8.40(b).

<table>
<tr><td>Illinois Distinction: Selection</td></tr>
<tr><td>Illinois allows officers to be elected, appointed by the board of directors, or chosen in any other manner prescribed in the bylaws. 805 Ill. Comp. Stat. 5/8.50.</td></tr>
</table>

C. AUTHORITY

An officer's authority can be actual, implied, or apparent. Actual authority wielded by an officer is defined by the corporate bylaws or set by the board of directors. An officer has implied authority to perform those tasks that are necessary to carry out the officer's duties by virtue of her status or position, so long as the matter is within the scope of its ordinary business. However, the officer does not have the authority to bind the corporation by extraordinary acts. In determining whether a transaction is extraordinary, the court might consider the economic magnitude of the action in relation to corporate earnings and assets, the extent of the risk involved, the time span of the action's effect, and the cost of reversing the action. Finally, an officer has apparent authority if the corporation holds the officer out as having authority to bind the corporation to third parties.

D. DUTIES—CARE AND LOYALTY

The specific duties of an officer are defined by the corporate bylaws or set by the board of directors. RMBCA § 8.41. The duties of care and loyalty that are imposed on the directors of a corporation are also owed by the officers of a corporation. Moreover, all employees, as agents of the corporation, owe the corporation these duties of care and loyalty. RMBCA § 8.42.

1. Financial Reports—Sarbanes Oxley Requirements

The CEO and CFO of a publicly traded corporation must certify the accuracy of the corporation's financial reports that are filed with the SEC. Sarbanes-Oxley Act 302. In addition to facing criminal penalties for filing a false report, a CEO and CFO must forfeit incentive-based pay, and return profits from stock sales for a year when financial reports must be restated due to such misconduct. Sarbanes-Oxley Act 304.

E. LIABILITY

As an agent of the corporation, an officer does not incur liability to third parties merely for the performance of duties to the corporation. Of course, an officer can be liable to a third party if the officer has acted in his personal capacity (e.g., guaranteed a corporate loan), or has engaged in purposeful tortious behavior.

F. INDEMNIFICATION AND INSURANCE

An officer is entitled to indemnification to the same extent and subject to the same restrictions as a corporate director. Similar insurance rules apply as well.

G. REMOVAL

An officer may be removed at any time with or without cause. RMBCA § 8.43. The existence of an employment contract between an officer and the corporation does not prevent the removal of the officer, but may give rise to contractual remedies such as damages if removal constitutes a breach of contract.

Illinois Distinction: Removal

An officer may be removed by the board of directors if, in its judgment, the best interests of the corporation will be served by the removal. The removal of an officer is without prejudice regarding the contract rights of the removed party. Contract rights are not created solely by the election or appointment of an officer. 805 Ill. Comp. Stat. 5/8.55.

H. OTHER EMPLOYEES

An employee who is not an officer is an agent of the corporation and is subject to the responsibilities of an agent. In turn, the employee is owed duties by the corporate principal. As an agent, the employee has the ability to act on behalf of the corporation to the extent of the employee's authority and is usually protected as an agent from liability for actions undertaken in accord with that authority.

VII. MERGERS AND ACQUISITIONS

A. MERGERS

1. Definition

A **merger** is the combination of two or more corporations such that only one corporation survives. The surviving corporation may be created as a result of the merger, rather than existing before the merger, in which case the process is referred to as a **consolidation**. RMBCA §§ 1.40, 11.01, 11.02.

2. Procedure

While the business aspects of effecting a merger can be complex, the statutory procedure is simple. In order to merge:

i)   The board of directors for each corporation must approve of the merger;

ii) The shareholders of each corporation must usually approve of the merger; and

iii) The required documents (e.g., plan of merger, amended articles of incorporation) must be filed with the state.

RMBCA § 11.04.

a. Shareholder approval

1) Voting requirements

Shareholder approval requires a majority vote, meaning a majority of the shares entitled to vote, but the shareholders' meeting at which the vote is taken is subject to a quorum requirement, which is usually a majority of shares entitled to vote. RMBCA § 11.04.

Illinois Distinction: Voting Requirements

The merger or consolidation must be approved by at least two-thirds of the votes of either the shares entitled to vote or the class of shares entitled to vote unless the articles state otherwise, but not less than a majority of votes entitled to be cast must approve. 805 Ill. Comp. Stat. 5/11.20.

---

2) Voting by class

If the corporation has more than one class of stock and the amendment would affect the rights of a particular class of stock, the holders of that class of stock must also approve of the amendment. RMBCA § 11.04.

3) Mergers without shareholder approval

a) Parent-subsidiary merger

A merger between a parent corporation and a subsidiary corporation when the parent owns at least 90% of the voting power of each class of outstanding stock of the subsidiary may occur without the approval of the shareholders of the subsidiary. A parent corporation may also effect a merger between two 90% or more owned subsidiary corporations without the need for approval by the shareholders of either corporation. In all these mergers, approval by a subsidiary's board of directors is also not required. RMBCA § 11.05.

Illinois Distinction: Parent-Subsidiary Merger

In Illinois, both the parent corporation and the subsidiary corporation must be solvent. The board of directors of the parent corporation must approve a merger plan, and a copy of the plan must be mailed to all shareholders of the subsidiary corporation, along with a notice informing them of their right to dissent. If there is no dissent filed within 30 days of mailing the merger plan, the articles of merger must be filed by the parent corporation with the Secretary of State. 805 Ill. Comp. Stat. 5/11.30.

---

b) Minnow-whale merger

A merger of a small corporation (i.e., a "minnow") into a large corporation (i.e., a "whale") may not require approval of the shareholders of the surviving large corporation. Approval is not required if the merger cannot result in an increase of more than 20% in the voting power of the outstanding stock of the surviving corporation, the articles of incorporation of the surviving corporation will not differ from the articles before the merger, and the pre-merger shareholders of the surviving corporation are otherwise unaffected by the merger. RMBCA §§ 6.21(f), 11.04.

Illinois Distinction: Mergers Without Shareholder Approval

In Illinois, unless the articles state otherwise, shareholder approval from the surviving corporation is not required if:

i) The merger plan does not amend the corporation's articles of incorporation;

ii) Each outstanding share immediately prior to the effective merger date has the same designations, preferences, qualifications, limitations, restrictions, and special rights immediately after the effective date; and

iii) Either no common shares of the surviving corporation and no shares, securities, or obligations convertible into such shares are to be issued under the merger plan or the authorized unissued common shares of the surviving corporation or those initially issuable upon conversion exceed 20% of the outstanding common shares of the corporation prior to the effective merger date.

805 Ill. Comp. Stat. 5/11.20.

---

3. Corporate Assets and Liabilities

All assets and liabilities owned by a corporation that are merged into another corporation are then owned by the surviving corporation after the merger. RMBCA § 11.07.

B. ASSET ACQUISITION

The sale or other transfer of a corporation's assets does not require approval by the shareholders or board of a transferor corporation. However, asset transfers that resemble a merger may require approval by both the board of directors and the shareholders of the transferor corporation.

1. Applicable Transfers

A transfer involving all, or substantially all, of the corporation's assets outside the usual and regular course of business is a fundamental corporate change for the transferor corporation. Thus, the corporation must follow the fundamental change procedures.

2. Approval Procedure

The approval procedure for an asset transfer follows the approval procedure for a merger, except that only the transferor corporation's board of directors and shareholders are entitled to vote on the transaction. RMBCA § 12.02.

3. Transferor's Liabilities

a. Transferor's continued responsibility

Apart from an agreement with a creditor that releases the transferor corporation from liability, the transferor corporation remains liable for its debts, including the ones associated with the transferred assets. The transferor may be able to obtain indemnification from the transferee for such liability.

b. Transferee's escape from liability

Unlike a merger, the transferee corporation is generally not responsible to the transferor's creditors for the liabilities of the transferor corporation, unless the transferee corporation assumes such liabilities.

C. STOCK ACQUISITION

A corporation may acquire stock in another corporation and thereby secure control of that corporation without going through the process of effecting a statutory merger. The two primary means by which a corporation can acquire stock in another corporation is by exchanging its own stock for that stock or by paying cash or other property for the stock.

1. Stock-for-Stock Exchange

A corporation may offer its own stock to shareholders in another corporation in exchange for their stock in that corporation (i.e., a stock swap). Generally, a shareholder in the other corporation may retain his stock and not participate in the stock swap. However, the RMBCA sets out a procedure, labeled a "share exchange," which parallels the procedure for a merger. If followed, this procedure requires all shareholders to participate in the stock swap. As with a merger, dissenting shareholders are given the right of appraisal. RMBCA § 11.03.

Illinois Distinction: Stock-for-Stock Exchange

An Illinois corporation may acquire all of the issued or outstanding shares of another corporation if the board of directors of each corporation approves an exchange plan by a majority vote and the plan sets forth:

i)   The name of the corporation whose shares will be acquired and the acquiring corporation's name;

ii) The terms and conditions of the exchange;

iii) The manner of exchanging the shares; and

iv) Any other necessary or desirable conditions, including abandonment prior to the filing of the articles.

Additionally, the corporations may agree to a voluntary share exchange. 805 Ill. Comp. Stat. 5/11.10.

---

2. Stock Purchase

A corporation may purchase stock in another corporation on the open market or make an offer to buy the stock from the current shareholders (i.e., a tender offer).

D. DISSENTING SHAREHOLDER'S RIGHT OF APPRAISAL

A shareholder who objects to a merger or acquisition may be able to force the corporation to buy his stock at a fair value as determined by an appraisal. This right is also available for shareholders whose rights are materially and adversely affected by an amendment of the corporation's articles of incorporation. RMBCA §§ 13.01-.31.

Illinois Distinction: Dissenting Shareholder's Right of Appraisal

In Illinois, a shareholder who makes a demand for payment retains all other shareholder rights until such rights are canceled or modified by the completion of the proposed corporate action. 805 Ill. Comp. Stat. 5/11.70.

---

1. Qualifying Shareholders

A shareholder who is entitled to vote on a merger, acquisition, or amendment of the corporation's articles of incorporation has appraisal rights. In addition, a minority shareholder in a short form merger can exercise appraisal rights, even though such a shareholder cannot vote on the merger. RMBCA § 13.02(a).

If a shareholder can sell his stock in a market that is both liquid and reliable, such as the New York or American Stock Exchange, the shareholder does not have a right of appraisal because the market is providing him with the opportunity to sell his stock at its fair value. RMBCA § 13.02(b).

2. Procedure

a. Notice to corporation

In order to exercise the right of appraisal, a shareholder must send a written notice to the corporation of the shareholder's intent to do so. This notice must be delivered to the corporation **before** the shareholders vote on the proposed action. RMBCA § 13.21(a).

b. No favorable vote

When the proposed corporate action is submitted to the shareholders for their approval, the shareholder must not vote in favor of the action (i.e., she must abstain or vote "no"). RMBCA § 13.21(a).

c. Demand for payment

After the proposed corporate action has been approved, the shareholder must make a written demand upon the corporation for payment. RMBCA § 13.21.

d. Fair market value

The corporation must pay shareholders what it estimates as fair market value. If the corporation and the shareholder do not agree on a price for the shareholder's stock, the fair value of the stock is determined through a court action.

3. Exclusivity of Remedy

A shareholder who has an appraisal right cannot challenge the corporate action except on the grounds of fraud or illegality. RMBCA § 13.02(d).

VIII. TERMINATION OF CORPORATE STATUS

A corporation may terminate its status as a corporation either voluntarily by agreement or involuntarily by court order or state action.

A. VOLUNTARY DISSOLUTION

1. Procedure Prior to Issuance of Stock

Prior to the issuance of stock, a corporation may voluntarily dissolve by a majority vote of the incorporators or initial directors. RMBCA § 14.01.

Illinois Distinction: Procedure Prior to Issuance of Stock

As long as either a majority of the incorporators or initial directors approve, voluntary dissolution may occur prior to the issuance of stock if:

i) The amount, if any, paid on the subscriptions, less any part disbursed for expenses, has been returned;

ii) There are no outstanding debts; and

iii) Written notice of the dissolution has been given to all incorporators or directors not less than three days before the execution of the articles of dissolution.

805 Ill. Comp. Stat. 5/12.05.

Voluntary dissolution may also be authorized by the unanimous written consent of all shareholders entitled to vote on dissolution. 805 Ill. Comp. Stat. 5/12.10.

---

2. Procedure After Issuance of Stock

A corporation that has issued stock may voluntarily dissolve if (i) the board of directors adopts a proposal for the dissolution of the corporation and (ii) the majority of shareholders approve. RMBCA § 14.02.

3. Effect of Dissolution—Winding Up

A dissolved corporation may continue to exist as a corporation for the limited purpose of winding up its affairs and liquidating its business. This includes (i) collecting assets, (ii) disposing of property that will not be distributed to shareholders, (iii) discharging liabilities, and (iv) distributing property among shareholders according to their interests.

It does not include (i) transferring title to the corporation's property, (ii) preventing transfer or shares or securities, (iii) changing quorum or voting requirements, (iv) terminating the authority of the registered corporate agent, or (v) preventing commencement of a proceeding by or against the corporation. RMBCA § 14.05.

4. Dissolution Distribution

The directors of a corporation are responsible for distribution of the corporate assets and may be liable for improper distributions. Such assets must be distributed in the following order:

i) To creditors of the corporation to pay the debts and other obligations of the corporation, including bona fide obligations owed to shareholders;

ii) To shareholders of stock with preferences in liquidation; and

iii) To shareholders of other stock.

RMBCA § 14.09.

B. INVOLUNTARY DISSOLUTION

1. Petitioner

Either a shareholder or creditor of a corporation may bring an action for involuntary dissolution of a corporation.

a. Creditor

A creditor may pursue the involuntary dissolution of a corporation only if the corporation is insolvent. RMBCA § 14.30(c).

b. Shareholder

A shareholder may pursue the involuntary dissolution of a corporation if:

 i) The corporate assets are being misapplied or wasted;

 ii) The directors or those in control of the corporation are acting illegally, oppressively, or fraudulently;

 iii) The directors are deadlocked in the management of the corporation's affairs, the shareholders are unable to break the deadlock, and irreparable injury to the corporation is threatened or being suffered; or

 iv) The shareholders are deadlocked in voting power and have failed to elect successors to the directors whose terms have expired.

RMBCA § 14.30(b).

2. Court's Power

Upon the petitioner's establishment of the necessary grounds, the court may dissolve the corporation. RMBCA § 14.30(a). The court has equitable powers to issue injunctions, appoint a receiver, and take other steps necessary to preserve the corporation's assets. RMBCA § 14.31. If the court orders the dissolution of the corporation, the distribution of the corporation's assets generally adheres to that of a voluntary distribution unless equity requires otherwise.

Illinois Distinction: Court's Power

In an action by the Attorney General, the court may dissolve a corporation if it is established that:

i) The corporation filed its articles of incorporation fraudulently;

ii) The corporation exceeded or abused its lawful authority or has otherwise violated the law after notice has been given; or

iii) Any interrogatory has been answered falsely or not fully within 30 days after the mailing of such interrogatories.

805 Ill. Comp. Stat. 5/1.35. Additionally, a court may dissolve a corporation if it is established that dissolution is reasonably necessary because the corporation can no longer conduct business to the advantage of its shareholders. 805 Ill. Comp. Stat. 5/12.50.

C. FORFEITURE/ADMINISTRATIVE DISSOLUTION

The state may force a corporation to forfeit its right to exist or administratively dissolve the corporation if the corporation has (i) failed to pay fees or taxes, (ii) failed to file required reports or notices, or (iii) has abused its powers. RMBCA §§ 14.20–14.21, 14.30(a). Continuing to operate as a corporation after forfeiture can result in the personal liability of the operators.

IX. SPECIAL TYPES OF CORPORATIONS

A. CLOSELY-HELD AND CLOSE CORPORATIONS

The terms "closely-held corporation" and "close corporation" are frequently used interchangeably to refer to a corporation with only a few shareholders and a more relaxed style of governance. Shareholders often serve as both directors and officers of the corporation. Stock of such a corporation is not publicly traded, and many states allow shareholders to do away with many of the corporate formalities.

B. FOREIGN CORPORATION

A foreign corporation is a corporation that is incorporated in another state. In order to do business in a state other than its state of incorporation, a corporation is required to register with that state and receive a "certificate of authority." Failure to do so prevents the foreign corporation from suing, but not from being sued, in state courts until registered. However, it does not impair the validity of corporate acts or contracts or prevent the corporation from defending any proceeding within the state. A number of actions, such as a holding board meetings, maintaining bank accounts, and selling through independent contractors, do not constitute doing business within a state. RMBCA §§ 15.01–15.32.

C. PROFESSIONAL CORPORATION

A professional corporation is a corporation with a purpose that is statutorily limited to the rendering of a professional service. A shareholder in a professional corporation must be a member of the applicable profession. In addition, a professional corporation does not shield an employee from liability arising from her own malpractice. However, it may provide protection against vicarious liability arising from malpractice by other professionals in the corporation.

D. S CORPORATION

A corporation is usually subject to tax as a "C corporation," which is a separate taxable entity from its shareholders, causing the corporation to face double taxation. The corporation pays taxes first on profits and again as shareholders on distributions received from the corporation. However, a corporation may elect to avoid double taxation as an "S corporation" when the income and expenses of the corporation are passed through to its shareholders (who are then taxed on such items directly). 26 U.S.C. § 1361, et. seq.

In order to become an S corporation for federal tax purposes, a corporation must file IRS Form 2553 and the IRS must approve the application. Companies that file as S corporations can have no more than 100 shareholders. Only individuals, estates, certain exempt organizations, or certain trusts may be shareholders and the shareholders must all be either U.S. citizens or resident aliens (nonresident aliens are not permitted). The S corporation may not have more than one class of stock. Each shareholder must consent to the S corporation election for a corporation to become an S corporation.

X. LIMITED LIABILITY COMPANY

A limited liability company ("LLC") is a legally recognized business entity that enjoys the pass-through tax advantage of a partnership but also the limited liability of a corporation. An LLC also provides flexibility in managing the entity. Many of the rules applicable to corporations and corporate governance have counterparts applicable to LLCs (e.g., the name of an LLC must include the words "limited liability company" or some abbreviation thereof). Some of these rules are detailed below.

A. CREATION

An LLC is created by filing articles of organization with the state. An LLC may adopt an operating agreement that governs any or all aspects of its affairs. This operating agreement generally takes precedence over contrary statutory provisions.

B. MEMBERSHIP

An LLC is not restricted as to the number of members it may have. However, a person cannot become a member of an LLC without the consent of all other members of an LLC.

C. MANAGEMENT

An LLC may provide for direct management of the LLC by its members. Alternatively, an LLC may provide for centralized management of the LLC by one or more managers who need not be members of the LLC.

D. LIABILITY OF MEMBERS AND MANAGERS

A member of an LLC is generally **not** liable as a member for an LLC's obligations. If a member renders professional services in an LLC, the member, as well as the LLC, may be liable for torts committed while rendering such services.

A manager or a managing member of an LLC is not personally liable for obligations incurred on behalf of the LLC. Members of a manager-managed LLC do not have the right to maintain a direct action against the manager of the LLC when the alleged misconduct caused harm only to the LLC.

Managers (or members in a member-managed LLC) owe a duty of care to the LLC. However, they are not liable for simple negligence. The duty of care consists of refraining from engaging in grossly negligent conduct or reckless conduct, intentional misconduct, or a knowing violation of law. However, some state statutes reject the gross negligence standard and impose an ordinary negligence standard when determining breaches of a duty of care. In these states, the business judgment rule may apply to protect LLC managers from liability when decisions are made in good faith. *See* ULLCA § 409(c); Revised Uniform Limited Liability Company Act § 409(c) (2006).

E. ALLOCATION OF PROFITS AND LOSSES

Typically, the operating agreement of the LLC determines the manner in which profits and losses will be allocated among the members of the LLC. In the absence of such an agreement, profits and losses are allocated and distributions are made according to each member's contributions to the LLC.

F. TRANSFER OF MEMBERSHIP

The transfer of a membership interest to another person does not automatically give that person the right to participate in the management of the LLC. Instead, the transferee merely acquires the transferor's right to share in the LLC's profits and losses.

G. TERMINATION OF MEMBERSHIP

Withdrawal of a member from an LLC does not automatically trigger dissolution of the LLC. The LLC may elect to liquidate the fair value of that person's interests, as of the date the person ceased to be a member, based upon the person's right to share in distributions from the LLC. The continuing members of the LLC following the withdrawal of a member will be deemed to have entered into an operating agreement in effect immediately prior to the withdrawal, and the members bound by the operating agreement shall be only those members who have not withdrawn.

H. MERGER AND DISSOLUTION

As with the case for other business entities, an LLC may merge with another LLC or another business entity (e.g., partnership, corporation). An LLC may dissolve upon the occurrence of various events, such as mutual consent of the members or the lack of any members.

Equity

EQUITY

Table of Contents

EQUITY

I. INTRODUCTION

A. DEVELOPMENT OF EQUITY

Historically, courts of equity arose in England to address situations in which damages in the common-law courts did not constitute full and adequate relief. Judges sought to achieve fairness where the remedies at law (basically, monetary damages) would not lead to a fair result. If a person complained that he could not get justice in the common-law courts, he would "pray" the king for equitable relief. Over time, courts of chancery arose with the power to provide equitable remedies.

This outline includes a description of the various **forms** of modern-day equitable relief including: (i) injunctions; (ii) specific performance; (iii) rescission and reformation; and (iv) miscellaneous common equitable remedies. In addition, it includes a discussion of substantive disputes that often give rise to claims for equitable relief and describes the defenses to equitable relief and the enforcement of equitable remedies.

B. LEGAL REMEDY INADEQUATE

Understanding the distinction between legal and equitable relief is important. Most significantly, **equitable relief is not available where an adequate legal remedy exists**. A litigant may not seek an equitable remedy unless she can first prove that a legal remedy is unavailable or inadequate. Note, though, that legal and equitable causes of action may be joined and pled in the same action. Ill. Sup. Ct. R. 135.

A legal remedy may be inadequate or unavailable when:

i) Money damages are insufficient to fully compensate for irreparable harm;
ii) Damages are uncertain or unfairly speculative;
iii) The subject matter of the lawsuit is unique (e.g., a contract for the sale of specific land);
iv) The defendant is insolvent;
v) Compensation for the harm would require the filing of successive lawsuits; or
vi) The nature of the defendant's conduct is willful.

C. EQUITABLE RELIEF: PERSONAL, ENFORCEABLE, DISCRETIONARY, COERCIVE

There are four other characteristics of equitable relief, all of which are important to success on the bar exam.

1. Personal

Equitable remedies are **personal**; that is, they compel or prohibit conduct by a party or parties.

2. Enforceable

Courts will not award equitable relief if such relief is not **enforceable**. For example, a court will not grant specific performance of a contract for personal services because, among other reasons, the court cannot exercise continuing control over the employment relationship.

3. Discretionary

Equitable relief is **discretionary**. Even where no adequate legal remedy exists, the court may refuse to grant equitable relief; it will not be granted as a matter of right.

4. Coercive

Unlike money judgments, equitable remedies are **directly enforceable by the court**. Usually, when a plaintiff is awarded money damages, she receives a judgment that she must then seek to satisfy. The court will not directly enforce that judgment on plaintiff's behalf. In contrast, when equitable relief is granted, the court may directly enforce its order by coercive means, such as contempt proceedings.

II. INJUNCTIONS

A. IN GENERAL

An injunction is a court order that commands an action (a mandatory injunction) or prohibits an action (a prohibitory injunction). It may be sought as the primary form of relief. For example, where a plaintiff brings suit on a claim of discrimination, the remedy she seeks may be an injunction against future discrimination by the defendant.

1. Mandatory Injunction

A mandatory injunction is one that requires an affirmative act by the defendant. They are most frequently sought in cases of nuisance, trespass, and protection of easements.

Example: In a suit by a state government against the EPA, the court may order the EPA to develop regulations for the reduction of carbon dioxide emissions.

2. Prohibitory Injunction

A prohibitory injunction forbids a defendant from engaging in harmful or illegal conduct. They are often sought in cases of harassment or discrimination, and in intellectual property cases.

B. TEMPORARY VS. PERMANENT RELIEF

Injunctive relief can be temporary (e.g., a preliminary injunction or a temporary restraining order) or it can be permanent. Temporary restraining orders and preliminary injunctions are available prior to the resolution of a controversy on its merits. In contrast, a permanent injunction is the order of a court following a hearing on the merits.

Temporary injunctive relief (whether a temporary restraining order or a preliminary injunction) is almost always prohibitory. That is, courts are generally willing to prohibit harmful conduct by the defendant pending a full hearing on the merits. It is very difficult to get any type of temporary injunctive relief that is mandatory.

1. **Temporary Injunctive Relief**

   a. **Preliminary injunction**

      1) **In general**

         A preliminary injunction is intended to preserve the status quo until a case requesting a permanent injunction can be heard on its merits. A preliminary injunction remains in effect pending a trial on the merits, after which it expires, or by further order of the court, becomes permanent.

         A preliminary injunction is an extraordinary remedy, the use of which is applicable only to situations where serious harm would result in the absence of the injunction.

      2) **Requirements**

         In order for a preliminary injunction to issue, a plaintiff must establish that:

         i) She possesses a clearly ascertained right that needs protection;
         ii) She will likely suffer irreparable harm without the injunction;
         iii) There is no adequate remedy at law for her injury; and
         iv) She is likely to be successful on the merits of her action.

         Levitt Homes, Inc. v. Old Farm Homeowners' Ass'n, 444 N.E.2d 194 (Ill. App. 2d 1982).

      3) **Balancing the hardships**

         In deciding whether to issue a preliminary injunction, courts also generally determine whether the "balance of hardships" to the parties justifies the granting of preliminary injunctive relief. A court will not issue an injunction if the benefit to be obtained does not warrant the hardship imposed. Accordingly, **the benefit to the plaintiff generally must greatly outweigh the burden on the defendant** in order for the preliminary injunction to issue. Note that if the defendant's conduct was **willful**, there will generally be no balancing of interests.

         Courts also look to whether or not the injunction will be injurious to the general interest of the public. Generally, when the issuance of an injunction will cause serious public inconvenience or loss without a corresponding great advantage to the plaintiff, no injunction will be granted, even though, as against the defendant, the plaintiff would be entitled to its issuance.

         > **EXAM NOTE:** Balancing of hardships is generally a key discussion point when considering an injunction involving nuisance, trespass to land, or encroachment.

      4) **Appeal**

         The trial court has discretion regarding whether or not to grant a preliminary injunction, based on the facts of the particular case. A reviewing court will only reverse the trial court on factual matters if it finds that granting the preliminary injunction was against the manifest weight of the evidence.

b. Temporary restraining order

A temporary restraining order is an emergency remedy issued in order to preserve the status quo while the court hears evidence to determine whether a preliminary injunction should issue.

A key difference between a temporary restraining order and a preliminary injunction involves the requirement for notice. Illinois law prohibits the entry of a preliminary injunction without notice. 735 Ill. Comp. Stat. 5/11-102. A temporary restraining order, however, may be issued without notice. 735 Ill. Comp. Stat. 5/11-101.

1) Without notice

A temporary restraining order without notice to the adverse party (i.e., *ex parte*) may not be issued unless immediate and irreparable injury, loss, or damage will result before notice can be served on the opposing party and a hearing held. 735 Ill. Comp. Stat. 5/11-101.

A temporary restraining order issued without notice to the adverse party will generally expire by its terms within 10 days after the signing of the order, unless for good cause shown it is extended by the court for a like period or the party against whom the order is directed consents that it may be extended for a longer period. *Id.*

2) With notice

If notice of the motion is provided, there is no 10-day limit applicable to the order.

3) Requirements

As with the issuance of a preliminary injunction, the party seeking issuance of a temporary restraining order must show that:

i)   She possesses a clearly ascertained right that needs protection;
ii) She will suffer irreparable harm without the injunction;
iii) There is no adequate remedy at law for her injury; and
iv) She is likely to be successful on the merits of her action.

Bartlow v. Shannon, 927 N.E.2d 88 (Ill. App. 5th 2010).

Note that unlike with a preliminary injunction, there is no balancing of harms analysis done with a temporary restraining order. A hearing for a motion for a temporary restraining order is generally a summary proceeding, and only the complaint is considered.

4) Appeal

The granting or denial of a temporary restraining order rests in the sound discretion of the trial court. The trial court's decision is an appealable order under Illinois Supreme Court Rule 307. If the temporary restraining order was entered *ex parte*, a motion to vacate must first be presented in the trial court. Ill. Sup. Ct. R. 307(b). Appellate review of a temporary restraining order is limited to determining whether the trial court abused its discretion.

c. Bond

The court hearing the application for a temporary restraining order or a preliminary injunction may require the applicant to give a bond in an amount and under conditions that are deemed proper by the court. The bond is intended to protect the adverse party from any costs or damages incurred in the event that the injunction was wrongful. No bond can be required of any governmental office or agency.

d. Modification and dissolution

Courts of equity have the inherent power and retain continuing jurisdiction to modify or dissolve a temporary restraining order or preliminary injunction based on changed circumstances, including a change in the law.

By statute, for temporary restraining orders, on two days' notice to the party who obtained the temporary restraining order without notice or on such shorter notice to that party as the court may order, the adverse party may appear and move for its dissolution or modification.

Whether to modify or dissolve a preliminary injunction or temporary restraining order rests within the discretion of the court.

2. Permanent Injunctions

a. In general

A permanent injunction is the final judgment of a court after adjudication on the merits. Permanent injunctions may not be entered without a trial on the merits if the defendant is not in default.

b. Requirements

A party applying for the injunction must demonstrate at a hearing on the merits that he: (i) possesses a certain and clearly ascertainable right in need of protection; (ii) has no adequate remedy at law; and (iii) would suffer irreparable harm without the requested relief. The court must also balance the harms, as described for preliminary injunctions, above.

c. "Permanency"

A permanent injunction is of unlimited duration and alters the status quo, meaning that it adjudicates rights between the interested parties.

While called "permanent," a permanent injunction does not necessarily last forever and can be modified or dissolved based on changed circumstances.

The issuance of a permanent injunction will not be set aside on appeal unless the trial court is found to have abused its sound discretion.

C. IMMEDIATE INJURY OR LIKELY FUTURE INJURY

A party may seek to enjoin a clear violation of her rights that has resulted in a substantial injury, or an activity that may lead to substantial harm in the future. The right to injunctive relief rests on actual or presently threatened interference with another's rights. Generally, the injury sought to be enjoined must be likely, not merely possible.

D. NO ADEQUATE REMEDY AT LAW

To be adequate and make injunctive relief unavailable, a remedy at law must be as clear, complete, practical, and efficient as the equitable remedy.

If a party's injury can be adequately compensated through monetary damages, then he will have an adequate remedy at law. A remedy at law will be inadequate and injunctive relief will be needed if:

(i) Money will be insufficient to compensate for the injury;

(ii) The injury cannot be properly quantified in terms of money;

(iii) Money damages are too speculative; or

(iv) The defendant is insolvent (and therefore money damages cannot be collected).

E. IRREPARABLE HARM

Whether an injury is irreparable will depend on the facts and circumstances of each specific case. Typically, irreparable harm is found if the injured party cannot be adequately compensated in damages or if the damages cannot be measured by any certain pecuniary standard. If an injury is of a continuing nature and is constant and frequent, that will generally be enough to establish irreparable harm.

F. LIKELIHOOD OF SUCCESS ON THE MERITS

A plaintiff seeking a preliminary injunction or a temporary restraining order is not required to make out a case that would entitle him to judgment at trial. Rather, the plaintiff need only show that he has raised a "fair question" about the existence of his right and that the court should preserve the status quo until the cause can be decided on the merits.

G. FRAMING THE ORDER

Every order granting an injunction or temporary restraining order must set forth the reasons for its entry, be specific in terms, and describe in reasonable detail (not by reference to the complaint or other document) the acts sought to be restrained. 735 Ill. Comp. Stat. 5/11-101. It must be reasonable and should go no further than is necessary to safeguard the plaintiff's rights.

H. WHO WILL BE BOUND BY AN INJUNCTION

Injunctive relief, whether temporary or permanent, is binding only upon the parties to the action, their officers, agents, employees, and attorneys, and upon those persons in active concert or participation with them who receive actual notice of the order by personal service or otherwise. 735 Ill. Comp. Stat. 5/11-101.

III. INJUNCTIVE RELIEF IN TORT CASES

EXAM NOTE: The following is a survey of commonly tested areas of **tort law** where equitable remedies are often sought and granted. Be mindful that in answering bar exam questions, you must methodically apply the principles of equity stated above. Be sure you consider the following:

i) Are damages measurable? If so, equitable relief will generally not be available.

ii) If damages are difficult to measure (i.e., the harm is of a type that cannot be compensated with money), equitable relief may be available.

iii) When considering injunctive relief, consider whether a TRO, preliminary injunction, or a permanent injunction should be sought.

iv) Whatever form of injunctive relief is sought, you must meet the requirements for that form of relief, discussed in § II, *supra*.

v) Finally, you should inquire whether the defendant may assert any equitable defenses. *See* § VI, *infra*, for a discussion of equitable defenses.

A. TRESPASS AND DAMAGE TO LAND

1. Trespass

In most instances, trespass, even without damage to the land, is compensable with money damages. However, where the trespass is **continuous**, equity may enjoin the harm in order to prevent a multiplicity of lawsuits.

Example: Golf balls from a neighboring golf course continually enter a plaintiff's property. A court might award injunctive relief ordering the golf course to keep golf balls off of the plaintiff's property.

2. Nuisance

An act by a defendant that interferes with a plaintiff's use and enjoyment of her land constitutes the tort of nuisance. A private nuisance is one that interferes with a specific plaintiff's use and enjoyment, while a public nuisance is one that harms numerous persons coming within the zone of harm created by the defendant.

An injunction may be available against a private nuisance, but equity *will not* enjoin a public nuisance unless the plaintiff can prove special harm not suffered by the public generally.

EXAM NOTE: Be wary of the situation where the nuisance is created by the operation of a factory or other business enterprise. In such circumstances, the **balance of hardships** factor becomes paramount. Most courts will *not* grant an injunction where the economic consequences to the business outweigh the economic consequences to the plaintiff. In other words, the courts will be reluctant to grant an injunction that prohibits operation of the factory or business. Damages will have to suffice.

3. Waste

An act (or the failure to act) by a person in lawful possession of property that causes *unjustifiable diminution of a future interest* in the property constitutes waste. Generally, money damages are sufficient, measured by the reduction in value of the future interest caused by the harmful acts (destructive waste) or the failure to act (permissive waste).

However, harm cannot always be easily measured in dollars. The destruction of a stand of trees, for example, cannot be measured by the value of the resulting lumber. In such a case, a prohibitory injunction may issue.

4. Encroachment

a. Intentional encroachment

When a defendant's structure intentionally encroaches on a plaintiff's property, a mandatory injunction to remove the structure may issue (assuming damages at law are inadequate). For an encroachment to be intentional, it must be either deliberate or in willful disregard of the rights of the adjoining property owner. An encroachment will be regarded as deliberate when made after due warning. Willful disregard of the adjoining property owner's rights may result from culpable negligence (i.e., the failure to take ordinary and reasonable precaution to ascertain the boundary line).

b. Unintentional encroachment

Where a defendant's act of encroachment is unintentional, injunctions rarely issue; in the balance of hardships, the removal of the structure often creates a greater hardship to the defendant than a benefit to the plaintiff.

B. NON-POSSESSORY INTERESTS IN LAND

Courts often grant equitable relief to protect a plaintiff's non-possessory interests in land.

Example: The plaintiff has an easement appurtenant that allows use of a neighbor's road to access a public highway. If the neighbor obstructs the road, money damages would not make the plaintiff whole. Accordingly, a prohibitory injunction may issue.

If a plaintiff has a profit, that is, a right to remove part of another's land (e.g., sand or gravel), acts of obstruction by the landowner may be enjoined.

C. UNIQUE CHATTEL

A plaintiff may seek injunctive relief if the defendant wrongfully obtains or converts unique chattel. The legal remedy is inadequate because the chattel is unique (i.e., it **cannot be duplicated in the market**). The court may issue a temporary restraining order or preliminary injunction to prevent the defendant from selling the property pending trial. The court may issue a permanent mandatory injunction after trial, requiring the defendant to return the property to the plaintiff.

D. DEFAMATION/INVASION OF RIGHT TO PRIVACY

Generally, equitable relief will not issue in cases of defamation or in right to privacy actions based on publication (e.g., commercial appropriation, false light, and publication of private facts). The primary reason is based on First Amendment grounds. Courts are reluctant to restrain conduct or speech that falls within the protection of the First Amendment. Damages are generally considered sufficient.

However, if a defendant is threatening to repeat a statement that has already been found defamatory in a court of law, a prohibitory injunction may issue. In addition, an action based on the fourth prong of the right to privacy—intrusion upon seclusion—may warrant the issuance of a prohibitory injunction.

E. ABUSE OF PROCESS

Courts have the power to issue injunctions to prohibit the parties before them from filing or proceeding with related actions in other courts in order to prevent the maintenance of vexatious and harassing litigation. The prosecution of a later-filed suit may be enjoined if it appears likely to cause undue interference with the progress of the original action. An injunction may also be sought to restrain a suit brought in another state based on a fraudulent claim of jurisdiction.

Note that such injunctions restrain the litigant(s) from moving forward, but not the other court. One court cannot enjoin the exercise of an out-of-state court's jurisdiction.

F. BUSINESS/COMMERCIAL/INTELLECTUAL PROPERTY INTERESTS

Equity will protect business, commercial, and intellectual property interests that have economic value. Damage to these types of interests is difficult to measure in money, and conduct aimed at harming intangible rights is often recurring. Accordingly, a legal remedy is often unavailable.

1. Interference with Contracts/Business Relationships

Generally, conduct intended to induce another to breach a contract or interfere wrongfully with a business relationship is subject to equitable relief. However, after the breach of contract occurs or the business relationship is harmed, the plaintiff's remedy is ordinarily reduced to only damages unless she can show that the harmful conduct will continue in the future.

2. Unfair Competition

Conduct that is deceptive or confusing as to the source of a product may be subject to a prohibitory injunction. When a defendant "passes off" his product as the product of another or "free rides" on the reputation of another's product, the courts may enjoin such conduct upon a proper showing by the plaintiff.

3. Trade Libel

A defamatory statement about another's business may be enjoined in equity, especially where the utterance is intended to directly harm another's business by taking away business and giving it to another.

4. Trade Secrets

Destruction or misappropriation of another's trade secrets (i.e., information that has independent economic value from not being known to others) may be enjoined. 765 Ill. Comp. Stat. 1065/3 (Illinois Trade Secrets Act). Injunctive relief may be available when the trade secret is improperly obtained, and may be imposed against both the "taker" of the trade secret and the person who receives it with the intent to use it.

An injunction may even be available *before* a trade secret is disclosed under the **inevitable disclosure doctrine**. Showing that a former employee's new employment will inevitably lead the former employee to rely on the plaintiff's trade secrets may cause a court to issue an injunction prohibiting such disclosure, though the fact that a former employee has taken a similar position with a competitor of the former employer is not alone sufficient to demonstrate inevitable disclosure. See § IV.F., *infra*, for a further discussion of trade secrets in contracts cases.

5. Trademarks

A trademark (as defined by federal law) is any word, name, symbol, or device used by a person to identify and distinguish his goods from those manufactured or sold by others and to indicate the source of the goods. The protected property interest is the mental association between the product and its source created in the minds of consumers.

Where a trademark is infringed, injunctive relief may be available. Infringement occurs when use of another's mark or a deceptively similar mark creates the **likelihood of confusion** in consumers.

Trademark dilution may also be enjoined, even in the absence of a likelihood of confusion. If another's use of a similar trademark creates a negative association with or negative economic effect on the trademark holder (tarnishment), such use may be enjoined. If the trademark is a famous mark, and its use by another blurs the distinctive quality of the mark, such use may also be enjoined.

6. Copyright

Copyrights are primarily governed by federal law, and protection applies automatically to original works of authorship that have been fixed in a tangible medium. Protected works include books, drawings, designs, musical compositions, artistic performances, and art works. Copyright law grants to the copyright holder the right to reproduce and perform the work, and to create derivative works. Others seeking to intrude upon such use are infringers and may be subject to prohibitory injunction (and damages), but registration of the work is a prerequisite for suit.

7. Right to Publicity

The common law recognizes a right of celebrities to protection against use of their likeness, name, or unique style of performance (e.g., a catchphrase). Accordingly, an injunction may be available to prevent unauthorized use by others.

8. Patents

Patent protection is governed solely by federal law. Any invention that is novel and useful may be patented by the inventor. Once patented, only the inventor (or her designee) may use the invention. Any infringing use may be enjoined, and the infringer may also be subject to a claim for damages.

Even upon a finding of patent infringement, a court must still weigh the four factors traditionally used to determine if an injunction should issue.

G. ENJOINING CRIMINAL CONDUCT

Generally, equity will not enjoin a crime. However, when criminal conduct is also a tort (e.g., assault) a court may enjoin such conduct.

H. POLITICAL RIGHTS

Courts will generally not grant injunctive relief when the exercise of political rights is involved. In other words, a court cannot issue an injunction to prevent the holding of an election or passage of legislation. However, statutes can give a court the power to enforce political rights by injunction.

IV. SPECIFIC PERFORMANCE IN CONTRACT CASES

The primary form of equitable relief given in contract cases is **specific performance**, whereby one party is directed to perform according to the terms of the contract. In essence, specific performance is a mandatory injunction in a contract dispute. In applying specific performance, the court has no authority to force a party to do something different from that which, by contract, the party has agreed to do.

In order to establish a right to specific performance a plaintiff must establish *all* of the following:

i)   The existence of a valid contract and the fulfillment of all its conditions;

ii) The inadequacy of legal remedies;

iii) That enforcement is feasible and fair;

iv) Mutuality of performance—specific performance will be denied where the injured party has not yet performed his part of the bargain or his performance cannot be secured by the court's order; and

v)   The absence of any defenses.

The remedy of specific performance of a contract rests in the sound discretion of the trial court and is determined from all surrounding facts and circumstances of each case.

Even if parties have contractually agreed to the remedy of specific performance, court of equity has an independent duty to determine whether the contract can be specifically performed without inordinate monitoring or supervision by the court.

A. VALID CONTRACT

The first requirement for a plaintiff seeking specific performance is to establish the existence of a valid, enforceable contract.

There must be an offer, acceptance, and consideration. The contractual terms must be definite and certain so that the court will know what is to be done. In the context of an equitable action for specific performance, contractual terms generally must be described with greater precision than is required for an action at law.

All conditions precedent must have been fulfilled, and all conditions concurrent will be readily performed.

The subject matter of the contract must not be illegal.

> **EXAM NOTE:** Accordingly, when confronted with a specific performance question on the bar, you must resort to basic contract law principles including those relating to contract formation. Before suggesting the remedy of specific performance, always be certain that the contract to be specifically enforced is valid and the terms with regard to the parties' performance are definite and certain.

B. INADEQUACY OF LEGAL REMEDY

1. The Subject Matter of the Contract—Rare or Unique

Specific performance will more likely be granted where the subject matter of the contract is rare or unique. Where property is unique, the legal remedy of damages will almost always be inadequate because simply providing money damages would not put the non-breaching party in as good a position as the performance of the contract would; damages would not allow the plaintiff to go out and purchase the property. Specific enforcement is generally the only remedy that would give the plaintiff adequate relief.

a. Real property

Real property is always considered unique. Each parcel of real property is deemed to have its own individual character.

b. Personal property

In the case of personal property, the chattel must be rare or unique, must be of personal significance to the buyer (applying the reasonable person objective test), or must be in short supply. Patents, copyrights, and other intangibles that are not readily available on the open market are also generally deemed unique.

While corporate stock is generally considered fungible and damages will therefore be sufficient, if the stock is of a closely-held corporation, its value is uncertain or unascertainable, or the stock is sought for purposes of control of the corporation, a contract to sell or purchase such stock will generally be subject to specific performance.

Example: Ari formed a closely-held corporation, issuing himself all 1,000 shares of its stock. He subsequently agreed to sell his friend Beth 500 shares of the stock. The 500 shares would be considered rare or unique in an action for specific performance by Beth, as they are not available on the open market and are likely difficult to value.

2. Defendant Insolvent

A legal remedy will generally be inadequate if the defendant is insolvent or judgment-proof. The burden is on the plaintiff to establish insolvency.

Example: Carl, a creditor of David, could specifically enforce an assignment for the benefit of creditors where David is found to be insolvent, even if the assignment involves personal property that is not considered to be unique.

3. Damages are Speculative

A legal remedy of money damages generally will be found inadequate if an accurate calculation of money damages is impossible or speculative. The failure to perform requirements or output contracts generally results in only speculative damages.

Example: Sara agrees to supply all of Ben's requirements of oil for a five-year period. At the end of the first year, Sara repudiates the contract. Ben can likely obtain specific performance of the requirements contract, as damages for failure to supply Ben with oil for the next four years would be considered highly speculative.

4. Necessity for Multiple Lawsuits

If a complete remedy would require the prosecution of several lawsuits against several defendants, a court may find the legal remedy to be inadequate and be willing to decree specific performance.

5.   Effect of Liquidated Damages Clause

Where the contract contains a liquidated damages clause, courts will still consider the award of specific performance unless the parties agreed that liquidated damages are the *sole* remedy. Note that the aggrieved party generally cannot have both the liquidated damages and a decree of specific performance.

C.   FEASIBILITY OF PERFORMANCE

Certain types of contracts cannot feasibly be enforced by specific performance. *See* § IV.F. *infra.*

A court may refuse to order specific performance where the supervision of performance by the court will be unduly burdensome. Generally, a court of equity will not decree specific performance where the contract calls for a succession of acts that cannot be consummated by one transaction and requires supervision and direction by the court. A requirement of continuous supervision, though, will not automatically prevent a court from exercising its equitable jurisdiction to enforce specific performance of a contract if the injustice from a refusal to enforce the contract outweighs the potential burden of supervision.

D.   ABSENCE OF DEFENSES

Standard contract defenses may defeat a claim for specific performance, including improper contract formation, mistake, impracticability, misrepresentation, fraud, duress, and incapacity. Specific performance cannot be enforced by a party that has repudiated his part of the contract by denying the other party's rights.

In addition, because specific performance is an equitable remedy, equitable defenses can apply to prevent its application. *See* § VI, *infra*, regarding equitable defenses.

E.   PERSONS AGAINST WHOM SPECIFIC PERFORMANCE MAY BE ENFORCED

1.   A Party or One in Privity with a Party

Specific performance of a contract generally may be enforced against a party to the contract or a person in privity with a party.

2.   Undisclosed Principal of an Agent

In general, specific performance of a contract may be enforced against an undisclosed principal of a contract with regard to the sale or purchase of real property that was entered into by the principal's authorized agent, acting within the scope of her agency. If, however, the agent has acted without proper authorization, the contract that was entered into generally cannot be specifically enforced against the principal unless she has ratified it.

F.   TYPES OF CONTRACTS SUBJECT TO SPECIFIC ENFORCEMENT

1.   Land Sale Contracts

Because of the unique nature of real property, land sale contracts are subject to specific performance. Either the seller or the buyer may be awarded specific performance.

a. Writing

1) In general

The Statute of Frauds is binding on both courts of law and courts of equity. Thus, generally, a contract for the sale of land must be in writing and signed by the party to be charged in order to be specifically enforced.

2) Exception—part performance

If the contract has been performed by the party seeking specific performance in such a way that the parties cannot be returned to the status quo or have damages awarded that would constitute adequate compensation, specific performance may be appropriate.

> **EXAM NOTE:** This will be highly fact-specific. Look for facts such as the purchaser having taken possession and having made valuable improvements to the property.

3) Exception—statute of limitations has expired

Specific performance may be decreed if the statute of limitations prevents the party seeking specific performance from obtaining a recovery in an action at law.

4) Exception—fraud

Courts of equity have also been willing to specifically enforce oral agreements to sell real property when the assertion of the Statute of Frauds would result in perpetration of a fraud.

b. Definite terms

For specific performance compelling the conveyance of real property, the contract must be definite and contain the names of the seller and buyer, a sufficient description of the property, the price, the terms and conditions of sale, and the signatures of the parties to be charged.

c. Who can be compelled to perform a contract of sale for real property

Only the owner of real property can be compelled to specifically perform a contract of sale. A subsequent purchaser who takes with notice of a prior sale of the property can generally be required to specifically perform the contract of sale. *Stein v. Green*, 128 N.E.2d 743 (Ill. 1955). A purchaser without notice of a prior sale cannot be required to specifically perform a contract of sale. *Boone v. Graham*, 74 N.E. 559 (Ill. 1905).

d. Partial specific performance with an abatement

If a seller's title to real property is encumbered so that she cannot fully convey it, the buyer may obtain partial specific performance with an abatement in the purchase price for what cannot be performed. If the nature of the interest is fundamentally different than what was understood by the parties, specific performance may be unavailable.

> **Example:** Stan contracts to sell Blackacre to Betty. Betty's title search reveals that Blackacre is encumbered by an easement that Stan had not disclosed to Betty. Betty establishes that the value of Blackacre is reduced by 10 percent as a result of the easement. A court of equity may order specific performance with a ten percent abatement in the contract price. If Betty's title search had revealed that Stan actually only owned a life estate in Blackacre, rather than a fee simple absolute, specific performance would likely be denied.

e. Doctrine of equitable conversion

1) In general

During the executory period between the signing of the land sale contract and the closing, the buyer is the equitable owner of the land and the seller is the equitable owner of the balance of the purchase price. Therefore, each party has a basis upon which to seek specific performance upon a breach by the other.

> **Example:** Silas contracts to sell his house to Brenda. During the executory period (the time between the sale and the closing), the house is destroyed by a fire. Silas is still entitled to the purchase price and may seek specific performance.
>
> **Example 2:** Silas has a change of heart and refuses to convey his home to Brenda. Brenda, as equitable owner, may seek specific performance. Note that this result may be different in states that have enacted the Uniform Vendor and Purchaser Risk Act, such as Illinois.

2) Uniform Vendor and Purchaser Risk Act

Illinois has adopted the Uniform Vendor and Purchaser Risk Act, in which liability for loss during the executory period is determined by whether the seller transferred legal title and possession to the purchaser before the loss. If neither has been transferred to the purchaser, the seller cannot enforce the contract and the buyer is entitled to recover any portion of the purchase price she has already paid. 765 Ill. Comp. Stat. 65/1.

> **Example:** Silas contracts to sell his house to Brenda. The parties agree that Brenda may live in the house and take legal title to the house during the executory period. If the house is destroyed, Silas is entitled to the purchase price.
>
> **Example 2:** This time, Silas retains possession and legal title to the house. If the house is destroyed, Brenda does not have to perform, and is entitled to any part of the purchase price that she has already paid.

3) Death of party to contract

a) Seller's death

Upon the seller's death during the executory period, the right to the balance of the contract price passes to the seller's estate. The executor may seek specific enforcement if the buyer refuses to purchase the property.

b) Buyer's death

Upon the buyer's death during the executory period, her heir(s) may specifically enforce the contract upon the seller's refusal to convey. Upon the granting of specific performance, the buyer's executor is required to pay the purchase price out of the buyer's personal estate.

4) Testamentary direction to sell

The doctrine of equitable conversion can also be applicable to a testamentary direction to sell real property and distribute the proceeds of the sale. If the direction is mandatory and leaves the decedent's executor with no discretion, the real property is treated as personal property as soon as the will becomes effective.

2. Covenants Not To Compete

In Illinois, covenants not to compete are enforceable if the terms of the agreement are **reasonable and necessary** to protect an employer's **legitimate business interest**. These determinations are based upon the facts of each case.

a. Formation

A covenant not to compete can only be enforced if it is ancillary to an existing transaction or relationship. This means that an agreement between two merchants who have no relationship other than being in the same profession will be void because it is against public policy; the agreement harms the public and the promisor, and serves no protectable interest of the promisee.

Like all contracts, covenants not to compete must be based on valid consideration. Continued employment for a substantial period of time is sufficient consideration.

b. Legitimate business interest

Illinois courts recognize two circumstances in which an employer has a legitimate business interest in preventing an employee from competing with the employer in the future. The first is when an employee acquires **confidential information or trade secrets** during the employment and tries to later use that information to compete against the employer. The second is when the employer has a **near-permanent relationship** with a customer and the employee would not have had contact with the customer but for his relationship with the employer.

1) Trade secrets

A trade secret is confidential information relating to a business that provides the business with a competitive advantage. The information must not be generally known to or discoverable by the public, and the business must take steps to ensure its continued confidentiality. Some of the factors used to determine whether a trade secret exists are:

  i)   The extent to which the information is known outside of the business;
  ii) The extent to which the information is known by employees and others within the business;

iii) The extent of measures taken to safeguard the information from disclosure;

iv) The value of the information to the employer and its competitors;

v) The amount of effort or resources spent to develop the information; and

vi) The ease or difficulty with which the information could be properly acquired or duplicated by others.

Confidential information that is commonly the subject of a covenant not to compete is a business's **customer list**. If the employer develops a list of customers over a number of years at great expense, and closely guards the list from disclosure, it may be entitled to protection. Whether a customer list is sufficiently confidential depends on factors such as whether the list is kept locked in a safe, whether access to the list is limited to certain employees, and whether the list is marked "confidential." An employer may use a covenant not to compete to prevent an employee from disclosing or using the list to later compete with the employer.

2) **Near-permanent customer relationships**

In certain businesses, developing customers takes significant time and effort. As a result, an employee that has built a relationship with a customer while working for his employer will be at a significant advantage if the employee terminates his employment and tries to lure the customer away from the employer. This is especially true if the employee would not have had any reason to contact the customer but for his employment with the employer. In such cases, a court will protect the employer's relationship with its customer by enforcing a covenant not to compete.

Courts often weigh the following seven factors to determine whether a near-permanent relationship exists:

i) The number of years required to develop the customer relationship;

ii) The amount of money spent to develop the customer relationship;

iii) The difficulty of acquiring customers;

iv) The extent of contact between the employee and the customer;

v) The extent of the employer's knowledge of its customers;

vi) The duration of the customer relationship; and

vii) The continuity of the customer relationship.

Agrimerica, Inc. v. Mathes, 557 N.E.2d 357 (Ill. App. 1990).

Alternatively, courts may look to the "nature of the business" to determine whether a near-permanent relationship exists. Under this test, professionals and plaintiffs who provide a unique product or service are more likely to establish a near-permanent relationship than others. *Office Mates 5, North Shore, Inc. v. Hazen*, 599 N.E.2d 1072 (Ill. App. 1992). Note that a relationship need not be exclusive to be near-permanent.

c. Reasonableness

Covenants not to compete must be reasonable in scope and duration, which is a highly fact-specific inquiry generally measured by its hardship to the employee, its effect on the general public, and the reasonableness of the time, territory, and activity restrictions.

One-year and two-year limitations have been upheld when the employer typically took one to three years to establish a customer relationship.

Territory restrictions are generally reasonable if the employee is excluded only from the territory where he was able to establish relationships with the former employer's customers.

Activity restrictions should be limited to restricting an employee from using information learned from the employer or from performing tasks the employee performed during the employment. An activity restriction need not have a geographic limitation.

3. Unique Chattels

Courts will often find legal remedies inadequate in cases involving contracts for the sale of rare or unique personal property. In such cases, specific performance is the appropriate remedy. The Uniform Commercial Code, as applicable in Illinois, provides for specific performance where the goods are unique or in other proper circumstances. *See* 810 Ill. Comp. Stat. 5/2-716.

4. Contracts to Make Testamentary Dispositions or Mutual Wills

In the case of both contracts to make testamentary dispositions and contracts to make mutual wills, courts have found legal remedies to be inadequate and have awarded specific performance.

G. TYPES OF CONTRACTS NOT SPECIFICALLY ENFORCED

1. Personal Service Contracts

A court of equity will not generally specifically enforce a contract for personal services. The enforcement of these contracts is thought to be akin to involuntary servitude in violation of the 13th Amendment. In addition, it is difficult (if not impossible) for a court to supervise its decree of specific enforcement since it cannot ensure that the defendant will perform with the requisite skill and expertise.

Example: Edward, an award-winning actor, contracts to perform *Hamlet* on Broadway. Subsequently, Edward refuses to perform. While Edward may be liable for damages at law for his refusal to perform, a court of equity will not order him to perform in the play.

If a personal services contract has been fully performed by the party rendering the services, the contract may be specifically enforced if a failure to carry out the agreement of the parties would constitute fraud.

2. Construction Contracts

As with personal services contracts, courts are reluctant to order specific performance of construction contracts because of the difficulty of supervision. In these cases, the courts generally find a legal remedy that is adequate to compensate the plaintiff.

3. Employment Contracts

Courts are reluctant to grant orders that they cannot enforce or supervise. Therefore, neither the employer nor the employee may be granted specific performance of an employment contract. Legal damages are usually adequate.

V. RESCISSION AND REFORMATION OF CONTRACTS

A. RESCISSION

Rescission voids a contract and leaves the parties as if no contract had ever been made. By definition, the grounds for rescission must have occurred prior to or contemporaneous with the formation of the contract. At law, the procedure is extra-judicial. A plaintiff would simply announce rescission of a transaction and then sue for damages or be sued for damages for breach of contract. In equity, the plaintiff sues for a decree of rescission or cancellation and the court must specifically issue a decree that voids the contract. In general, courts of equity are reluctant to order rescission unless both parties can be put in the same position that they were in prior to the contract or transaction.

1. Mutual Mistake

If both parties are mistaken as to a **material fact** (i.e., one that goes to the **essence** of the contract), the contract may be rescinded. A mistake by one party (a unilateral mistake) will *not* result in rescission unless: (i) the non-mistaken party was aware of the mistake and took advantage of it; or (ii) the mistaken party would suffer severe hardship if forced to accept the bargain.

2. Misrepresentation

Misrepresentation by one of the parties may be grounds for rescission where the misrepresentation is **material**, is either intentional or unintentional, and is **relied upon** by the other party. A misrepresentation is material if it relates to a matter on which the plaintiff could be expected to rely in determining whether to engage in the conduct in question.

If the misrepresentation was unintentional, the party seeking rescission will generally be required to have reasonably relied on the misrepresentation. If the misrepresentation was intentional (i.e., fraudulent), the party seeking rescission need only show that she actually relied on the misrepresentation, not that it was reasonable to do so. For example, a mistake as to the quality of a good would not be grounds for rescission, but if there were implied or express representations as to the quality or fitness of the goods, rescission may be an appropriate remedy.

3. Rescission Defenses

Rescission will be denied when there is an equitable defense (e.g., laches or unclean hands). It may also be denied when, in the case of fraud, a plaintiff has an election of remedies: money damages or rescission. The plaintiff may not have both.

B. REFORMATION

A contract may be reformed to conform to the true intent of the parties. While the court can effectuate the true intent of the parties, it cannot make a new contract for them.

Reformation presupposes that the **original contract was valid**. If the original contract was defective and voidable, there is nothing to reform.

Accordingly, the requirements for reformation are:

i)   A valid original agreement;
ii) The original agreement must have been in writing; and
iii) The original agreement fails to accurately express the intent of the parties.

> **Example:** Alice contracts to sell Barbara 100 acres known as Blackacre. The deed, however, conveys 90 acres. Barbara accepts the deed, only to learn later that fewer than 100 acres were conveyed. Because the original deed was not based on fraud, it was enforceable as written, but did not comport with the intent of the parties. Barbara is entitled to reformation, and the court will revise the deed to reflect the intent of the parties.

1.   Grounds for Reformation

a.   Fraud

Where one party induces another to execute a contract by misrepresenting its contents, the other party is entitled to reformation of the document to comport with his true intent.

b.   Mutual mistake of fact

A court of equity will reform an instrument on the basis of mutual mistake of fact. Instead of seeking rescission, the parties may agree to revise the agreement pursuant to court order.

c.   Unilateral mistake

In general, a unilateral mistake will not constitute grounds for reformation in the absence of fraud by the other party to the contract. However, when one party is aware of a mistake in the agreement and does not tell the other party, reformation may be granted.

2.   Burden of Proof

The plaintiff must establish the requirements for reformation by clear and convincing evidence.

3.   Defenses to Reformation

a.   General equitable defenses

These include the defenses of unclean hands, laches, and undue hardship. *See* § VI, *infra*, discussing equitable defenses.

b.   Sale to bona fide purchaser

Where the instrument subject to reformation is sold to a bona fide purchaser without notice of the right to reformation, reformation will *not* be allowed.

4. No Defense to Reformation

a. Negligence of the plaintiff

Where the plaintiff was negligent, she is not barred from seeking reformation (e.g., where the plaintiff failed to identify a mistake in the document).

b. Parol evidence rule

The parol evidence rule does not apply in reformation actions.

c. Statute of Frauds

The majority rule is that the Statute of Frauds does not apply in reformation actions.

VI. EQUITABLE DEFENSES

A. UNCLEAN HANDS

A plaintiff seeking equitable relief must not have engaged in any wrongdoing toward the defendant or the subject matter of the litigation. The plaintiff is said to have "unclean hands" if her wrongdoing (i) relates to the **specific transaction** that is the subject matter of the litigation **and** (ii) causes **prejudice** to the defendant. Misconduct of the plaintiff that is independent of the parties or distinct from the action between the parties does not constitute the defense of unclean hands.

The defense of unclean hands cannot be waived and can be applied by the court on its own initiative.

B. LACHES

1. In General

Where a party unreasonably delays in initiating or pursuing her claim, the doctrine of laches will bar the lawsuit if the defendant is prejudiced by the delay, even if the statute of limitations has not yet run. Laches cannot be a bar to an action at law; it is a defense only in actions seeking equitable relief.

Remember that mere delay is not enough to establish laches. The delay must have prejudiced the party seeking to apply the defense.

2. Affirmative Defense

Laches is an affirmative defense and must be pleaded by the defendant or it will be waived.

3. Knowledge Required

For a defendant to successfully plead laches (i.e., to find that the plaintiff failed to exercise due diligence in bringing suit), the plaintiff must have failed to seek prompt relief after having knowledge of the facts upon which the plaintiff's claim is based. While actual knowledge is generally required, if a reasonable person would have made inquiry concerning the facts known to the plaintiff, the plaintiff will be charged with knowledge sufficient to support a defense of laches.

4. Not Applicable to Minors or Incompetents

Laches cannot be applied to a person who is mentally incompetent or to a minor.

C. UNDUE HARDSHIP

On occasion, a plaintiff may establish all of the prerequisites for the granting of equitable relief, but the court may refuse to impose an equitable remedy if to do so would cause undue hardship to the defendant. In such a situation, the plaintiff's only remedy, if at all, is at law.

The standard that courts apply in determining undue hardship will differ slightly depending on the nature of the case.

1. When Injunctive Relief is Sought

When a party seeks an injunction in tort cases (e.g., private nuisance, trespass) courts generally engage in a "balancing-of-the-equities" analysis whereby the relative hardships of the parties are reviewed.

Example: A plaintiff seeks the closure of a polluting factory in a private nuisance case. The court will balance the economic effect of the closure against the injury to the plaintiff. The court may refuse to grant a prohibitory injunction against operation of the factory if it judges the economic cost to the defendant to be too high.

2. When Specific Performance is Sought

Undue hardship is often an issue in cases involving land sale contracts and casualty loss. At common law, the risk of casualty loss during the executory period falls upon the buyer. If the property is destroyed by a hurricane (a casualty loss), the buyer must still pay the purchase price to the seller under the doctrine of equitable conversion. In cases where the buyer has not insured himself against such loss, courts will sometimes deny specific performance to the seller because of the undue hardship to the defendant buyer, who now has a worthless property for which he must otherwise pay the full purchase price.

D. EQUITABLE ESTOPPEL

When a party makes a misrepresentation of a material fact, and another party reasonably relies on the misrepresentation to his detriment, the party may later be estopped from denying the truth of the statement. Specifically, the elements of equitable estoppels are:

i) A party misrepresents or conceals material facts, knowing that the representations were untrue;

ii) The party claiming estoppel did not know that the representations were untrue;

iii) It was reasonably foreseeable that the party claiming estoppel would rely on the representations; and

iv) The party claiming estoppel reasonably relied upon the representations to his detriment, and would be prejudiced if the speaker is permitted to deny the truth of her statement.

It is not necessary that the speaker intentionally mislead or deceive the other party. Rather, all that is necessary to invoke equitable estoppel is that the other party reasonably relied on the speaker's conduct or representations.

VII. ADDITIONAL FORMS OF EQUITABLE RELIEF

A. SUIT TO QUIET TITLE TO REAL PROPERTY

1. In General

A plaintiff in possession of land may bring an equitable action to remove a cloud on title or to resolve a dispute with regard to ownership of property. If the plaintiff is successful, a court may "quiet title, " and the plaintiff may rely on that ruling to resolve any future disputes concerning title to the property. In general, anyone with a substantial interest in the property who will be materially affected by the court's decree should be made a party to the action.

2. Cloud on Title

A complaint to quiet title will not apply to oral claims regarding title. It can apply only to written instruments (e.g., a deed, a will, a contract for the sale of land) that appear to cast doubt on the validity of the record title. A "cloud on title" exists only where the claim of title or encumbrance at issue appears to be valid on the face of the instrument creating it.

3. Actual Controversy Required

There must be an actual controversy in order to properly bring a suit to quiet title in equity.

4. Plaintiff Must Be in Possession or Property Must Be Unimproved or Unoccupied

In general, an action to quiet title to real property can only be maintained when the plaintiff is in possession of the property or when the property is unimproved or unoccupied. Possession must be actual and not merely constructive.

5. Equitable Defenses

Equitable defenses (e.g., laches, unclean hands) can prevent a party from bringing a suit to quiet title.

B. CONSTRUCTIVE TRUST

1. In General

A **constructive trust** may be imposed to prevent unjust enrichment where title to property is obtained by fraud, mistake, breach of fiduciary duty, undue influence, duress, misrepresentation, etc. The imposition of a constructive trust acts to transfer legal ownership of the property to the plaintiff in order to avoid unjust enrichment of the defendant. It declares the defendant trustee of the property, whose sole purpose is to convey title to the plaintiff. (*See the Themis Trusts outline for further discussion of constructive trusts*.)

2. Requirements

There are three requirements that must be met before a constructive trust may be imposed by the court:

i) The defendant must have legal title to property belonging to the plaintiff;

ii) The defendant will be unjustly enriched if title remains in him; and

iii) There must be no adequate legal remedy.

Remember, if legal damages are available and would constitute an adequate remedy, the imposition of a constructive trust would not be appropriate.

3. Equitable Defenses

A constructive trust may be **denied** where an equitable defense applies.

4. Transfer to a Bona Fide Purchaser for Value

Where legal title has been transferred to a bona fide purchaser for value without notice of the fraud, mistake, etc., the plaintiff's equitable title will be cut off, both with respect to the purchaser and with respect to anyone who takes title from or through that purchaser, even if the person subsequently taking title has notice of the fraud, mistake, etc.

Example: Frank, Victor's business partner, fraudulently transfers title to an office building owned by the partnership to himself. Frank subsequently sells the property to Bert, a bona fide purchaser for value who has no notice of the fraud. Victor's equitable title is cut off as against Bert and a constructive trust with regard to the building would not be decreed. Note that if Victor can trace the proceeds of the sale to Frank, Victor would be entitled to a constructive trust with regard to the proceeds of the sale.

C. EQUITABLE LIEN

An **equitable lien** is another vehicle to prevent unjust enrichment. It may be imposed by a court on property of the defendant when the defendant has unlawfully obtained other property of the plaintiff. Such a lien gives the plaintiff **priority over other creditors** because the imposition of the equitable lien **relates back** to the point in time when defendant unlawfully obtained title to the property.

Unlike a constructive trust, an equitable lien *does not require transfer of title* to the property to the plaintiff. Instead, the plaintiff receives a security interest in the property that may be used to satisfy the debt.

Example: Don converts some of Paul's dairy cows, sells them, and uses the proceeds to purchase Whiteacre. Paul may *not* seek the imposition of a constructive trust against Whiteacre because title to that property was not obtained unlawfully from the grantor. Nevertheless, Don has been unjustly enriched by the conversion of the cows. Paul may therefore seek the imposition of an equitable lien against Whiteacre as security to recover the value of his converted cows.

D. SUBROGATION

Subrogation is another equitable doctrine intended to prevent unjust enrichment. When one party involuntarily discharges the debt or other obligation owed by the defendant, he may seek repayment (subrogation) from the defendant.

Equity accomplishes this by essentially reviving the discharged obligation and placing the plaintiff in the shoes of the original creditor. The plaintiff may then recover all that the original creditor was entitled to recover from the defendant.

E. EQUITABLE ACCOUNTING

1. In General

An action for equitable accounting seeks a money decree for benefits that were obtained by one person at the expense of another. Generally, to obtain an accounting in equity, the plaintiff must allege the absence of an adequate remedy at law and one of the following: (i) the breach of a fiduciary relationship between the plaintiff and the person being required to account; (ii) a need for discovery; (iii) fraud; or (iv) the existence of a mutual account that is of a complex nature.

> **Example:** Peter, the general partner in a limited partnership, embezzles funds that were earned by the partnership. The amount embezzled is not known. Larry, a limited partner in the partnership, would be entitled to an equitable accounting, a decree requiring Peter to account for the money received and managed by him in his fiduciary capacity as the general partner.

2. Equitable Defenses

Equitable defenses (e.g., laches, unclean hands, etc.) can bar a party from bringing an action for equitable accounting.

VIII. ENFORCEMENT OF EQUITABLE REMEDIES

A. CONTEMPT PROCEEDINGS

A contempt proceeding may be brought against a defendant who disregards an equitable decree. However, constitutional due process requires that the equitable decree be sufficiently specific as to inform the defendant of the requirements imposed upon him by the court.

1. Civil Contempt

When a defendant violates either a mandatory decree (one requiring him to act) or a prohibitory decree (one prohibiting certain acts), he may be subject to civil contempt. The defendant may be imprisoned until he complies with the decree. Note, however, that a defendant *may not* be imprisoned for non-payment of a debt.

A sanction in a civil contempt proceeding must specify how the defendant may clear herself of contempt and may not be imposed where it is not possible for the defendant to comply with the order the court is seeking to enforce.

2. Criminal Contempt

As an alternative to civil contempt, a court may impose an order of criminal contempt against the defendant. Unlike civil contempt, which is imposed for the purpose of causing the defendant to act (or refrain from acting), criminal contempt is intended to punish the defendant. In other words, civil contempt is remedial, while criminal contempt is punitive.

3. Erroneous Order is No Excuse

The fact that an injunction or other order is erroneous or was improperly entered by the court is not a defense in an action for contempt for violating the order. The correct approach in such an instance is a motion for reconsideration or an appeal. If the court had no jurisdiction over the defendant, however, the defendant can use that as a defense in an action for contempt.

4. Right to Jury Trial

In general, there is a constitutional right to a jury trial in proceedings for criminal contempt, but no right to a jury trial for civil contempt.

B. WRITS OF ASSISTANCE

Where a defendant is ordered to deliver possession of real or personal property, a writ of assistance may issue to law enforcement personnel (i.e., a sheriff) to ensure that plaintiff is placed in possession of the property. A writ of assistance allows a court of equity to carry out its judgment or decree.

C. WRITS OF SEQUESTRATION

A writ of sequestration is a device that may be used to deprive the defendant of income, rents, etc., from real property by holding the property until the defendant complies with the court's decree.

Family Law

FAMILY LAW

Table of Contents

FAMILY LAW

I.   GETTING MARRIED

In most states, marriage is defined as a civil contract between a man and a woman. Similar to most contracts, marriage involves parties who are legally capable of consent, the exchange of consideration in the form of mutual promises, and the imposition of rights and obligations. Conversely, unlike most contracts, a marriage contract cannot be modified or terminated without state intervention. *Maynard v. Hill,* 125 U.S. 190 (1888). A marriage is valid if there is a license and a solemnization of the marriage (i.e., a ceremony).

There are typically two types of marriages recognized by law: ceremonial (or statutory) marriage, and common-law marriage.

A.   CEREMONIAL MARRIAGE

A ceremonial or statutory marriage requires that the parties obtain a license to get married. The couple must meet several requirements to obtain this license.

1.   Licenses

a.   Requirements

1)   Age restrictions

Most jurisdictions will impose some statutory requirements in order to be married. As parties are required to have the capacity to marry, most states impose **minimum age restrictions** and require parental consent for younger persons to marry. Most states prohibit marriages of persons younger than 15, even with parental consent. Statutory age requirements for marriage have withstood constitutional scrutiny. *See, e.g., Moe v. Dinkins,* 669 F.2d 67 (2d Cir. 1982) (the rational basis test applies to the minimum age requirement to marry, and the state's important interest in promoting the welfare of children by preventing unstable marriages among those who lack capacity is a legitimate state interest).

2)   Waiting period

Additionally, most states impose a **waiting period** between the date of the marriage and the date of the marriage ceremony. The waiting period may typically be waived by the court in cases of an emergency. According to the Uniform Marriage and Divorce Act (UMDA), a marriage license is effective three days after the license has been issued, but expires after 180 days. UMDA § 204.

3) Premarital medical testing

Some states also require a form of **premarital medical testing**. The requirements range from filing a health certificate or certifying the absence of a venereal disease to the testing of blood for certain diseases, including measles, tuberculosis, and sickle cell anemia. While a state can mandate the testing, a state cannot condition the issuance of the license on the results of the test. *See T.E.P. v. Leavitt*, 840 F. Supp. 100 (D. Utah 1993) (invalidating a Utah statute prohibiting marriage of an HIV inflicted individual as unconstitutional under the Americans with Disabilities Act).

Illinois Point of Law: Requirements

Age restrictions: In Illinois, parental consent is required for a party who is 16 or 17, but may be waived by the court. Persons younger than 16 cannot be married.

Waiting period: The waiting period for a marriage license in Illinois is one day, but it may be waived by the court upon a showing of just cause. The license is valid for 60 days.

Premarital testing: Illinois has abolished the requirement of premarital medical testing.

---

b. When not issued

A marriage license will *not* be issued when:

i) One of the parties is **married to someone else**;

ii) The parties are **too closely related** as defined by statute;

iii) The parties entered into the marriage as a **sham**;

iv) The parties are **incapable of understanding** the nature of the act; or

v) The parties are of the **same sex** and such marriages are not permitted under the law of that jurisdiction.

UMDA § 207.

Most jurisdictions further provide that marriage licenses will not be issued when, at the time the license was sought, one or both parties were **under the influence** of alcohol, drugs, or another substance that rendered the person(s) incapable, or when a party lacked consent due to duress or fraud.

c. Same-sex marriage

Currently at issue in some states is the right of parties of the same sex to marry. Marriage between parties of the same sex is not recognized by the federal government in part due to the enactment of the Defense of Marriage Act ("DOMA"). 1 U.S.C. § 7 (1996). As of this writing, the following jurisdictions have legalized same-sex marriage and are either performing said ceremonies or will do so in the near future: Connecticut, District of Columbia, Iowa, Massachusetts, New Hampshire, New York, Vermont, and Washington. Additionally, same-sex marriages from other states are recognized (to varying extents) by, but not performed in, California, New Jersey, Maryland, and Rhode Island. As a result of the enactment of DOMA, states do not need to recognize same-sex marriages performed in other states under the Full Faith and Credit Clause of the United States Constitution. Although several challenges to the constitutionality of DOMA have been filed, the United States Supreme Court has declined to accept review of the cases.

While the majority of states currently have a constitutional ban prohibiting same-sex marriages, approximately 15 states have created legal unions and/or domestic partnerships offering some of the same rights and responsibilities offered to married couples under the law.

Illinois Point of Law: Same-Sex Marriage

In 2011, Illinois passed the Illinois Religious Freedom Protection and Civil Union Act, 750 Ill. Comp. Stat. 75/1 *et seq*. This act mandates that "party to a civil union" means and is included in any use of the term "spouse" or "family member" throughout the law. 750 Ill. Comp. Stat. 75/10. Parties to civil unions are entitled to the same legal obligations, protections, and benefits as spouses. 750 Ill. Comp. Stat. 75/20.

Parties to a civil union (1) must be 18 years old; (2) may not be in a marriage or civil union with another party; (3) may not be an ancestor and descendant; whole- or half-blood or adopted siblings; aunt, uncle, niece, and nephew; or first-cousins. 750 Ill. Comp. Stat. 75/25.

Illinois will recognize same-sex marriages, civil unions, and similar legal relationships (other than same-sex common-law marriages), legally entered into in another jurisdiction, as an Illinois civil union. 750 Ill. Comp. Stat. 75/60.

---

2. Solemnization

Most states do not prescribe a particular form of the marriage ceremony, but many require that any ceremony solemnizing the marriage be performed in front of at least two witnesses. Some states even allow for a proxy to stand in for one of the parties who cannot attend the ceremony as long as the party provides written authorization for the third person to act as a proxy. Additionally, in most jurisdictions, a judge, political official, or member of the clergy of a recognized religious organization must solemnize a marriage. The marriage license must be completed and filed with the appropriate government office.

Illinois Point of Law: Solemnization

Solemnization: The majority of counties in Illinois do not require that the solemnization be in front of any witnesses, but some require the presence of two witnesses.

B. COMMON-LAW MARRIAGE

Common-law marriages are defined as marriages when the parties:

i) **Agree** they are married;

ii) **Cohabit** as husband and wife; and

iii) **Hold themselves out** in public as married.

UMDA § 209.

Unlike a ceremonial marriage, no ceremony takes place and no license is issued for a common-law marriage. A common-law marriage is not valid if either party was married to someone else at the time the common-law marriage was entered into. UMDA § 209.

1. Recognition of Common-Law Marriages

Most states have abolished common-law marriages. Common-law marriages are only recognized in Alabama, Colorado, District of Columbia, Iowa, Kansas, Montana, Rhode Island, South Carolina, Texas, and Utah. Some states (Georgia, Idaho, Ohio, Oklahoma, and Pennsylvania) allow common-law marriages that occurred within the state before a certain date to be "grandfathered" into recognition.

Even though most states do not permit common-law marriages, as a result of the Full Faith and Credit Clause of the U.S. Constitution, all states recognize common-law marriages entered into in a jurisdiction that does recognize such relationships. Under conflict-of-law principles, a marriage valid under the law of the place in which it was contracted will be valid elsewhere unless it violates a strong public policy of the state that has the most significant relationship to the spouses and the marriage. If a man and woman are domiciled in a state that permits common-law marriage and their conduct meets the requirements of that state's laws for establishing such a marriage, recognition of the marriage does not violate a strong public policy. Jurisdictions conflict, however, as to the degree of contact necessary with the common-law marriage state before it is necessary to recognize the marriage. Some jurisdictions recognize a common-law marriage when the parties only had a short, transitory visit to the permitting state, while other jurisdictions require that the parties be domiciled in the permitting state. Some jurisdictions consider the inquiry on an individual basis, weighing the harm to the claimant seeking recognition and the state's policy against such marriage.

EXAM NOTE: On the bar exam, assume that the jurisdiction has abolished common-law marriage, unless the question states otherwise.

2. Mental Capacity

In order for two parties to enter into a common-law marriage, they both must have the mental capacity to do so. The threshold to determine mental capacity is the same used to determine eligibility to obtain a license in a ceremonial marriage.

3. Intent

Jurisdictions vary on the proof necessary to establish the requisite elements for a common-law marriage. *See, e.g., Buford v. Buford*, 874 So.2d 562 (Ala. 2004) (clear and convincing evidence); *Callen v. Callen*, 620 S.E.2d 59 (S.C. 2005) (preponderance of the evidence). The parties must produce evidence that they intended to enter into the marriage, and this must be evidenced by **words in the present tense** made for the purpose of establishing a valid legal marital relationship.

Words in the future tense that indicate the parties agree to get married at a later date are **not** valid to show intent.

In the event the parties are unable to show evidence of their intent to marry in present-tense words, the court may look to cohabitation or reputation to determine if the couple holds or held themselves out as husband and wife. The courts, however, have consistently held that cohabitation alone does not support a common-law marriage. *In re Thomas' Estate*, 367 N.Y.S.2d 182 (N.Y. Sur. 1975).

C. HEARTBALM ACTIONS

Traditionally, if a marriage failed to take place, the jilted party was permitted to file a heartbalm action, which is a civil suit for money damages based on the damage to the jilted party's reputation when the engagement was broken. Abolished by the majority of states, only nine jurisdictions (Hawaii, Illinois, Mississippi, Missouri, New Hampshire, New Mexico, North Carolina, South Dakota, and Utah) currently recognize heartbalm actions, which include actions for breach of promise to marry, seduction, alienation of affection, criminal conversation, and jactitation of marriage (falsely holding one's self out as married).

> **EXAM NOTE:** On the bar exam, assume the jurisdiction has abolished heartbalm actions, unless the question states otherwise.

Illinois Distinction: Heartbalm Actions

Illinois follows the minority rule and permits heartbalm actions, but limits damages only to monetary losses and not for pain and suffering.

D. THE MARRIAGE RELATIONSHIP

The relationship between a husband and wife brings with it a myriad of rights and responsibilities, as well as constitutional privacy issues that are germane to married couples. As the marriage relationship and individual rights continue to evolve, new law will more than likely continue to develop.

II. ENDING A MARRIAGE

A valid marriage, including a common-law marriage, can only be terminated by **annulment**, **divorce**, or **death**.

A. ANNULMENT

An annulment voids a marriage and declares it as having never been valid (as opposed to divorce, which terminates a valid marriage). An annulment action involves two types of relationships: void and voidable.

1. Void Marriage

A void marriage is treated as if it never happened. It does not need to be judicially dissolved and will not be legally recognized for any purpose. UMDA § 208.

a. Prior existing marriage

If either party has a valid prior existing marriage at the time that the subsequent marriage is entered into, the latter marriage is void. However, if one of the parties had a good-faith belief that the marriage was valid, some states allow the marriage to become valid once the impediment is removed. Other states require that once the impediment is removed, the parties must continue to cohabit and one party must still continue to believe in good faith that it is a valid marriage.

1) Good faith belief in death of spouse

Most states have adopted what is known as an "Enoch Arden" statute in bigamy cases. In those jurisdictions, there is a defense to bigamy if the parties had a good-faith belief that the previous spouse was dead. The courts differ in the treatment of such marriages. Some jurisdictions require a divorce proceeding from the original spouse once the existence of the spouse is determined as a prerequisite to validating the later marriage.

2) Presumption of validity

There is a presumption that the latest marriage is valid. This presumption is rebuttable by cogent evidence of the existence of a prior valid marriage at the time that the latest marriage was entered into.

b. Incest

Incest is marriage or sexual relations between people related within the prohibited degree of kinship. All states restrict marriages by consanguinity (blood relationships) and nearly half bar marriages between first cousins. Typically, most consanguinity statutes also prohibit marriages between relatives of half blood and many prohibit it when the relationship is by adoption. *But see Bagnardi v. Harnett,* 366 N.Y.S.2d 89 (N.Y. 1975) (marriage between adoptive father and daughter permissible); *Israel v. Allen,* 577 P.2d 762 (Colo. 1978) (unconstitutional to prohibit adoptive siblings from marrying).

c. Mental incapacity

A person must be able to understand the nature of the marriage contract, and its duties and responsibilities, to enter into a marriage. Note that a marriage contract entered into during a lucid moment is valid, as long as the person understood the nature of the contract at the moment the contract was executed.

Illinois Point of Law: Void Marriage

Prior existing marriage: There is a strong presumption in favor of the second marriage. If the impediment to the first marriage is removed (e.g., death of first spouse) and the parties thereafter cohabit, the second marriage will be deemed lawful as of the date the impediment is removed.

Incest: Ancestors and descendants, brothers and sisters of whole- or half-blood or adoption, and uncles and aunts, nephews and nieces are prohibited from marrying. Generally, marriages between first cousins are prohibited unless both parties are at least 50 or a certificate by a licensed physician attests that a party to the marriage is completely sterile.

---

2. Voidable Marriage

A voidable marriage is valid until one spouse seeks to legally void the marriage. There must be a **judicial decree** to dissolve the marriage. Grounds for a voidable marriage include age, impotence, intoxication, and fraud or duress. UMDA § 208.

a. Age

A party who is under the age of consent to marry and who did not seek consent of his parents or the court may apply to have the marriage annulled. If the partner, however, is of legal age to marry, the partner may not attack the validity of her marriage to an underage person. In many states, the declaration of validity may also be brought by the underage party's parents or legal guardian. Many courts, however, will prohibit the filing of an annulment based on age once the party who was not of legal age has attained such age and continued to freely cohabit with the other party as a married couple.

> **Example:** A, who is 16, marries B, who is 21, in a state that requires parental consent or court approval when a party is under the age of 18. Neither consent nor approval is obtained. Until A reaches the age of 18, only A, her parents, or her legal guardian may seek an annulment. If A turns 18 before seeking the annulment, the court will most likely deny the request.

b. Impotence

A marriage is voidable if one party is "naturally and incurably" impotent, unless the other party knew about the condition before the marriage.

c. Intoxication

If either party was under the influence of drugs or alcohol at the time of marriage, which made that party incapable of contracting into a marriage, that marriage may be annulled. In most jurisdictions, however, the parties must be able to demonstrate that they did not ratify the marriage by continuing to voluntarily live with each other after the ceremony.

d. Fraud, misrepresentation, duress, coercion, or force

Most states permit an annulment when the marriage was the result of a fraud that goes to the essence of a marriage. In order to annul a marriage based on fraud, it must be based on present—not future—facts. Most courts require that the parties immediately cease living together once the fraud is discovered. Concealment of defective morals, character, habits, fortune, and temper are typically insufficient grounds for an annulment. Jurisdictions have differed, however, on claims of misrepresentation when a woman has falsely claimed to be pregnant by a man, or on claims relating to a party's religious beliefs.

e. Lack of intent

Most jurisdictions permit annulment when the parties participated in the marriage ceremony as an act of jest or hilarity and do not have the requisite intention to be bound by the act. Most courts annulling marriages in such circumstances have determined that the interest of the public would not be served by requiring the parties to remain married. This also includes cases in which the parties, in advance, agree to only some, but not all, of the conventional aspects of marriage, including sexual and emotional fidelity, economic interdependence, and commitment to the relationship. Often seen in cases with immigration issues, this type of marriage is commonly referred to as a "limited purpose" marriage.

Illinois Distinction: Voidable Marriage

Age: As with many states, Illinois prohibits a party, or his parent or guardian, from filing for an annulment based on age once that party has attained legal age and has continued to freely cohabit with the other party as a married couple.

Mental incapacity: In Illinois, mental incapacity may result in the marriage being voidable as opposed to void. The incapacity can be based on a mental incapacity or infirmity or because of the influence of alcohol, drugs, or any other incapacitating substance. The action for annulment may be brought by either party or by the legal representative of the incapacitated party within 90 days of the petitioner obtaining knowledge of the condition.

Impotence: Lack of capacity to consummate the marriage is grounds for annulment. The statute of limitations is one year from the time the petitioner obtained knowledge of the condition.

3. Equitable Distribution of Property in an Annulment

Just because a marriage is terminated by annulment rather than divorce does not mean that parties to annulled marriages have no rights. The party seeking the annulment still has a right to request an equitable distribution of property and, in some cases, spousal support. That party may also seek child support, custody, attorney's fees, and other costs related to the dissolution of the marriage. Many jurisdictions have statutorily provided courts the ability to award spousal support. In states without this statute, courts will not award spousal support. However, many of these states allow temporary spousal support during the pendency of the suit. Also, most courts will not reinstate spousal support from a previous marriage.

4. Children

Children of an annulled marriage are nevertheless considered marital children.

5. Defenses

When a marriage is void, the only way to defend against the annulment is to deny the existence of the impediment that voided the marriage. Removing the impediment merely makes the marriage voidable, but will not necessarily prevent the annulment.

In annulling voidable marriages, courts recognize the equitable defenses of unclean hands, laches, and estoppel.

6. Putative Marriage Doctrine

Most jurisdictions, either by statute or common law, have adopted a version of the putative marriage doctrine. *See, e.g., Williams v. Williams*, 97 P.3d 1124 (Nev. 2004); *In re Marriage of Himes,* 136 Wash. 2d 707 (1998); Colo., Rev. Stat. Ann. § 14-2-111 (West 2003). The purpose of the doctrine is to protect a party who is unaware of an impediment to the marriage that makes it either void or voidable. Under the doctrine, a party who participated in a ceremonial marriage and believes in good faith that the marriage is valid may use a state's divorce provisions even if the marriage is later found void due to an impediment. UMDA § 209.

As a putative marriage is not technically a marriage, divorce is not needed to terminate a relationship. The doctrine, however, is normally invoked to provide equitable relief, including maintenance and property distribution.

B. DIVORCE AND SEPARATION

Divorce is a legal dissolution of a marriage.

1. Grounds for Divorce

Most jurisdictions recognize both fault and no-fault grounds for divorce. The no-fault statutes eliminate fault and wrong as a ground for dissolution.

a. No-fault

Every jurisdiction has a unilateral no-fault ground for divorce. The majority of the jurisdictions require a party to allege that the marriage is **irretrievably broken** and there is no prospect of reconciliation (e.g., irreconcilable differences). Despite the terminology, the fact that the discord stems from a curable condition will not prevent divorce on a no-fault ground.

Most courts also require a specific passing of time prior to the filing of the divorce action; some courts also require a waiting period before the divorce can be granted. The fact that one spouse wishes to reconcile may lengthen the time period for obtaining a divorce, but is not an absolute bar to a no-fault divorce. Some states also permit the filing of a bilateral, no-fault ground when both parties mutually consent to the divorce; the requirements are typically less than the unilateral no-fault statute.

Most jurisdictions have abolished the traditional defenses to divorce. The only defense would be to deny the grounds for the divorce. However, unless both parties agree, this is generally insufficient to prevent the divorce.

Illinois Point of Law: No-Fault

In Illinois, the no-fault ground is known as irreconcilable differences. The requirements are that:

i)   The parties must live separate and apart for a period of more than two years;

ii) The parties must have irreconcilable differences that have caused a permanent breakdown of the marriage;

iii) All efforts to reconcile must have failed; and

iv) Further attempts to reconcile are either impracticable or not in the family's best interest.

The two-year separation requirement may be waived upon the written stipulation of both parties and after a continuous separation of at least six months. If the parties attempt reconciliation after the six-month period or at any point during the two years of separation, it will count towards the required separation period if the reconciliation fails, if the parties attend counseling, or if it is pursuant to a written reconciliation agreement. Illinois does not require separate housing in order for the parties to separate.

---

b. Fault

Fault grounds for divorce include adultery, cruelty, desertion, bigamy, imprisonment, indignity, and mental disorder. Most jurisdictions retain some level of fault-based grounds, although some have removed it from the law since the adoption of no-fault grounds. The use of fault-based divorce grounds has decreased dramatically since the adoption of no-fault based grounds in most jurisdictions, although fault is often considered when awarding maintenance.

1) Adultery

Adultery is voluntary sexual intercourse with someone other than one's spouse. Because the details of adultery are rarely known to both parties, it is usually proven by circumstantial evidence. It must be shown that a party had the **opportunity and the inclination** to commit adultery. The facts of the case must provide enough evidence to conclude the person was guilty of the adulterous act.

2) Cruelty

To prevail on the grounds of cruelty or inhumane treatment, most jurisdictions require that the plaintiff demonstrate a course of conduct by the other party that is harmful to the plaintiff's physical or mental health, and which makes the continued cohabitation between the parties unsafe or improper. The conduct of the defendant must be serious and typically cannot be based on one isolated incident. The majority of jurisdictions permit divorces on the basis of cruelty in cases of physical abuse, while only some permit it in cases of only emotional abuse or mental cruelty.

3) Desertion

Desertion (also called abandonment) results when one spouse, without cause or the consent of the other spouse, voluntarily leaves the marital home with the intent to remain apart on a permanent basis. Most jurisdictions require that the abandonment be for a statutorily designated period of time. Some jurisdictions also find desertion when one spouse forces another out of the marital home, and there is a fear of harm if that spouse returns. If the parties separate by mutual consent, the ground of desertion will not apply.

4) Habitual drunkenness

Some states permit habitual drunkenness as a ground for divorce if it is the frequent habit of getting drunk that causes impairment in the marital relationship. There is no requirement that the defendant be an alcoholic or that she be constantly under the influence of alcohol, but **more than an occasional level** of intoxication is required. A possible defense to the grounds of habitual drunkenness may be assumption of the risk.

5) Bigamy

Bigamy, which in most jurisdictions is also grounds for annulment, occurs when one of the parties in the marriage **knowingly** entered into a prior legal and existing marriage before entering into the current marriage.

6) Imprisonment

Imprisonment of one spouse for a specified period of time may be grounds for divorce.

7) Indignity

Indignity grounds arise when one spouse exhibits negative behavior toward the other that renders that spouse's condition intolerable and life burdensome. Indignity can include: vulgarity, unmerited reproach, habitual laziness, neglect, intentional incivility, manifest disdain, abusive language, malignant ridicule, habitual humiliating treatment, repeated accusations of infidelity, sexually deviant behavior, serious temper tantrums, or violence. While it is still available in some states, indignity is no longer recognized in the majority of states.

8) Institutionalization

Institutionalization is grounds for divorce if a spouse's insanity or serious mental condition results in her being confined to a mental institution for a specified period of time prior to the commencement of the divorce, and there is **no reasonable prospect of discharge** or rehabilitation.

Illinois Point of Law: Fault

In addition to bigamy, adultery, and extreme and repeated mental or physical cruelty, Illinois recognizes the following fault grounds:

Desertion: In Illinois, the willful desertion must have lasted for a minimum of one year. The one-year requirement can include time spent by the parties in divorce litigation or separation, provided that the parties have separate residences. The abandonment must continue until the marriage is dissolved. In Illinois, refusal to have sexual intercourse does not constitute desertion.

Constructive abandonment: Illinois courts also recognize constructive abandonment, which occurs when a spouse unjustifiably forces the other spouse to leave the home, making the maintenance of the marriage impossible. One spouse locking the other out of the house for an extended period of time without justification constitutes constructive abandonment.

Habitual drunkenness: In Illinois, habitual drunkenness for a period in excess of two years is a ground for divorce. Although the statute does not require the drunkenness to have an impact on the plaintiff, it is an implicit consideration of the court in determining whether the ground has been established.

Conviction of a crime: In Illinois, the conviction of one spouse for a felony or "infamous crime" constitutes grounds for divorce. An infamous crime is an act, "the commission of which was inconsistent with the commonly accepted principles of honesty and decency, or one which involves moral turpitude." *Keenan v. McGuane*, 150 N.E.2d 168, 175 (Ill. 1958).

Sexually transmitted disease: Infecting one's spouse with a sexually transmitted disease is a ground for dissolution of marriage.

Natural impotency: Impotency is a ground for annulment or divorce in Illinois. The petitioner must demonstrate that the respondent was impotent at the time of the marriage and that the condition has continued until the time the dissolution action is brought. The impotency must be incurable and affect a person's physical ability to perform the act of intercourse. It does not include the inability to have children or sterility.

Habits relating to excessive drug use: Gross and confirmed habits relating to the excessive use of addicting drugs is a ground for divorce provided that the behavior has occurred for a minimum of two years. In order to qualify as an excessive use, the drug use must have become a controlling or dominating purpose in the life of the user. The types of behavior necessary to establish this ground have not yet been addressed by the Illinois courts, but likely would be similar to the standards used to determine habitual drunkenness.

Attempting to take the life of another: The ground of attempting the life of another arises when one spouse has attempted to take the life of the other spouse by poison or other means showing malice.

---

2. Defenses

Defenses only apply to a fault-based divorce and must be affirmatively pleaded when asserted.

a. Recrimination and unclean hands

Recrimination occurs when both spouses have committed a marital wrongdoing of like conduct. In other words, because both parties were guilty of the same offense (e.g., adultery) that would justify a divorce, a court could not grant the request. A similar defense is "unclean hands," when the plaintiff's own behavior or acts are questionable. Both of these defenses are most commonly seen in desertion, adultery, or cruelty cases.

b. Connivance

Connivance is consent to or participation in the marital wrong, usually adultery (e.g., allowing or benefitting from a spouse's prostitution).

c. Condonation

Forgiveness of a spouse is a defense to a fault-based divorce. There must be knowledge of the misconduct, forgiveness of the misconduct, and the party must resume marital relations with the guilty party. It is typically based on a promise not to engage in the misconduct again. At common law, once an act was forgiven, it could not become future grounds for divorce.

d. Collusion

Collusion occurs when both spouses "conspired to fabricate" grounds for divorce. Collusion defenses are not as common since the adoption of no-fault grounds in many jurisdictions.

e. Provocation

If misconduct is provoked by the moving party, it is not grounds for divorce.

f. Insanity

Insanity is a valid defense when one spouse does not know the difference between right and wrong or lacks the ability to understand that an act is wrongful.

g. Consent

Consent is a defense to desertion or adultery.

h. Justification

Justification grounds may be established if one party left the home because of the other's misconduct. This is a defense to desertion.

i. Religion

A litigant that challenges a divorce on religious grounds will fail in all jurisdictions.

3. Limited Divorce and Separate Maintenance

Limited divorce, known in some states as a "divorce from bed and board," is recognized in most jurisdictions, but rarely used. When utilized, it is often for religious or medical reasons, as the parties do not sever the marital tie and are still considered legally married. They are, however, permitted to live apart. As with an absolute divorce, the court will determine support and property division.

A separate maintenance action provides for a decree of support for a party, typically the wife and any minor children. It does not, however, authorize the parties to live apart. As with a limited divorce, the parties are still considered married and cannot remarry.

4. Finalizing Divorce

When a divorce is initially granted, many courts will not finalize the divorce until a specified period of time has elapsed. This is known as an "interlocutory" decree. During this interlocutory period, neither spouse can remarry.

C. MEDIATION

Mediation is a frequently-used, less expensive, and often more effective manner to resolve separation disputes. A neutral, court-approved mediator assists both parties with spousal and child support issues, as well as custody and visitation rights. Discussions during the mediation process and the written agreement derived from the discussions remain confidential, unless both parties agree to its disclosure. The court may approve the agreement and make it part of the final judgment. A mediator must conduct the mediation process in an impartial manner and disclose all and potential grounds of bias and conflicts of interest. A mediator must facilitate the participants' understanding of what mediation is. A mediator should recognize a family situation involving domestic abuse and take appropriate steps to shape the mediation process accordingly. Additionally, a mediator shall structure the mediation process so that the participants make decisions based on sufficient information and knowledge.

D. DIVISION OF PROPERTY

There are two methods relating to the distribution of assets in the United States: **equitable distribution** and **community property**.

1. Community Property

Community property is a method for the distribution of marital assets that is used in nine states: Arizona, California, Idaho, Louisiana, Nevada, New Mexico, Texas, Washington, and Wisconsin. The guiding principle behind community property is that **marriage is a partnership**. Most community property states require an equal division of the marital property.

2. Equitable Distribution

Most states follow a system of equitable distribution. The objective of the equitable distribution system is to order a **fair distribution** of all marital property, taking into consideration all of the circumstances between the parties. Unlike a community property division, an equitable distribution is not necessarily an equal division of marital assets. There are, however, a few states that presume that an equitable division is an equal division, but permit deviation when necessary to achieve a more equitable result.

3. Marital Property

In most states, all property acquired during the marriage is marital property and subject to equitable distribution. Some states subject all property owned by either spouse to equitable distribution (i.e., the "hotchpot" approach). The definition of marital property is typically broadly applied and includes retirement benefits and, under some circumstances, equity in non-marital property. Classification of the appreciation in non-marital property will typically depend on whether it remains separate property and if the appreciation can be attributable to spousal labor. Title to the property is immaterial. If a party claims that an asset is non-marital, and not subject to equitable distribution, the burden is placed on that party to prove the assertion.

a. Exceptions to marital property

Most states treat certain property as separate, rather than marital property. Among the types of property treated as separate property are the following:

i)   Property **acquired before marriage** or property acquired in exchange for property acquired before the marriage;

ii) Property **excluded by the parties' valid agreement** entered into before, during, or after the marriage;

iii) Property **acquired by gift or inheritance**, or property acquired in exchange for such property, except when it is between spouses;

iv) Property a party has **sold, granted, conveyed,** or otherwise disposed of in good faith and for value before the date of final separation;

v)   Property to the extent it has been **mortgaged or otherwise encumbered in good faith** for value before the date of final separation; and

vi) Any **award or settlement payment received** for any cause of action or claim that accrued before the marriage, regardless of when the payment was received.

Example: One spouse was in a car accident two years before the marriage. That spouse was granted a settlement of $200,000 for her pain and suffering and invested it in the stock market before the marriage. The $200,000 would not be marital property.

Illinois Point of Law: Exceptions to Marital Property

Illinois follows an equitable distribution of property. In Illinois, all property is marital property, unless it meets one of the exceptions below:

i) Property **acquired before marriage** or property acquired in exchange for property acquired before the marriage;

ii) Property **excluded by the parties' valid agreement** entered into before, during, or after the marriage;

iii) Property **acquired by gift or inheritance**, or property acquired in exchange for such property, except when it is between spouses;

iv) **Increase in the value of non-marital property**, regardless of whether the increase occurred because of the contribution of marital property, the personal effort of the spouse, or is subject to the right of contribution;

v) Property **acquired in exchange for separate property** or directly related to an increase in the value of separate property, less any contributions by the other spouse;

vi) Property acquired after a **judgment of legal separation**;

vii) Property obtained by a **judgment** awarded to a spouse from the other spouse; and

viii) Any income derived from any of the above methods, with some minor exceptions.

b. Factors in distribution of marital property

Courts consider the following factors in distribution of property:

i) Length of marriage;

ii) Prior marriages;

iii) Age, health, earnings, earning potential, liabilities, and needs of both spouses;

iv) Contributions to education;

v) Needs for future acquisitions;

vi) Income, medical needs, retirement of both spouses;

vii) Contributions to increases in marital property, including homemaking and child rearing services;

viii) Value of separate property;

ix) Reduction in valuation in marital property by one spouse;

x) Standard of living;

xi) Economic circumstances of each spouse at the time of divorce; and

xii) Custodianship of any minor children.

In most states, the fact that a divorce is granted on a fault ground, such as adultery, is not a factor in the distribution of the property. However, dissipation of marital property may be a factor. Dissipation occurs when one spouse uses marital property for his sole benefit after the marriage has irreconcilably broken down, such as the purchase of expensive gifts for a paramour.

Illinois Distinction: Factors in Distribution of Marital Property

In addition to the above factors, Illinois courts also consider the following in determining the distribution of marital property:

i)   Any award of maintenance or whether the distribution of assets is in lieu of maintenance; and

ii) Tax consequences to each party.

In determining the value of property, whether marital or non-marital, the court uses the date of trial.

In Illinois, when marital and non-marital property is commingled, the classification of the property takes on that of the receiving estate. If the commingling of property was not a gift to the marital estate, the contributing spouse will be reimbursed upon distribution.

Further, when a spouse contributes significant personal effort to non-marital property, which results in substantial appreciation of non-marital property, the personal effort is deemed a contribution to the marital estate, and the spouse contributing the effort shall be reimbursed. The court may provide for reimbursement out of marital property to be divided or by imposing a lien against non-marital property.

4.   Treatment of Specific Types of Marital Property

a.   Professional licenses or degrees

The majority of jurisdictions do not treat a professional license or degree as a distributable property interest. *Simmons v. Simmons,* 708 A.2d 949 (Conn. 1998); *but cf. Elkus v. Elkus,* 572 N.Y.S.2d 901 (1 Dep't 1991) (a professional degree is an asset subject to equitable distribution). Most courts look at advanced degrees or licenses as an acquisition of knowledge as opposed to a property interest. A court may, however, view an advanced degree or license as increased earning capacity, which may have an effect on the determination of alimony. A court may also use its equity power to award a spouse reimbursement for his actual contribution towards the other spouse's educational and related living expenses. This is often referred to as the cost-value approach.

b.   Retirement or pension benefits

Retirement or pension benefits acquired during the marriage are considered marital property and are subject to equitable distribution. This includes military pensions.

c.   Personal injury claim proceeds

Jurisdictions differ on the treatment of proceeds from personal injury claims and worker's compensation claims. There are three basic approaches:

1)   Marital property

In some jurisdictions, if the cause of action accrues between the date of the marriage and the final separation, the proceeds from the settlement or award are marital property. As long as the cause of action accrued during the marriage, the proceeds are marital property—even if the claim is paid after the final separation.

2) Separate and marital allocation

Other jurisdictions view the nature of the award to determine whether it is separate or marital property and allocate the award between non-marital and marital property. Compensatory damages for pain, suffering, disability, and loss are considered separate to the injured spouse. Consortium losses are considered separate property of the non-injured spouse. Awards for lost wages, loss of earning capacity, and medical expenses are typically split. The court calculates the portion of the award attributable from the time of the accident until the termination of the marriage, and treats that portion as marital property. Any part of the award attributable to loss of wages or medical expenses after the termination of the marriage is separate property.

d. Goodwill

The reputation and clientele of a professional practice (such as that of a doctor or lawyer) is considered marital property in some jurisdictions.

e. Accumulated sick and vacation days

Jurisdictions are split on the issue of whether vacation and sick days are marital property. Courts have held the following: (1) accrued vacation and sick days are marital property subject to division at the time of dissolution; (2) accrued vacation and sick days are marital property, but are subject to distribution when received, as opposed to the time of dissolution; and (3) accrued vacation and sick days are not marital property. *Presby v. Presby* 2004 Ohio 3050 (Ohio Ct. App. 2004) (accumulated days that can be cashed out are considered marital property to be distributed at the time of dissolution); *Ryan v. Ryan*, 261 N.J. Super 689 (1992) (when payment for the unused accumulated days was received at separation, it constituted marital property if the majority of the days were accrued during the marriage).

f. Future interest

A possible future interest in property (e.g., inheritance) is not distributable.

g. Social Security

Social Security benefits are not subject to equitable distribution. *Fleming v. Nestor*, 363 U.S. 603 (1960) (applying accrued property rights to the Social Security system would deprive it of the flexibility in adjustment which it demands).

h. Post-separation property

In most states, property acquired by one spouse until a divorce is granted can be marital property. Some states treat property acquired by a spouse after permanently separating from the other spouse as separate property. Still other states draw the line between marital and separate property on the date the divorce action is filed.

i. Stock options

Stock options acquired during the marriage are marital property even if they will not be exercised until after the marriage.

Illinois Distinction: Treatment of Specific Types of Marital Property

Personal injury awards: Illinois follows the analytical approach, providing for separate and marital allocation. *In re Marriage of Waggoner*, 634 N.E.2d 1198 (Ill. App. Ct. 1994).

Goodwill: In Illinois, goodwill is not treated as marital property.

Indirect contribution: An increase in the value of separate property that occurred during the marriage which can be linked to the indirect contribution of the other spouse, such as in a homemaker capacity, will not be considered marital property unless it results in substantial appreciation to the non-marital property and is a result of a substantial effort of the spouse.

Accumulated sick & vacation days: Accumulated sick and vacation days are considered separate property of the spouse due to their speculative nature and, as a result, their inability to be valued at the time of dissolution. Accumulated days, however, may be considered marital property if payment is received prior to dissolution of the marriage and the true value of the time is known. *In re Marriage of Abrell,* 923 N.E.2d 791 (Ill. 2010).

5. Tax Consequences of Equitable Distribution

Equitable distribution payments are not taxed in the same manner as regular income. Property that is transferred between divorcing spouses is tax free at that time. The transferee's tax basis is the same as the transferor's and the property becomes taxable when it is sold.

III. FINANCIAL SUPPORT OF SPOUSES AND CHILDREN

A. SPOUSAL MAINTENANCE

Spousal support (also called **maintenance** or **alimony**) is the obligation of one party to provide the other with support in the form of income. It is awarded in a divorce if one spouse cannot provide for his own needs with employment. Alimony payments can be made for a definite or indefinite period of time. Unlike property settlements, alimony obligations cannot be discharged in bankruptcy.

1. Factors

Each jurisdiction provides by statute the criteria to be applied by the court in determining the eligibility and amount of a maintenance award. The majority of jurisdictions consider some or all of the following factors when determining the support award.

a. Financial resources

Courts consider the financial resources of the spouse seeking support, including property to be awarded in the divorce and any child support. They also take each spouse's earning potential into account, as well as the ability of the spouse from whom support is sought to pay.

b. Standard of living

The couple's standard of living during the marriage is considered.

c. Time

Courts also consider the time it will take for a spouse to find employment or to complete any education or training necessary for a job.

d. Length of marriage

The length of the marriage is considered in determining spousal support.

e. Contributions to marriage

Contributions by one spouse to the marriage, particularly those that enhanced the earning potential of the other spouse (e.g., education, training), may be considered.

f. Age and health

The parties' age and health, both physical and mental, is considered in determining support.

g. Marital misconduct

Fault or marital misconduct may be taken into account in many states in determining spousal support. The weight the marital misconduct is given in determining alimony is dependent on the jurisdiction, with some considering it as a factor and others giving it a preclusive effect. *See Stevens v. Stevens*, 484 N.Y.S.2d 708 (3d Dep't 1985) (marital fault may only be considered when the conduct of the recipient is egregious); 23 Pa. Cons. Stat. § 3701(b) (marital misconduct is one of 17 factors to be considered when determining alimony).

Illinois Distinction: Spousal Maintenance

Illinois, which refers to spousal support as maintenance, considers the following factors in addition to those mentioned above in determining the award:

i) Which party has custody of the children and whether such award of custody and its circumstances make it appropriate for the recipient spouse not to seek employment;

ii) The tax consequences to each party;

iii) Impairment to the earning capacity of the recipient spouse due to domestic duties or delaying employment or education during the marriage;

iv) The agreement between the parties, if any; and

v) Any other factor that the courts finds just and proper.

See In re Marriage of O'Brien, 912 N.E.2d 729 (Ill. App. Ct. 2009).

Marital misconduct: Illinois does not consider marital fault or misconduct in determining a maintenance award.

---

2. Types of Support

Spousal support may be any of the following types:

a. Lump sum

A lump-sum spousal support award is a fixed amount and may not be modified.

b. Permanent

Permanent alimony is an award for the remainder of the dependent spouse's life, unless certain circumstances occur. The purpose behind permanent alimony is to compensate the dependent spouse for either the lost earning capacity or benefit conferred to the other spouse during the marriage. It is primarily used in cases when one spouse remained out of the work force for homemaking or child-rearing purposes. Permanent alimony is typically only awarded when the marriage was one of long duration. While jurisdictions differ on the definition of "long-term," it typically refers to a marriage of 15 years or more.

c. Limited duration

Limited-duration alimony is established for a limited period of time. Unlike rehabilitative or reimbursement alimony (discussed below), its purpose is not to facilitate an increased earning capacity of the dependent spouse or to compensate a spouse that has sacrificed. Limited duration alimony is typically awarded when the marriage was of short duration (making permanent alimony inappropriate), but there is still an economic need for support.

d. Rehabilitative

Rehabilitative support is for a limited period of time, such as until the spouse receives education or employment. The purpose of rehabilitative alimony is to enhance and improve the earning capacity of the economically dependent spouse. For example, a spouse may be required to pay rehabilitative alimony for a period of four years while a dependent spouse attends college. The payments would automatically terminate at the end of the four-year period.

e. Reimbursement

The purpose of reimbursement alimony is to compensate a spouse for financial sacrifices made during the marriage which resulted in a reduced standard of living in order to secure an enhanced standard of living in the future. Often, this type of alimony is only awarded in cases where one spouse did not work in order to secure an advanced degree or professional license. It is rarely used, and unlike the other forms of alimony, it is based on past contributions rather than present or future needs. Instead of reimbursement alimony, some jurisdictions treat this type of payment as property division.

f. Palimony

Only available in a few states, palimony is support provided by one unmarried cohabitant to another after the dissolution of their relationship. First recognized in 1976 by the *Marvin* decision, palimony is only available when the cohabitants have lived together in a stable, long term-relationship. *Marvin v. Marvin*, 557 P.2d 106 (Cal. 1976). The treatment of such cohabitation agreements and the resulting support of palimony vary among jurisdictions. A majority of jurisdictions distinguish between contracts that are based on sexual services and those in which the agreement is independent of the illicit relationship. Some courts also permit remedies to unmarried couples based on an implied-in-fact contract, resulting trust, constructive trust, or *quantum meruit* theories. In most states, the Statute of Frauds does not require that an express contract between cohabitants be in writing.

Alimony and spousal maintenance payments are generally taxable as ordinary income to the recipient and deductible by the payor.

Illinois Point of Law: Palimony

Illinois does not recognize implied marriage contracts. Further, Illinois is one of the few states that deny property rights to unmarried cohabitants absent an express agreement that is not meretricious in nature.

3. Modification of Support

In general, spousal support may be modified, even when it has been deemed permanent. The party seeking modification typically has the burden of establishing a significant change in circumstances in the needs of the dependent spouse or financial abilities of the obligor that warrant the modification. As with child support, a party who willfully or voluntarily reduces her income will not receive a reduction in her support payments.

a. Death

Spousal support generally continues until the death of a spouse. Support is usually not included as a liability of the deceased spouse's estate, unless specified by the court.

b. Remarriage

In most jurisdictions, if the receiving spouse remarries, spousal support may be terminated. A subsequent annulment of this marriage generally does not revive a spousal support obligation from a former marriage, even though an annulment usually results in a marriage being treated as invalid as of the date of its inception.

c. Cohabitation

If the receiving spouse cohabits with someone who is not family, spousal support may be modified if the recipient spouse's need for the support decreases as a result of the cohabitation. Support, however, typically is not automatically terminated, as the new cohabitant does not have a legal duty to support the alimony recipient. Cohabitation can also forestall the award of spousal support. The courts, however, will also consider the nature of the cohabitation, such as a same-sex roommate living in a separate room versus a dating relationship.

Cohabitation does not terminate alimony *pendente lite,* which is paid during the pendency of the divorce litigation.

d. Retirement

Jurisdictions differ on whether an obligor can seek a reduction in spousal support payments upon retirement. Some jurisdictions hold that the parties should have addressed the issue during the divorce proceedings and deny modification, while other jurisdictions find that the dependent spouse cannot expect to receive the same level of support after the supporting spouse retires.

Illinois Point of Law: Modification of Support

In Illinois, as in the majority of states, a party seeking a modification to a maintenance award must demonstrate a substantial change in circumstance. In evaluating a party's request to modify alimony, the court will also consider the following factors:

i)   Changes in the employment status of either party and whether the changes, if any, have been made in good faith;

ii) Any increase or decrease in the income of either party since the entry of the prior order;

iii) The duration of the maintenance payments, the number of payments previously made and remaining, relative to the duration of the marriage;

iv) Tax consequences of both parties relative to the maintenance payments;

v)   Impairment to either party's present or future earning capacity;

vi) Property acquired, including retirement benefits, under the judgment and subsequently obtained by each party and its present status;

vii) Efforts made by the recipient party to become self-supporting and the reasonableness of those efforts already made; and

viii) Any other relevant and just factor.

Cohabitation: In Illinois, cohabitation with a non-marital partner terminates a maintenance obligation if the cohabitation is on a continuing basis and is conjugal in nature.

Retirement: Illinois considers the issue of modification of maintenance upon retirement on a case by case basis.

4.   Support during Marriage

At common law, a husband was obligated to support his wife and the duty was enforceable under the necessaries doctrine. A necessary item was something suitable to the parties' station in life, including medically necessary care. Most jurisdictions have modified the necessaries doctrine to apply equally to both spouses and often refer to them as family expense statutes. A minority of jurisdictions has abolished the doctrine as a violation of equal protection rights.

In those jurisdictions retaining the doctrine, a creditor may sue either spouse for payment of necessaries, but may be required to first seek payment from the incurring spouse.

5.   Tax Consequences of Spousal Maintenance

The payor of spousal support payments may deduct those payments from income, while the recipient must include the support payments as income, unless otherwise stated in the divorce decree or separation agreement.

B.   JURISDICTION

As with a court hearing other matters, a court hearing a family-related dispute must generally have both subject-matter jurisdiction and personal jurisdiction. Most states have statutory residency requirements, typically ranging from six weeks to two years, in order for a court to have subject-matter jurisdiction. Full Faith and Credit applies to divorce decrees as long as one of the spouses was domiciled in the state that granted the decree.

Matrimonial courts have full equity powers in matrimonial actions, which include:

i) Division of property;

ii) Divorce or annulment;

iii) Custody;

iv) Support and alimony;

v) Award of attorney's fees;

vi) Enforcement of separation agreements; and

vii) All other matters related to matrimonial actions.

Illinois Point of Law: Jurisdiction

At least one spouse must be a resident of Illinois for 90 days prior to filing for divorce in the state.

1. Divisible Divorce Doctrine

Under the doctrine of divisible divorce, also known as ex parte divorce, a court may have sufficient jurisdiction to grant a divorce but lack such jurisdiction with respect to other divorce-related matters, such as property division, alimony, and child support. A court with subject-matter jurisdiction over the divorce action as well as personal jurisdiction over one spouse can grant a divorce, but cannot determine property division, alimony, or child-support issues without personal jurisdiction over the other spouse. If a court makes such a determination, the defendant can challenge the court's orders due to the court's lack of *in personam* jurisdiction over the defendant. *Estin v. Estin*, 334 U.S. 541 (1948); *Vanderbilt v. Vanderbilt*, 354 U.S. 416 (1957).

2. Collateral Attack on Jurisdiction

The only way for the non-resident defendant to attack the issuance of an *ex parte* divorce is to demonstrate that the plaintiff was not domiciled in the divorcing state at the time the judgment was granted or left the state's domicile immediately after the entry of the divorce. If the court had both personal and subject-matter jurisdiction over the parties and the attacking party litigated or had the opportunity to litigate, that person will be precluded from collaterally attacking the judgment in any jurisdiction. *Sherrer v. Sherrer*, 334 U.S. 343 (1948). This is often seen in cases where the parties colluded to obtain an out-of-state divorce. Although persons other than the party may collaterally attack a divorce if standing exists (i.e., a child), they will be precluded from attacking it if the third person is in privity with any party who would have been estopped from attacking the judgment themselves.

3. Issues Relating to Indigent Parties

Courts cannot require that an indigent party pay costs and fees in order to access the court system. Such requirements are unconstitutional. *Boddie v. Connecticut*, 401 U.S. 371 (1971). Although there is no legal right to counsel for indigent parties in divorce proceedings, the court has the discretion to award attorney's fees and costs if the party is unable to afford the services of legal counsel.

C. CHILD SUPPORT

1.   Child's Right to Support

Child support is the payment by one parent to the other for the support of a common child. The duration of child support varies with each jurisdiction. In all jurisdictions, both parents (custodial and non-custodial), regardless of marital status, are legally required to support their minor children (i.e., unemancipated and 18 years of age or younger). *Gomez v. Perez*, 409 U.S. 535 (1973) (state law basing the existence of a support obligation on marital status violates Equal Protection). Some jurisdictions, however, continue that obligation through college. Additionally, child support can also be continued, even indefinitely, for a child incapable of self-support, provided that the inability to support is linked to a physical or mental disability.

The payment of child support is entirely separate from visitation rights. Such rights cannot be denied for non-payment of support.

Parents cannot bargain away child support payments, regardless of whether they intended to have a child. Parents can enter into private agreements regarding the payments but cannot agree to any release or compromise that would negatively affect the child's welfare.

2.   Nonmarital Children

Nonmarital children historically were not entitled to child support or to inherit from their father's estate. Courts now use an intermediate scrutiny standard to analyze the constitutionality of government action, focusing on the purpose behind the distinction between marital and nonmarital children. As a result, child support, government benefits, and wrongful death claims may no longer be denied to nonmarital children, and nonmarital children may inherit from their father's estate so long as paternity was proved prior to the father's death.

Nonmarital children may change their status and become marital children under certain circumstances, including when:

   i)   The parents marry after the birth of the child;

   ii) The father consents to being named on the birth certificate;

   iii) The father holds himself out or in some way acknowledges that he is the child's father; or

   iv) A judicial decree establishes paternity.

3.   Paternity

The obligation of child support falls on the child's parents. Questions may arise, however, as to the identity of the child's father. Once his identity is established, the child's father has rights to custody and visitation, but is also under a duty to support the child. Paternity actions are confidential and not available to the public.

a.   Blood test

When there is a question as to the father of a child, a court may order blood tests of the child and the possible fathers to determine paternity. If a defendant involved in a paternity matter is indigent, he is entitled to blood testing at the state's expense to establish or disprove paternity. *Little v. Streater*, 452 U.S. 1

(1981). If the test disproves paternity, the case seeking child support must be dismissed.

b. **Other evidence**

In addition to the blood test, evidence such as (i) prior statements regarding paternity by deceased family members, (ii) medical testimony on the probability or improbability of conception, (iii) the defendant's acknowledgment of paternity, and, in some states, (iv) the resemblance of the child to the defendant are admissible to prove paternity.

c. **Unconstitutional time limit on paternity petition**

A time limit on the filing of a paternity petition in order to secure support from the purported father is invalid unless there is a reasonable opportunity to pursue such an action and the limit is substantially related to the government's interest in restricting such an action (e.g., prevention of fraudulent claims). Otherwise, the time limit is a violation of the Equal Protection Clause of the U.S. Constitution because it subjects illegitimate children to restrictions not imposed on legitimate children. *Picket v. Brown*, 462 U.S. 1 (1982). The suit may be brought by the child or the child's mother. Standard of proof varies by the jurisdiction, but could be as low as preponderance of the evidence or as high as clear and convincing proof.

d. **Marital presumption**

There is a marital presumption that a child born to a married woman is the child of that woman and her husband. Most states apply the presumption even when the wife is artificially inseminated, provided that the husband gave his consent to the procedure and the procedure is performed by a physician. In some states, a wife is estopped from denying her husband's paternity of her child, but approximately half of the states permit rebuttal of the marital presumption if the husband is impotent, sterile, or lacked access to his wife. When rebuttal is permitted, some states permit a court to exclude evidence rebutting the presumption if rebuttal is contrary to the child's best interests.

e. **Estoppel**

A husband who is not the biological father of his wife's child may be estopped from denying his obligation to pay child support. Under the doctrine of equitable estoppel, the husband may be required to pay child support when:

i) There is a representation by the husband that he would provide for the child;

ii) The wife relied on his representation; and

iii) The wife suffered an economic detriment as a result of the reliance (e.g., loss of opportunity to obtain child support from child's biological father).

Although many jurisdictions recognize the doctrine of paternity by estoppel, some jurisdictions will only permit it to be used as a basis to prevent a party from denying their obligation to support as opposed to preventing a biological father from asserting his rights. *See R.W.E. v. A.B.K.*, 961 A.2d 161 (Pa. Super. 2008). However, some states have recently begun placing greater emphasis on the interests of men who have been erroneously identified as fathers. In these jurisdictions, a husband's child support may be terminated and paternity may be disestablished, without regard to a child's financial interests. *Williams v Williams*, 843 So. 2d 720,723 (Miss. 2003); GA. CODE ANN. § 19-7-54 (2009).

Illinois Point of Law: Paternity

Acknowledgment: In addition to the marital presumption, a man can acknowledge paternity of a child by executing an acknowledgment of paternity. An executed acknowledgment of paternity is conclusive after the passage of 60 days from its execution or the date of a judicial proceeding regarding the child in which the person who signed the acknowledgment is a party. An executed acknowledgment of paternity may only be challenged on the basis of fraud, duress, or material mistake of fact, with the burden of proof on the challenging person. *Jackson v. Mannie*, 913 N.E.2d 1174 (Ill. App. Ct. 2009).

Testing: In Illinois, there is a presumption that the male is the father of the child if the blood genetic marker testing establishes paternity with a probability of 99.8% and a combined paternity index of 500. If the male is determined to be the father of the child, an order of support will be entered; if not, the case will be dismissed.

---

4. Personal Jurisdiction over Out-of-State Parent

With respect to proceedings to establish or enforce child support or to determine parentage, a court obtains personal jurisdiction over an out-of-state parent pursuant to a long-arm provision in the Uniform Interstate Family Support Act (UIFSA), which has been adopted by every state. The ways in which a court can obtain personal jurisdiction are:

i) Personal service on the defendant parent;

ii) Consent of the defendant parent, such as by entering an appearance in the action;

iii) Current residency with the child in the state;

iv) Past residency in the state and the provision of prenatal expenses or support for the child;

v) Residency of the child in the state as a result of acts or directives of the parent defendant;

vi) Parent defendant engaged in sexual intercourse in the state and the child may have been conceived by that act;

vii) Parent defendant asserted parentage in the putative father registry maintained by the state; or

viii) Any other basis consistent with federal and state constitutions for the exercise of personal jurisdiction.

It is important to note that the United States Supreme Court has not yet spoken on the constitutionality of UIFSA's long-arm provisions. Several states, however, have upheld the provision as meeting the requisite due process requirements. *See, e.g., Poindexter v. Poindexter*, 594 N.W.2d 76 (Mich. Ct. App. 1999); *County of Humboldt v. Harris*, 254 Cal. Rptr. 49 (Cal. Ct. App. 1988). In so holding, state courts have relied on the voluntary nature of the sexual act or conduct; that conception is a logical result of that conduct; and the state's strong interest in protecting its minor children in all regards, including financially. As the obligation to support a child extends to at least the age of majority, there is no time limit on the assertion of jurisdiction under this statute. UIFSA § 201, cmt.

For the jurisdictional requirements for the modification of child support order, *see* § III.E.3., *infra*.

D. AMOUNT OF CHILD SUPPORT

All jurisdictions have adopted child support guidelines to streamline the process by using objective bases for determining child support awards. Child support awards are typically based on income from any source and include wages, interests and dividends, rental income, and other income received including retirement benefits, capital gains, and social security income. The guidelines are applied in all cases regardless of marital status.

1. Calculating Support

a. Income-shares model

Most jurisdictions have adopted an income-shares model, which operates on the theory that a child should receive the same proportion of parental income as if the parties continued to live together.

b. Percentage-of-income model

Other jurisdictions have adopted a percentage-of-income model, which determines the minimum amount of child support by using a percentage of the supporting (i.e., noncustodial) parent's net income, determined by the number of children supported. Certain expenditures, such as taxes or necessary medical expenditures, may be excluded when calculating net income. *See, e.g.,* 750 Ill. Comp. Stat. 5/505.

c. Melson Formula

The Melson Formula is similar to the income-shares model, but takes into account six specific considerations, such as the minimum amount each supporting parent must retain, the number of the supporting parent's dependents, and a Standard of Living Adjustment (SOLA). *See, e.g.,* Del. Fam. Ct. Civ. R. 52(c).

d. Deviations from child support guidelines

In all jurisdictions, there is a rebuttable presumption that the amount calculated pursuant to the child support guidelines is correct. 42 U.S.C. § 667. Deviations, however, are permitted as the circumstances warrant. If the court determines that the amount set forth under the guidelines should be deviated from, it must set forth specific findings explaining and supporting the deviation, including the amount that would have been awarded under the application of the guidelines. If a parent is unemployed or underemployed, the court may impute an income in order to calculate the child support award. Conversely, if the parent(s) earn a significant income far exceeding the needs of the child, the court may modify the award to provide solely for the child's needs, but generously define the amount. Once a child support award has been paid, the obligor is not permitted to monitor how the money is expended.

Percentage-of-Income Model: Illinois determines the minimum amount of child support by using a percentage of the supporting parent's net income, determined by the number of children supported. If there is one child, the minimum amount of support is 20% of the supporting party's net income; two children, 28%; three children, 32%; four children, 40%; five children, 45%; six or more children, 50%.

In addition to taxes, social security, and similar required payments, certain expenditures are excluded when calculating net income, such as reasonable expenditures for the benefit of the child and other parent, necessary medical expenses, and expenses necessary for the production of income.

2. Other Considerations

Additional factors the courts consider in determining the amount of support include:

i) Ages of the children;

ii) Unusual needs and unusual obligations (e.g., special education);

iii) Support obligations of the parties;

iv) Assets of the parties;

v) Medical expenses outside of insurance coverage;

vi) Standard of living;

vii) Duration of marriage, for spousal support or alimony *pendente lite*; and

viii) Best interests of the child.

Illinois Point of Law: Other Considerations

The court has discretion to increase the amount of child support owed after considering the best interests of the child. The court may consider a variety of factors, including (i) the financial needs of the child, (ii) the financial resources and needs of both the custodial parent *and* the non-custodial parent, (iii) the standard of living the child would have enjoyed had the marriage not dissolved, and (iv) the physical, emotional, and educational needs of the child.

3. Medical Insurance

In most jurisdictions, the cost of providing medical insurance for the child is included in the child support award, if either of the parents have access to insurance. If there is no insurance available, the court may include provisions for the procurement and payment of insurance after consideration of the medical needs of the child, the cost of the coverage, and the availability of a plan to meet the child's needs. Any premiums associated with the medical coverage shall be subtracted from the net income of the parent who is responsible for the payment.

Illinois Point of Law: Amount of Child Support

Imputation of Income: Courts have the authority to impute income to the payor in order to compel parties to pay child support at a level commensurate with their earning potential. In Illinois, in order to impute income, a court must find one of the following: (i) the obligor is unemployed on a voluntary basis, (ii) the obligor is attempting to evade his child support obligation, either in full or in part, or (iii) the obligor has unreasonably failed to take advantage of an employment opportunity. *In re Marriage of Gosney*, 916 N.E.2d 614 (Ill. App. Ct. 2009).

College Expenses: In addition to child support, a child, even one who has attained the age of majority, may receive support for educational expenses, including college or other occupational training after graduation from high school. In determining whether a parent should be obligated to contribute to the educational expenses of the child, the court shall consider:

i)   The financial resources of all parties, including the child;

ii) The standard of living the child would have enjoyed had the marriage not been dissolved; and

iii) The educational and academic performance of the child.

In re Marriage of Baumgartner, 912 N.E.2d 783 (Ill. App. Ct. 2009). Any award of educational support automatically terminates upon the receipt of a degree.

E.   MODIFICATION OF CHILD SUPPORT

1.   Modification of Support

Most jurisdictions permit an award of child support to be modified. Although the statutory language varies, in general, modifications are permissible when there is a substantial change in circumstances regarding the child's needs or parents' financial situation. Examples include a parent's change in occupation, remarriage of a parent who now has additional family obligations, increase in income, or a decrease in health. The burden to substantiate the change in circumstances is on the parent requesting the modification. Some jurisdictions, however, permit a modification to a support order after a certain passage of time, such as for a cost of living increase. Typically, a modification award is made retroactive to the date of service of the motion on the opposing party, but support obligations that have accrued prior to that date generally may not be modified. 42 U.S.C. § 666(a)(9) (prohibiting retroactive modification of child support).

> **EXAM NOTE:** Be aware of fact patterns in which the obligor spouse voluntarily quits a job. The amount of child support may not be reduced simply because of the voluntary reduction in the obligor's pay. If this situation arises, discuss the obligor's earning capacity, which is the amount the person could realistically earn under the circumstances in consideration of the person's age, mental health, and physical condition.

Illinois Point of Law: Modification of Support

Illinois applies the change in circumstances standard. Only events that have occurred subsequent to the award are relevant. Child support arrears cannot be modified.

Additionally, without a substantial change in circumstances, a child support obligation may be modified when:

i)   There is an inconsistency of at least 20% but not less than $10 per month between the existing child support order and an order that would be rendered pursuant to the child support guidelines, (unless the existing order was a deviation from the guidelines), and:

   a)   There has not been a change in circumstances that resulted from the deviation;

   b)   At least 36 months have elapsed since the prior order;

   c)   The recipient of the child support is receiving public aid; and

   d)   The order is enforceable through the child support enforcement services; or

ii) There is a need to provide medical insurance for the minor child and it is not addressed in the current order.

2. Termination of Support

A parent's obligation to pay support usually ends when the child reaches the age of majority (typically 18 years of age). Some jurisdictions, however, have the authority to order support beyond the age of majority when the child is in college. An additional exception applies when an adult child is unable to support himself due to circumstances such as a mental or physical disability. In most jurisdictions, termination may also take place if the child marries, the parental rights are terminated, the child commences active duty in the military, or the parent or child dies. A court, however, does have the right to order that a parent obtain insurance on his life for the benefit of the children to provide future support after his death.

Additionally, support may be terminated if a child is **emancipated** before the age of majority. To be emancipated, a minor child must be established as a self-supporting individual beyond the sphere of influence of his parents or independent of parental control. The mere employment of the child does not, by itself, establish emancipation. Also, the birth of a child by an unemancipated child does not result in an automatic emancipation and termination of support. However, the support rights of an employable child are contingent on the compliance by the child with reasonable parental demands; an employable child who fails to comply risks loss of parental support.

> **EXAM NOTE:** If there is a question as to whether a minor child has been emancipated, discuss the totality of the circumstances. Emancipation of a minor is *fact specific.*

Illinois Point of Law: Termination of Support

In Illinois, a parent's obligation to pay support usually ends when the child reaches the age of 18, or, if the child is still attending high school, the age of 19. Support may end upon emancipation of the child. Parents owe an ongoing duty to support adult children unable to support themselves due to circumstances such as mental or physical disability.

The death of a parent paying child support will not terminate an award. Additionally, the right to petition for child support is not extinguished upon the death of the parent and may be awarded against and paid by the decedent's estate.

As to the emancipation of a child, in Illinois, a minor seeking emancipation under the self-supporting provision must be at least 16 years old and the parents must not object to the emancipation. Neither the birth of a child by an unemancipated child nor the incarceration of a child results in automatic emancipation and termination of support.

3. Jurisdiction for Modification of Support

Similar to the jurisdictional issues with child custody orders, a state court may not modify an order of child support rendered by a court of continuing jurisdiction in another state unless the parties, including the child, no longer reside in that state or the parties expressly agree to permit another state to exercise jurisdiction. A court order that fails to adhere to this jurisdiction rule does not qualify for enforcement under the Full Faith and Credit Clause of the U.S. Constitution. 28 U.S.C. § 1738B(a) (Full Faith and Credit for Child Support Orders Act); Uniform Interstate Family Support Act § 205.

As with enforcement, a child support order may be registered in another tribunal (e.g., order entered in Mississippi, but all parties moved to Minnesota and the order is then registered in Minnesota). It is important to note, however, that if an aspect of a child support obligation may not be modified under the law of the state that first imposed the obligation, that aspect of the obligation may not be modified under the laws of any other state. UIFSA § 611, cmt. *See also, C.K. v. J.M.S.*, 931 So. 2d 724 (Ala. Civ. App. 2005) (while amount of child support may be modified, the length of the obligation may not be changed as it is a non-modifiable aspect of the original order); *Wills v. Wills*, 745 N.W.2d 924, 926–29 (Neb. Ct. App. 2008).

4. Tax Consequences of Child Support

Neither the payor nor the recipient of the support may deduct the support from or include it in their income.

F. ENFORCEMENT OF AWARDS

Both child and spousal support orders are enforced through civil contempt orders, income withholding, or withholding of tax refunds.

1. Civil Contempt

Civil contempt requires compliance with a court order. An obligor with the ability to pay may be found in civil contempt and can be sent to jail and held until the amount owed is fully paid. Jurisdictions are currently split on whether the appointment of counsel is constitutionally required in civil contempt cases when the defendant is indigent. *Cf. Rodriquez v. Eighth Judicial Dist. Court,* 102 P.3d 41 (Nev. 2004) (Sixth Amendment right to counsel inapplicable); *Pasqua v. Council,* 892 A.2d 663 (N.J. 2006) (counsel for civil contempt obligors is required under the Due Process Clause and state constitution).

2. Criminal Contempt

Criminal contempt is a specific jail sentence imposed upon an obligor who willingly fails to pay the amount owed. When criminal contempt is sought by the court, the defendant is entitled to additional constitutional protections. *Hicks v. Feiock,* 485 U.S. 624 (1988) (violative of the Fourteenth Amendment Due Process Clause to place burden of proving inability to make support payments on the defendant).

3. Other Sanctions

Courts may impose other sanctions, such as issuing judgments, intercepting tax refunds, credit bureau reporting, suspending the obligor's driver's license or occupational license, seizing property or assets, garnishing the noncomplying party's wages, and ordering the payment of attorney's fees. Additionally, the Personal Responsibility and Work Reconciliation Act of 1996 permits the denial of a passport application when the noncustodial parent is more than $5,000 in arrears on his child support obligation. PRWORA § 312.

Illinois Point of Law: Enforcement of Awards

In addition to the mechanisms addressed above, in Illinois, if an obligor is more than 90 days in arrears, her motor vehicle license may be suspended until she is in compliance with the support order. These remedies are also available without judicial intervention if the order is for child support and payable

---

through a Support Collection Unit. Additionally, there is no statute of limitations on child support judgments; accordingly, they may be enforced at any time.

4. Enforcement in Other Jurisdictions

Every jurisdiction has adopted the **Uniform Interstate Family Support Act** (UIFSA) to simplify collection of support payments when the obligor or child resides in a jurisdiction different than the one in which the original order was issued. Once an order is registered in another state, it is enforceable in the same manner and to the same extent as a child support order issued by the original state. UIFSA § 603(b). If properly registered, the Full Faith and Credit Clause of the U.S. Constitution applies to the order. UIFSA § 603(b).

Only the issuing state may modify the original support order; the other state's responsibility is simply to enforce the order. If there is no personal jurisdiction over the obligor, there is a two-state procedure that can be employed. Under this approach, an enforcement order can be obtained in the issuing state by filing an enforcement petition in the initiating state that will be forwarded to the issuing state's court. UIFSA § 203.

> **EXAM NOTE:** The modification and enforcement of interstate child support is always governed by UIFSA, which has been adopted in every jurisdiction. If more than one state is involved in a fact pattern, always discuss UIFSA, as the failure to follow its requirements does not result in its enforcement under the Full Faith and Credit Clause of the Constitution.

G. TAX CONSEQUENCES OF SUPPORT

Alimony is considered taxable income to the recipient and is deductible by the payor. A parent cannot, however, deduct child support payments as alimony or include them as income. The custodial parent automatically gets the child dependency exemption, unless the parties agree otherwise. Often the parties agree to alternate the exemption. The parent that pays medical expenses may deduct them.

IV. CHILD CUSTODY

A. DEFINITION OF CUSTODY

Having custody (i.e., control) of a child can mean having **legal custody** or **physical custody, or both.** Either or both of these types of custody can be shared under a **joint custody** arrangement.

1. Legal Custody

Legal custody is the right of a parent to make major decisions, as contrasted to everyday decisions, regarding the minor child. Typically, areas of health, education, and religion are encompassed.

2. Physical Custody

Physical custody is the right to have the child reside with a parent or guardian and the obligation to provide for routine daily care and control of the child. As with legal custody, physical custody may be shared by both parents under a joint custody arrangement.

3. Joint Custody

Joint custody generally requires that the parents are both willing and able to cooperate with respect to the well being of the child. Usually joint custody is not imposed over the objections of one parent, but, even when it is, the arrangement must meet the best interest of the child standard.

Under a typical joint legal custody arrangement, neither parent has a superior right to make major decisions; instead, joint custody arrangements typically spell out a procedure for resolving conflicts. Joint legal custody is the outcome in the majority of cases. In fact, many jurisdictions have a statutory presumption in its favor.

Joint physical custody does not necessarily require a 50-50 time-sharing arrangement. It encompasses any situation in which the child maintains a residence at the home of each parent and spends a significant amount of time with each parent.

Illinois Point of Law: Joint Custody

In applying the best interests of the child standard, which is discussed in more detail below, Illinois requires that the following factors be considered in determining whether joint custody is appropriate:

i) The desire and the ability of the parents to participate and cooperate in a joint custody arrangement, including agreement on important decisions involving the child;

ii) The residential circumstances of the parties; and

iii) Any other factor deemed relevant to the best interests of the child.

The capacity of the parents to communicate and reach joint decisions that have an impact on the child's welfare is the most important factor relevant to the determination of joint custody.

B. UNIFORM CHILD CUSTODY JURISDICTION AND ENFORCEMENT ACT (UCCJEA)

The purpose of the Uniform Child Custody Jurisdiction and Enforcement Act (UCCJEA) is to prevent jurisdictional disputes with courts in other states on matters of child custody and visitation. Almost all states have enacted the UCCJEA. Adjudication under the UCCJEA requires that the court possess subject matter jurisdiction.

1. Initial Custody Determination (Home State Jurisdiction)

A court has subject matter jurisdiction to preside over custody hearings and either enter or modify custody or visitation orders if the state is:

i) The child's **home state** and has been the home state for a period of **six months** or since birth, if the child is less than six months old; or

ii) Was the child's home state in the **past six months** and the child is absent from the state, but one of the parents (or guardians) continues to live in the state.

2. Significant Connection Jurisdiction

A court can enter or modify an order if (i) **no other state** has or accepts home state jurisdiction, (ii) the child and at least one parent have a **significant connection** with the state, **and** (iii) there is **substantial evidence** in the state concerning the child's care, protection, training and personal relationships.

3. **Default Jurisdiction**

If no state has jurisdiction through home state jurisdiction or substantial connection jurisdiction, a court in a state that has appropriate connections to the child has jurisdiction.

4. **Exclusive Continuing Jurisdiction**

Courts that make the initial ruling in a custody case have exclusive jurisdiction over the matter until the court determines that:

   i) The **parties no longer reside** in the state; or

   ii) The **child no longer has a significant connection to the state** and any substantial evidence connected to the child's condition is no longer available in the state.

5. **When Courts Can Decline Jurisdiction**

If a court has either initial or exclusive continuing jurisdiction, the court may decline to exercise such jurisdiction if it finds the forum to be inconvenient after considering the following factors:

   i) Whether **domestic violence** has occurred and is likely to continue in the future, and which state could best protect the parties and the child;

   ii) The **length of time** the child has resided outside of the jurisdiction;

   iii) The **distance** between the competing jurisdictions;

   iv) The parties' relative **financial circumstances**;

   v) Any **agreement of the parties** regarding which state should assume jurisdiction;

   vi) The **nature and location of the evidence** required to resolve the pending litigation, including the child's testimony;

   vii) The ability of each state's court to decide the issue expeditiously and the **procedures necessary** to present the evidence; and

   viii) The **familiarity of each state's court** with the facts and issues in the pending litigation.

A court may also decline to exercise its jurisdiction if a party has "engaged in unjustifiable conduct," such as wrongfully removing a child from another state.

6. **Temporary Emergency Jurisdiction**

A jurisdiction that does not otherwise have jurisdiction may obtain temporary emergency jurisdiction and enter an order if the child is in danger and requires immediate protection. If a prior custody order is in existence, the court rendering the emergency order must allow a reasonable time period for the parties to return to the state of original jurisdiction and argue the issues at hand before that court. If there is no prior custody order, the emergency order remains in effect until a decision is rendered by the child's home state. If no future determination is made, the emergency order continues in full force and effect.

7. **Enforcement of Another State's Orders**

   a. **Registration of order**

   A custody order from another state can be registered with or without a simultaneous request for enforcement. Typically, most jurisdictions require at least one certified copy of the order from the appropriate entity. The registering court can then grant any relief available for enforcement of the registered order.

   b. **Expedited enforcement of child custody determination**

   The UCCJEA utilizes a process similar to habeas corpus. After a petition is filed, the respondent must appear in person at a hearing held on the **first judicial day after service of the order** or, if that date is impossible, on the first judicial day possible. The petitioner will be awarded immediate physical possession of the child unless:

      i)   The custody or visitation order was not registered; and

         a)   The issuing court did not have jurisdiction;

         b)   The order had been stayed or vacated; or

         c)   The respondent was entitled to notice, but notice was not given before the court issued the order for which enforcement is sought; or

      ii) The order was registered and confirmed, but the order was stayed, vacated, or modified.

   c. **Warrant for child custody**

   The court may issue a warrant, upon a petitioner's request, for the petitioner to take physical possession of a child if it finds the child is likely to suffer serious physical injury or be removed from the state.

   d. **Law enforcement**

   The UCCJEA allows any law enforcement official to take any lawful action to enforce a custody order or obtain the return of a child if (i) the official believes the person holding the child has violated a criminal statute, or (ii) if requested to do so by a court of law.

C. **UNIFORM CHILD CUSTODY JURISDICTION ACT (UCCJA)**

Enacted prior to the UCCJEA, the UCCJA was established to create a uniform system to resolve interstate custody matters. Although the UCCJA was adopted by all 50 states, by the time of its adoption, Congress had enacted the Parental Kidnapping Prevention Act (PKPA), which conflicted in application to the UCCJA despite its common goal. In its original form, the UCCJA operated on principles that established jurisdiction over a child custody case in one state and protected a custody order of that state from being modified in any other state as long as the original state retained jurisdiction. Unlike the UCCJEA and PKPA, the UCCJA did not give first priority to the home state of the minor child. Similar to the PKPA, the UCCJA did not address enforcement of visitation rights. Almost all states have now replaced the UCCJA with the UCCJEA.

D. PARENTAL KIDNAPPING PREVENTION ACT (PKPA)

The Parental Kidnapping Prevention Act (PKPA), despite its name, applies not only to parental kidnapping cases but also civil interstate custody disputes, including visitation rights. Under the Supremacy Clause of the United States Constitution, the PKPA takes precedence over any conflicting state law. *See, e.g., Murphy v. Woerner*, 748 P.2d 749 (Alaska 1988). The PKPA discourages forum shopping between states and allocates the powers and duties between states when a child custody dispute arises. 28 U.S.C. § 1738A. If a jurisdiction fails to follow the PKPA's rules regarding jurisdiction, which are substantially similar to the UCCJEA rules (*see* § IV.B., *supra*), the order of the non-compliant jurisdiction is not entitled to full faith and credit.

The International Parental Kidnapping Crime Act (IPKCA) prohibits a parent from taking a child outside the U.S. and obstructing the other parent's physical custody of the child. The Hague Convention requires the return of a child wrongfully taken or retained in a foreign country, and allows the custodial parent to file suit. The exception to this is if bringing the child back into the country would expose the child to grave physical or psychological harm.

E. BEST INTERESTS AND WELFARE OF THE CHILD STANDARD

The standard for determining child custody is the **best interests and welfare of the child**. Generally, a parent is in the best position to care for a minor child, unless the parent is determined unfit.

There is no longer a presumption for custody in favor of the mother.

Many courts consider who the primary caretaker of the child was during the marriage, separation, and prior to the divorce, as a factor in determining who should have custody. *See, e.g., Garska v. McCoy*, 167 W.V. 59 (W. Va. 1981); *but cf. Gianvito v. Gianvito*, 975 A.2d. 1164 (Pa. Super. 2009) (the primary caretaker doctrine encompasses not only the day-to-day care of the child, but also includes the quantity and quality of the time spent with the parent at the time of the hearing, rather than in the past). The primary caretaker factor is based on a child's need for a stable and continuous relationship with the primary parent.

> **EXAM NOTE:** For any fact pattern about a proceeding involving children, be sure to discuss the best interests and welfare of the child standard in determining custody.

Illinois Point of Law: Best Interests and Welfare of the Child Standard

In Illinois, there is a presumption that the maximum involvement and cooperation of both natural parents regarding the child's emotional, physical, mental, and moral well-being is in the best interest of the child. Some of the factors the court may consider in determining the best interests of the child are as follows:

i)   The interaction between the child and his parents, siblings, and others who have a significant effect on the child's life;

ii) The physical and mental health of all involved individuals;

iii) The willingness of the parent to promote a relationship with the other parent and child;

iv) The adjustment of the child to his home, school, and community;

v)   The wishes of the parents and child, if of a mature age;

vi) The presence of ongoing domestic violence, whether directed at the child or another person; and

vii) Any other factor the court deems relevant.

750 Ill. Comp. Stat. 5/602.

Domestic violence: Illinois has statutorily created a rebuttable presumption that custody should not be awarded to a party who has been found to have committed abuse against a minor child.

1. Race or Religion

In most jurisdictions, the courts cannot use race or religion as a factor in determining custody.

Illinois Distinction: Race or Religion

Unlike the majority of jurisdictions, Illinois case law provides that race may be considered in custody disputes, but may not outweigh all other relevant factors.

2. Parents' Sexual Conduct

In many, but not all, jurisdictions, courts may not consider the parents' prior sexual conduct, including gay or lesbian relationships, in making a custody decision, unless it can be determined that the conduct of the parent has or will have a negative impact on the child.

3. Third-Party Rights

Legal parents are presumptively entitled to custody of their children in cases against third parties, including grandparents or step-parents, unless it can be established that the legal parent is unfit or that awarding custody to the legal parent would be detrimental to the child.

If a natural parent has had little or no contact with a child, or if the child has lived with the third party for an extended period of time, courts have employed the terms "parent by estoppel" and "*de facto* parent" in order to get around the presumption.

A minority of the jurisdictions apply the best interests standard in all custody cases, even those between a parent and third party. However, such a standard may run afoul of a parent's constitutional rights (*see* § IV.F., *infra*).

As with support obligations, custody rights may also turn on paternity issues (*see* § III.C., *supra*).

Illinois Distinction: Third-Party Rights

Although Section 602 of the Illinois Marriage and Dissolution of Marriage Act provides that a non-parent with standing may seek custody, there is a presumption that it is in the best interest of the child to give custody to the natural parent; the stepparent must rebut this presumption. In order to have standing, a non-parent seeking custody of a child may only file a petition for custody if the child is not in the custody of one of its natural parents or if the petitioner satisfies one of the below tests.

Stepparent: If the third party is a stepparent, the following prongs must be satisfied before custody may be sought:

i) The stepparent provided for the child's care and welfare prior to commencing the proceeding;

ii) The child for whom custody is sought is a minimum of 12 years old and desires to live with the stepparent;

iii) The stepparent and the custodial parent were married for a period of at least five years and the child resided with them during that time;

iv) The custodial parent cannot provide for the needs of the child, care for the child, or perform the duties required of a parent due to death or disability; and

v) It is alleged to be in the child's best interest to live with the stepparent.

The same requirements apply when a stepparent is seeking visitation with a stepchild.

Grandparent: If one of the parents is deceased, a grandparent who is the parent or stepparent of the deceased parent may file for custody if one or more of the following circumstances apply at the time of the death of the natural parent:

i) The living parent has been absent from the marital residence for at least one month and the deceased spouse was unaware of his location;

ii) The living parent is incarcerated or under the custody of the state or federal government;

iii) The living parent has been convicted of or received supervision for an enumerated criminal act against the deceased parent or child for whom custody is sought; or

iv) The living parent has been convicted of or received supervision for violating a domestic violence order of protection issued in favor of the deceased parent or child for whom custody is sought.

4. Child's Preference

Most courts will consider the **wishes of the child** if the court can determine that the child has a sufficient maturity to express a preference. Although age is not the sole factor in determining whether a child should be consulted, it is considered by the court. If children are consulted, the court evaluates the reasons behind the preference.

5. Guardian *Ad Litem*

In a highly contested child custody case, legal counsel may be appointed for the child. This attorney's duty is to advocate for the child's preferences and act on her behalf. The attorney's fees are usually paid by the parents.

6. Siblings

Courts traditionally avoid separating siblings from each other in order to maintain stability and promote sibling relationships.

7. Domestic Violence

Nearly every jurisdiction requires the court to consider the presence of domestic violence between the parties when awarding custody. Some jurisdictions have created rebuttable presumptions in favor of the non-abusive spouse.

F. VISITATION AND PARENTING TIME

Generally, the noncustodial parent is allowed reasonable visitation (or "parenting time") with a minor child. Because parents have a constitutional right to have contact with their children, the denial of visitation is very unusual and typically only an issue when it would seriously endanger a child's physical, mental, or emotional health. The court will, however, place restrictions on the exercise of visitation, such as supervised parenting time or a denial of overnight visits. The parents, by agreement, usually determine the time, place, and circumstances of the visitation. If the parties cannot agree on the circumstances, the court will determine the particular circumstances surrounding the parenting time.

1. **Third Parties**

In some situations, third parties, such as grandparents, stepparents, or gay or lesbian non-biological co-parents, may seek parenting time. Visitation is sometimes granted to stepparents and same-sex non-biological co-parents, but is typically limited to those cases in which they have acted *in loco parentis* with the child prior to the divorce. Absent such a relationship, there are no protected rights of a stepparent or non-biological co-parent to have ongoing contact with the child(ren) after divorce or death of the natural parent.

a. **"Special weight" to fit parent's decision**

A fit parent has a fundamental right to the care, custody, and control of his children. *Troxel v. Granville*, 530 U.S. 57 (2000). *Troxel* requires that state courts must give "special weight" to a fit parent's decision to deny non-parent visitation; "special weight" has been held to mean a very significant difference.

b. **Grandparent visitation**

Although the majority of jurisdictions have statutes regarding grandparent visitation, they differ among states and often do not guarantee the right to visit. In *Troxel*, the Supreme Court specifically implicated a fit parent's fundamental right to the care, custody, and control of the children in relation to grandparent visitation. Courts examining the request of grandparents for visitation will focus on the decision of the fit parents, statutory factors, and what is in the best interest of the child.

c. **Unwed biological father**

An unwed biological father has a substantive due process right under the U.S. Constitution to have contact with his child. However, this right exists only when the father demonstrates a commitment to the responsibilities of parenthood (e.g., participation in child rearing or providing financial support). *Lehr v. Robertson*, 463 U.S. 248 (1983). In addition, many states have imposed a two-year limit on the establishment of paternity by an unwed biological father. Further, if the mother is married to another man and refuses to join in a paternity petition, a state may preclude the purported biological father from pursuing the paternity petition. *Michael H. v. Gerald D.*, 491 U.S. 110 (1989).

2. **Sexual Relationship or Cohabitation**

Courts are unlikely to restrict visitation because of a parent's cohabitation with another or a parent's sexual relationship unless the cohabitation has an adverse impact on the children. Although jurisdictions differ in their handling of gay and lesbian relationships, the majority of jurisdictions do not prohibit overnight visitation unless the opposing parent can demonstrate a specific danger to the child's physical or emotional health.

3. HIV/AIDS

Courts cannot deny visitation merely because a parent has HIV/AIDS. *Noth v. Noth*, 648 A.2d 1025 (Md. App. 1994).

4. Interference

Interference or refusal to comply with a visitation order may be remedied by a change in custody or by contempt proceedings.

Illinois Point of Law: Visitation and Parenting Time

Convicted Sex Offender or Murderer: Illinois prohibits courts from awarding visitation to any incarcerated person if that party has been convicted of any sex offense involving a person under the age of 18. Visitation may only be considered upon release and after the successful completion of a court-approved treatment program.

Additionally, unless such visitation is in the best interest of the child, the court may not grant visitation to any person who has been convicted of the first-degree murder of the parent, grandparent, great-grandparent, or sibling of the child, and must revoke visitation already granted.

G. ENFORCEMENT

1. Sanctions

A party seeking enforcement of child custody and visitation orders can request assistance though the court system. The court hearing the case may impose a variety of sanctions, including compensatory visitation, attorney's fees, court costs, fines, and jail time. Tort damages may also be awarded to a parent for the period of time the child is wrongfully out of the parent's custody. In most states, a party cannot be denied parenting time for his failure to pay child support, or based merely on a child's wishes.

2. Habeas Corpus Proceedings

While not available for child custody disputes or visitation rights, a habeas corpus proceeding is a way in which a person who claims to have custody of a child, but does not have physical custody of the child, can be heard by the court. In addition, during these proceedings, many jurisdictions will revisit the issue of which placement is in the best interest of the child.

Less limiting than habeas corpus is a suit in equity action, which enjoins conduct in violation of custody order. The current trend has been to use suits in equity over habeas corpus proceedings.

3. Enforcement of Foreign Decrees

Custody and visitation orders between states are enforceable under the Full Faith and Credit clause if the other state's decree has been registered in the state seeking enforcement (*see* § IV.B.7., *supra*). Generally, a local court cannot modify an out-of-state decree, unless (i) the foreign court declines jurisdiction and the local court has proper jurisdiction, and (ii) the out-of-state party is given sufficient notice of the hearing in the local court.

H.   MODIFICATION

Once a custody order has been entered, absent relocation, a state retains subject matter jurisdiction to modify the order while the child remains a minor. The majority of jurisdictions apply a change in circumstances standard, requiring some substantial and unforeseen change since the issuance of the prior order. Some jurisdictions have also applied time barriers before an application for modification can be filed absent consent or endangerment. The purpose behind requiring time barriers or a substantial change in circumstances is to promote stability in the child's life. The violation of a child visitation order does not automatically change who is designated as the custodial parent; it is a factor to consider in modification of an order. The failure to pay child support is not a basis to withhold visitation or modify an existing child custody order.

If the custodial parent is proposing to relocate with the minor child and the relocation will significantly impair the non-custodial parent's ability to see the child under the court-ordered visitation schedule, it will almost always constitute a substantial change in circumstances warranting a modification. Note that prior to discussing the modification, if any, the court must provide the custodial parent with permission to relocate after applying the below factors.

1.   Relocation

The law regarding whether a parent can modify a custody order and relocate with a minor child is diverse. Some jurisdictions consider the relevant facts, but place the predominant weight on the best interest of the child. *See, e.g., Pollock v. Pollock*, 889 P.2d 633, 635 (Ariz. Ct. App. 1995). Other states apply a presumptive right to relocate with the child, provided that the rights and welfare of the child are not prejudiced. More often, the custodial parent seeking relocation bears the burden of demonstrating that the relocation is for a legitimate and reasonable purpose, as opposed to restricting the non-custodial parent's visitation. *See, e.g.,* Conn. Gen. Stat. 46b–56d. Some states, however, will place the burden of proof on the parent objecting to the relocation, typically the non-custodial parent, to demonstrate that the move will not serve the child's best interests or that the move would also cause harm to the child. *See, e.g., Pennington v. Marcum*, 266 S.W.3d 759, 768–69 (Ky. 2008).

Provided that a legitimate purpose for the move can be ascertained, the trend of the courts is to permit the custodial parent and child to relocate. An application to relocate, however, should be made in advance of the relocation, and must be based on anticipated present facts, not speculative ones. *See, e.g., Arthur v. Arthur*, 54 So. 3d 454 (Fla. 2010). Applications made after the relocation has taken place are often highly criticized by the court. Among the factors considered by the various jurisdictions are the following:

i)   The nature, quality, and involvement with the child of the parent who is not seeking relocation;

ii) The age and needs of the child and the impact the proposed relocation will have on that development, including any special needs of the child;

iii) The ability to preserve the relationship with the non-relocating parent and the child through visitation arrangements;

iv) The child's preference, if the child is of sufficient maturity;

v) Whether the parent seeking relocation has any history of promoting or preventing parenting time with the non-relocating parent;

vi) Whether the relocation will enhance the child's quality of life and the parent seeking relocation;

vii) The reasons each parent has in requesting or opposing the relocation; and

viii) Any other factors that affect the best interests of the child.

It is important to note that the applicable standards may be even more restrictive when the parents share joint custody of the minor child. *See, e.g., O'Connor v. O'Connor*, 793 A.2d 810 (N.J. Super. Ct. App. Div. 2002); Tenn. Code Ann. § 36-6-108 (2005). In those jurisdictions, the standard is often more protective of the parent who is not seeking the relocation. Mediation can often be very useful in assisting with resolving child custody issues.

Illinois Point of Law: Relocation

In Illinois, the predominant consideration in determining whether relocation is permissible is the best interest of the child. The burden of proving that such relocation is in the child's best interest is on the party seeking to remove. The rights and needs of the child must outweigh the rights of both the custodial and noncustodial parent. When granted, the court may order the removing parent to provide reasonable security to guarantee the return of the child.

In deciding whether relocation is in the child's best interests, a determination that must be made on a case-by-case basis, the court must consider the following factors:

i) The likelihood that the proposed move will increase the quality of life for the child and the custodial parent;

Illinois Point of Law: Relocation (cont'd.)

ii) The motives of the parents in requesting and opposing the removal;

iii) The effect, if any, on the non-custodial parent's visitation rights; and

iv) Whether a reasonable visitation schedule can be achieved for the non-custodial parent if the relocation is granted.

The above factors, however, are not exclusive and a court may consider other evidence relevant to the circumstances of the individual case.

---

2. **Cohabitation**

Some states permit a hearing to consider a change in custody when the custodial parent is living with a nonmarital partner. However, a change in custody is generally not granted unless there is a showing that the cohabitation is having an adverse impact on the child.

I. TERMINATION

A child custody order terminates upon the custodial parent's death or upon the child reaching the age of majority. In cases of death, the surviving parent generally receives custody of the child.

J. PARENTAL CONSENT

In certain circumstances, such as medical procedures, parental consent must be obtained. This policy holds regardless of the parents' marital status. A doctor who performs surgery on a minor child without parental consent is liable in tort. There are some exceptions to this general rule, such as in the case of an emergency, where time is of the essence. Some states may permit an exception to the general rule of consent when the child is older or deemed mature, or when the medical concern is related to public health, such as the treatment of a venereal disease.

1. Religious Beliefs

At times, the parent's religious beliefs can conflict with what may be in the child's best interests. Often seen in cases where medical treatment contradicts religious beliefs, the court can intervene, under the theory of *parens patriae*, to protect a child when necessary medical care is needed to prevent serious harm to the child's health. *Prince v. Massachusetts*, 321 U.S. 158, 170 (1994) ("Parents may be free to become martyrs themselves. But it does not follow they are free...to make martyrs of their children."). In those situations, a child can be declared neglected and the medical treatment ordered.

In some states, there are exemptions to the finding of abuse or neglect which permit the state to order the requisite medical care without finding the parent at fault. Such action by the court is typically only taken when the medical treatment is life-threatening, and only after the court balances the risks and benefits of the medical treatment. The home state has jurisdiction if it has been the home state of the child within the six months prior to the beginning of the custody proceeding.

2. Upbringing

A parent has a right to raise her child as she sees fit. *Wisconsin v. Yoder*, 406 U.S. 205 (1972). This right of parents extends to decisions relating to the religious upbringing of a child.

V. MARITAL AGREEMENTS

EXAM NOTE: Marital agreements are subject to the principles of contract law, just as other legal agreements are. When you see a bar exam question dealing with marital agreements and a violation of contract principles, be sure to raise the issue as you would in a contracts question.

A. TYPES OF MARITAL AGREEMENTS

1. Premarital Agreements

A premarital (also known as "prenuptial" or "antenuptial") agreement is a contract made before the marriage, typically containing terms that relate to division of property or spousal support in the case of a divorce and at death. As with any contract, consideration is required. A valid marriage is sufficient consideration for a premarital agreement.

Many jurisdictions have held that a premarital agreement must expressly state its applicability to divorce proceedings. Additionally, the majority of jurisdictions find clauses relating to child custody and support unenforceable. Adopted in 27 states, the Uniform Premarital Agreement Act (UPAA) is a uniform law that relates specifically to these types of contracts and imposes the same standards that are discussed below at § V.B., Validity of Marital Agreement.

When there is an issue as to which state's law will govern whether a premarital agreement is enforceable, most states apply the law of the state with the most significant relationship to the agreement and the subsequent marriage. Some states apply the law of the state where the agreement was executed.

Illinois Point of Law: Premarital Agreements
Illinois has adopted the UPAA, codified at 750 Ill. Comp. Stat. 10/1 *et seq.*

2. Separation Agreement

Separation agreements are made between a husband and wife who are planning for divorce. These agreements can define property division, spousal support, child support, custody, and visitation. The court generally will enforce spousal maintenance and property division provisions so long as the agreement is not unconscionable or based on fraud. Provisions related to child support and custody, on the other hand, are modifiable by the court if the initial terms are not in the best interest of the child. These agreements are generally merged into the final judgment for divorce, as long as they are based on full and fair disclosure. When no merger occurs, enforcement is based on contract law rather than judgment enforcement.

3. Property Settlement Agreement

The purpose of a property settlement agreement is to settle the economic issues of the marital estate. It is entered into by the parties *before* a divorce decree is issued.

B. VALIDITY OF MARITAL AGREEMENTS

A premarital agreement is enforceable if there has been **full disclosure**, the agreement is **fair and reasonable**, and it is **voluntary**. The agreement must be in **writing** and **signed** by the party to be charged. The agreement may be amended or revoked after the marriage provided both parties sign a written agreement to that effect. The burden of proving its invalidity is by clear and convincing evidence.

If the marriage is voided, a premarital contract is enforceable only if it will avoid an inequitable result.

1. Full Disclosure

Premarital agreements must provide full disclosure of financial status, including income, assets, and liabilities of all parties. Disclosure is an important consideration to the court, as it demonstrates that each party exercised a meaningful choice when they agreed to the terms of the contract. Absent full disclosure, a court will generally refuse to enforce the agreement.

2. Fair and Reasonable

The current trend is for courts to enforce contractual agreements that may not be fair as long as there has been fair disclosure. To determine if a premarital contract's terms are reasonable, the courts consider the parties' wealth, age, and health. An agreement obtained by fraud, duress, or undue influence may be set aside as unfair. When a mediator participates in the creation of a settlement agreement, misconduct by the mediator (e.g., bias towards one spouse) can give rise to grounds for setting aside the agreement. If a confidential relationship between the spouses exists, the burden of proving the fairness of the agreement or the absence of undue influence may be placed on the dominant spouse.

Most courts evaluate fairness at the time of execution of the contract and a minority of jurisdictions will evaluate it at both the time of execution and enforcement.

Illinois Point of Law: Fair and Reasonable

Illinois follows the majority rule and will evaluate the fairness at the time of execution of the contract.

3. Voluntary

The parties must enter into the contract voluntarily (i.e., free of fraud, duress, or misrepresentation). Courts consider factors such as time-pressure, the parties' previous business experience, and the opportunity to be represented by independent counsel.

A party's insistence on the agreement as a condition to marriage is *not* considered duress.

EXAM NOTE: Be sure to discuss whether procedural fairness exists if one party was not independently represented. Address the question of voluntariness by discussing whether the individual was both informed of her right to counsel and given the opportunity to consult counsel.

4. Impoverished Spouse

Even if a valid agreement has been voluntarily executed and it meets the test for reasonableness, fairness, and full disclosure, the agreement may be set aside if its result winds up leaving one spouse woefully impoverished to the extent he becomes dependent on the state (i.e., welfare). It is irrelevant if abrogation of the exact terms of the agreement results.

5. Modification of Marital Agreements

While a court may uphold a provision in a marital agreement that prevents modification of property rights, including spousal support, a court may always modify child support provisions in a marital agreement even if the agreement states that no modifications may be made.

C. AGREEMENTS BETWEEN UNMARRIED COHABITANTS

1. Cohabitation Agreements

Contracts between unmarried persons are invalid if the only consideration is sexual relations. Agreements in which other consideration, such as full-time companionship or cooking, is exchanged for financial support will generally be enforced. These contracts may be express, regarding earnings or property rights, or implied. However, courts are less likely to enforce an implied contract.

2. Property Division between Unmarried Cohabitants

When there is no express contract, courts will generally provide for equitable distribution of property based on a resulting trust, constructive trust, or quantum meruit theory to avoid unjust enrichment.

VI. RELATIONSHIP BETWEEN THE FAMILY AND THE STATE

A. ADOPTION

Adoption is a statutory legal action in which the previous parent-child relationship is terminated and a new parent-child relationship is established. Once the adoption has been completed, a new birth certificate with the adoptive parents' names is issued for the child. The records for most adoptions are sealed and kept confidential, but many states allow the adopted child to receive medical information on the birth parents. Additionally, most states have residency requirements for the county in which the adoption will take place and prohibit the payment of money to the natural parents other than costs related to medical care connected with the pregnancy.

1. Termination of a Natural Parent's Rights

For an adoption to be valid, the parental rights of the biological parents must be terminated. In order those rights to be terminated, one of the following circumstances must occur.

a. Voluntary termination

The biological parents may **voluntarily** give up their rights as parents of the minor child and consent to the child's adoption by the adoptive parents.

1) Consent of unwed fathers

a) Consent by failure to register

Some jurisdictions have created adoption registries for the purpose of determining the identity and location of putative fathers and providing notice in the event of an adoption. A putative father's failure to register within a statutorily-prescribed period of time constitutes a waiver of his right to notice of the adoption and irrevocably implies his consent to the adoption. *See, e.g., In Re J.D.C.*, 751 N.E.2d 747 (Ind. App. 2001); *Robert O. v. Russell K.*, 604 N.E.2d. 99 (N.Y. Ct. App. 1992). Termination in this fashion typically applies only to cases in which the father and child never developed a relationship. A situation in which the child is a newborn gives the unwed father a constitutional right to have an opportunity to develop a quality relationship with the child.

b) Limitations on right to object

The right of an unwed father to object to an adoption may be denied if the father does not demonstrate a commitment to the responsibilities of parenthood, but cannot be denied if such a commitment has been made. *Quilloin v. Walcott*, 434 U.S. 246 (1978); *Caban v. Mohammed*, 441 U.S. 380 (1979).

2) Consent of prospective adoptee

In most jurisdictions, the prospective adoptee must consent to his adoption if he is over 14 years of age; some jurisdictions lower the age to 12.

3) Withdrawal of consent

Prior to a final decree of adoption, the parents' consent to adoption may be withdrawn with court approval. After the final decree is entered, however, no withdrawal of consent is allowed.

Illinois Point of Law: Voluntary Termination

Consent by failing to register: In Illinois, a putative father's failure to register within 30 days of the birth of the child will waive his right to notice of the adoption. The failure to register also irrevocably implies his consent. The putative father's rights are not terminated if he can show by clear and convincing evidence that it was impossible to register within the statutorily prescribed period of time due to no fault of his own. The lack of knowledge of the pregnancy or birth is an insufficient reason for failure to register.

Surrender: In Illinois, parents must voluntarily terminate their rights in favor of an authorized adoption agency in an agency adoption, except when the termination is a part of an abuse and neglect proceeding. A surrender of parental rights is irrevocable if given after 72 hours elapsed since the birth of the child, absent fraud or duress. A father's surrender may be taken prior to the birth of the child, but only becomes irrevocable after a period of 72 hours has elapsed since the birth. The statute of limitations to void a parent's surrender based on fraud or duress is 12 months from the date the surrender was executed.

Illinois consent requirements: A child who is above the age of 14 must consent to the adoption in writing unless unable to do so due to mental deficiency or because the child is in need of medical treatment. Illinois has modified the consent requirements of the natural father in certain circumstances involving a nonmarital child. Consent of the natural father is not required when he has previously executed an instrument denying paternity or surrendered his parental rights.

i) Child more than six months of age: If the child is more than six months old, consent is only required when the natural father has maintained substantial and continuous or repeated contact with the child as manifested by the payment of reasonable support and visitation at a minimum of a monthly basis, unless financially or physically unable to do so, in which case the father must regularly communicate with the child or agency providing care. A father who has openly lived with the child for six months of the year preceding placement will satisfy the criteria.

ii) Child less than six months of age: If a child is less than six months old, consent is only required when the natural father has made a good faith effort to pay a reasonable amount of the expenses associated with the birth and support of the child for the first thirty days following the birth of the child, unless financially unable to do so. A father who has openly lived with the child or the child's mother for a period of 30 days after the birth of the child and has openly held himself out as the father will satisfy the criteria.

iii) Registration: In lieu of satisfying the above criteria, the consent of a natural father will be required when he has been identified as the father under an order of parentage, executed an acknowledgment of paternity, or timely registered with the Putative Father Registry and within 30 days of the date of such registration filed a proceeding to establish paternity.

b. Involuntary termination

Unlike consensual termination of parental rights, only a court can involuntarily terminate one's constitutional right to parent a child. The involuntary termination of parental rights typically occurs as a part of an abuse, neglect, or dependency case after the state has intervened and made attempts to rectify the situation. Also, if consent is unreasonably withheld, the court will waive such consent.

1) Requirements

Each jurisdiction provides the statutory grounds and requirements for termination of parental rights. They can include abandonment, incapacity, abuse of a sibling, termination of parental rights over a sibling, and abuse and neglect of the child over a period of time. Additionally, under the Adoption and Safe Families Act, a state can move for termination of parental rights when the child has been placed outside of the home and not with a relative for 15 of the past 22 months, provided certain reunification attempts have been provided by the state.

Because the termination of parental rights has constitutional implications, it is considered an extreme remedy. The standard for determining whether termination is appropriate is clear and convincing evidence.

2) Adoption

Some jurisdictions also apply the traditional law of adoption, which permits an adoption upon the finding that a parent has abandoned the parent-child relationship. Jurisdictions vary on the use of a subjective versus objective test. When an objective standard is applied, the key is whether the parent has failed to act in a way that indicates a commitment to maintaining the parent-child relationship (e.g., visitation and support). When a subjective standard is applied, the key is whether the parent subjectively intended to abandon the parent-child relationship; objective evidence of a parental loss of interest in the relationship is insufficient.

Illinois Point of Law: Involuntary Termination

Grounds: Illinois law provides the following circumstances in which the court can seek termination of parental rights:

i) Abandonment, which is evidenced by intent to forgo parental rights and obligations, and can include no visitation or communication despite an ability to do so, for a period of twelve months preceding the action;

ii) Substantial neglect of the child on a continuous or repeated basis, or which results in the death of a child in the household;

iii) Inability to provide basic care due to mental retardation or mental deficiency;

iv) Extreme or repeated cruelty to child;

v) The parent has been convicted of felony assault, aggravated or heinous battery, murder, or manslaughter of the child or a sibling of the child;

vi) Habitual drunkenness or addiction to drugs for a period of one year preceding the action;

---

vii) Adultery or fornication on an open and notorious basis;

viii) Depravity, or a parent's conviction or incarceration for specific felony crimes; and

ix) Other aggravated circumstances warranting termination as in the child's best interests.

Additionally, under the Adoption and Safe Families Act, a state can move for termination of parental rights when the child has been placed outside of the home, and not with a relative, for 15 of the past 22 months provided certain reunification attempts have been made by the State.

Process: In Illinois, the involuntary termination of parental rights is a two-step process. First, the court must find, by clear and convincing evidence, that a parent is an unfit person as defined under the Act. If a finding of parental unfitness is made, the court must then consider the best interests of the child in determining whether parental rights should be terminated. It is important to note that the procedures and grounds in regard to involuntary termination of parental rights equally apply to parents who themselves are still minors.

c. Approval of adoption

After a thorough investigation regarding the fittingness of the adoptive parents, the courts either approve or deny the adoption. The investigation may be waived if the adoptive parents are close family members of the child.

2. Legal Effects of Adoption

Once an adoption takes place, the adoptive parents have all of the rights and responsibilities the biological parents would have had (e.g., support, custody, visitation, and inheritance), and the adopted child has all of the rights and responsibilities a biological child would have had (e.g., intestate rights in the adoptive parents' estate). As the adoptive parents stand in the shoes of the adoptee's biological parents, the vast majority of jurisdictions will not permit visitation between the adoptee and her biological parents. A few states do authorize visitation between an adoptee and a non-parent, typically a stepparent, but only when there is a substantial relationship between the child and non-parent and the visitation is in the child's best interests.

Generally, an adoption may not be dissolved, although some states have permitted dissolution in limited circumstances, such as the discovery of an undisclosed mental or physical illness. In evaluating dissolution claims, courts typically consider the length of the relationship, the child's needs, and the parent's motives.

Illinois Point of Law: Adoption

Confidentiality of records: Under Illinois law, the birth parents and adoptive parents may consent to exchange vital medical information during the life of the adoptive child. Additionally, identifying information may be kept by the State and provided to the adoptee upon request with the written mutual consent of the birth and adoptive parents.

Persons who may adopt: In Illinois, the following classes of people may adopt a child or an adult:

i) An unmarried adult;

ii) Married couples;

iii) A person separated from her spouse either by legal separation or living apart for a period of 12 months or more; and

iv) A minor, upon the showing of good cause and with leave of court.

Although Illinois law permits an adult to adopt another adult, the adult seeking to adopt must have lived with the adoptee for a continuous period of more than two years preceding the adoption proceeding or be related to the adoptee within a degree designated by statute. When a separated party adopts, the non-adopting spouse does not become the parent or stepparent of the child and has no rights or obligations to the child.

Jurisdiction: Any person seeking to adopt may initiate an adoption proceeding in the circuit court where the adoptor or the adoptee resides, was born, or the parents of the adoptee reside. The jurisdictional requirements do not apply to any person seeking to adopt a related child or a child from an agency.

B. ADOPTION ALTERNATIVES UNDER THE UNIFORM PARENTAGE ACT (UPA)

The Uniform Parentage Act (U.P.A.) is a set of uniform rules for establishing parentage. As of this writing, the U.P.A. has been adopted by 19 state legislatures.

1. Assisted Reproduction

The U.P.A. defines "assisted reproduction" as implanting an embryo or fertilizing a woman's egg with a man's sperm without sexual intercourse. U.P.A. § 102. This may include in vitro fertilization, when fertilization occurs outside the woman's body, and the fertilized egg is then implanted into the woman's uterus. The donor is the man or woman who produces the sperm or egg used in assisted reproduction, but is not considered the parent of the prospective child. Maternity is determined by the woman who gives birth to the child, unless a gestational agreement states otherwise. U.P.A. § 201. Likewise, the husband of the woman who is determined to be the mother of the child is the child's father, unless the husband pursues an action to declare he did not consent to the assisted reproduction. This action must commence within two years after the husband learns of the birth of the child. U.P.A. § 705. If either the egg donor or sperm donor dies before implantation of the embryo, or before conception, that donor is not a parent of the resulting child, unless a writing by the deceased party states otherwise. U.P.A. § 707.

2. Gestational (Surrogacy) Agreement

Sometimes used interchangeably with the term "surrogacy," a gestational agreement is one in which a woman, known as the gestational mother or surrogate, agrees to carry a pregnancy, either through artificial insemination or by surgical implantation of a fertilized embryo, as a substitute for intended parents who cannot conceive. The intended parents are the individual or individuals who provide the egg or sperm of one or both of them used to implant into the surrogate. The intended parents agree to be the parents of the resulting child, with all the rights and obligations of parenthood. This agreement involves the gestational mother, and her husband if she is married, giving up all parental rights and obligations to the child being conceived.

All parties involved must petition the court for approval of the agreement. The court must have jurisdiction, which continues until the resulting child is six months old, and the appropriate government agency must perform a home study of the intended parents to determine their fitness. All parties must have entered the agreement voluntarily, and made provisions for the proper medical care associated with the surrogate agreement. The agreement may not limit the right of the gestational mother to make health care decisions concerning herself or the embryo she is carrying. Consideration to the gestational mother, if any has been promised, must be reasonable. The agreement may be terminated for cause by any of the parties, including the court, prior to the gestational mother becoming pregnant. An agreement that is not approved by the court is not enforceable.

Once the court approves the agreement, a child born to the surrogate mother within 300 days after the assisted reproduction is presumed to be the product of the assisted reproduction. A subsequent marriage of the gestational mother has no effect on the validity of the agreement. The intended parents must file a notice of the child's birth in order for the court to declare them to be the legal parents.

It is important to note that in many of the states that have adopted legislation regarding assisted reproduction, gestational agreements are not given effect.

Illinois Distinction: Gestational (Surrogacy) Agreements

Illinois does recognize and enforce surrogacy agreements. To be enforceable, the agreement must be (i) in writing, (ii) witnessed, and (iii) executed before performance of any medical procedures (other than screenings and evaluations). The surrogate must be at least 21 years old and have given birth before. Additionally, if an intended parent or surrogate is married, both spouses must execute the contract.

The surrogate and the intended parents must be represented by separate counsel, and the Illinois Gestational Surrogacy Act sets forth terms that must be explicitly included in the contract. *See* 750 Ill. Comp. Stat. 47/1 *et seq.*

3. "Frozen Embryo" Issues

A "frozen embryo" is the result of in vitro fertilization which is cryogenically preserved. Issues concerning ownership and parentage are complex and continue to be unresolved. Additional problems surface when one of the individuals who provided the egg or sperm dies, or the individuals get divorced. Absent an agreement, the decision as to whether or not transplantation will take place is made by weighing the interests of the parties. Ultimately, resolution of these issues may turn on whether the embryo is classified as a person or as property.

C. DOMESTIC VIOLENCE

Every jurisdiction has some type of statute granting civil relief to victims of domestic violence. Although each jurisdiction has its own definition of what constitutes domestic violence, the definitions typically focus on physical abuse, as opposed to mental or emotional abuse.

1. Scope of Statute

Virtually every jurisdiction requires that the perpetrator of the violence be in a relationship with the victim or be a household or family member. Jurisdictions differ, however, on the scope of coverage. Most states include spouses, former spouses, children, unmarried parents of a common child, and household or family members. Some jurisdictions also cover same-sex relationships and dating relationships. *See, e.g.,* N.J.S.A. 2C:25-19d. These statutes tend to focus on a continuum of behavior, but depending on the level of violence, a single episode may qualify for court protection.

2. Relief Granted

The major relief granted under most of the statutes is an injunctive order prohibiting the defendant's further abuse of and contact with the victim. It can, and typically does, include exclusive possession of the residence for the period of time, child custody and parenting time, and support. In most jurisdictions, the application for a protective order is a two-step process. The applicant must obtain an *ex parte* order with limited injunctive relief, followed by a hearing, after notice has been given to the defendant, for a permanent order. The duration of the order depends on the jurisdictional statute and ranges for a period of one year to an indefinite length of time. The penalties for violating a protective order are criminal in nature and range from a fine to imprisonment.

> **EXAM NOTE:** In bar exam questions, a typical example of the relief obtained by a protective order is that the defendant not abuse the petitioner and have no contact with her.

Illinois Point of Law: Domestic Violence

Who is covered? Under Illinois law, the following relationships are eligible for relief:

i) A victim related to the perpetrator by blood or current or former marriage, including step-relations;

ii) Current or former cohabitants;

iii) Parties who have or allegedly have a child in common;

iv) Parties who share a blood relationship through a child;

v) Parties who have dated more than casually; and

vi) High-risk adults or disabled adults and their caregivers.

Although disabled or high-risk adults do not need to be adjudicated incompetent to receive protection, a complaint may not be brought over the adult's objection unless a legal guardian has been appointed and consents to the action.

Illinois Point of Law: Domestic Violence (cont'd.)

Abuse Defined: Illinois defines abuse as physical abuse, harassment, intimidation of a dependent, and interference or the willful deprivation of personal liberty (except reasonable direction between a parent and a minor child). It also includes neglect if the petitioner is a high-risk or disabled adult. In Illinois, there is a rebuttable presumption that certain acts cause emotional distress and constitute harassment, including:

i) Creating a disturbance at the petitioner's workplace or school;

ii) Repeated telephonic communications to the petitioner's residence or place of employment;

iii) Repeated following or surveillance of the petitioner either in public or by remaining outside a location occupied by the petitioner;

iv) Concealing or repeatedly threatening to conceal the petitioner's minor child from the petitioner or threatening to remove the petitioner's minor child from the jurisdiction;

v) A single threat to conceal or remove the petitioner's minor child from them or the jurisdiction with an attempt to do so provided that the respondent was not fleeing from domestic violence; and

vi) A single or repeated threat of physical force or restraint.

Mutual protective orders: In Illinois, the issuance of mutual protective orders is statutorily prohibited.

Emergency or temporary *ex parte* protective order: If there are reasonable grounds to believe a person who is eligible for relief has suffered abuse, the court may enter a temporary *ex parte* order (also known as an emergency order). The temporary order will be in effect for a period of 14 days, but not more than 21 days, unless extended by the court upon the request of the petitioner and a showing of good cause. If the petitioner testified under oath on an *ex parte* basis, an order may be entered if the petitioner proves by a preponderance of the evidence that there are reasonable grounds to believe that the alleged abuse occurred. The respondent must be served with the order. If both parties appear at the emergency hearing, the court may waive the temporary hearing and conduct a 30-day interim hearing.

Relief: If the temporary order is granted, immediate relief may be obtained by the petitioner. Depending on the individual facts, the relief may include:

i) Prohibiting further abuse or contact between the victim or other family members;

ii) Awarding exclusive possession of the residence and ordering the respondent to vacate said residence provided that the petitioner has a right of occupancy and the presumption of hardship is in favor of the petitioner;

iii) Awarding temporary care and custody of a minor child to the petitioner;

iv) Awarding possession or protection of personal property, including animals;

v) Permitting law enforcement to seize the respondent's weapons and prohibiting the respondent from possessing weapons; and

vi) Prohibiting the respondent from being near certain locations, including residences of family members, places of employment, schools, or other applicable locations.

The balance of hardships is presumed to be in the favor of the petitioner. The presumption may be rebutted by the preponderance of the evidence upon demonstration by the respondent that her own hardships substantially outweigh those of the petitioner and any minor child or dependent adult in the petitioner's care. If the respondent is awarded possession, she may be required to provide the petitioner suitable alternative housing.

Standard: In determining whether or not to grant specific relief, the court considers the nature, frequency, severity, and consequences of the respondent's past abuse and the likelihood of future abuse to the petitioner or any member of the petitioner's family, and also, danger to any minor child.

Interim Protective Order: A person eligible for relief may seek a petition for an interim protective order if (i) notice of the hearing has been served on the respondent, (ii) the respondent has issued a general appearance, or (iii) service on the respondent is being diligently attempted by the petitioner. An interim protective order is effective for up to a period of 30 days. The relief that can be granted is identical to the relief available under a temporary protective order, but can include the award of legal custody of a minor child, require the respondent to undergo counseling, the payment of support, or the payment of other monetary obligations if the respondent has been properly served or filed an appearance.

Plenary or Final Protective Order: If an emergency or interim protective order is granted, a hearing for a plenary order (also known as a final protective order) will be held after the respondent has been served with the order or made a general appearance, and the respondent has answered or defaulted. If issued, the final order may last for a period of up to two years, unless later extended by the court upon the request of the petitioner and a showing of good cause. All of the relief available under an emergency or interim order is available under a plenary order.

Violations: The Illinois statute encourages the court to impose a minimum penalty of 24 hours of imprisonment for a first offense and a minimum of 48 hours for a second or subsequent offense. Additional penalties shall include fines, restitution, payment of attorney's fees, and community service.

D. RIGHTS AND OBLIGATIONS OF CHILDREN

Children are provided with special rights and limitations compared to adults. These distinctions are meant to protect children as well as provide them with expanded rights when necessary. In many cases, as with property and contracts, children may convey property or enter into contracts as minors, but upon the age of majority they have the option of disaffirming the transaction. Conversely, a child does not have the capacity to make a valid will.

1. Right to Consent to Medical Care

A child's rights regarding medical care vary depending on the age of the child and the medical procedure. Children over a certain age may be able to provide the consent needed for treatment. Otherwise, parental consent is almost always necessary before a child can receive emergency medical treatment, even though the state may override the parent's failure to consent when the child's life is at risk. Nevertheless, in non-emergency situations minors are allowed to consent to abortions, treatment for sexually transmitted diseases, and obtain birth control without the consent of their parents.

2. Liability for Torts and Criminal Acts

Generally, children are judged by a more moderate standard than adults when determining the liability for tortious behavior. Criminal acts, as well, generally are limited to adjudication in juvenile courts under juvenile laws. The purpose for this is to provide the child with supervision and rehabilitation. Usually, the decision regarding the extent of punishment is dependent on the age of the child; the younger the child, the more likely the court will show leniency.

3. Emancipation

In a few situations, a child no longer lives with his parents and is self-supporting. In such a case, the child may petition the court for a decree of emancipation. This means the child is no longer considered a minor in the eyes of the law and therefore has all the duties and obligations of adulthood. Parents no longer have a duty to support them, and in fact, some jurisdictions require the children to support their parents in later years. Married minors are also considered to be emancipated in most states.

4. Limits on Parental Authority

A parent's authority over his child is not absolute. Laws are in place to protect children from harm, whether or not that harm is intentional. Child abuse and neglect laws, as well as compulsory school attendance statutes, are in place to ensure a child is well taken care of and supervised appropriately. As has been discussed, the state may terminate parental rights despite parents' constitutional right to raise their children when it is in the best interest of the child. Grounds for termination include abandonment, neglect, failure to support, or inflicting serious harm, among others. The state must prove these allegations by clear and convincing evidence because of a parent's right to due process.